TWENTY

FORTY

FIVE

THE GROWING
DEMOGRAPHIC
CRISES

Written By Dr Clint R Laurent for
Global Demographics Ltd

Copyright @ 2021 by Global Demographics Ltd

Published by Global Demographics Ltd

1108 Tai Yau Building, 181 Johnston Rd, Hong Kong

ISBN 978-1-3999-0390-5

The Big Issues

Introduction

The 116 countries included in this analysis account for 91% of the world's population as estimated by the United Nations and 95% of the world's GDP as estimated by the World Bank in 2019.

The world divides into 4 groups of countries

- Older Affluent Countries – GDP per capita over US$20,000 p.a. and median Age over 35 years (25 countries)
- Older Less Affluent – GDP per capita between US$6,000 and US$20,000, median age over 25 years (22 countries)
- Family Stage Low Income GDP per capita between US$3,000 and US$10,000, median age between 25 and 35 years (34 countries)
- Young Poor – GDP per capita less than US$3,000 and median age below 25 years (32 countries)

Total population

- The overall population of the 116 countries included in this analysis is projected to grow from 7.27 billion persons in 2019 to reach 8.67 billion in 2045.
- 70% of that growth is in countries where the average GDP per capita is US$1,500 and none are above US$4,000 per capita. The other 30% is in the family stage countries where the average GDP per capita is US$4,400 per annum.
- The total population of the young poor countries is projected to grow at 2.1% per annum, taking it from 1.33 billion persons in 2019 to 2.31 billion by 2045. That is an additional 1 billion persons in 25 years.

- In total, the older countries, which accounted for 78% of global consumption in 2019, are declining in the number of consumers. Their expenditure growth is also slowing. This has implications for the future demand for goods and services and ultimately demand for workers globally.
- China's population is 1.411 billion persons in 2020. It is projected to peak in 2024 at 1.433 billion and then decline to 1.354 billion persons by 2045 – even after allowing for relaxation of the one-child policy.

Global Age Profile

- In 60 of the 116 countries covered in this analysis, the under 40-year age groups are now stable or declining in the absolute number of persons. The youth markets of these countries may still be large, but they are no longer growth markets (in terms of the number of consumers).
- **The older regions of the world are now approaching 'peak aged'** thereby reducing growth in future demand for health and social systems. The projected growth rate of the 40 years and above population (the age at which the need for health services starts to increase) is 0.3% per annum from 2030 to 2045. That compares to 1.4% per annum for the decade to 2019.
- **Some areas of the world normally described as 'young' such as India and most of South America are becoming middle-aged** by 2045 and with that a growing health care need. In India, the 40 years and above population is projected to grow at 2.5% per annum to 2030. In contrast, the under 40-year age group is projected to decline marginally.
- **Nearly every country in the African continent has a median age of less than 25 years**. Some are as young as 14 years (Niger). The total number of 0 to 14-year-olds in this region is projected to increase from 551 million to 776 million in the next 25 years.

Population Dynamics (Births, Deaths, and Migration)

- In the countries where 50% of adults are educated to lower secondary or above, birth rates are stable at around 40 to 50 births per thousand women aged 15 to 49 years. In these same countries the number of women aged 15 to 49 is projected to decline and with that so will total births. As the women aged 15 to 49 in 2035 are already alive in 2019 (albeit aged 0 to 34 years now) this decline is non-reversible at least until then.
- **For many of the younger countries, the births are 'out of control'.** The number of family stage couples is projected to increase at a rate that more than offsets the declining birth rate. For example, in Nigeria, the number of women 15 to 49 years of age is projected to increase from 46 million in 2019 to 90 million in 2045 and even though the birth rate declines from 166 to 137 per thousand, total births per annum are projected to increase from 7.7 million to 12.4 million.
- This high number of births in the young poor countries means the projected global total births per annum is almost unchanged between 2020 and 2045. That is 125 million in 2020 and a projected 124 million in 2045. This is despite declining birth rates.
- **In China – the number of women aged 15 to 49 will decline (at least to 2035 as they are already alive) and with that a decline in total births is inevitable.** Birth rates would need to increase by 50% just to maintain the current level of births per annum. This is unlikely to happen
- The movement of labour to affluent countries from poor countries is effectively 'de-skilling' the less affluent countries and limiting their ability to grow. In the decade 2009 to 2019 Greece lost 376,000 working-age persons through emigration and 3.5% of its 2009 workforce (and perhaps 7% of its skilled workforce).
- Migration is also confronting moral issues. Is it right for Britain (for example), with 1 doctor for 356 persons, to offer employment to a Nigerian (trained and qualified) doctor on anything other than a training basis? In Nigeria, there are 2,631 persons per doctor.

- Data for countries with a historic high rate of immigration show that while immigration may grow both the total working-age population and Gross Domestic Product of a country the number of dependents per worker remains almost the same as does GDP per capita.

Education

Education breaks the poverty trap.

The problem with education is that it takes time to first implement and then be effective

- **China is an example of how this is done properly**. The One-Child Policy was introduced in 1979 and meant the number of children needing to be educated levelled out by 1984. This meant that from that year China could afford to introduce compulsory education for every child.

  By 2000 there was a significant pool of around 20 million persons each year able to move from being in an agricultural village doing low productivity agricultural work to urban areas and enter manufacturing and tertiary level jobs which significantly enhanced productivity and hence GDP and household incomes. Without constraining births this could not have happened.
- **Education is a *necessary but not sufficient* driver of affluence. No poorly educated country is affluent**. But in well-educated countries, there is a distinct difference in productivity (and hence household incomes) depending on the level of Fixed Capital Investment behind each (educated) worker.
- There is a pool of countries– specifically Eastern European and some Asian countries (Vietnam) – where the education standard is high, but the country has not attracted sufficient Fixed Capital Investment per worker to leverage it sufficiently. One might expect rapid economic growth in those countries in future if they change their approach to investment (domestic or foreign)

- There are grounds to be optimistic about the availability and quality of education globally. The cost of delivery is going down and its value is getting better understood. However, the reality is, that it takes over 20 years to take effect – so for some time, the poor will remain poor.

BUT....

- **There is an unfortunate propensity for countries with the lowest education index values to be also spending a below-average share of GDP** on education (after adjusting for the proportion of the population that is school-aged). Of the 42 countries that are regarded as poorly educated, only 9 are spending a higher than average (for all countries) share of GDP on education.
- And the number of school-age children (5 to 14-year-olds) in these same countries is projected to increase dramatically. From 344 million in 2020 to 498 million in 2045 as a result of the projected trend in births. Just to maintain current availability and quality the education budget has to increase by 45%.

Employment

- *China*. Despite a declining total population, the urban working-age population and labour force are projected to continue to increase through to 2045. This is a result of ongoing (but declining) rural to urban migration.
- *The older (and Affluent) countries of the world*. For these countries, **the definition of working-age is now age 15 to 74 years. Not 64 years**. With increasing life span, education, and pension insecurity an increasing proportion of 65 to 74-year-olds are staying in employment. In some countries, they account for 10% of the labour force already. Additionally, the 65 to 74-year age group is one of the fastest-growing age segments. As such **the dependency ratio of the older affluent countries remains low and they do not need migrant labour to sustain GDP per capita.**

- **The Demographic Dividend.**
  - This is often touted as the item that will drive the economies, and well-being, of the poorer and younger countries. For young countries (essentially the African continent) the number of persons of working age is quite reliably forecast to increase from 742 million in 2019 to 1,418 million in 2045.
  - Currently, 64% of the working-age population in these countries is in work. If that rate of employment is to be maintained, the number of employed persons would need to increase from 475 million to 918 million. That means **443 million extra jobs need to be found by 2045 to leverage this 'demographic dividend'.**
  - A similar situation exists for the family stage countries (India, South Asia, and South America particularly). The number of working-age persons is projected to grow in total from 2.1 billion in 2019 to 2.46 billion in 2045. Given that 58% are typically employed, these countries need an additional 248 million jobs.

But they are not achieving that growth in jobs. Already India's propensity to be employed has dropped from 58% in 2005 to 50% in 2019 - in short, *the demographic dividend is not paying out nor is it likely to in future* because.....

- **The global equilibrium of growing consumer demand and the number of people seeking work is potentially ending in this decade.**
  - Between 2020 and 2030 the number of the middle class and affluent consumers living in countries that collectively account for 78% of the world's consumption expenditure is projected to slow in growth. After 2030 they are projected to decline in number. In addition, they are getting older and typically become more careful spenders.
  - The number of consumers under 40 years of age in these affluent countries is projected to decline.

- As a result, **the growth of global total household consumption spending is expected to slow** from 2.64% per annum from 2009 to 2019 to 2.16% from 2019 to 2030, 1.65% per annum from 2030 to 2040 and 1.42% per annum from 2040 to 2045.
  - At the same time, **the productivity of the average (global) worker is expected to continue to increase**. It has been growing at 1.67% per annum for the last decade and with ongoing improvements in education, fixed capital investment, robotics, and AI this can be expected to continue at least at that rate.

- The combination of slowing growth of consumption expenditure and increased productivity per worker means **the global demand for workers is projected to be less than the number of people seeking work.**

- This is a serious sociological issue.
  - **The global demand for workers is projected to peak in 2034 at 3.3 billion persons. It then declines to 3.24 billion in 2045.** However, this compares with 3.467 billion seeking work in 2034 and 3.638 billion seeking work in 2045. **In 2034 there is a projected shortfall of 166 million jobs and by 2045 it is 400 million missing jobs.** That is a large number of people wishing to be employed but who will not be able to find work and support themselves and their families.
  - But it is not just the 400 million missing jobs – it is also the dependents of the workers that are expected to have those jobs. Typically, 2 or more dependents per worker. That means **a total of 1.6 billion people will potentially be unable to support themselves.**
  - The search for jobs is going to be intense. The countries where there is massive growth in the number of persons seeking work have low education standards and a limited competitive edge except where natural resources (including water) play a role. This may cause intercountry conflict.

- It will inevitably result in mass migration to the point that it could overwhelm the societies/countries to which they wish to migrate. Either from South America or the African Continent. This is going to cause political issues and changes in social attitudes in the target countries. The resolution, if any, is not going to be easy. The 'Trump Wall' and 'Greece Wall' (along its border with Bulgaria) may be just the start of a new reality.

- *Migration will become a matter of survival not of choice.*

The Distribution of income

- Income levels are strongly correlated with the level of education and fixed capital investment per worker. An increase in affluence requires both but education is a prerequisite to attracting investment,
- **Countries with existing poor education standards for their workforce will not be able to lift their incomes for at least 20 years assuming they invest heavily in education now**. A child cannot be educated overnight. The dichotomy between countries is going to last for at least one or two generations.
- Many of the countries that are low income are under-investing in education (as a share of GDP) so the prognosis for them is not very good.

For those reasons, **the dichotomy between the rich and the poor is expected to increase.** The number of households with an income over US$50,000 almost doubles by 2045, but the number of households with an income below US$5,000 declines only marginally by 2045. From 702 million to a projected 645 million in 2045.

The projected high growth consumer segments are

- Over US$125,000 in the older countries. The number of such households is projected to increase by 73% by 2045. Their spending is projected to increase by 88% and will account for 24% of global spending by 2045 – so important.
- The middle class of China is projected to shift in definition and size dramatically through to 2030. Currently, there are 101 million urban households earning between US$15,000 and US$25,000. By 2045 middle class is projected to be 134 million urban households with an income between US$25,000 and US$50,000 per annum. In total, the consumer spending of households in urban China is projected to increase from US$3.5 Trillion to US$8.6 trillion by 2045. But most of this growth takes place by 2033. After 2033 the growth of consumer spending slows dramatically.
- The emerging middle class of India is households with an income between US$7,500 and US$25,000. It is projected to grow from 65 million households to 215 million in the next 25 years. That is a growth rate of 4.7% per annum in the number of households.
- The upper-middle class in the Family Stage Low-Income Countries other than India will nearly double in size in the next decade. That is half a billion more consumers (and 146 million more households) with a projected household income of over US$15,000 pa.

Consumption Expenditure

- **The rate of growth in global household consumption expenditure is projected to slow.** From 2.64% per annum for 2009 to 2019, then 2.16% for 2019 to 2030, 1.65% per annum to 2040 and 1.42% to 2045.
- This is particularly a function of the lack of growth in the population of the older affluent countries. These countries account for 62% of global consumption. In the next 25 years, their total population is projected to grow in absolute terms by just 4%. Add to that a changing age profile with an increasing proportion moving towards retirement and the under 40 years of age population declining in number and growth in total spending will be impacted.
- A similar scenario exists for the older less affluent countries and particularly China where total population growth is negative from 2024. The number of under 40-year-olds is projected to decline, and the growth of the high spending 40 to 64 years old (working-age empty nesters) slowing dramatically to 2030 and then declining thereafter.
- For the period to 2030 urban China and India and the Young Poor countries are where consumption growth is going to grow most (circa 4% per annum). After 2030 Urban China drops to 2.4%, India to 3.2% and the growth is now concentrated in the Young Poor countries at 4.9% per annum.
- But this assumes that they can find employment – which is considered unlikely as while there is significant 'local' consumption the reality of it is that these countries account for just 3% of global consumption in 2020 and are projected to reach 8% by 2045 if full employment is achieved. That is not sufficient to offset the declining growth elsewhere in the world and provide sufficient additional employment.

Health

- There is a relationship between the demand for health services and the age of the population. For that reason, health needs and expenditure have grown significantly in the older countries over the last two decades and have not been such an issue elsewhere in the world. That now changes.
- **The older countries are approaching peak aged, and marginal demands on health and social services are reducing.** The existing services/infrastructure is close to having sufficient capacity for the future aged population. The emphasis can shift to lifting quality rather than quantity of healthcare. Also, these countries can all afford to lift their current expenditure per case and stay within 15% of GDP being spent on health.
- **The future growth sector for health is the family stage countries (in South Asia and South America particularly) as they are entering middle-aged** (over 40 years of age) and with that experiencing a significant increase in the number of persons developing chronic conditions. Based on the changing age/gender profile of the population and the trend in incidence/prevalence of chronic conditions, the demand for health treatment is projected to grow at 4.8% per annum for these countries.
- Those most able to afford to pay for their health care (with household incomes over US$20,000 per annum) have the greatest government support. In contrast, those least able, that is, countries where the average household income is below US$10,000, get the least government support.

Table of Contents

Chapter 1
Introduction

Gaining a Perspective

Assuming yesterday was an average day, across the globe an estimated 349,127 people were born during that day. Sadly 159,899 other people died on the same day. This means a net addition to the world's population of 189,229 persons. This continues for 365 days of the year. That means an additional 69 million persons by the end of this year – that is the equivalent to 2.5 Australia's in a year.

Unless something catastrophic happens, trends in births and deaths indicate that an average of 54 million persons will be added to the world's population per annum for the next 25 years. By 2045 there will be an additional 1.34 billion persons.

By 2045 there will be an additional 1.34 billion persons living in the 116 countries included in this analysis (Which include 91% of the Global Population in 2019 based on the United Nations Global Population estimate.)

There is the obvious issue of whether the planet can sustain such an increase. People are becoming increasingly aware that more and more humans are not necessarily good for the environment. Perhaps ongoing growth in the population is a danger to the ecological system? It is not aeroplanes – it's people in the planes! Simply by existing we pollute.

In addition, this continuous growth of the population is quite dichotomous in terms of where it is taking place. It is projected that 70% of the global population growth from 2020 to 2045 will be in just 32 of the 116 countries included in this analysis.

Overlay on that

- the ongoing process of the changing age profile of populations,
- differences throughout the world in the provision of education, healthcare, employment, and
- availability of resources to lift worker productivity and

the world of 2045 is going to be very different from what it is today.

NOTE: The 116 countries included in this analysis account for 91% of the global population as estimated by the United Nations and 95% of the Global GDP as estimated by the World Bank for 2019.

The purpose of this book is to help people understand what is happening, and the diversity of potential outcomes. Some countries will be experiencing very little, or even negative, population growth, others will double in size. Obviously, at the same time, age profiles will change and with that the nature of lifestyles. Consider the difference in the overall lifestyle between a country where half the population is under the age of 15 years (Mali) and a country where half the population is over the age of 46 (Italy).

With these changes in the age profiles of countries will come changes in capability. Fortunately, education standards are improving generally, which should improve both employability and productivity. Employability is important as the number of persons that need to be in work if their country's economies are to be sustained will increase significantly in many countries.

In that respect, there are 'clouds on the horizon'. The absolute number of consumers in the countries that account for 78% of the world's consumption expenditure is projected to decline. Particularly consumers under the age of 40. That could significantly impact future demand for items that are manufactured and ultimately the demand for workers. Will there be enough jobs for the growing working-age population?

*The persons that account for 78% of global consumption are
projected to decline in absolute number. This will at the very least
reduce the growth rate in consumption and employment prospects.*

The changing age profile and size of the population not only impact
employment needs, consumption patterns, and demand for housing and
education but also health needs. Will the increasingly aged population
(that is persons over 40 years in respect of a demand for health services)
overwhelm the health system of some societies? If so, which ones?

Finally, by way of setting the scene, be aware that the dichotomy across
the globe in terms of income, employment, health care, etc, is probably
going to increase rather than decrease. That potentially could cause
political issues. The world is a very long way from every child receiving
adequate health care and education. This will create other pressures, not
least of all migration.

The need to find better opportunities for the individual will continue.
With that will come migration flows. But is it right? Should affluent
countries (who can pay more) take the talent (better educated and skilled
workers) from poor countries? Even if the individual migrant wants to
move?

*Is it right for Britain (for example) with 1 doctor for 356 persons to
offer employment to a Nigerian (trained and qualified) doctor on
anything other than a training basis? In Nigeria, there are 2,631
persons per doctor.*

As individuals, we tend to focus on the immediate environment that is
relevant to our lives today and perhaps do not look beyond that as much
as we should. We do not always have time to find out about, and fully
comprehend, how much the world is changing around us – until it is
obvious. Individual time is precious.

The purpose of this book is to address that need by showing compactly and clearly the demographic and socio-economic changes likely to take place across the world over the next 25 years.

The purpose of this book is to show compactly and clearly the demographic and socio-economic changes likely to take place across the world over the next 25 years.

Demographics (age, gender, household formation, education) and socioeconomics (employment, incomes, consumption) tend to follow stable trends. The shape of today's socio-demographics very significantly determines the shape of tomorrow's. For example, a change in birth rates in a country today starts to determine the size of the labour force in 15 years, when the newborn reaches working age.

We understand that in our 'local' context, but what is difficult for us to comprehend is how much this is changing on a global basis. Some examples that may not be appreciated:

1. Nigeria is projected to nearly double its population in the next 25 years (from 207 million to 380 million persons).

2. That the number of persons of working age in the world is projected to increase by 16% in 25 years. But it will double in the countries with the lowest education standards.

3. The population of most of the more affluent countries is now stable in number, whereas for the poor it is growing. Rapidly!

4. How adequate education is not available to so many young people – and the consequences of that.

5. The number of persons who are over 40 years of age in the world will increase from 2.8 billion in 2020 to 3.9 billion in 2045 which will have a significant impact on the potential demand for health care. Can this demand be met, and where is that demand located?

Demographic forecasts are not infallible, but they tend to be reasonably accurate because, as mentioned, the key drivers tend to follow stable trends rather than experience abrupt changes. This applies to birth rates, death rates, age of marriage/partnership, propensity to be employed, education profile (which is particularly important but also particularly slow to change), earning capabilities and even migration policies.

They do change, but generally predictably and steadily. Yes, governments can introduce or remove birth policies and immigration policies – and that needs to be kept in mind. But that tends to be the exception rather than the rule. Perhaps the most volatile influence is the presence or absence of a stable and effective government. That can impact employment (investment) and hence access to education and health – and that sadly is not predictable. Unfortunately, so many countries are already at the low end of the scale in terms of having capable government and governmental agencies.

So how is this book (discussion) structured? The following pages describe what each Chapter is about and highlights some of the key issues arising in each. The intention is to 'paint' the background to the total picture which is multifaceted. The possible outcomes, particularly at a social level, because of the projected changes, are considerable in number and for the reader to ponder.

By having a view of the world and the variables at play you can then assess the possible alternative outcomes and the risk associated with each.

Chapter Two – Segmentation and a Global Perspective

This book uses the data of 116 countries, and therefore it is necessary to develop a structure for identifying the trends that are emerging without descending into an incomprehensible level of detail. The purpose of this Chapter is to explain how the world has been segmented into four meaningful groups of countries which provide the basis for much of the subsequent analysis and discussion.

Prior work with demographics has identified two key drivers which differentiate countries. They are median age and Gross Domestic Product per capita. Why these two variables?

Median age

This is the age where half the population is older than that age and half is younger. It is a reliable indicator of the overall life stage profile of the population. If the median age is (as for some countries) under 20 years of age it means that most persons in that country are children or young adults. The bias for households will be toward parents and never married children living in the home. Obviously in such countries, the aged population (over 64 years of age) will be in a minority and probably at this stage only growing slowly in number. In terms of lifestyle, it will be biased to family and the concerns of a family.

Conversely where the median age is over 40 years then the bias of the population lifestyles is towards the older household - probably empty nesters – and the child/youth market is relatively small and probably declining in size. Also, there will be a change in consumption patterns – from buying things to buying experiences as the older population already has the 'things' it needs to live. However, saving is also a big concern for these populations.

The age profile of a population also gives a good indication of the future trend in births, new household formation, projected size of the working-age population and hence labour force.

Gross Domestic Product per Capita

This is the second key variable for differentiating between countries and is used as a measure of *relative* affluence or quality of lifestyle the average person can afford.

While it is tempting to use *household income per capita*, the problem with that is it does not reflect the wider social benefits an individual can receive from society. That is free or subsidised education, health, infrastructure, etc. That varies significantly across countries.

In addition, there is less controversy over what the Gross Domestic Product of a country is than there is over what the average household income is. The measure and definitions of Gross Domestic Product are more clearly defined.

The Country Segments

Using the **2019 value** of these two global variables, the 116 countries included in this analysis are divided into four key segments of about the same size in terms of the *number* of countries. However, the four segments do differ quite a lot in terms of share of GDP and share of the total population. This is inevitable with a few countries having particularly large populations (for example China and India) or high affluence (United States of America and Japan).

The four groups of countries identified by the segmentation process are:

1. The Older Affluent – there are 25 countries in this segment, and they have a median age of over 35 (but twenty are over 40) years and a GDP per capita of more than US$20,000 in 2019 values (Twenty of these countries have a GDP pc of more than US$40,000).

2. The Older Low Income – Twenty-Two countries fall into this segment. They are also Countries with a median age of over 35 years (14 are over 40 years) but their GDP per capita ranges from US$6,000 to US$20,000 in 2019 with an average of US$11,000. This segment includes (and is numerically dominated by) China so in some situations, the analysis of this segment excludes China – which is then discussed separately.

3. The Family Stage Low Income – these are countries where the median age is between 25 years and 35 years (typically the age range at which people form their own households and relationships) and GDP per capita is between US$3,000 and US$10,000. There are 32 countries

in this segment including several large ones – specifically India, Indonesia, and Brazil.

4. The final segment is the Young Poor Countries. The median age is under 25 years and GDP per capita is less than US$3,000 but mostly less than US$2,000. There are 32 countries in this segment.

Only three countries fall outside these definitions.

Figure 1-1 shows graphically the segmentation that exists.

The differences between the four Country Segments on a range of relevant variables such as birth rates, life expectancy, incomes, health, education, and employment are considerable. The world is not homogeneous and neither are the future trends.

The definition and details of these Country Segments and an overview of how they are projected to change in terms of population and income by 2045 are the subjects of Chapter Two. The differences between the Country Segments on a range of relevant variables such as birth rates, life expectancy, incomes, health, education, and employment are quite considerable. As a result, the projected outcomes for the four segments by 2045 are very different.

Figure 1-1: Segmentation of Countries by Age and GDP per cap

Older Affluent

	2019	2030	2,045
Population Mns	991	1,025	1,030
Population Growth rate pa	0.5%	0.3%	0.0%
Share of Global Population	13.5%	12.7%	11.8%
Median Age	42	44	46
GDP US$ Bn	48.7	59.8	71.9
GDP Real Grwoth Ratepa	1.8%	1.9%	1.2%
Share of Global GDP	56.9%	52.2%	46.7%
GDP per cap (US$)	49,146	58,414	69,765
GDP per cap grwoth rate pa	1.3%	1.6%	1.2%

Older Low Income

	2019	2030	2,045
Population Mns	1,821	1,837	1,740
Population Growth rate pa	0.4%	0.1%	-0.4%
Share of Global Population	24.9%	22.8%	19.9%
Median Age	39	43	47
GDP US$ Bn	19.7	30.8	44.7
GDP Real Grwoth Ratepa	6.0%	4.2%	2.5%
Share of Global GDP	23.0%	26.9%	29.0%
GDP per cap (US$)	10,793	16,787	25,674
GDP per cap grwoth rate pa	5.6%	4.1%	2.9%

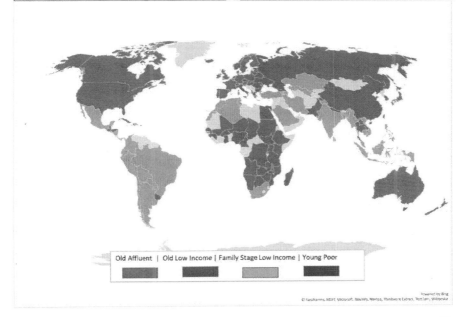

Old Affluent | Old Low Income | Family Stage Low Income | Young Poor

	2019	2030	2,045
Population Mns	3,122	3,425	3,595
Population Growth rate pa	1.2%	0.8%	0.3%
Share of Global Population	42.7%	42.5%	41.1%
Median Age	29	33	38
GDP US$ Bn	13.7	18.3	26.7
GDP Real Grwoth Ratepa	3.9%	2.6%	2.6%
Share of Global GDP	16.1%	16.0%	17.3%
GDP per cap (US$)	4,398	5,338	7,421
GDP per cap grwoth rate pa	2.7%	1.8%	2.2%

	2019	2030	2,045
Population Mns	1,332	1,717	2,309
Population Growth rate pa	2.5%	2.3%	2.0%
Share of Global Population	18.2%	21.3%	26.4%
Median Age	19	21	23
GDP US$ Bn	2.0	3.4	7.1
GDP Real Grwoth Ratepa	4.1%	4.9%	5.1%
Share of Global GDP	2.3%	2.9%	4.6%
GDP per cap (US$)	1,494	1,953	3,078
GDP per cap grwoth rate pa	1.6%	2.5%	3.1%

Chapter Three - Births Deaths and Migration

The size and age profile of the future population of a country is significantly determined by three items. The birth rate (that is the propensity of a woman aged 15 to 49 years to have a child in any one year), the number of such women by age, and the propensity of a person dying in any one year by age and gender. There is a fourth factor, migration, but while important for a few countries it is not significant for most.

This chapter examines the trends in all four of these variables and their implications for the future size and age profile of the relevant populations. Except for migration, which is subject to government decisions, the relevant variables all tend to have quite stable trends and as such the forecasts have a high degree of reliability.

In the case of death rates, they are very much a function of the nutritional, emotional, and educational experience of the individual when they were a child. For that reason, they change slowly, and the trend is not easily influenced by the government or society albeit subject to the availability of healthcare.

Typically, the trend is downward *within* an age group due to improved understanding of wellness, nutrition, and healthy lifestyles along with greater availability of healthcare facilities. But do note that the average death rate of a society or country goes up as the population ages.

Similarly, the trend in birth rates is difficult to change. Except for China, where the government could impose an abrupt change, a government's attempts to lower/increase the rate of births are generally of limited success. It requires a shift of attitude in society and that happens generationally rather than instantly.

Finally, the number of women of childbearing age is predetermined for the next 15 years as all those women are already alive. That is, the 15 to 49 years of age cohort in 15 years time are the 0-to-34-year age cohort today. A small number will die – but death rates in that age range are low – and some will migrate but not sufficient to significantly change the absolute number.

It might be noted that China did not achieve a 'One Child Policy'. For the last 20 years, the average number of births per woman aged 15 to 49 years has been 1.4. Under the original policy, a very high proportion of the population could have a second child if the first was female.

The number of women of childbearing age is a very significant variable – more so than the birth rate. An example of this is China. As explained in Chapter Ten on China – it has now relaxed the 'One-Child Policy' to what is now effectively an 'Up to Three Child Policy' for any couple.

However, in the next 15 years, the number of women of childbearing age will decline by 28% from 334 million women in 2020 to a reliably estimated 282 million in 2035 and a projected 238 million by 2045. (This forecast to 2045 assumes an increased birth rate of 47 per thousand by then as a result of the relaxed birth policy.) The reduction in the number of women aged 15 to 49 is a function of the earlier implementation of the One-Child Policy. It is this decline in the number of women, rather than a change in birth rates, that will result in total births declining from 15 million in 2019 to 11 million in 2035 and stay at around that level through to 2045. For this not to happen would require a significant increase in the 2019 birth rate (from 44 births per thousand women aged 15 to 49 years to 63 per thousand).

There is a belief by some that 'more people' is better for an economy, and for that reason discuss the importance of countries maintaining birth rates. The belief is that failure to do so will lead to economic doom.

However, this chapter shows that this is not necessarily the case by providing a comparison of two different projected birth rates for Nigeria – one scenario is the passive trend and the other assumes a significant reduction in the birth rate by 2030 and that continues through to 2045.

This demonstrates that the assumption that things will be worse if the population is not growing may not be valid. It shows how dramatically the demand for education *places* reduces under such a change and the consequent potential for a focus on the quality of education rather than scrambling to keep up with ever-growing demand. As shown, this ultimately has a payoff in that while the workforce may be smaller, it is better educated, healthier and more productive than it would otherwise have been, and total GDP is maintained and GDP per capita increased.

The least predictable of the variables determining the size and age profile of a country's future population is migration. Inward migration is very much a function of Government policy, and this can change very rapidly. Indications are that there is a general trend towards tightening borders. Perhaps this should be encouraged as there appears to be good data showing how the affluent countries (who pay better wages) are attracting skilled workers from poorer countries to the extent that is damaging those economies. The forecasts used in this analysis are for migration to moderate – because of restricted access rather than a lack of desire to migrate.

Greece's labour force has declined from 4.5 million to 3.8 million in the last 10 years – which given that the loss is almost certainly biased to the more skilled worker leaving for higher-paying locations within the European Union – is catastrophic for the economy.

As a result of the trend in these variables, there are very different outcomes projected in terms of the future population size by Country Segment as well as by country. This is summarised in Figure 1-2.

The Older Affluent countries are projected to be virtually unchanged in population size by 2045 with inward migration offsetting a small decline in natural population growth. The Older Low Income Segment declines in absolute number as natural population growth is negative and migration is low or negative. China, for reasons discussed above in terms of a declining number of births, reduces by 79 million persons. The Family Stage Low Income Segment, not surprisingly given it is the Family stage, grows, but at a moderate pace – as does India.

The standout segment is, of course, the Young Poor. Very simply, the population of this Country Segment is projected to almost double in the next 25 years. That of course has many implications in terms of education, health care, employment, and incomes per capita as discussed in subsequent chapters.

Figure 1-2: Current and Projected Total Population of the Four Country Segments. 2019 and 2045.

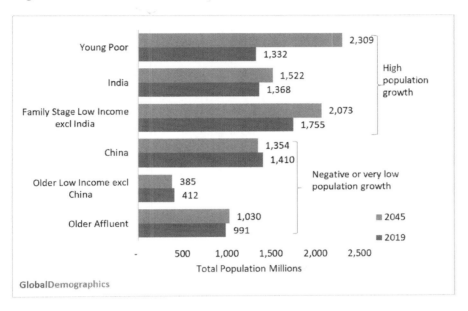

GlobalDemographics

Chapter Four. The Global Age Profile

The key point of this Chapter is to demonstrate that the 'age profile' of the global population (and consumers) will go through a significant change through to 2045. There will be quite dramatic changes in the trends of individual age groups, and except for the youngest age group they are largely inevitable and have significant implications for the economies of the world. Consumption patterns and volumes will change – as will growth rates.

In many respects, the projected changes pivot around what is termed the Working-age Empty Nester Segment (ages 40-45 to 64-70 years, no dependent children at home). Age groups below that are typically stable or declining in size and age groups over 69 years are increasing in size. Especially in the countries that account for most of the global consumption expenditure.

There will be quite dramatic changes in the trends of different age groups, and they are inevitable and have significant implications for the economies of the world. Consumption patterns and volumes will change – as will growth rates.

As shown in Figure 1-3, within the Older Affluent Countries (which accounted for 62% of household consumption expenditure in 2019) the Working-age Empty Nester Segment grew from 273 million persons in 2005 to 324 million by 2020, with an additional 51 million persons in a key spending segment. By 2020 it was 33% of the total population.

Figure 1-3: Relative Size and Projected Trend in Key Age Segments in The **Older Affluent Countries** *Who Accounted For 62% Of Global Consumption Expenditure In 2020.*

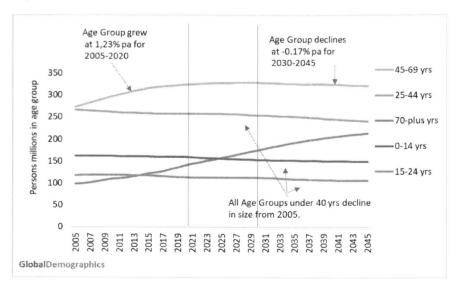

That, combined with increased household incomes, made this consumer segment very important over the last decade in terms of both growth and value. But from 2020 to 2030 this segment is projected to show virtually no growth in the absolute number of persons – peaking at 329 in 2028 – and then decline steadily thereafter. This is a significant change in trend.

But the issue of changing consumer demand does not stop there. In the same Country Segment (Older Affluent) the younger age consumers (0 to 39 years) have been in a slow decline in absolute number for the last decade (down from 543 million to 531 million. This trend is projected to continue to 2045 when there would be 496 million. The 'Youth/Young' market is not a 'growth' opportunity in the 'Affluent' part of the world.

The decline in the number of potential consumers is not, however, confined to the Older Affluent Countries. An almost identical trend is happening in the Older Low-Income Countries which collectively account for a further 18% of total household consumption expenditure in the world. Furthermore, in percentage terms, the decline is even greater.

The decline in the number of core consumers may not mean less consumption expenditure because, as detailed subsequently in the chapter on incomes, they are still growing in affluence. But it almost certainly means *slower growth* of total consumption expenditure compared with the previous decade for this segment of countries.

In aggregate the youth market (0 to 39 years) globally, outside the very poor countries, is now in decline in terms of the absolute number of persons. It is now the 'age of the older middle-aged!'

In contrast, in the Young Poor Country Segment, the total number of consumers in all age groups is increasing, and rapidly. The 0-14 added 107 million in the last decade and is projected to add nearly the same number in the next decade. The 15 to 39 age group is projected to add 152 million consumers. The problem is that in 2020, due to their low incomes/earning power this group of countries collectively accounted for just 3% of total household consumption expenditure. As such their impact on total global consumption and hence the demand for workers is not likely to be significant.

Chapter Five – Education

Education influences the overall development of a country. First, it impacts the propensity to have children. As education standards go up so does the propensity to have children go down. In countries where the education level of the adult population is high, the birth rate is typically below 50 per thousand women of childbearing age. This reflects an understanding of life's choices and contraception, and an awareness of the cost of a child versus responsibility to the child.

The Existing age profile, and trends in birth rates, death rates and migration 'size' a society. Education 'shapes' it. Unfortunately, while it is critically important as a variable, it is also one of the slowest to change

---

Education impacts our lifespan. Better educated people have a greater understanding of hygiene, nutrition, and wellness. This is reflected in better diets, exercise and ensuring their society has a functioning healthcare system. The result of this is already evident in the difference in life spans of the societies that have had a functioning universal education system versus those that do not.

Finally, education impacts affluence and hence lifestyle choice. A better-educated person is more employable and typically more productive, in that they can make greater use of capital equipment. The data across 116 countries for the last 15 years indicates that investment in equipment that enhances productivity *follows* education. Until society has an education level where at least half the population has a lower secondary education or better, fixed capital investment remains relatively low per worker.

The benefits of education are considerable and self-evident. What is the problem?

Simply put, it takes time to implement. A child is not educated overnight. To get a child from entering the school at age 5 to being a lower secondary graduate at age 12 takes, by definition, seven years. To upper secondary, it typically takes an additional 3 to 4 years. This means a change in the availability of education will not even begin to impact the quality of the labour force until at least 10 years later. It can take a further ten years before the overall education profile of the labour force is significantly improved to attract fixed capital investment. That is a long time in the life of a politician – who is the determinant of the funds for such facilities.

A change in the availability of education will not even begin to impact the quality of the labour force until at least 10 years later. It can take a further ten years before the overall education profile of the labour force is significantly improved. That is a long time in the life of a politician.

This chapter examines the availability of education within the Country Segments as well as in individual countries. It shows how there are four groups of countries that transcend the earlier defined Country Segments. That is,

- countries that already have a good education profile and are aggressively investing further in education;
- those countries that are coasting because education is already high and that advantage does not disappear in the short term;
- those with weak education now but doing the right thing by spending relatively more (than most countries) on education to lift the countries (children's) prospects and finally;
- those countries with a weak education profile and who appear to not care as they underspend on it (in terms of share of GDP) relative to other countries. (They also underspend on health!).

This failure of some countries to provide adequate education has significant implications for the world, not just the countries where it is happening. The youth in these countries emerge from their childhood with limited capability to gain employment and to live a reasonable lifestyle. This is not good for those societies or the others they choose to emigrate to.

It is estimated that in 2020 about 36 million persons will turn 15 years of age but with limited education and are looking for work. This increases to 52 million persons per annum in 2045. Will they find work? If not, what will they do?

As shown in Figure 1-4 there is also a significant difference between countries (and Country Segments) in terms of the trend in demand for education.

Figure 1-4: *Projected Trend in Number of School-Age Children by Country Segment.*

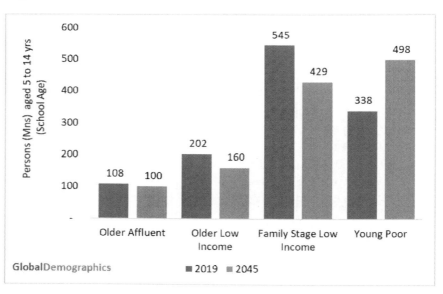

For most countries, the number of school-age persons (5 to 14 years) is actually in decline. That means the same education budget enables a greater spending per student and hence a lift in quality.

However, for some countries, the number of school-age persons is projected to increase significantly (circa 50%) which means those countries have to increase their education spending by a similar amount just to stand still in terms of availability and quality. Unfortunately, these also tend to be countries where education is currently at a low standard.

Finally, this Chapter on education looks at how the overall level of education of the adult population can be expected to improve in the future. It demonstrates how long it takes for change to be effective and compares India (which only in the last few years has introduced universal education – that is all males, females, urban and rural aged 6 to 12 years are required to attend school and it is free) with China who introduced that same policy in 1984. The difference in the current education profile of adults (and workforce) is considerable – as are the capabilities of the economies. Furthermore, it is hard to close the gap.

Chapter Six - Employment

Employed persons are, of course, the 'engine' of the economy. The greater the proportion of the population that is in work the stronger the economy. Not only in terms of total productivity (Gross Domestic Product) but also in household incomes because there would be more workers per household.

This chapter highlights the two different stories in terms of employment that exist across the countries covered in this analysis.

In the older (and generally more affluent) countries the total labour force is not projected to grow relative to the population, and in some cases, it declines. As such the pressure to create *additional* jobs is low to non-existent. This minimises unemployment. It means the focus moves to lifting productivity per worker.

Nor, for most of these countries, is the ratio of workers to dependents (old or young) expected to decline precipitously. It is important to be aware that in Older Affluent countries, the definition of working age is changing, and this has significant implications for the size of the workforce in those countries.

Working-age now extends to age 74. Already in the USA, 24% of males aged 70 to 74 years are in full-time employment. The same in Japan and some other countries with similar life expectancy and affluence levels. Age 65 to 74 is typically the fastest-growing age group, and the inclusion of workers from this age range is projected to largely offset the declining number of young entrants into the labour force. The proposition by some that these countries need migrants to sustain the economy does not have credibility.

Working-age is no longer 15 to 64 years. It now extends to age 74 in the more affluent countries, and they are not running out of workers.

This chapter demonstrates how a very different picture exists for the Young Poor Country Segment. The number of persons of working age (in this case years 15 to 64 inclusive due to shorter life expectancy) is projected to increase substantially. Currently, there are 742 million persons in this age range living in countries where the GDP per capita is below US$10,000 and education standards are low. This is projected to increase to 1.00 billion in 2030 and 1.42 billion by 2045.

Currently, 475 million of these people are employed – that is 64% of the 742 million aged 15-to-64-years. If that rate of employment is to be maintained, then an **additional** 443 million jobs need to be found in the next 25 years. This ignores any possibility of increased participation rates as would be required if female participation is to increase.

The obvious question is, will those jobs be found or even available? Competition between the countries for low skilled workers will be intense as the downside is unemployment and possible civil unrest. The inability to find enough work opportunities at an adequate pay level also drives the level of emigration. This is a real issue for the African Continent and South and Central America. Their (more skilled) workforce leaves.

Slower growth in the number of affluent consumers and their incomes combined with increased productivity per worker indicates that global consumption will require an additional 303 million workers by 2045. Unfortunately, there will be an additional 725 million persons looking for work by that year. This is a catastrophic scenario.

Chapter Seven – Household Incomes

Household income (or revenue available to save or spend – as it can be from other sources than just wages) is important as it determines the nature of lifestyles that can be afforded in a country.

It is a difficult variable to measure. For many households, their income comes from multiple sources, not just paid employment, and that needs to be considered. Therefore, this chapter starts with a detailed explanation of how household income has been determined for this analysis. The analysis shows the estimated average household income across all 116 countries and its distribution within countries. There is a huge difference in the income distribution of the four Country Segments (let alone by individual countries). Interestingly it shows how inequality of income within countries is worse in poor countries than it is in affluent countries. Figure 1-5 shows the difference between Country Segments in both the average and median household income.

Given the generally positive GDP forecasts used for this analysis, *average* household incomes are projected to increase – albeit at different rates depending on the nature of the country.

Figure 1-5: Estimated Average and Median Household Income by Country Segment in 2019 (US$s per household)

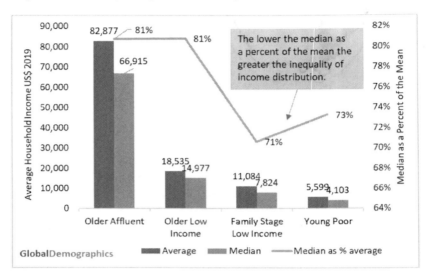

GlobalDemographics

While claims are made about the growth of a middle class in the Young Poor Countries, this hides an unfortunate truth – the lowest income segment was also growing. Globally, the lowest income segment (under US$5,000 pa) increased by 28 million households in the last decade.

Obviously, in an ideal world, this disparity in incomes would be less, but that is not, and will not, be the case. However, it is interesting to question why it exists. It is argued that the key differentiator in terms of outcomes is the level of education.

China is a good example of the value of education. It introduced compulsory education for all 6 to 12-year-olds in 1984 irrespective of gender or whether they were urban or rural-based. From 1998 onward around 20 million younger persons were moving from low paying rural employment to higher-paid/more productive manufacturing and tertiary employment, thereby lifting incomes. If only other countries followed this example!

Chapter Eight – Consumption Expenditure

The world has just gone through a consumption boom. In the last decade, total expenditure by all households grew at 2.6% per annum. However, as shown in Figure 1-6, the older countries – who are the biggest spenders – were the slowest growing. The Older Affluent grew at 1.6% per annum and the Older Low Income Country Segment (excluding China) grew at 1.9% per annum.

Figure 1-6: Historic and Projected Growth Rate Per Annum for Consumption Expenditure by Country Segment and China.

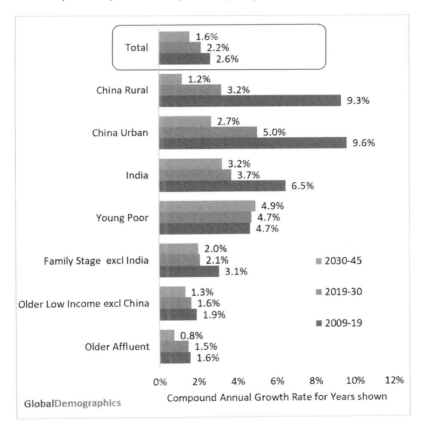

The major driver of consumption growth in the older countries was, as shown in Figure 1-6, urban China where real private consumption expenditure grew at 9.6% per annum from 2009 to 2019.

For the next decade to 2030 and then through to 2045 the older countries (Older Affluent, Older Low Income and China) who combined, account for 78% of all consumption expenditure in 2019 are projected to show much slower growth. This is very much a function of the projected declining number of consumers in these countries as detailed in the previous chapter and the slower rate of income growth.

Even urban China, which accounted for so much consumption growth in the last decade, is expected to show a significant reduction in the growth rate of its consumption expenditure. Down from 9.6% for 2009 to 2019 to 5.0% for the decade to 2030 and then 2.7% for 2030 to 2045. The reasons for this are discussed in Chapter 10 but are essentially a function of the inevitable changing age profile of the population. (Note, urban China accounts for 81% of consumer spending within China).

This analysis shows that the growth area of consumption expenditure after 2030 is going to be the consumption spending by India and the other Younger Countries. These new consumers are very different from the ones who drove consumption in the past. While the total spending is considerable, compared with the older countries the spending per household will be significantly lower and biased to the needs of a very young population. So expect a consumption shift.

Projections indicate that the annual growth rate of expenditure by the 'Older Affluent' falls to 0.8% from 2030 to 2045. These people currently account for 62% of all consumption.

However, the older countries dominate consumption expenditure and as a result, the rate of global growth in consumption expenditure is expected to slow. At the same time, the productivity of workers is increasing (globally at 1.67% per annum) and is projected to continue to improve over time. This means that the number of workers needed to meet the consumption demand does not grow as rapidly as needed to ensure ongoing employment.

The resulting gap is substantial. The difference between those expecting to be in work (persons of working age multiplied by the trend in the propensity to be employed) and the number that find work is estimated to be 400 million by 2045. That is a significant shortfall and indicates that the propensity to be employed in the Young Poor countries could fall to 38%.

The slower growth in consumption expenditure means the difference between those expecting to be in work (persons of working age multiplied by the trend in the propensity to be employed) and the number that find work is estimated to be 400 million by 2045. That is a significant shortfall and indicates that the propensity to be employed in the Young Poor countries could fall to 38%.

Chapter Nine – Health

This is an important chapter in the context of the future. It starts by combining the trends in incidence/prevalence of chronic health conditions by age and gender with the trends in the age/gender profile of the population. By doing so it identifies where demand for health services is likely to grow.

The demand for health care by an individual typically starts to increase more rapidly after age 40. But the over 40 years of age population in the older countries is no longer increasing rapidly in size. In comparison, the young countries are now transitioning to being middle-aged. As a result, the 40 plus age groups are the growth age segment. This means that the projected rate of increase in demand for health services is greater for the younger (and typically less affluent) countries than it is for the older affluent countries.

Figure 1-7 shows the projected increase in demand by Country Segment based on the number of persons by age and gender and probability of having a chronic health condition. The age projections are quite reliable and the probability of having a health condition is probably conservative.

The year 2019 sums to 100 so the index values show change from that year.

As is apparent between 2019 and 2045 the projected demand for each country segment except the Older Affluent is expected to increase by over 60%. In contrast, the index of demand for health services in the Old Affluent countries is projected to only increase from 21 to 28 by 2045. The advantage of already being old.

Whereas demand for health services is projected to double in the less affluent countries (due to ageing) in the Older Affluent countries demand will grow by just 28% (they are already old).

Figure 1-7: Indexed trend in Demand for Health Services 2009 to 2045.

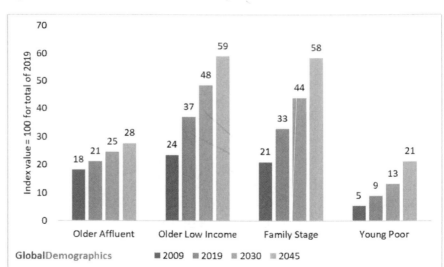

Healthcare expenditure tends to increase in line with affluence – be it GDP per capita of the country or household income. However, it is constrained in that there are other demands on the funds available.

Analysis indicates that the Older Affluent countries can afford to increase their spending *per health condition* by 1% per annum through to 2045 and stay under the 'normative' 15% share of GDP level. This suggests that the future demand for healthcare in those countries is probably affordable.

The younger countries with much higher growth rates in demand for healthcare, fortunately also have higher projected GDP growth rates. They could sustain a 2% increase per annum in health care expenditure per health condition and stay within a 10% share of GDP. Consequently, this is where one might expect faster growth of total health expenditure in absolute terms for the next 25 years.

However, there are some very significant differences between Country Segments (and within them) in terms of expenditure per relevant person. (Relevant person is the number of persons aged either 0 to 4 years or 40 years and above as those are the age ranges where health conditions are most prevalent).

Figure 1-8 shows the total health expenditure per (relevant) capita for each of 2005 and 2019. The fastest-growing in terms of expenditure per relevant person was the Older Low Income – and effectively China.

As demonstrated in Figure 1-8 it has increased significantly (4.4% per annum). The Family Stage Low Income increased at 1.5% per annum then Young Poor at a rather concerning 1.7% per annum.

This leads to the other key issue in terms of health, that is, who pays? The government or the individual (private)? It is perverse that the countries where the individual is best able to afford reasonable health care (i.e., the Affluent) are typically the ones where social medicine (i.e., paid by the government) is most available. In those countries, 61% of the total health spending is paid for by the Government – making it a political issue as it typically accounts for 20% of Government expenditure. In many of these countries, the share paid by the government exceeds 70%.

Figure 1-8: Health Expenditure per relevant Capita by Country Segment. 2009 and 2019.

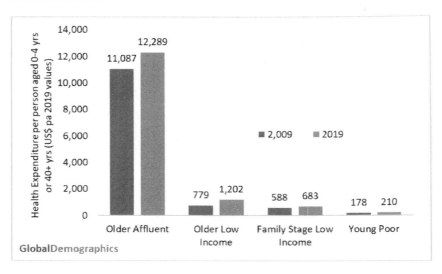

In poor countries, the government share of health expenditure is quite low (the average for these countries is 29%) indicating that the burden rests with the individual household. This is unfortunate as these households have very low incomes and cannot afford anything but the most basic treatment. These countries also allocate below average GDP to health (and education!)

It is perverse that the countries where the individual is best able to afford reasonable health care (i.e., the Affluent) are typically the ones where social medicine (i.e., paid by the government) is most available.

Chapter Ten – China

This and the next chapter (which is about India) are necessary. With 1.4 billion persons in 2020 for China and 1.38 Bn (increasing to 1.52 Bn by 2045) persons for India, they account for a very large proportion of the global population. As such their Demographic Trends are important – but they are very different stories.

China is in many respects a success story. While clearly, it has a way to go before it can be described as an affluent country it has over the last two decades significantly improved the affluence of its citizens and with that, their lifestyle. How did that happen?

This chapter examines the real nature of the 'One Child Policy' (it was not) and how that combined with the introduction of compulsory schooling for all 6- to 12-year-olds (urban and rural, male, and female) in 1984 enabled the mass migration (average of 19 million persons a year for the last decade) from rural to urban locations and occupations> This lifted productivity per worker by a factor of 3 or more. This resulted in a rapid increase in household incomes and improved lifestyles.

This chapter shows how China, like Japan and most of the Older Affluent countries, is moving from the 'pyramid' to the 'square' population profile. With the number of young people stable, such countries can shift their focus from supplying an increasing quantity, to increasing the quality, of social services such as education and health with the same budget.

The changes in the Chinese Government's policy on births are described in detail in this chapter. The Government has moved from the 'One-Child Policy' to a 'Three-Child' Policy. With that, there will be a marginal lift in the birth rate. It is marginal as even under the 'One-Child Policy' a high proportion of couples could have a second child – and did (the average woman had 1.45 children in the last decade).

It is projected that the average number of births per thousand women will lift marginally from 44 to 47 but that will not offset the 'locked in' decline for the next 15 years of the number of women of childbearing age because of the earlier restrictions on births. The number is projected to decline in number from 334 million women aged 15 to 49 years in 2020 to

298 million in 2035 and then to 239 million by 2045. This means that total births are projected to decline from the current level of 15 million in 2019 to 11 million in 2035 and stay at around that level to 2045. (In 2020 and 2021 it dropped to 12 million but that is off-trend because of the COVID-19 pandemic).

This means China's total population will peak in 2028 and gradually decline after that. In addition, its working-age population is already in decline. This does raise the issue of whether the unavoidable reduction (over the next 15 years) in the working-age population will impact China's economic growth?

China's total population will peak in 2028 and gradually decline after that. Its working-age population is already in decline.

Analysis shows that it is rural rather than the urban working-age population (and labour force) that is in decline. As shown in Figure 1-9 the urban labour force is projected to continue to grow, albeit at a reducing rate, for the next 25 years (to 2045) as a result of the ongoing rural to urban migration and the younger profile of the urban population. This indicates that while the overall GDP growth rate may slow it probably will not go negative.

Rural-Urban migration means that while China's total labour force will decline in future, the urban labour force continues to grow to 2045. Urban workers are nearly three times more productive than the rural labour force.

The impact of rural to urban migration has had a significant impact on the relative age profile of the urban and rural populations. It has resulted in the Working-age Empty Nester segment (40 to 64 years of age) in urban China exhibiting explosive growth over the last decade.

Figure 1-9: Historic and Projected Trend in the Size of China's Urban and Rural Labour Forces.

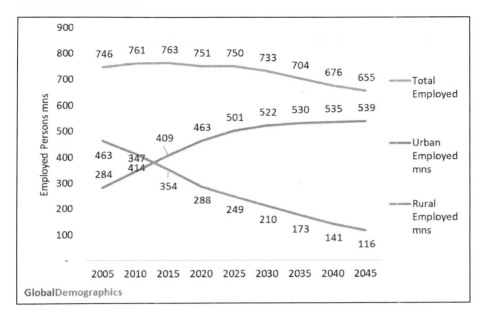

GlobalDemographics

Given that Working-age Empty Nesters tend to have a higher level of discretionary spending power, this probably drove the rapid growth in retail and particularly discretionary retail, (including services as well as goods) for the last decade. However, the numerical growth of this consumer age group is projected to slow into the next decade and then decline. This will have implications for the retail market of China. Especially as the total number of young people is also in slow decline.

An issue that China is going to have to deal with is the male bias of the marrying age population for the next 25 years. By 2045 it is estimated that there will be 28 million males who are in or have passed through, marrying age (25 to 34 years) and were not able to form a family of their own. Being a family person is a significant stabilizer for society, so this is a potential social issue – for which there is no apparent easy solution.

Chapter Eleven – India

The expectation of India in many people's minds is that it will be 'Another China'. India with its large, young population is expected to replicate what happened in China – that is, the rapid growth of an (urban) workforce (the so-called 'Demographic Dividend') which has greater productivity than the rural workforce, and hence drive-up affluence.

This chapter examines how the dynamics of a growing working-age population, improving education profile and propensity to find work will play out in the context of India.

Importantly it deals with the issue of the demographic dividend. It shows how the evolving age profile of India, impacted in part by a significant reduction in birth rates in the last decade, will play out in terms of the number of additional working-age persons. This is summarised in Figure 1-10.

Figure 1-10: The Evolving Age Profile of India to 2045.

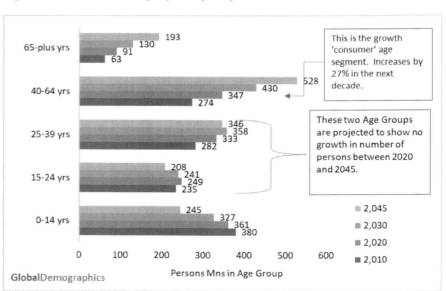

It shows how India is no longer a 'young' country. Rather it is transiting to middle age and away from the Pyramid model, with its constant scramble to provide enough social needs to meet an ever-growing young population, to a population where middle-age is the norm and growth is in the over 40-year aged segment.

In short, it shows how the India of the next 25 years is going to have very different dynamics from the India of the past two decades. In that respect, it is important to note that the 'demographic dividend' has largely been played out and the inability to maintain earlier levels of employment meant that there was no dividend.

India in the next 25 years is going to have very different population dynamics from the India of the past two decades.

This chapter also addresses the key strategic weakness of India – education. It has been late moving to universal education (that is education is available free to all 6 to 12 years olds irrespective of gender or urban/rural location). This is now improving dramatically, but as shown in this chapter, and stated earlier in the chapter on education, it takes time to educate a child – there is no quick fix.

The implications of this for employment over the last decade and the next 25 years are examined. The ability to leverage the remaining years of the demographic dividend depends on lifting the education profile of the workforce. The competitive set of countries to India in terms of skill (education) and wages also has an increasing number of persons looking for work – and this will have implications for India's Future.

Finally, it shows that although India's total population grows continuously through to 2045, the rate of growth slows significantly as a result of a significant decline in birth rates (initially) and then the number of couples of childbearing age. This in turn has implications for the size and nature of the future consumer segments in India.

To Conclude

It is intended that the subsequent Chapters, covering the subjects detailed above, provide a good understanding of how the socio-demographic aspects of the world *may* change over the next 25 years.

As mentioned, overall demographic trends are relatively stable so the projections in terms of the number of people, age profile, working-age population and number of households are quite reliable. Even the pandemic of 2020 will have only a minor impact, not observable in the gross data.

Financial data, specifically household incomes and expenditure are a function of GDP forecasts which themselves are impacted by levels of employment and a wide range of external factors. The projected absolute levels of income in future years are less reliable than the projections for demographic data. We publish our GDP forecasts in an Appendix to this Book, and to the extent that this is correct in future, so much the better. But it will not be correct, and it may be necessary to revise the forecasts of household income and expenditure up or down depending on your level of optimism regarding the Gross Domestic Product growth of a specific country.

Subject to that caveat, the analysis given in the subsequent chapters shows that there will be quite dramatic, and inevitable, changes in the profile of the world's population over the next 25 years. Nearly half the countries (typically those with older populations) are projected to have no further population growth and are moving away from the 'population pyramid 'concept to a 'population square' concept.

It is argued that this is sociologically preferable. An ever-expanding (pyramid-shaped) population profile is not good for the earth. Nor is it good for a country. It needs to cater to maintaining standards for an expanding population (and dependents) rather than improving the quality of life for the existing population.

Population growth is projected to take place in what are the young (and also, unfortunately, the poor) countries. They will almost double in population in the next 25 years. Unfortunately, the projected increase in productivity that takes place is not sufficient to offset the increase in the number of persons and dependents and as a result quality of life does not improve significantly.

Given that these countries are typified as having inadequate education and health facilities and generally failing governmental systems this is not good and is going to create a significant social issue in the future. Probably reflected in internal strife as well as significant (illegal) migration waves by people who simply want to live safely and decently.

As also shown in the subsequent Chapters, it is not just a story about increasing or declining populations. There are some very significant sub-stories in terms of the changing age profile of the populations. We divide the population into five key age segments which represent at a macro level, key shifts in an individual's lifestyle as they age. From a child through to a retired older adult. Where a country is today in terms of the relative emphasis of its population on these stages, and how that will change over the next 25 years is a significant factor in determining the future path of the country.

It is also a story about balance. In some respects, the world has been fortunate in the way different needs and capabilities have balanced out in the past. The obvious one is the growth of consumption which has created work for the growing working-age population globally. In reading the subsequent chapters the reader will see where there is the potential for that 'balance' to be upset. Particularly in terms of availability of work. It remains to be seen just how significant these will be.

The subsequent chapters should be treated a little like following a journey as new issues emerge, and potential conflicts of forces arise. We hope it makes you think.

The differences between the four Country Segments on a range of relevant variables such as birth rates, life expectancy, incomes, health, education, and employment are considerable. The world is not homogeneous and future trends are quite diverse.

Chapter 2
The World at a Glance

Introduction

This book examines how the demographic and socio-economic profile of 116 countries is likely to develop over the next 25 years. These countries account for 91% of the world's estimated total population (by the United Nations), so while not strictly global it is sufficiently encompassing for it to identify any major issues that are evolving in the world. The missing countries typically have smaller populations and economies and are hence unlikely to disturb the trends evident in the countries included here.

The 116 countries included in this analysis account for 91% of the world's population as estimated by the United Nations and 95% of the world's GDP as estimated by the World Bank in 2019.

It would be time-consuming to reach any sort of conclusion about the future shape of the world if all 116 countries were discussed individually. What is needed is a useful framework within which to group the countries so that key trends can be properly identified and discussed.

The obvious route for that is to group them on the two variables which appear to influence future demographic and socio-economic outcomes most significantly. That is:

- Age and

- Affluence (as measured by GDP per capita)

The Age Dimension

In the case of age, the best summary statistic is 'median age' rather than the 'average age'. Median age is the age at which half a country's population is younger than it, and the other half is older than it. A country with a median age of 25 has half its population under the age of 25 years and a half above 25 years.

Age is important as it does significantly determine the relative importance of the different lifestyle stages in a country. If the median age of a country is young (e.g., close to 25 years) then it means a significant proportion of the population is still in their formative years. Family size is probably larger (over 3 persons and probably 4) and the aged population (those over 65 years) is a relatively small proportion of the total population. It also means that the number of entrants into working age (if not the actual workforce) is likely to remain strong if not increase in number in the next 25 years depending on birth rates.

In contrast, a country with a high median age, for example, 40 years, has a very different profile. Probably the number of persons reaching working age (15 to 18 years depending on the availability of education to higher stages) is flat or declining. The average family is two-person or three with either a single older child or older relative, and the aged population (over 64 years) is a significant and growing proportion of the total population.

These two countries, one at each extreme of the age profile, will evolve very differently over the next 25 years. They will also have quite different consumption patterns.

The Affluence Dimension

In terms of affluence, we have selected to use Gross Domestic Product per capita rather than Household Income per capita, for segmenting the countries. This is for the following reasons.

1. GDP per capita is widely reported and a relatively reliable measure.

2. It reflects the total funds available per person and not just their earnings. It encompasses possible benefits from the State in terms of infrastructure, health care etc. and as such normalizes the impact of different political systems (and tax rates) on an individual's welfare.

Global Age/Affluence Segments

We have grouped the 116 countries on these two criteria and the result is shown in Figure 2-1. A listing of the countries in each group is given later in this Chapter.

Figure 2-1: Top Level Segmentation of Countries.

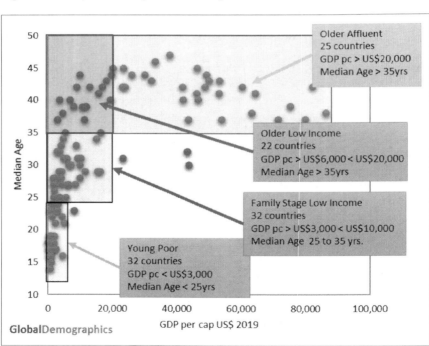

As shown in Figure 2-1 there are four segments. Two of them are very distinctive on both dimensions – older and affluent or very young and poor. The other two differ more in the age dimension than the affluence dimension. But this age difference has a significant impact on the future demographic profile of countries and hence the distinction between the two groups.

The four Country Segments are as follows:

1. The Older Affluent countries. This segment consists of countries where the median age is *over* 35 years and the average GDP per capita is *more than* US$20,000 p.a. in 2019. It contains 25 of 116 countries. As shown in Figure 2-1, while the age profile is relatively similar across these countries there is a significant difference within this segment in terms of GDP per capita. Their unweighted[1] average age is 40 years and the average GDP per capita is US$49,146.

2. The Older Less Affluent countries. This segment consists of countries where the median age is *over* 35 years and the average GDP per capita is *below* US$20,000 p.a. but mainly *over* US$6,000 p.a. This segment contains 22 countries, one of which is China.

3. Family Stage Low-Income countries. This is where the median age is *between* 25 years and 35 years and GDP per capita is *below* US$10,000, and typically over US$3,000 p.a. This segment contains 33 of the 116 countries. India is included in this Segment.

4. The Young Poor countries. The median age of the populations in these countries is *below* 25 years (with some below 20 years) and GDP per capita is mainly below US$3,000 per annum. This segment contains 32 countries.

Three countries fall outside the definitions of the four groups, and they are younger and affluent. They are all in the Middle East – namely Saudi Arabia, UAE, and Israel.

---

[1] Unweighted age/GDP per Capita is where all the countries are treated equally. Weighted is where their relative population size/GDP is considered.

The following pages summarize the details of each of the four Country Segments. It also provides a 'glimpse' of the degree of change that is expected to take place over the next 25 years.

What is interesting is that three of the segments have quite a distinct geographical underpinning. This is demonstrated in the discussion on each of the four segments subsequently in this Chapter.

The 'Older Affluent' are Western Europe, North America, Northeast Asia, and Australasia. The Older lower income is China, Russia, and Eastern Europe (socialist or ex-socialist states predominate). The 'Young Poor' segment is strongly biased toward Africa (North and South) supplemented by some developing Asia and Central American countries.

In contrast, the 'Family Stage Low Income' segment is widely spread – including South America, South Asia (India and Bangladesh), stretching down into Southeast Asia and across the Middle East. In many ways, this is a more diverse segment geographically and sociologically.

The Older Affluent Segment

The countries in this segment are relatively concentrated geographically. They currently have a total population of just under 1 billion persons, with the largest being the United States of America at 329 million persons and then Japan at 127 million persons. Iceland at 339,000 is the smallest – by a significant margin. Figure 2-2 shows the geographical spread of them.

Figure 2-2: Geographical Spread of the Older Affluent Country Segment.

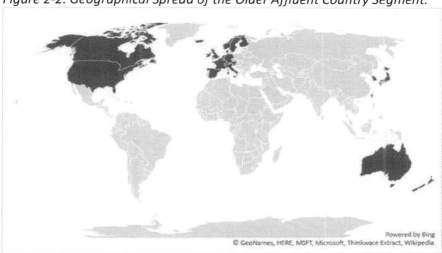

Table 2-1 summarizes the countries included in this segment and their key statistics and obviously, the interesting aspect of Table 2-1 is the degree of change that potentially could take place. While the total population of this Country Segment is projected to grow by only 3.5% in total over the next 25 years, the total GDP will lift in absolute terms by 48%, which also results in them being 42% more affluent individually (GDP per capita).

Age is a distinguishing characteristic of this Country Segment. They have a median age of 40 (the lowest is 37) and the oldest is, as one might expect, Japan, at 47 years of age, closely followed by Italy at 46 years and Germany at 45 years. In total, 19 of these 26 countries have a median age of over 40 years and this has significant implications for the nature and size of their future workforce and consumer profile as discussed later.

Table 2-1: The Current and Projected Future Profile of the Older Affluent Countries.

Country	Actual 2019				Projected 2045			
	Population (000s)	Median Age	GDP per cap	Total GDP US$ Bns	Population (000s)	Median Age	GDP per cap	Total GDP US$ Bns
Australia	25,141	37	53,842	1,354	30,739	41	83,394	2,563
Austria	8,932	43	49,977	446	10,478	45	61,223	642
Belgium	11,513	41	46,008	530	12,818	43	48,769	625
Canada	37,359	40	46,480	1,736	44,778	45	47,872	2,144
Denmark	5,770	42	60,325	348	6,150	43	70,887	436
Finland	5,523	42	48,676	269	5,415	47	60,098	325
France	65,074	42	41,738	2,716	66,847	45	45,804	3,062
Germany	83,179	45	46,242	3,846	93,304	45	51,473	4,803
Hong Kong	7,458	44	49,076	366	8,321	51	69,577	579
Iceland	339	37	71,356	24	373	43	125,028	47
Ireland	4,878	37	79,704	389	6,179	42	161,602	999
Italy	60,400	46	33,140	2,002	56,758	52	43,512	2,470
Japan	126,628	47	37,724	4,777	109,301	54	60,633	6,627
Macao	639	38	86,245	55	787	51	98,464	77
Netherlands	17,091	43	53,201	909	17,085	46	70,226	1,200
New Zealand	4,780	37	43,502	208	5,471	42	60,226	329
Norway	5,372	39	75,081	403	6,335	44	68,297	433
South Korea	51,173	43	32,095	1,642	48,798	54	98,402	4,802
Singapore	5,792	41	64,234	372	6,146	53	163,239	1,003
Slovenia	2,075	44	25,903	54	2,030	48	57,974	118
Spain	46,687	44	29,867	1,394	43,480	53	67,929	2,954
Sweden	10,027	41	52,939	531	11,840	41	53,057	628
Switzerland	8,571	42	82,027	703	10,133	46	97,749	990
United Kingdom	67,412	40	41,938	2,827	74,891	43	46,374	3,473
USA	328,801	38	63,206	20,782	351,963	43	86,826	30,559
Total/Average	990,613	40	49,146	48,685	1,030,420	45	69,765	71,887

With an average GDP per capita of US$49,146 per annum in 2019 (and in 2019 values) the older and more affluent countries account for 62% of the world's GDP but only 14% of the world's population.

These countries have a longer life expectancy than those in the other Country Segments and with that, their propensity to stay in employment is longer. Already in the United States of America, Japan and South Korea, 24% of males aged 70 to 74 years are still in full-time employment. This means that for this Country Segment we define retirement as generally starting after age 69 rather than 64. By 2045 age 74 will likely be 'retirement age'. *(Please note that age segments portrayed for this segment -as in Figure 2-3 - differ from that of the other Country Segments for this reason).*

Slow population growth is a function of the age profile of the population. Natural population change (births minus deaths) is low or negative and where there is growth it is typically a function of immigration. As these countries are all relatively well-off, migration is essentially inward.

Figure 2-3 shows how the different age groups of these countries are projected to change in absolute size over the next 25 years. These forecasts are very reliable. Except for the youngest two age groups, all the people in these calculations are already alive today.

Even Covid-19 has had only a marginal impact as the deaths associated with it are significantly biased to persons over 70 years of age and hence does not impact births or workforce size. Also, in a *relative* sense, the number of deaths is quite small.

The only source of error is potentially wrong assumptions about birth rates and perhaps migration. In terms of immigration, for reasons discussed later in this book, we expected that to reduce - because of constraints by these countries rather than because of supply – and this moderates the projected total population growth of this segment of countries.

Figure 2-3: Historic and Projected Trend in the Size of Key Age Segments of Older Affluent Country Segment.

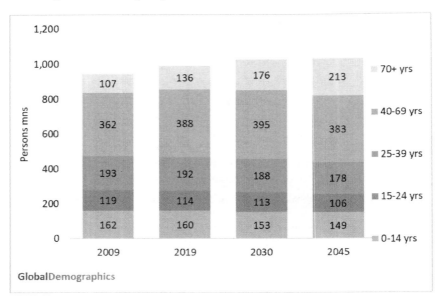

GlobalDemographics

The key headline to take from Figure 2-3 is that the three younger age groups are projected to be in slow decline (-0.03% pa) from 2020 onward. Furthermore, the total population only lifts marginally (4% absolute increase), and migration is a significant factor behind that.

In the Older Affluent Country Segment, every age group except those over 69 years of age is projected to decline in size (less than 0.4% per annum) by 2045. Accounting for 62% of global consumption this has implications for consumer demand.

The over 69-year segment is expected to grow at an average rate of 1.7% per annum. However, do note that even this age group has a slowing growth rate over time. For the decade to 2030 it grows at 2.3% per annum and then for the subsequent decade the growth rate is a more modest 1.8% per annum. From 2040 to 2045 – the last five years of our time horizon – there is almost zero growth in this age group except for 6 countries. This suggests that the Older Affluent Countries are approaching (in 2040) 'Peak Aged'.

The Older Affluent Countries are approaching (in 2040) 'Peak Aged'. That is the oldest age segment is no longer growing rapidly in the number of persons. This has implications for the health and social care sectors.

There is an important economic message that flows from this chart and that **is the total number of affluent consumers is now in slow decline**.

This must-have implications for global demand. In 2019 these countries accounted for 62% of global consumption expenditure.   There were 694 million persons aged 15 to 69 years in 2019 and this is projected to be 695 million in 2030 and 668 million in 2045. So not a massive decline in absolute size, but not a growth segment either.

As shown in Table 2-1, they are expected to achieve a significant increase in individual affluence over the same time, (Gross Domestic Product per capita up 42% in absolute terms) but due to changing consumption habits as the population gets older this may not translate into increased consumption of goods. There are indications (but no hard data) that with the ageing of these populations there is a shift in the pattern of purchases – from things to experiences (clothing to travel) – with implications for demand for workers and an increased propensity to be careful spenders.

We revisit this issue in a later chapter on the nature of consumers, but it is important to note how simple demographic trends can be significant in terms of global impact. Insufficient growth in consumption by the affluent countries can (and is expected to) lead to significant unemployment elsewhere in the world (where the factories are). Unless that consumption is replaced by other regions (see later) there could be a lack of growth in employment opportunities for the global workforce.

The Older Less Affluent Segment

This segment is also relatively concentrated geographically as shown in Figure 2-4. Furthermore, it contains China – which with 1.4 billion persons in 2020, rather dominates the profile of this segment. China is interesting in that it had an explicit policy in terms of births, and it would not be unreasonable to expect it to have a somewhat different age profile from the other countries of the same affluence (GDP per capita). But as demonstrated elsewhere in this book, its age profile is not significantly different from other countries in this segment.

Figure 2-4: Geographical Spread of the Older Lower Income Segment.

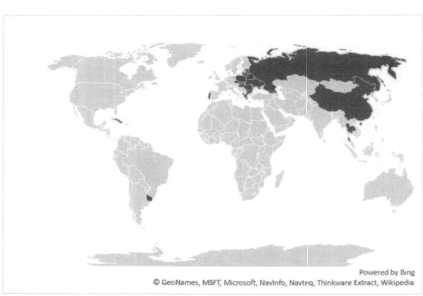

Powered by Bing
© GeoNames, MSFT, Microsoft, Navinfo, Navteq, Thinkware Extract, Wikipedia

Given the Older, Low-Income countries have a relatively high education standard they have a significant resource advantage which will be difficult for other less affluent countries to match in the medium (10 years) term.

In total, an estimated 1.82 billion persons are in this segment but except for China, Russia, Thailand, Ukraine and Poland, the other countries in this segment are relatively small with individual populations under 20 million in 2019.

They also tend to have one other characteristic in common – a lot of them either are, or have been, socialist/communist countries and the reality is, that they encouraged, and invested in, education. As such the gap between these countries and the previous segment in terms of education is not as great as one might expect given differences in relative affluence. This is discussed in greater detail in Chapter Five which looks at education globally.

This is very important as investment follows education. While it is relatively easy to build a factory in a year, educating an individual takes at least 10 years. These countries have a significant resource advantage of well-educated (that is, 44% are educated to upper secondary at least) working-age persons which will attract investment. It will be difficult for countries with poor education profiles to match in the forecast period.

Table 2-2 lists the countries in this segment and shows how their population, age, and GDP per capita are projected to change between 2019 and 2045.

China with a median age of 39 in 2019 is one of the youngest countries in this segment. The fact that China is in this segment of countries is a testament to the success of its compulsory education program and One Child Policy (which helped facilitate it). Otherwise, without its higher GDP per capita, it would be in the next segment to be discussed – Family Low Income.

The average GDP per capita of these countries in 2019 ranges from US$23,739 (Estonia) down to US$2,838 for the Republic of Moldova, but only four of the countries in this segment are below US$6,000 per capita. The average is US$10,793 per capita. However, this Country Segment is generally expected to show good economic growth. In terms of total Gross Domestic Product China is expected to achieve an average annual growth rate of 3.6% per annum. The other countries in this segment are projected to increase their total Gross Domestic Product by 1.7% per annum.

Table 2-2: The Current and Projected Future Profile of the Older Low-Income Countries.

Country	Actual 2019				Projected 2045			
	Population (000s)	Median Age	GDP per cap	Total GDP US$ Bns	Population (000s)	Median Age	GDP per cap	Total GDP US$ Bns
Albania	2,880	35	5,305	15	2,394	48	28,107	67
Belarus	9,437	40	6,684	63	9,071	43	11,993	109
Bulgaria	6,992	44	9,715	68	5,671	47	17,548	100
Cuba	11,324	42	8,815	100	10,323	48	9,460	98
Czechia	10,680	42	23,080	246	10,687	46	57,538	615
Estonia	1,322	42	23,739	31	1,324	46	82,265	109
Georgia	3,989	38	4,448	18	3,839	36	9,225	35
Greece	10,454	45	20,079	210	8,705	54	39,923	348
Hungary	9,673	42	16,641	161	8,510	48	33,096	282
Latvia	1,898	43	17,982	34	1,312	51	58,651	77
Lithuania	2,760	44	19,649	54	1,767	53	39,814	70
Mauritius	1,270	37	11,169	14	1,183	46	25,964	31
Poland	37,818	41	15,658	592	32,960	51	28,926	953
Portugal	10,219	45	23,265	238	8,599	54	57,972	498
Rep of Moldova	4,037	37	2,838	11	3,390	49	5,873	20
Romania	19,349	42	12,925	250	15,424	48	32,189	496
Russia	145,426	39	11,689	1,700	146,850	39	11,355	1,667
Slovakia	5,451	40	19,345	105	5,031	49	48,538	244
Thailand	69,566	39	7,815	544	67,566	47	17,435	1,178
Ukraine	43,872	40	3,505	154	37,096	46	5,430	201
Uruguay	3,460	35	16,200	56	3,624	40	17,083	62
China	1,409,581	39	10,633	14,993	1,354,380	48	27,617	37,404
Total/Average	1,821,456	39	10,793	19,659	1,739,709	45	25,674	44,665
excl China	411,875	40	11,327	4,665	385,329	47	18,844	7,261

A characteristic of this group of countries is that, like the preceding segment, population growth is not taking place. The current projection is that the total population will decline from 1.82 Bn persons in 2019 to 1.74 Bn by 2045 a drop of 81 million persons.

China is a significant contributor to this reduction in total population (see Chapter Ten on China). The impact of the restrictive birth policy is working through the age profile of that country's population and is impacting the number of women of childbearing age. As a result, the total population of China is projected to peak at 1.433 Bn persons in 2028 and then decline to 1.35 Bn by 2045. This is after taking into account the relaxation of the 'One Child Policy' to a 'Three Child Policy'. In total between 2020 and 2045 China's population is projected to decline by 55 million persons.

However, it is not just China that is experiencing a population decline. For the other countries in this Country Segment, life expectancy has not been increasing as rapidly as might be expected, and birth rates have been declining steeply. Together with emigration (particularly from some countries within the European Union), the total population of most countries in this Segment is in decline.

Greece, for example, is being plundered of its skilled working-age population by the affluent countries in the European Union. It has lost 326,000 working-age (and presumably better skilled) persons in the last 15 years. This is great for the affluent countries in the EU but it is effectively 'de-skilling' Greece.

The free movement of labour within the European Union is advantageous for the affluent countries in the European Union but is effectively 'de-skilling' the less affluent.

These factors impact the projected age profile of the population in the next 25 years.

Because China is such a significant proportion of this segment's total population it is shown separately from the rest of this segment in Figure 2-5. The projected population age profile of the other countries in this segment is shown in Figure 2-6. The similarity between the two charts is quite surprising. Especially as China has engaged in quite specific population management policies whereas the others have not.

Again, the projected trend in the age profiles of these countries does have important economic implications. As for the previous Country Segment (Older Affluent Countries), the number of 'younger' consumers in these countries is projected to decline in number, and the important segment of 40-to-64-year old's (the Working-age Empty nester) with high discretionary expenditure is stable for the next ten years then declines significantly.

Figure 2-5: Historic and Projected Trend in the Size of Key Age Segments of **China**.

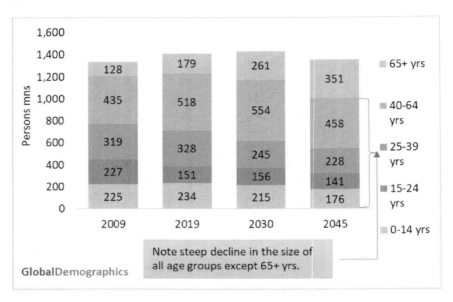

Figure 2-6: Historic and Projected Trend in the Size of Key Age Segments of Older Less Affluent Segment **excluding China**.

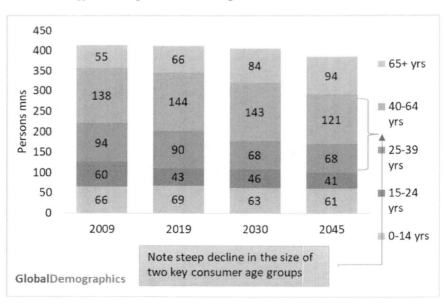

In total (that is including China as well) the core consumer base (15 years to 64 years) declines by 17% over the next 25 years which needs to be offset by either increased affluence or propensity to spend. But do note that, most of this decline is in the rural population of China.

The Family Stage Low Income Segment

This segment differs from the other three country segments in that it is far more geographically diverse. This is shown in Figure 2-7. It does have a predominance in South and Central America, but it also includes countries in North Africa, the Middle East, South Asia (including India) and what might be referred to as Developing Asia. Table 2-3 lists the countries included in this segment and their key characteristics. It includes 34 countries in total and is the largest of the four segments in terms of the total population at 3.122 billion persons in 2019.

Figure 2-7: Geographical Spread of the Family Stage Low Income Segment.

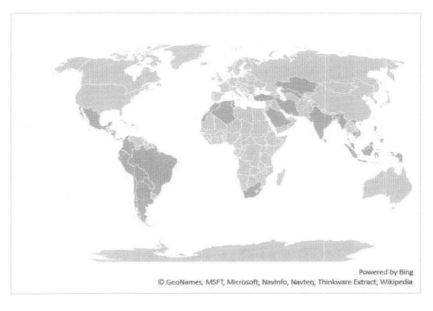

India dominates this segment with a population of 1.368 billion persons, but as shown in Table 2-3 there are five other countries (Indonesia, Brazil, Bangladesh, Mexico, and the Philippines) with populations over 100 million persons. In contrast to the previous Country Segment where most of the countries had a total population of less than 20 million, only a third of the countries in this segment are below 20 million total population.

Table 2-3:: Listing of Countries in Family Stage Low Income.

Country	Actual 2019 Population (000s)	Median Age	GDP per cap	Total GDP US$ Bns	Projected 2045 Population (000s)	Median Age	GDP per cap	Total GDP US$ Bns
Algeria	43,087	28	3,945	170	65,721	29	3,762	247
Argentina	44,763	31	10,045	450	52,628	37	12,295	647
Armenia	2,950	34	4,635	14	2,833	42	23,533	67
Azerbaijan	10,027	31	4,792	48	11,421	38	19,304	220
Bangladesh	163,115	27	1,846	301	175,654	39	5,948	1,045
Bolivia	11,536	25	3,545	41	14,092	35	3,760	53
Brazil	210,946	33	8,722	1,840	227,692	43	10,930	2,489
Cambodia	16,494	25	1,642	27	19,633	34	2,416	47
Chile	18,884	34	14,950	282	23,640	44	19,676	465
Colombia	50,188	30	6,452	324	61,503	42	7,030	432
Dominican Rep	10,752	27	8,272	89	12,604	35	20,202	255
Ecuador	17,362	27	6,188	107	23,502	36	5,825	137
El Salvador	6,454	27	4,187	27	6,275	38	5,702	36
India	1,367,932	28	2,116	2,895	1,521,754	38	4,691	7,138
Indonesia	270,785	29	4,133	1,119	333,374	35	5,228	1,743
Iran	82,816	31	5,686	471	99,506	39	20,210	2,011
Kazakhstan	18,530	30	9,723	180	26,285	28	15,916	418
Malaysia	31,931	29	11,422	365	37,934	41	21,861	829
Mexico	127,573	28	9,863	1,258	149,893	37	11,107	1,665
Morocco	36,495	29	3,253	119	45,005	36	6,253	281
Myanmar	54,176	28	1,501	81	56,196	37	6,105	343
Nicaragua	6,547	26	1,912	13	7,765	35	2,366	18
Panama	4,250	29	15,259	65	6,032	35	16,105	97
Paraguay	7,046	25	5,414	38	8,010	36	6,857	55
Peru	32,483	30	6,984	227	46,205	47	8,450	390
Philippines	108,218	25	3,482	377	129,664	35	4,789	621
Saudi Arabia	34,175	31	23,203	793	42,056	42	25,759	1,083
South Africa	58,607	27	5,996	351	76,150	32	6,167	470
Sri Lanka	21,325	33	3,940	84	22,700	37	6,622	150
Tunisia	11,689	32	3,556	42	13,903	36	6,367	89
Turkey	83,131	31	9,075	754	105,997	40	9,194	975
Uzbekistan	32,963	27	1,757	58	41,476	34	3,349	139
Venezuela RB	28,885	29	16,027	463	20,478	36	25,821	529
Viet Nam	96,380	32	2,718	262	107,464	40	13,905	1,494
Total/Average	3,122,495	28	4,398	13,734	3,595,045	36	7,421	26,679
excl India	1,754,563	29	6,178	10,839	2,073,291	37	9,425	19,541

Unlike the previous two Country Segments, this Country Segment is projected to have positive population growth. It is estimated to have had a total population in 2019 of 3.122 billion and projections indicate that it will reach 3.595 billion by 2045 – an increase of 473 million persons in 26 years. India accounts for 154 million of this increase. As shown in the next chapter, this is a function of natural population growth (births exceeding deaths). Migration plays no role. However, the rate of natural population increase is projected to slow as the population ages (more deaths) and births decline in number.

India

Because India is a particularly large proportion of this segment, its projected age profile is shown separately from the sum of the other countries in this segment. This is Figure 2-8 below.

Figure 2-8: Historic and Projected Trend in the Size of Key Age Segments of India.

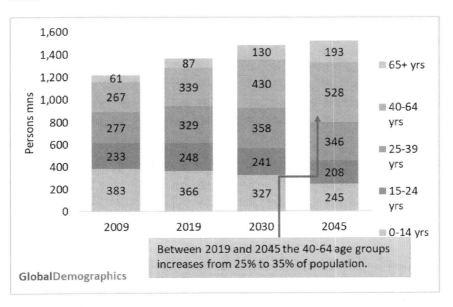

What is particularly noticeable here (and discussed in greater depth in the next two chapters) is the changing age profile. There is a steady decline in the youngest age group (0- to 14-year-olds) reflecting a significant decline in birth rates. This forecast does assume that this decline in birth rates – evident over the last 10 years - continues. In addition, from 2019 the 40-to-64-year age group significantly increases in importance. From 25% of the total population to 35% in 2045.

Probably the most important issue in terms of India is the projected size of the working-age population (15 to 64 years in this case). Much has been made about its 'demographic dividend'. That is, an increasing proportion of the population is of working age *and* employed. This reduces the dependency ratio while at the same time increasing the absolute size of the economy (through production).

In total, the working-age population in India grew significantly since 2005 when it was 718 million persons. By 2019 it had added nearly 200 million persons to this age range to reach 916 million. The projection to 2045 indicates the working-age population will lift to 1.029 billion by 2030 (an increase of 101 million working-age persons) and then grow marginally (0.3% pa) to 1.083 Bn by 2045.

In short, the growth of the working-age population is projected to slow dramatically for the next decade and then stabilize. The big opportunity was in the last decade. To the extent that there is any dividend left, it must be realized in the next decade. That is a function of being able to turn those working-age persons into *employed* working-age persons. The record over the last decade for doing that is not good.

However, it must be noted that the productivity of the workforce is projected to show positive trends and as shown in Table 2-3, India is expected to achieve significant gains in GDP per capita which will improve lifestyle and assist consumption. This is partially driven by expected improvements to education and aggressive Fixed Capital Investment.

The other Countries in this Segment

India was dealt with separately from the other countries in the Segment because of its relative size. However, as is obvious from comparing Figure 2-8 with Figure 2-9, the overall pattern of population change for the next 25 years is almost identical. The 40-to-64-year age groups come into dominance, the 0 to 14 age range is in decline and the 15 to 39 age range is almost unchanged in size.

This does mean that the size of the working-age population starts to stabilize. In 2019 there are estimated to be 1.18 billion persons defined as working-age (15 to 64 years) and it is projected to peak at 1.383 billion in 2045 – but with very little increase in size after 2030. So again, the 'demographic dividend' must be realized (in terms of maintaining employment rates) in the next decade.

Figure 2-9: Historic and Projected Trend in the Size of Key Age Segments of Family Stage Low Income Country Segment Excluding India.

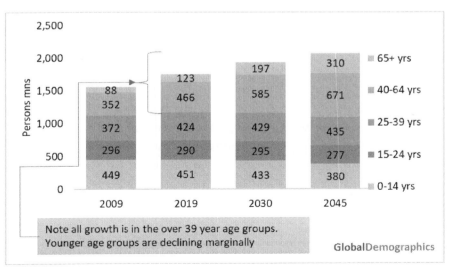

77

The key issue for all the countries included in this Country Segment (including India) is education and then ultimately - employability. The current standard of education of the existing adult population is relatively poor. An estimated half of those aged 15 years and above have only primary or less education.

The existing adult population in the Young Family Stage countries have relatively poor education. Half of those aged 15 years and above have only primary or less education and thereby are poorly equipped to work in higher productivity jobs.

Clearly, with increased education facilities, this issue will be reduced but not significantly as the number of new entrants into the workforce is projected to decrease (as a result of fewer young people) and it takes ten years before they are a sufficient proportion of the total labour force to effectively change its 'education' profile. This issue is addressed in greater detail in the subsequent chapters on education and employment. However, it is reflected in the GDP per capita of these countries.

Overall, this Country Segment is no longer made up of 'young growth' markets. The 0-to-24-year age range is estimated at 1.354 billion persons in 2019. The projections indicate that it will decline to 1.11 billion by 2045. The growth segment in terms of age is now the 45-to-64-year old. From 805 million in 2019 to a projected 1.2 billion in 2045.

The countries in the Family Low Income Country Segment are transiting from being growing youth markets to growing 40- to 64-year-old markets. This is a significant shift in consumer emphasis – and tastes/needs.

The Young Poor Countries

This final Country Segment is very much one of growth. It consists of 32 countries and has an estimated total population in 2019 of 1.33 billion persons. However, such is its population 'dynamics' that the total population is projected to increase by 73% in the next 25 years to reach 2.31 billion persons. That is an additional 978 million persons.

Figure 2-10 highlights how different this Country Segment is from all the others included in this analysis. Specifically:

1. Every age group is projected to increase in absolute size in the next 25 years. Age segments over 39 years of age are projected to double in size.

2. 41% of the population in 2019 is under the age of 15 years, declining to 34% by 2045, but increasing in absolute number by 231 million (or 42%)

3. The aged population (65 years plus) is just 3% of the total population and remains a low proportion through to 2045.

Overall, this Country Segment is adding an average of 38 million persons to its population every year for the next 25 years. All the countries in this segment that are in Africa (north or South) have a projected population growth rate of more than 2% per annum for the next decade and most of them for the next 25 years.

As shown in Figure 2-11 the countries included in this segment are significantly biased toward the African continent, and then what is generally referred to as 'Developing Asia' and Pakistan. Pakistan and Nigeria each have just over 200 million persons in 2019 and just under half of the remaining countries have populations over 20 million.

Figure 2-10: Historic and Projected Trend in the Size of Key Age Groups in the Young Poor Country Segment.

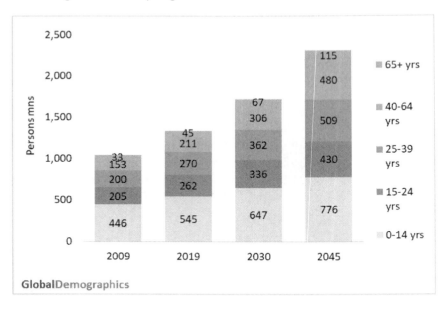

Figure 2-11: Geographical Spread of the Young and Poor Countries.

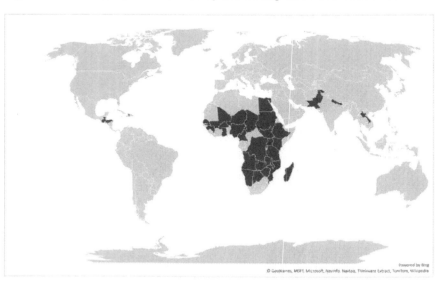

Table 2-4 lists the 32 countries in this segment. The standout statistic in this Table is the number of these countries where the median age is 20 years or below – 22 countries in total, with Niger, with a median age of 14 being the youngest.   That is, half of Niger's population in 2019 was under the age of 14 years!

Clearly, in that context (a lot of children) the concern with these countries is education. Available data indicates that 56% of the adult population have Primary or less education and just 29% have more than lower secondary education. Unfortunately, as detailed in Chapter Five, the propensity of these countries to spend on education is low – as measured by the share of GDP devoted to it. This is a serious issue, as without improving education these countries cannot evolve.

Furthermore, birth rates are projected to remain high and therefore the pressure on the education system also remains high. As shown earlier in Figure 2-10 the number of persons aged 0 to 14 years is projected to continue to grow rapidly, from 545 million in 2019 to reach 776 million in 2045. This means an absolute increase of 42% in the education budget is required just to *maintain* the existing availability of education. It needs to double to improve the availability and quality in a meaningful way.

On the positive side, the proportion of the population that is of working age and therefore potentially able to contribute to the economy increases from 56% in 2019 to a projected 61% by 2045. Provided they can find work this will lift the GDP per capita (and total GDP) significantly as shown in Table 2-4.

Table 2-4: Listing of Young Poor Countries.

Country	Actual 2019				Projected 2045			
	Population (000s)	Median Age	GDP per cap	Total GDP US$ Bns	Population (000s)	Median Age	GDP per cap	Total GDP US$ Bns
Angola	32,177	16	4,415	142	68,621	19	5,787	397
Botswana	2,311	23	7,937	18	3,565	30	8,468	30
Burkina Faso	20,520	17	767	16	38,798	21	835	32
Cameroon	26,110	18	1,485	39	44,930	23	1,984	89
Chad	16,173	16	700	11	30,035	21	1,256	38
DR Congo	87,907	16	538	47	200,143	18	492	99
Egypt	100,457	24	2,932	295	162,797	25	4,233	689
Ethiopia	112,660	19	823	93	179,253	27	9,314	1,670
Ghana	30,551	21	2,193	67	48,264	25	3,142	152
Guatemala	17,600	22	4,359	77	23,233	34	7,401	172
Guinea	12,892	17	1,054	14	22,749	23	1,169	27
Haiti	11,308	23	712	8	12,751	34	735	9
Honduras	9,751	23	2,574	25	12,123	36	6,252	76
Kenya	52,792	19	1,809	96	78,570	29	2,804	220
Lao PDR	7,183	23	2,794	20	8,459	35	13,162	111
Madagascar	27,099	19	520	14	44,966	25	737	33
Malawi	18,760	17	409	8	31,381	25	632	20
Mali	19,926	15	879	18	41,490	18	1,184	49
Mozambique	30,668	17	487	15	60,419	20	495	30
Namibia	2,505	21	4,937	12	3,858	24	5,494	21
Nepal	28,756	24	1,068	31	34,371	41	1,513	52
Niger	23,632	14	547	13	63,196	15	527	33
Nigeria	203,158	17	2,295	466	379,696	19	5,608	2,129
Pakistan	217,775	22	1,162	253	308,199	29	1,651	509
Rwanda	12,670	19	788	10	19,961	27	1,018	20
Senegal	16,389	18	1,439	24	31,081	21	1,826	57
South Sudan	11,227	18	1,142	13	13,946	21	1,094	15
Sudan	43,122	19	573	25	74,388	23	638	47
Uganda	44,479	16	780	35	91,432	23	918	84
Tanzania	58,487	17	1,104	65	120,410	20	1,251	151
Zambia	18,005	17	1,281	23	33,772	23	1,366	46
Zimbabwe	14,733	18	4	0	22,626	20	5	0
Total/Average	1,331,782	18	1,494	1,990	2,309,483	24	3,078	7,108

It is projected that under the assumptions made in terms of population age profile, the propensity of working-age to find work and improvements in education, this Country Segment will achieve a 106% absolute lift in GDP per capita. Given the growing population, this results in a 257% lift in total GDP. That is growth rates of 3.4% and 3.2% per annum, respectively.

However, the vulnerability of this forecast is the availability of work. The growth of the population and changing age profile forecasts are reliable. The improvement in education is with confidence but maybe on the optimistic side given the rapid increase in demand for educational facilities. It may be a case of working hard to stand still.

But it is the availability of work that is of concern. Whereas in 2019 there are 475 million employed persons in these countries this would need to increase to 918 million by 2045 to maintain the existing participation rate of 64%. That is an additional 443 million jobs or an average of 18 million a year.

For countries, whose populations on average are poorly educated and not well supported in terms of infrastructure and investment, this is a challenge. Especially in a world where the number of affluent consumers is no longer growing, and robotics and artificial intelligence are providing an efficient on-shore alternative to low-cost unskilled overseas labour.

There are some serious issues that the countries in this segment need to confront, and this will become increasingly evident as we progress through the topics of education, employment, and healthcare in this book.

The Young Poor countries will need to find an additional 18 million jobs every year for the next 25 years to simply maintain present rates of employment.

In Summary

The differences between the four Country Segments in age profile and relative affluence are quite considerable. That means that they can be expected to develop in quite different directions over the next 25 years in terms of size, age profile, growth segments and rate of change.

Given present trends, the 116 countries included in this analysis are projected to add 54 million extra persons to the global population every year for the next 25 years. Will they receive adequate healthcare, education, and work opportunities? If not, the implications are worrying.

Table 2-5 gives a summary of the degree of difference between the four Country Segments on the two key variables – age and affluence. The differences are substantial and for obvious reasons mean that the future directions of the segments will be very different.

Some basic summary points.

1) Two of the Segments account for nearly all population growth in the future. Not surprisingly they are the youngest segments/ countries.

2) The level of population growth is concerning for two reasons. First is the ecological point of view. How many more humans can the planet sustain? Second, and more specifically how many more people can these countries sustain? Already in many, access to water, let alone food, health, and education are serious issues.

3) The ability to change course on issues such as population growth and education has a significant lag. India and Kenya are two good examples of this (see later). In both cases, birth rates have declined significantly and yet total births will keep increasing for

at least a decade for other reasons. In terms of education, many countries are trying to improve, but again it takes ten years for the improvement to even reach the workforce let alone productivity and household income. For these reasons, there are significant delays in changes in population trends or incomes (GDP per capita). However, when the change happens it can be quite dramatic. India's total births per annum after 2030 are a case in point.

4) There is a need to recognise some fundamental changes in the nature of populations – because when change happens it tends to happen quite rapidly. The perception that countries such as India are 'Young' is no longer correct. They are becoming middle-aged. With that comes a change in priorities, lifestyles, and consumption patterns. As such the population for the next 25 years is quite different from that of the last 25 years.

To focus on India, no longer can you regard it as a 'Young' country. In 10 years, time (and already) it will be middle-aged. The youth age segment is now in decline in absolute size, and the society of 2030 in India is a middle-aged, family person with the

5) In a similar vein, while trends may continue, they can and do change in terms of speed of change. The aged (persons over 64 years) was a rapidly growing segment in the last decade in the older countries. However, these countries are now old and the number of persons reaching 64 years of age is declining. Suddenly the retired age group is now growing at a much slower rate.

6) The changing life span, healthiness and education are changing other dimensions- and specifically, attitudes to when to marry/form a partnership, have children, and retire. These changes are not always appreciated. For example, many seem to not understand that the working-age in the USA, Japan, South Korea, and many Northern European countries is now to age 69, and increasingly age 70. (Just consider the age of the candidates for the Presidential elections in the USA in 2020).

The demographic and socio-economic world is changing around us in various directions and at different rates from what we were used to for the last decade. We need to understand what these changes are (directionally and speed) and their implications. That is the purpose of the subsequent chapters.

Table 2-5 shows the projected changing pattern of population and wealth from 2019 to 2045. The specific GDP Growth rates behind this are included in Appendix B.

Table 2-5: Relative Share of Population and GDP by Country Segment.

	2019 share of total population	GDP	GDP per Capita	2045 share of total populatio	GDP	GDP per Capita	CAGR GDP per Capita
Older Affluent	14%	57%	49,146	12%	47%	69,765	1.4%
Older Middle Inco	25%	23%	10,793	20%	29%	25,674	3.5%
Family Stage Low	43%	16%	4,398	41%	17%	7,421	2.1%
Young Poor	18%	2%	1,494	26%	5%	3,078	2.9%

Summary Profile – Diversity of the World's Base Demographics

Older Affluent

	2019	2030	2,045
Total Population Mns	991	1,025	1,030
Pop Growth rate % pa	0.5%	0.3%	0.0%
Births (mns)	10	10	10
Births Growth rate % pa	-0.5%	-0.1%	-0.2%
Birth Rate per 000	47	47	49
Births-Deaths 000	808	-958	-3,310
Migration 000s	0.08	0.09	0.08
Average Age yrs.	41	43	45
Median age yrs.	42	44	46

Older Low Income

	2019	2030	2,045
Total Population Mns	1,821	1,837	1,740
Pop Growth rate % pa	0.4%	0.1%	-0.4%
Births (mns)	19	17	16
Births Growth rate % pa	-0.8%	-1.2%	-0.6%
Birth Rate per 000	44	44	50
Births-Deaths 000	3,053	-2,515	-10,700
Migration 000s	-0.02	-0.01	-0.01
Average Age yrs.	39	42	45
Median age yrs.	39	43	47

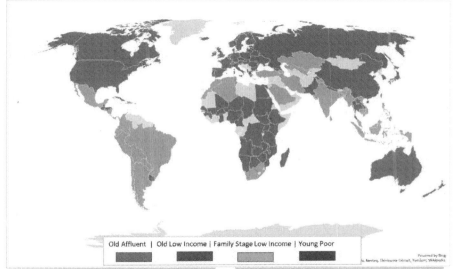

Old Affluent | Old Low Income | Family Stage Low Income | Young Poor

Powered by Bing
s, Kerton, Thinkware Extract, Tomtom, Wikipedia

Family Stage Low Income

	2019	2030	2045
Total Population Mns	3,122	3,425	3,595
Pop Growth rate % pa	1.2%	0.8%	0.3%
Births (mns)	54	48	39
Births Growth rate % pa	-0.6%	-1.1%	-1.3%
Birth Rate per 000	66	54	45
Births-Deaths 000	33,034	21,260	1,935
Migraton 000s	0.00	0.00	0.00
Average Age yrs	31	34	38
Median age yrs	29	33	38

Young Poor

	2019	2030	2045
Total Population Mns	1,332	1,717	2,309
Pop Growth rate % pa	2.5%	2.3%	2.0%
Births (mns)	44	50	59
Births Growth rate % pa	1.5%	1.2%	1.1%
Birth Rate per 000	137	118	101
Births-Deaths 000	33,531	37,636	41,315
Migraton 000s	0.07	-0.02	-0.02
Average Age yrs	23	25	27
Median age yrs	19	21	23

Chapter 3
Births, Deaths and Migration

Introduction

On an average day, this year there will be 343,218 new-born and a net addition (after deaths) to the global population of 183,354 persons. For the year it comes to 66,924,036 additional persons. Sounds improbable? Well in the last 5 years to 2021 the total global population of the countries included in this book grew from 6.66 billion persons to 7.42 billion – giving an average annual growth of 75.8 million for that period. (The good news is the rate of increase is slowing – hence the discrepancy between the average for the last five years and the total addition for the latest year)

Today there will be 343,218 new-born and after allowing for deaths, a net addition to the global population of 183,354 persons.

Not only is the annual growth in the absolute size of the global population concerning but so also is the location of this increase. Just over one in three of the births this year (that is 41 million) are taking place in a country where the GDP per capita is less than US$5 per day and education and health care (and a functioning government) are virtually non-existent. As such these persons have no real prospect of having a fulfilling life. To just survive will be an achievement. Why is this happening? Can the course of humanity be changed for the better?

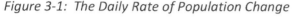

Figure 3-1: The Daily Rate of Population Change

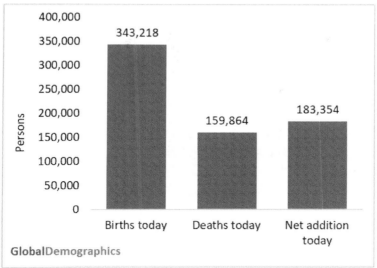

GlobalDemographics

Also of concern is that the projection of the total number of births per annum does not decline significantly in the next 25 years. It is projected to reduce from its current level of 128 million (in 2019 – that year is used as Covid has impacted births in 2020) to 124 million in 2045. That is a total drop of just 4 million or 3% over 26 years. The main cause of the decline in overall population growth *rates* is deaths, not fewer births. With the ageing of the population, this is increasing quite rapidly. From an expected 57 million per annum in 2019 to a projected 94 million deaths in 2045. The shape of society is changing.

The shape and size of the future population of a country are determined by four key items.

- The number of women of childbearing age – defined as ages 15 to 49 years. This is a crucial variable, and its size for the next 15 years is known as these women are already alive (albeit some are 1 year old this year).
- The propensity of those women to have a child in any one year (Birth rate)
- Death rates by gender and age group. These tend to be entrenched trends that change slowly over time.

- Finally, migration which is generally controllable by Governments.

This chapter looks at the expected trends for each of these variables and the implications of those trends for the future size of the total population and its age profile.

The total number of births per annum is projected to stay at close to the same level for the next 25 years. It is expected to reduce from its 2019 level of 128 million to 124 million in 2045. This is despite declining birth rates.

Births

In examining the future shape of a population, it is best to start by looking at the trend in the propensity to have a child (birth rate) and the number of persons able to have a child in any one year (women/couples aged 15 to 49 years).

Birth rate varies significantly throughout the world – but historically within an individual country, the trend is usually negatively correlated with education and income. As they increase, birth rates decline.

As education and income are themselves closely correlated it is not possible to properly identify their individual impact. But as a rule, an improvement in education precedes a lift in income (educated people attract more investment and hence can produce greater value). This would suggest that education is probably the real driver in this instance. Education also, of course, provides awareness of contraception availability and methods.

Figure 3-2 shows the relationship between the overall standard of education of the adult population and the birth rate per thousand women of childbearing age (15 to 49 years) for 103 countries included in the database which reports both education and birth rate data (out of 116 countries).

Figure 3-2: The Global Relationship Between Education and Birth Rates 2019.

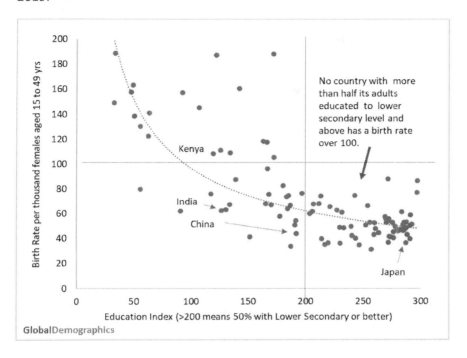

GlobalDemographics

Education Index Defined:

> *To summarize the relative level of education of the workforce of the 103 countries for which we have data, an index has been created with '0' applied to the proportion that have none/not completed primary, 1 to those completed primary level, 2 to lower secondary, 3 to upper secondary and 3 also to vocational and or tertiary. This value has been multiplied by the percentage of the adult population that has achieved each stage. The range is zero – no one has an education level above primary – to 400 – everyone has a tertiary/vocational qualification. A value of 200 typically means that around 66% of the adult population have lower secondary and above. A more detailed explanation is given later in the Chapter on Education.*

Cultural and religious issues impact this relationship to some extent and hence the variation around the best-fit line. As a result, a perfect fit between education and birth rates cannot be expected, but Figure 3-2 does demonstrate the general nature of the relationship.

Figure 3-2 shows that until at least half of the population has at least lower secondary education (typically 200+ on the Education Index), the birth rate will probably be high. In contrast, without exception, in all countries where over half the adult population have lower secondary or better education, birth rates are below 100 per thousand females aged 15 to 49 years (and typically the rate is within the 35 to 60 range).

It is an observable fact that every country in the top left quadrant of Figure 3-2 is in the 'Young Poor' Country Segment as defined in the previous Chapter. That is, they have a median age below 25 years and a GDP per capita of less than US$3,000 per annum.

In doing this analysis it should be noted that there is no, or insufficient, education data for 14 of the 116 countries covered. The missing ones are all countries where the GDP per capita is low, as is productivity per worker. It is therefore indicated that their education standard is also low and would be at the top left of the chart in Figure 3-2 if the data were known.

The Young Poor Country Segment

The worry for the world is the Young Poor countries. Of the 32 countries in this segment, only 24 report education data and, of these, 21 are in the top 23 in terms of birth rates and at the bottom in terms of the education standard of the adult population.

These high birth rates are concerning as they mean a future tsunami of children in countries ill-equipped to educate them and hence give them the *prospect* of an acceptable standard of living. Furthermore, most of these countries have a form of governance that is unlikely and unable to cause the sort of change that can break this cycle that perpetuates poverty. It is important to explain the 'trap' that these countries are in.

Figure 3-3 shows the extent to which the birth rate per thousand females aged 15 to 49 years is decreasing in the Young Poor Countries. In the last decade, the unweighted birth rate of this Country Segment declined from 155.7 in 2009 to 134.8 by 2019. This is a 15% decrease which is good, but is it enough?

Figure 3-3: Historic Trend in Birth Rates for Young Poor Countries.

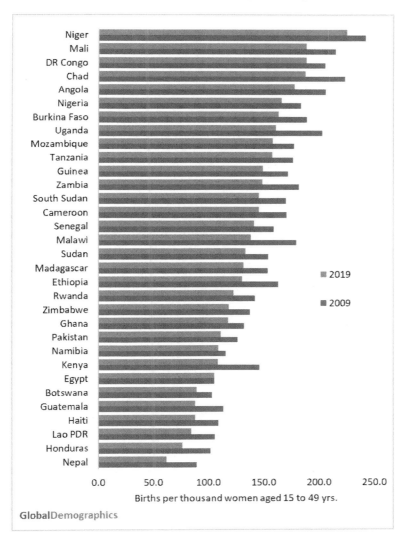

These high birth rates mean a future tsunami of children in countries ill-equipped to educate them and hence give them the prospect of an acceptable standard of living.

Analysis of the historic trend for other countries which now have lower birth rates (under 100) indicates that the rate of decline will typically continue at a linear pace until the birth rate is below 100 per thousand women of childbearing age. After which the rate of decline slows and eventually levels out at around 40 births per 1000 women of childbearing age.

As such, the *average* rate of births for countries in the Young Poor Country Segment is projected to be 112.8 by 2030 and 91.7 by 2045. This is a significant improvement and does assume increasing education availability as discussed subsequently in Chapter Five.

However, that improvement is not enough in itself. There is a lagged effect of the historic high birth rate in the form of an increasing number of women of childbearing age.

To state the obvious, total births are a function of two variables.
1) The propensity of a woman of childbearing age to have a child and
2) the number of women of childbearing age.

Unfortunately, in the countries of concern, the number of women of childbearing age is increasing because of the historic high birth rates. This largely offsets the decline in the birth rate for the subsequent ten to fifteen years such that total births continue to increase, exacerbating the problem even further in future years.

Figure 3-4 shows the historic and projected trend in these two variables from 2005 to 2045 for the Young Poor Country Segment. The total number of women in this Country Segment aged 15 to 49 years is projected to increase from 330 million in 2020 to 479 million in 2035 and then reach 584 million in 2045.

All women aged 15 to 49 years in 2035 are already alive today (albeit aged 0 to 35 years in 2020) so unless there are catastrophic death rates of younger females (unlikely) this number of women aged 15 to 49 years is a highly reliable projection to that year. The projection for the subsequent period to 2045 is also of high confidence as it is determined by the expected trend in birth rates to 2030 and those trends tend to be quite stable.

Figure 3-4: Historic and Projected Trend in Birth Rates and Number of Women aged 15 to 49 years – Young Poor Country Segment.

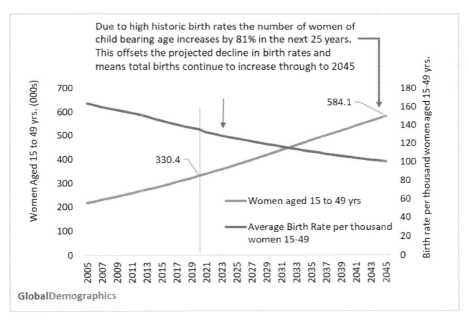

Figure 3-5 shows the collective impact of these two variables on total births per annum for this Country Segment. In 2019 total births were reported as 44.1 million. By 2030 the combined trends in the number of females aged 15 to 49 years and births per thousand women of that age range results in 50.2 million births and by 2045 it is projected to reach 58.9 million births per annum.

Figure 3-5: Historic and Projected Total Births (mns) per annum for the Young Poor Country Segment.

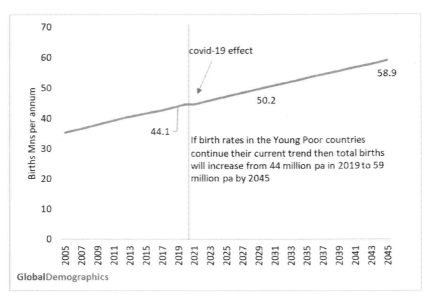

In short, the projected decline in the birth *rate* is not sufficiently steep to offset the inevitable increase in the number of women (and couples) of childbearing age. To stabilize total births at the current (2019) level the average birth rate would need to drop to 103 in 2030 and 76 by 2045 compared with current 'trend' values of 118 and 101, respectively.

Due to the age profile of the population, total births in the poorest countries of the world are projected to increase from 44 million per annum in 2019 to reach 59 million per annum in 2045 despite the birth rate declining over the same period.

It needs to be reinforced; the number of women aged 15 to 49 years for the years 2020 to 2035 is unchangeable. They are alive. It is the propensity to have a child that must be changed. That in turn is very much a function of education and social pressures. The historic positive

96

trend in education indicates that the average birth rate will decline. But it is not declining with sufficient speed to reduce the otherwise projected tsunami of children.

Kenya – A Specific Example

The story varies quite a lot between countries – averages can be misleading. For that reason, we look at one country - Kenya – to demonstrate the dynamics of these three variables. That is the birth rate, number of women aged 15 to 49 years and total births.

As Figure 3-6 shows, the number of women of childbearing age increases over the next 25 years. As explained, this is inevitable as the new entrants to this age range over the next 15 years are already alive and the number for the subsequent 10 years is a function of the slowly declining birth rate from 2020 to 2030. At the same time, it is expected that the birth rate will decline from 106 in 2020 to 51 per thousand by 2045 – a substantial decline.

But there is an important point to be made here. Even a substantial improvement in birth rate does not have any real impact on total births per annum until nearly a decade later due to the increasing number of women aged 15 to 49 years. In Kenya between 2019 and 2045, the projected number of such women increases from 13.7 million to 22.3 million, but the rate of increase slows significantly after 2035 when it has reached 18.9 million.

However, as shown in Figure 3-7, total births per annum do not start to decline significantly until after 2030 when the combined effect of declining birth rate and slower growth in the number of women aged 15 to 49 (and particularly 15 to 30 years) begins to take effect. After 2030 total births per annum are projected to decline from 1.4 million to 1.1 million by 2045. Still a large number but a significant reduction in the number of children needing education and health care.

Figure 3-6: Kenya – Women of Childbearing age (mns) and Birth rates per thousand. 2005 to 2045.

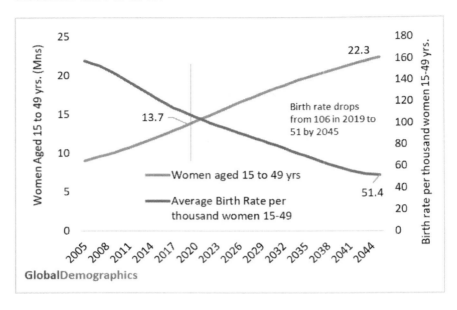

Figure 3-7: Kenya: Births (mns) per annum 2005 to 2045.

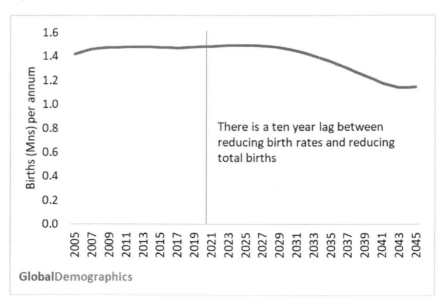

The Economic Implications of Slowing the Birth Rate

Some argue that a high birth rate is good for a country – it builds a supply of future workers which will help the economy grow and ultimately make the working-age population constitute a larger proportion of the total population (provided births subsequently slow down). As such it is referred to as the 'Demographic Dividend'.

But that 'dividend' is only going to be realised if the extra working-age persons can gain employment and that in turn is a function of their skill level (education) and neural and physical well-being. These are very much a function of good nutrition and health care in the early years. It also assumes that these workers can lift their productivity enough to meet the needs of the *ever-growing* (under this scenario) young (and old) population.

How serious is the high birth rate in Young Poor countries? The current trend indicates that the total population of these countries nearly doubles over the next 25 years. The number of 'school age' children will increase by 45% and the number of persons of working age will double from 742 million in 2019 to 1.418 billion in 2045.

This means that the number of school places must increase by 45% just to maintain current education availability and standard, let alone improve it. In addition, the availability of work opportunities must at least double if the demographic dividend is to be realized and living standards are to be improved. Both those factors – employability and employment – are at risk.

This raises the question of what would happen to the long-term development of a country if the birth rate were suddenly reduced (perhaps through policy intervention such as in China with the 'One-Child Policy'?)

This is tested by running such a scenario for Nigeria which is one of the largest countries in the Young Poor Country Segment. It also has a high birth rate that is declining only slowly.

Table 3-1 compares the scenario of ongoing current trends in the birth rate with one where, for whatever reason, the birth rate drops to 90 per thousand women of childbearing age by 2035 and then to 70 by 2045.

The table shows 2020 (base case) then 2035 and 2045. Why 2035? Assuming people do not enter the workforce until they are 15 years of age, then the change in the birth rate only affects the labour force and hence the economy after 2035.

Impact by 2035

> For the first 15 years, the impact of a reduction in birth rates is only on the household structure. That is the cells that are shaded yellow in the 2035 scenario version. The second column of the right-hand block of data in Table 3-1.
>
> There are fewer babies brought into the household, so the total population does not grow as fast and, perhaps more importantly, household size declines. In this example, from 4.63 persons per household in 2020 to 3.75 by 2035. In the Passive case household size would also decline (to 4.15) as that scenario also assumes some, but a very modest, decline in birth rates (from 165 to 147).

Table 3-1: The Impact of a Dramatic Decline in Birth Rates on Long-term Population and Economic Profile. Nigeria.

	Base Case			Dramatic Change			
	2020	2035	2045	2020	2035	2045	
Birth rate per 000s	164.7	147.4	146	164.7	90	70	← The Change
Total Births in yrs. Mns	7.83	10.46	13,162	7.83	6.39	6.34	
Females 15-49 yrs. Mns	47.56	70.96	90,180	47.56	70.96	84.68	
Total population (Mns)	207.58	301.33	384.23	207.58	272.76	220.03	
Households (Mns)	44.85	72.65	93.58	44.85	72.65	94.44	Household Size
Household size	4.63	4.15	4.11	4.63	3.75	2.33	← drops
Working age pop (Mns)	110.85	168.14	214.4	110.85	168.1	203.3	
Total employed (Mns)	54.55	83.94	117.1	54.55	83.94	111.9	
Employment rate	49%	50%	55%	49%	50%	55%	
Workers per household	1.21	1.15	1.25	1.21	1.15	1.18	
GDP per worker (US$ pa)	8,617	15,733	17,641	8,617	15,733	19,208	Productivity Improved over base case due to workers starting to be better educated
aFCI per worker (US$) **	7,232	15,373	18,189	7,232	15,373	19,783	
wages as % GDP	75%	75%	77%	75%	75%	73%	
Average Wage (US$ pa)	6,474	11,731	13,639	6,474	11,731	13,990	This is the big gain 67% increase in per capita household income
Average HH income (US$)	7,903	13,745	17,445	7,903	13,745	16,571	
HH^ Inc per cap (US$)	1,708	3,314	4,249	1,708	3,720	7,113	
Total GDP (US$ Bn)	469	1,319	2,065	469	1,319	2,148	Demand for school places levels out. Emphasis can move from Quantity to Quality
School age 0-14 (000s)	91,087	124,176	157,452	91,087	95,580	71,947	

** Average Fixed Capital Investment per worker over 10 years depreciated
^ HH is Households

This is important as it impacts household income *per capita* as shown further down in the table. With no change *from the base case* in the size of the labour force or its productivity, per capita household income is 12.2% higher in real terms (US$3,720 compared to US$3,314) over what it would have otherwise been and doubles over what it was in 2020 (in real terms) at US$1,708.

That is significant as such an increase means more money can be spent on the welfare of the (fewer) children. That is, on nutrition, health, and education. That in turn starts the upward lift of the quality of the population's lifestyle.

Also, note that the total number of persons who are 0 to 14 years of age stabilizes at 95.6 million in this scenario (last row of the table). This enables the health and education services to invest in quality rather than quantity. Under the base case scenario, the number of persons aged 0 to 14 years would increase from 91.1 million in 2020 to reach 124.2 million by 2035. That means that the number of school places needing to be provided must be increased by 36% just to stand still in terms of education provision. That must inhibit quality improvement.

Impact of Lower Birth Rate by 2045

After 2035 additional forces are coming into play as the change in the birth rate in the preceding years now starts to have an impact on the size of the labour force and productivity.

The change scenario also assumes that there is some improvement in the education standard of the people leaving school and entering the labour force after 2020. This is based on the not unreasonable assumption that the stabilization of the number of children needing education in the previous 15 years (2020 to 2035) has resulted in more education funding per child – that is, smaller class size, better textbooks, better-trained teachers.

As shown in Table 3-1, the downward trends in the size of households and total births continue, and by 2045 the average household is now 2.33 persons – a major reduction from 4.6 in 2020 and 4.1 in the passive forecasts for 2045. It means that after 2035 many households are Working-age Empty Nester households with no dependent children in them.

The additional changes taking place after 2035 are in the size of the labour force. After 2035, the working-age population (15 to 64 years of age in this case) starts to decline from the base case and by 2045 is down to 203 million in the new scenario compared with 214 million under the base case. A difference of 5% in the total working-age population.

Assuming the propensity to be employed increases from 49% to 55% under both scenarios although it should be better for the change scenario as the children are better educated, the total labour force in 2045 is 111.9 million in the scenario case compared with the expected 117.1 million under the base case.

Here an additional assumption is made which differentiates the scenario from the base case. That is, after 2035 the worker is better educated because of the reduction in the number of school-age children. This results in more fixed capital investment and productivity per worker lifting from US$17,641 under the base case to US$19,208 under the scenario (in 2019 US Dollar values). The impact of this increase in productivity is offset slightly by the worker getting a lower share of it as more goes back to the provider of the equipment which is enhancing productivity. The average wage is projected to increase under this scenario but not quite at the same rate as productivity.

The combination of fewer workers per household compared to the base case (1.18 compared to 1.25 in 2045) but limited gain in average wage means total average household income is lower than it would be under the base case. That is US$16,571 compared with US$17,445. However, under the scenario case household size has reduced significantly so income per capita increases. In 2045 it would be US$7,113 compared with US$4,249 per capita under the base case. This is very significant.

That is the real payoff of this change. The increase in income per capita translates into increased capabilities of the population (As a result of better education, nutrition, and healthcare), which in turn leads to better lifestyles.

Note under the base case scenario the number of 0-14-year-olds in 2045 is projected to be 157 million. This means to just maintain the present quality of education and child health care the budget would need to have almost doubled over its 2020 level. Under the revised scenario the number needing these services declines and that permits quality development.

Finally, do note that the total real GDP in 2045 is the same under both scenarios. There is no loss in total affluence, and it is now spread over fewer people.

The conclusion from this example is that a stable or even declining population does not lead to economic loss. The total economy can still grow and more to the point the well-being of the individual is significantly improved. In Nigeria's case, the per capita household income lifts by 67% and GDP per capita by 82%.

Scenario analysis indicates that the so-called Demographic Dividend is a Poverty Trap.

The Older Affluent Country Segment

This Country Segment has a significantly different demographic profile from the Young Poor Country Segment. The populations of these countries are much older with 50% being over the age of 40 years.

In addition, they have had a history over the last two decades of a declining, and now stable, birth rate. This is now low at around 47 per thousand women aged 15 to 49 years. That will impact future births and the population's age profile.

Figure 3-8 shows the historic and projected trends in both the average birth rate and the total number of women aged 15 to 49 years in these countries. The birth rate has settled at 47 per thousand women aged 15 to 49 years and is showing a slight lift over time as the propensity of older women to have children increases. The forecast is that the birth rates will stay at around this level through to 2045 as there is unlikely to be any significant change in the (high) standard of education of the population (a key driver of lower birth rates).

The other obvious trend is the steady reduction in the number of women aged 15 to 49. For reasons explained earlier, this is not going to change significantly – at least for the next 15 years. Between 2019 and 2035 the projected reduction is 16% which is not excessive and slows marginally to a 15% reduction in the subsequent 10 years to 2045. Figure 3-9 shows that total births per annum are projected to decline very marginally from 10.4 million in 2019 to 10 million in 2045.

Figure 3-8: Historic and Projected Birth Rate and Females aged 15 to 49 yrs. (000s) in the Older Affluent Country Segment.

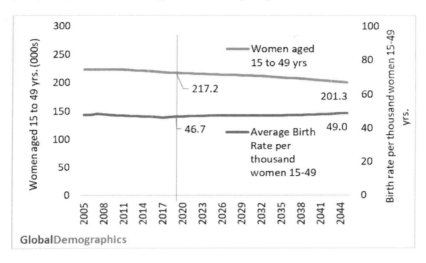

GlobalDemographics

Figure 3-9: Historic and Projected Total Births(mns) for the Older Affluent Country Segment.

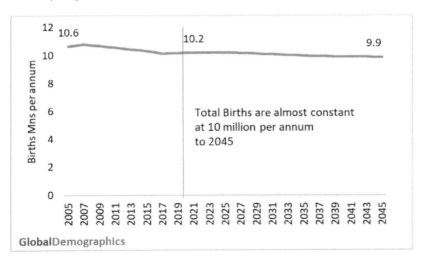

GlobalDemographics

The Older Lower Income Country Segment

This segment is dominated numerically by China. In addition, China has been active in terms of birth policy in the form of the 'One-Child Policy'. As such, China's scenario needs to be dealt with separately. It is discussed in some detail in Chapter Ten and summarised below.

China – a Brief description

China's One-Child Policy historically allowed the average woman of childbearing age to have 1.43 children. Those with a rural Hukou (which was the majority of the population when introduced and not tied to where they now live or their occupation) could have two children if the first was a female. The policy has now been relaxed to 2, and then 3, children per couple irrespective of the gender of the first child or whether they are rural or urban Hukou.

Figure 3-10: Historic and Projected Trends in the Number of Women (mns) Aged 15 to 49 Years and Total Births (mns) in China. . (Note this uses a 'positive' scenario for 2nd and 3rd childbirth rates – see Chapter 10)

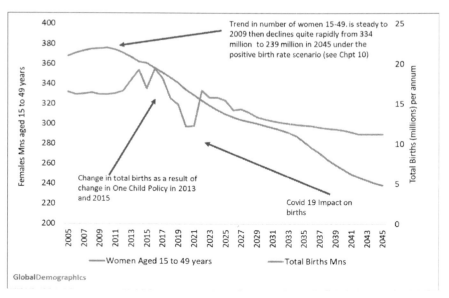

While the initial change to allowing 2 children caused a 2-year blip after each stage of relaxation (2012 and 2015) in total births, the birth rate and birth trend returned to their earlier level by 2019. In 2019 the birth rate was 44 per thousand women of childbearing age, the same level as when the one-child policy was in force. This is also in line with other countries with a similar education standard as China.

The birth policy has now (January 2022) been relaxed to a three-child policy. There is no evidence as to what extent this will impact total births. The expectation is the propensity to have a second child will be high based on past behaviour, but uncertainty as to the propensity to have a third.

However, a scenario analysis (from low uptake to a high uptake of a second and third child shows the sensitivity is very low. The difference in total births between 2024 and 2045 between a scenario where the birth rate is 46 and one where the birth rate is 68 per thousand women aged 15 to 49 years is 68 million. In the context of total births over that period being 281 million it is not significant. Even the optimistic case does not offset the growing number of deaths due to an ageing population and the total population is still projected to decline in size. The middle scenario (and the one used for this publication) indicates total births will peak at 17 million in 2022 and decline to 11.3 million by 2045.

The decline in total births is not entirely the result of a declining birth rate. It is more a function of the inevitable decline in the number of women of childbearing age. The earlier restricted birth rate has resulted in the total number of women of childbearing age declining significantly over the next 15 years and probably 25 years. Declining from 334 million in 2020 to 282 million in 2035 – inevitable as all these women are already alive (just younger and 15 in 2020). The middle scenario in birth rates indicates the number of such women will decline further to 239 million by 2045.

Note in 2020 and 2021 births dropped to 12.2 million, presumably a result of the Covid Pandemic. In the absence of any data on post-pandemic year behaviour, the forecasts assume birth rates return to trend in 2022).

The Other Countries

In the case of the remaining countries in this Segment, the average birth rate in 2019 was 46.7. This is not surprising as they are like the Older Affluent Country Segment in terms of education profile which appears to be a key driver of birth rates.

Where this Country Segment is different from the Older Affluent Country Segment is that the proportion of women of childbearing age that are under 35 years of age is increasing. The younger women have a higher probability of having a child. This results in the birth rate lifting after 2035.

Figure 3-11: Historic and Projected Birth Rate and Females aged 15 to 49 years (000s) in the Old Low Income Country Segment (excluding China).

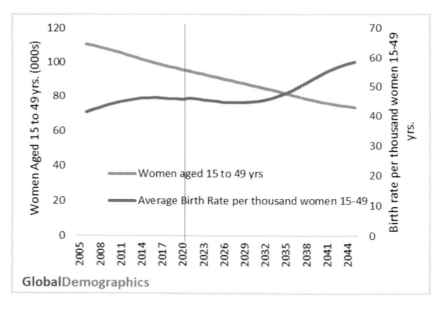

This counters the effect of a declining number of women in the relevant age range and total births also start to increase marginally after 2035 –

from a low of 4.2 million in 2030 to a high of 4.7 million in 2045. So basically, total births for this Country Segment excluding China vary over a small range of 4.2 to 4.7 million a year on a population of 412 million in 2019 (excluding China). Figures 3-11 and 3-12 summarise this situation.

Figure 3-12: Historic and Projected Total Births (mns) for Older Low Income Country Segment (excluding China)

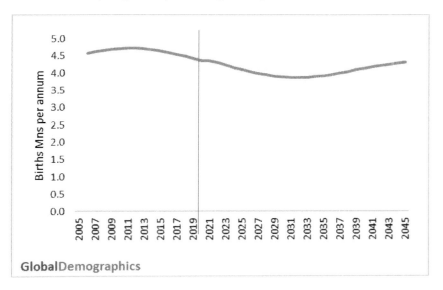

GlobalDemographics

The Family Stage Low Income Segment

This segment consists of countries where the population is at the family stage in age profile. That is, biased to ages 25 to 39 years. While this segment is numerically dominated by India, the pattern for the individual countries within it is sufficiently homogeneous to not justify separating India out in this instance.

Reflecting the education profile of this population and their level of income the average birth rate is 65.9 births per thousand women aged 15 to 49 years in 2019. This compares to a birth rate averaging 45 per thousand for the two older and better-educated Country Segments.

In the case of this Country Segment, the average birth rate has been showing a steady decline – which is desirable as it was 85 per thousand in 2005. The average rate has lowered to 66 by 2019 and is projected to reach a more 'normal' 45 births per thousand females aged 15 to 49 by 2045. It is argued that this is a result of the improvements in education over the preceding and current period. Figures 3-13 and 3-14 summarise the situation for this Country Segment.

This is decline in the birth rate is good, as this group of countries has an ongoing increase in the number of women of childbearing age and without the decline in birth rates total births would be climbing steeply.

As it is, the projected total births for this Country Segment decline – and at an increasing rate. By 2045 it is anticipated that population growth for the Country Segment will be close to zero. That is a significant change from the present situation.

Figure 3-13: Historic and Projected Birth Rate and Females aged 15 to 49 years (000s) in the Family Stage Low Income Country Segment.

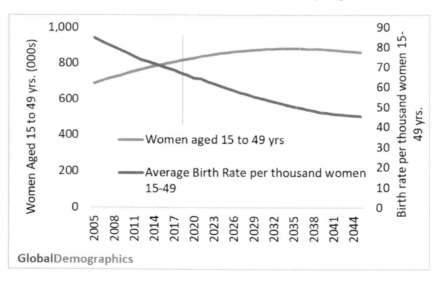

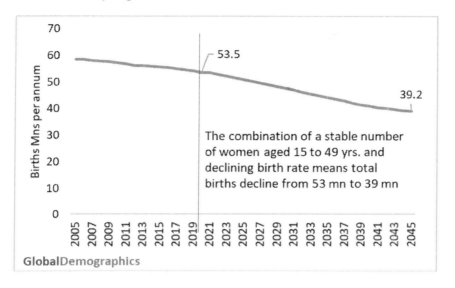

Figure 3-14: Historic and Projected Total Births for the Family Stage Low Income Country Segment.

Deaths

It is a strange thing to say, but a significant factor behind total population growth is that people are not dying soon enough. Despite declining total births some countries still have a growing total population because of extended life expectancy.

With the improvement in health care, nutrition, and an increased understanding of the concept of 'wellness and exercise' people's life expectancy is increasing. As such the rate of death *within* all age groups is in decline. Do note, that in the older countries the *average* death rate for the entire population is going up. That is simply a function of there being more old people (with higher death rates) and not a decline in the standard of healthcare.

There is little about this variable that can be changed – life expectancy is very much a function of the quality of life of the child in the first 8 years followed by the nature of the environment the individual lives in during adult life. A heavily polluted urban environment is not good for the individual as demonstrated by the life expectancy of 50-year-old urban males in China (73 years).

The pattern of death rates tends to be consistent across countries but the age at which it starts to increase does differ by levels of affluence and this is demonstrated in Figure 3-15 which compares four countries – one from each of the four Country Segments. As can be seen, there is little difference between the four countries in terms of deaths per thousand in the 40 to 50-year age range. It is low for all four of these countries (and for most countries).

Figure 3-15: Trend in Deaths Per Thousand Persons (Male) in 2019 for China, Germany, Indonesia, And Kenya.

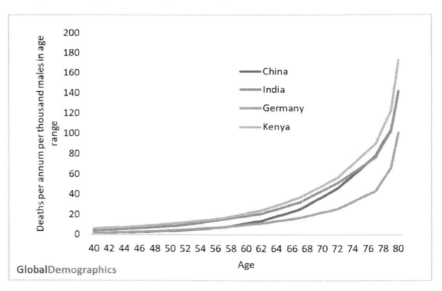

Note: the age range (horizontal axis) for this chart has been truncated to age 40 and above to show the differences in death rates in the older age groups. Death rates are very low for younger age groups.

However, between the age of 40 and 45, the death rate starts to climb quite steeply, for all but Germany. In many respects the deaths in the age range of 45 to 65 years are a function of the onset of chronic conditions rather than ageing and the difference between countries reflects their overall wellness and nutritional history. This becomes more apparent after age 64 where Germany (more affluent and better educated) lags behind the others quite significantly.

In the case of China, it is interesting to note how at age of 60 it is in line with Germany (a more affluent country), but for older age groups the death rate is much higher. This reflects the fact that the older people in China went through a period when there was political turmoil which had consequences in terms of quality of nutrition and health care when they were young. This has an impact on life expectancy.

Migration

This is a difficult variable when dealing with forecasting population change. It is influenced by unpredictable factors. Also, it is difficult to measure reliably. Illegal migration is not reported but it is significant in number.

Therefore, for the Population Model, the assumption is that births and deaths are reported with acceptable accuracy in most countries. Similarly, most countries have had a reasonably reliable census in recent years, such that they know the total population count.

Using those assumptions, net migration is the residual between the reported total population for the latest and the previous census figure plus recorded births and subtracting recorded deaths over the inter census years. The residual gives an estimate of the net number of persons leaving/entering the country (migrants) in the intervening years which can then be expressed as a percentage of the total population.

Migration flows are almost invariably from poor and/or unstable regions to affluent/more stable regions. Figure 3-16 shows the migration rate (as a percentage of the total population) relative to the GDP per capita of a country for the 116 countries in this analysis. A negative rate is people leaving and a positive rate is people arriving. Not surprisingly it shows the pattern is towards affluence. There are, of course, exceptions to this.

Turkey, a relatively poor country, nonetheless is showing positive migration because of people moving from its war-torn neighbour.

Countries receiving a lot of migrants as a percentage of their population are Singapore, Switzerland, Norway, Australia, Canada, Austria, Sweden, Belgium, Hong Kong, Germany, Denmark, New Zealand, Finland, Turkey, and the United Kingdom. However, in the absolute number of immigrants per annum, the United States of America is the largest, followed by Germany, Turkey, Canada, the UK, and Australia.

In contrast, Georgia, Lithuania, El Salvador, and Latvia are the biggest losers as a percentage of their population. It is also noticeable that relatively prosperous countries in the Economic Union, specifically Spain, Portugal and Greece are also experiencing significant negative migration rates reflecting the impact of the EU policy of free movement of labour.

The non-predictable factors in terms of forecasting migration are essentially social attitudes about migration and a subsequent (generally) political stance that can arbitrarily change the extent to which migrants enter the country.

Figure 3-16: Immigration Relative to GDP Per Capita of Country.

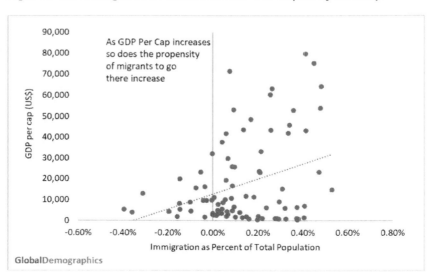

This is, of course, hard to forecast but the assumption in our model is that generally, it is getting more restrictive. There is an increasing awareness of the very large number of persons wanting to move from poor/unstable/corrupt regions to stable and typically more affluent regions. This raises concerns about the impact of that on society. As such we assume a gradual decline in the permitted immigration rates of receiving countries.

One of the factors influencing this is a 'moral issue'. Is it correct for a wealthy country such as the United Kingdom to attract health workers from poor countries when the latter has paid for the development and training of the individual and has a singularly understaffed health system? The loss of their domestic skill to the United Kingdom is not helpful.

Is it right for Britain (for example), with 1 doctor for 356 persons, to offer employment to a Nigerian (trained and qualified) doctor on anything other than a training basis? In Nigeria, there are 2,631 persons per doctor.

While the movement is understandable from the individual's point of view – average wages are significantly higher in the UK – is it morally correct for the UK to take such people. It is correct from an economic rational point of view but...

The moral issue is expected to increase in relevance and constrain migration. Especially as the access to professional services changes with the increasing availability of the internet.

The net conclusion from the above discussion is that it is assumed that migration is going to slow over time and hence the growth of the populations of more affluent countries taking migrants will slow as well.

The Greek Dilemma

It is interesting to look at the implication of emigration for the long-term development of a country. Those who migrate tend to be better skilled and this impacts the economic capability of the country *losing* these individuals. Greece is a good example of this, but it applies equally to Spain, Italy, Poland, and Romania as well as most other countries suffering emigration.

The European Union has, as one of its key principles, free movement of labour. This will probably continue. This is disastrous for the less affluent countries in the bloc and great for the more prosperous countries.

The latter gets a ready supply of skilled workers without having had to invest in their training. In contrast, the less affluent countries are being gutted in terms of their skilled workforce. Why would a skilled engineer stay in Greece when by simply getting on an overnight train they can work in Germany or France and earn 2 to 3 times as much? Figure 3-17 compares the age profile of Greece for 2009 with that of 2019 after 'ageing the 2009 population by 10 years so that the chart is comparing the same age cohort of persons. It demonstrates the hollowing out of this country's working-age population.

In terms of the traditional working-age definition (15 to 64 years) the 2009 total population of 5 years to 54 years of age is 7.10 million persons. Therefore the expected 2019 total of the 15 to 64 age group would be 7.05 million after allowing for deaths – but it is 6.7 million. That indicates that Greece lost 376,000 persons of working age in a decade through emigration. It is probably a higher percentage of the skilled worker category as those are the ones most able to move countries. (Note: the death rate for this age is very low).

Figure 3-17: Loss of Working-age Population in Greece – 2009 to 2019.

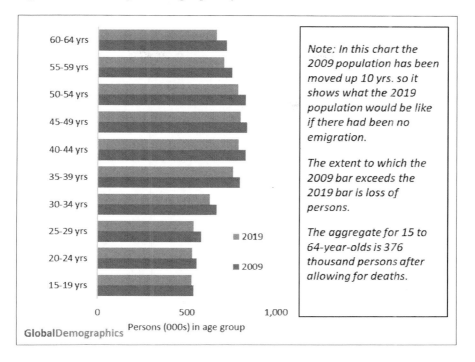

GlobalDemographics

In the decade 2009 to 2019 Greece lost 376,000 working-age persons through emigration. Given a 54% propensity of that age range to be employed, that is approximately 200,000 workers and around 5% of its 2009 workforce (and perhaps 8% of its skilled workforce).

This of course is not good for the long-term development of Greece – it is losing its 'engine'. That is younger, skilled productive workers. But the damage to Greece does not stop there.

Those emigrating are typically at the 'family' stage of life and as a result, there are fewer families in the childbearing age range left in the 'home' country - Greece. Total births in 2019 are 78,000. By 2045 it is projected to have declined to 59,000 even though the birth rate is projected to increase from 35 to 41. The cause is that under the projections for the

117

population the number of women of childbearing age decreases significantly from 2.2 million in 2019 to 1.4 million by 2045 due, in part, to migration.

The net effect of this is that Greece suffers what might be called a catastrophic loss of population. The current trends indicate that the total population of Greece will decline from 10.4 million in 2019 to 8.7 million in 2045. Furthermore, the loss will be mainly in its younger, better-skilled population. This is well demonstrated in Figure 3-18 which shows the long-term age profile of Greece under these assumptions.

The chart shows how all age groups under 60 years of age are projected to decline quite significantly in the number of persons between 2019 and 2045. That is its working-age and family population and then, ultimately, the number of births. The only growth age groups are 65 years and above.

Figure 3-18: Long term Dynamics of Greece's Population Age Profile.

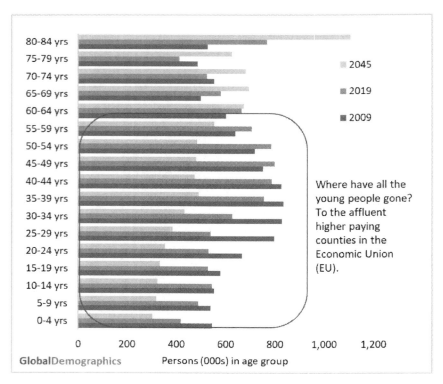

The relative Trends in Births, Deaths and Migration by Country Segment and Individual Countries

The following table summarises each of the four Country Segments' historic and projected changes in the population from 2009 to 2045 as a result of the trends and issues outlined in the previous sections of this Chapter. Please note that the total population column is in millions, whereas the columns for births, deaths and migration are in thousands (000s) as is the annual average for the period covered.

Older Affluent

The important trend in this set of countries is how, over the three blocks of time shown in Table 3-2, the total deaths are initially smaller than total births and then ultimately exceed total births. These countries move from 'natural' population growth to natural population decline. Total population size is sustained in the period 2030 to 2045 entirely by immigration into a small (10) subset of these countries.

But this may change. As mentioned earlier, attitudes towards immigration can and have changed quite suddenly – and in either direction. So clearly migration is a critical variable to the nature of these countries in future. At the time of writing, indications are that it is more likely to be constrained and selective. For that reason, the migration forecast for these countries is downward.

	2009 Total Pop mns	Average for 2010 to 2019 (000s of persons pa)			2019 Total Pop mns	Average for 2020 to 2030 (000s of persons pa)			2030 Total Pop mns	Average for 2031 to 2045 (000s of persons pa)			2045 Total Pop mns
		Births	Deaths	Migration		Births	Deaths	Migration		Births	Deaths	Migration	
Australia	21.8	315	159	184	25.1	337	195	127	28.1	361	259	75	30.7
Austria	8.4	84	86	57	8.9	93	98	71	9.6	96	114	74	10.5
Belgium	10.8	126	113	54	11.5	127	121	52	12.2	135	143	53	12.8
Canada	33.7	386	274	252	37.4	418	340	258	41.1	441	460	267	44.8
Denmark	5.5	60	56	21	5.8	67	65	18	6.0	67	74	17	6.1
Finland	5.3	55	54	17	5.5	50	62	17	5.6	46	72	15	5.4
France	62.5	758	590	91	65.1	724	659	74	66.6	731	786	72	66.8
Germany	80.9	736	924	413	83.2	809	996	595	87.7	851	1,091	616	93.3
Hong Kong	7.0	77	47	17	7.5	79	58	36	8.1	65	87	38	8.3
Iceland	0.3	4	2	0	0.3	4	3	1	0.4	4	4	1	0.4
Ireland	4.5	67	29	3	4.9	59	36	27	5.4	68	49	31	6.2
Italy	59.0	497	634	273	60.4	441	697	183	59.6	436	789	164	56.8
Japan	128.4	1,012	1,317	125	126.6	864	1,544	156	120.9	788	1,681	122	109.3
Macao	0.5	7	2	7	0.6	6	3	5	0.7	5	7	6	0.8
Netherlands	16.6	175	147	20	17.1	176	173	25	17.4	168	214	25	17.1
New Zealand	4.3	61	32	17	4.8	63	40	13	5.2	64	52	8	5.5
Norway	4.8	60	43	38	5.4	62	50	31	5.8	64	63	32	6.3
Sth Korea	49.4	413	291	55	51.2	373	377	40	51.6	333	558	41	48.8
Singapore	5.0	51	24	54	5.8	46	34	25	6.2	35	62	23	6.1
Slovenia	2.0	21	20	4	2.1	19	23	3	2.1	21	27	3	2.0
Spain	46.3	427	418	28	46.7	343	464	63	46.1	324	554	59	43.5
Sweden	9.3	117	93	49	10.0	130	106	45	10.8	144	121	47	11.8
Switzerland	7.7	85	68	67	8.6	92	80	55	9.3	98	101	57	10.1
United Kingdom	62.8	790	618	294	67.4	803	695	258	71.4	843	802	190	74.9
USA	305.8	3,947	2,727	1,081	328.8	3,967	3,271	937	346.8	3,747	4,079	678	352.0
Total	942.8	10,330	8,768	3,221	990.6	10,155	10,190	3,116	1,024.5	9,934	12,252	2,712	1,030.4

Another important aspect of these countries is that they have moved to a population 'square' rather than a 'pyramid'. This means that the size of the age groups moving up the square over time is relatively consistent. This means demand for education and health care (and other social needs) is stable over time. The focus can move to quality and increased availability with a consequent positive impact on affluence and lifestyle. This view is supported further by the awareness of the impact of humanity on the planet (and climate in particular) and that more people (higher birth rates) may not be a desirable option.

The Older Less Affluent Country Segment

This Country Segment is, in many respects, like the previous except that migration plays a significantly smaller, and in some cases a negative, role (that is, emigration rather than immigration).

For the period to 2019 total births exceeded total deaths, but the situation is marginally reversed for the period to 2030. Thereafter the number of deaths *significantly* exceeds the total births. It should be noted that this trend applies to China as well as the segment overall.

However, unlike the Older Affluent Segment, this shortfall in natural population growth is not offset by migration. There can be multiple reasons for this. One is that these countries are relatively less affluent than the previous Country Segment. As such, there is less incentive for persons from less affluent countries to migrate to them. The other reason, of course, is China, which dominates the numbers in this segment and inward migration to that country is constrained.

Table 3-3: Drivers of Population Size. Older Less Affluent Country Segment.

	2009 Total Pop	Average for 2010 to 2019 (000s of persons pa)			2019 Total Pop mns	Average for 2020 to 2030 (000s of persons pa)			2030 Total Pop mns	Average for 2031 to 2045 (000s of persons pa)			2045 Total Pop mns
		Births	Deaths	Migration		Births	Deaths	Migration		Births	Deaths	Migration	
Albania	3.0	35	22	-23	2.9	28	27	-11	2.8	16	34	-8	2.4
Belarus	9.4	112	124	12	9.4	104	120	10	9.4	105	134	9	9.1
Bulgaria	7.5	66	111	-2	7.0	58	111	2	6.4	57	110	1	5.7
Cuba	11.2	121	97	-16	11.3	107	118	-4	11.2	94	148	-2	10.3
Czechia	10.5	111	112	23	10.7	106	126	27	10.8	113	144	27	10.7
Estonia	1.3	14	16	1	1.3	13	16	4	1.3	13	17	4	1.3
Georgia	4.1	56	53	-16	4.0	51	52	-5	3.9	56	56	-5	3.8
Greece	10.9	90	114	-25	10.5	71	120	-7	9.8	63	132	-6	8.7
Hungary	9.9	91	126	8	9.7	86	131	11	9.3	77	141	10	8.5
Latvia	2.1	21	29	-16	1.9	17	28	-11	1.7	13	27	-9	1.3
Lithuania	3.2	30	40	-31	2.8	25	39	-23	2.3	17	38	-18	1.8
Mauritius	1.2	14	10	-1	1.3	12	12	1	1.3	9	16	1	1.2
Poland	38.3	378	384	-43	37.8	315	417	-10	36.6	259	494	-7	33.0
Portugal	10.6	85	110	-11	10.2	70	119	1	9.7	59	134	1	8.6
Republic of Mold	4.1	43	47	-2	4.0	33	50	2	3.9	24	59	2	3.4
Romania	20.6	196	258	-68	19.3	170	260	-49	17.8	153	273	-40	15.4
Russian Federati	143.5	1,854	1,922	258	145.4	1,695	1,912	280	146.1	1,901	2,115	263	146.8
Slovakia	5.4	57	54	2	5.5	51	61	5	5.4	45	75	5	5.0
Thailand	66.9	744	512	38	69.6	682	627	55	70.8	580	852	57	67.6
Ukraine	45.9	457	697	32	43.9	372	668	56	41.2	362	684	46	37.1
Uruguay	3.4	48	33	-5	3.5	47	35	-1	3.6	43	39	-1	3.6
China	1,334.5	17,127	11,416	1,799	1,409.6	14,261	12,621	383	1,431.8	11,923	17,511	424	1,354.4
Total	1,747.7	21,749	16,287	1,916	1,821.5	18,375	17,670	716	1,837.1	15,985	23,231	754	1,739.7

Family Stage Low Income Country Segment

This is a segment with strong, but declining, natural population growth. Even from 2030 to 2045, the projections indicate that births will significantly exceed deaths. This, of course, is a function of their historically high birth rates.

But the birth rates are declining, in some cases (India) quite rapidly, and because the population is ageing, total deaths are increasing. The projected differential between births and deaths declines significantly between 2019 and 2045.

Again, because their affluence level is relatively low, these countries are not a natural target for migration and to the extent that it is positive it is very low relative to the total population size.

This scenario means that the population of these countries is projected to grow over the forecast period but at a slowing rate. Between 2009 and 2019 the total population of the countries in this Country Segment increased by 345 million persons. From 2030 to 2045 the projected increase is 170 million.

Table 3-4: Drivers of Population Size. Family Stage Low Income Country Segment.

	2009 Total Pop Mns	Average for 2010 to 2019 000s of persons pa			2019 Total Pop mns	Average for 2020 to 2030 000s of persons pa			2030 Total Pop mns	Average for 2031 to 2045 000s of persons pa			2045 Total Pop mns
		Births	Deaths	Migration		Births	Deaths	Migration		Births	Deaths	Migration	
Algeria	35.6	990	188	-48	43.1	1,054	234	4	52.2	1,231	342	14	65.7
Argentina	40.5	752	333	5	44.8	733	379	27	49.0	677	464	31	52.6
Armenia	2.9	43	29	-10	2.9	34	30	-2	3.0	30	38	-2	2.8
Azerbaijan	9.0	172	65	-2	10.0	143	76	10	10.9	141	115	11	11.4
Bangladesh	146.3	2,996	873	-444	163.1	2,532	1,014	-344	176.0	1,727	1,371	-381	175.7
Bolivia	9.9	248	76	-12	11.5	230	85	-9	13.0	182	104	-7	14.1
Brazil	194.0	2,955	1,281	17	210.9	2,700	1,592	102	224.3	2,273	2,166	122	227.7
Cambodia	14.2	367	95	-43	16.5	316	111	-24	18.5	250	150	-23	19.6
Chile	16.9	240	108	67	18.9	236	138	124	21.3	223	197	128	23.6
Colombia	44.8	743	260	60	50.2	700	333	217	56.6	583	482	226	61.5
Dominican Rp	9.6	208	62	-31	10.8	198	75	-25	11.8	175	99	-24	12.6
Ecuador	14.8	331	83	8	17.4	336	105	41	20.4	313	152	48	23.5
El Salvador	6.2	119	44	-45	6.5	101	50	-35	6.6	69	60	-33	6.3
India	1,220.5	24,653	9,504	-404	1,367.9	22,083	11,209	-80	1,486.7	16,887	14,731	184	1,521.8
Indonesia	239.9	4,934	1,673	-176	270.8	4,858	2,049	52	302.3	4,887	2,906	94	333.4
Iran	73.1	1,472	382	-120	82.8	1,347	458	-17	92.4	1,188	724	9	99.5
Kazakhstan	16.1	386	141	-6	18.5	392	145	-4	21.2	535	191	-6	26.3
Malaysia	27.7	513	148	60	31.9	490	200	60	35.8	377	299	65	37.9
Mexico	112.6	2,255	698	-60	127.6	2,127	905	-1	141.0	1,856	1,274	9	149.9
Morocco	32.1	694	181	-70	36.5	655	214	-28	41.0	614	326	-23	45.0
Myanmar	50.4	957	442	-140	54.2	882	496	-136	56.9	711	640	-120	56.2
Nicaragua	5.8	135	31	-25	6.5	123	38	-18	7.3	104	54	-18	7.8
Panama	3.6	79	20	8	4.2	83	26	13	5.0	89	37	16	6.0
Paraguay	6.2	142	37	-18	7.0	126	45	-15	7.8	92	60	-17	8.0
Peru	28.8	574	165	-43	32.5	580	220	218	38.8	504	359	346	46.2
Philippines	92.8	2,266	589	-135	108.2	1,997	752	-6	121.8	1,585	1,062	-1	129.7
Saudi Arabia	26.7	608	108	244	34.2	485	148	186	39.9	300	253	95	42.1
South Africa	50.7	1,196	561	151	58.6	1,185	618	171	66.7	1,219	787	197	76.1
Sri Lanka	20.1	347	134	-93	21.3	327	170	-76	22.2	335	229	-74	22.7
Tunisia	10.6	204	71	-20	11.7	190	85	5	12.9	184	124	7	13.9
Turkey	71.5	1,308	431	285	83.1	1,248	524	327	94.7	1,154	761	361	106.0
Uzbekistan	28.2	689	185	-28	33.0	623	219	7	37.5	586	334	14	41.5
Venezuela RB	28.1	557	187	-288	28.9	416	230	-472	25.7	296	279	-369	20.5
Viet Nam	87.3	1,579	568	-100	96.4	1,425	701	-33	104.0	1,268	1,017	-18	107.5
Total	2,777.5	55,712	19,752	-1,458	3,122.5	50,959	23,673	239	3,425.3	42,645	32,187	861	3,595.0

For all three periods total births exceed deaths - but the difference is reducing substantially.

The Young Poor Country Segment

This is the Country Segment where the median age is less than 25 years. As such it is not surprising that the ratio of births to deaths is very high. In the decade to 2019, there were 4 births for every death. This resulted in the total population of this Country Segment increasing by 345 million people despite 1.5 million emigrants.

As shown in Table 3-5, nearly every country has significant levels of emigration. This is probably understandable in the context of opportunities in these countries relative to that in other countries. It is good for the individual, but it does mean that these countries are in all probability losing a significant proportion of their more skilled workforce. This can inhibit the growth of the domestic economy. For these countries to lose over a million people a year is perhaps a point of concern.

However, emigration aside, the extreme difference between the number of births and deaths per annum means that these populations will grow robustly. While some may consider this desirable (it potentially creates a demographic dividend – providing the new working-age population can find employment) the reality is that it means basic social services are scrambling to keep up. As shown in a subsequent Chapter on Education, in total these countries need to provide an additional 154 million extra school places over the next 25 years just to *maintain* existing educational opportunities. That is nearly a 50% increase. A similar impact exists on health services.

This raises the question of how they will be educated and provided for in terms of water, food, housing, clothing, healthcare, and ultimately work opportunities. The inevitable growth of these populations is a serious issue for global stability. Yet the basis for it happening is already in place. It cannot be averted easily, if at all.

Table 3-5: Drivers of Population Size. Young Poor Country Segment.

	2009 Total Pop Mns	Average for 2010 to 2019 Births	Deaths	Migrat- ion	2019 Total Pop mns	Average for 2020 to 2030 Births	Deaths	Migrat- ion	2030 Total Pop mns	Average for 2031 to 2045 Births	Deaths	Migrat- ion	2045 Total Pop mns
		000s of persons pa				000s of persons pa				000s of persons pa			
Angola	22.9	1,189	263	-2	32.2	1,473	282	-5	45.2	1,917	371	15	68.6
Botswana	2.0	56	14	-7	2.3	58	14	3	2.8	63	18	5	3.6
Burkina Faso	15.4	717	166	-37	20.5	852	182	-34	27.5	1,028	239	-37	38.8
Cameroon	20.1	861	239	-18	26.1	973	264	-9	33.8	1,082	342	1	44.9
Chad	11.8	619	187	7	16.2	738	219	-8	21.8	829	282	2	30.0
DR Congo	63.6	3,271	803	-34	87.9	4,287	934	-21	124.6	6,295	1,291	34	200.1
Egypt	81.7	2,536	554	-111	100.5	2,745	675	33	123.6	3,512	953	55	162.8
Ethiopia	86.1	3,394	728	-8	112.7	3,656	782	14	144.4	3,208	953	66	179.3
Ghana	24.4	853	215	-19	30.6	935	251	-5	38.0	1,026	346	3	48.3
Guatemala	14.4	417	79	-15	17.6	384	94	-7	20.7	299	127	-5	23.2
Guinea	10.1	433	110	-44	12.9	499	118	-8	17.0	536	148	-4	22.7
Haiti	9.9	273	96	-33	11.3	241	102	-34	12.5	171	118	-34	12.8
Honduras	8.2	206	40	-7	9.8	183	50	-6	11.1	142	72	-5	12.1
Kenya	41.2	1,476	292	-25	52.8	1,484	310	-10	65.6	1,277	412	0	78.6
Lao PDR	6.2	167	46	-21	7.2	144	50	-13	8.1	103	67	-11	8.5
Madagascar	20.7	813	159	-17	27.1	912	184	-4	35.1	905	251	5	45.0
Malawi	14.3	605	132	-27	18.8	662	128	-21	24.4	641	154	-21	31.4
Mali	14.8	759	193	-58	19.9	950	210	-54	27.5	1,277	276	-67	41.5
Mozambique	23.2	1,052	278	-28	30.7	1,299	289	-12	41.6	1,637	385	0	60.4
Namibia	2.1	69	21	-7	2.5	75	21	-4	3.0	85	26	-5	3.9
Nepal	26.8	575	181	-202	28.8	449	201	85	32.4	260	262	132	34.4
Niger	16.2	958	196	-15	23.6	1,341	223	-10	35.8	2,134	314	5	63.2
Nigeria	156.9	7,132	2,351	-152	203.2	8,553	2,650	-120	266.8	11,039	3,468	-43	379.7
Pakistan	177.1	5,792	1,440	-284	217.8	5,954	1,661	-233	262.4	5,380	2,141	-188	308.2
Rwanda	9.9	372	67	-27	12.7	392	69	-12	16.1	361	91	-11	20.0
Senegal	12.5	528	92	-44	16.4	620	103	-20	21.9	779	140	-23	31.1
South Sudan	9.2	381	117	-61	11.2	389	119	-149	12.6	379	126	-160	13.9
Sudan	34.1	1,303	295	-105	43.1	1,521	347	-58	55.4	1,790	462	-61	74.4
Uganda	31.9	1,567	293	-16	44.5	1,856	313	145	63.0	2,073	414	233	91.4
Tanzania	43.6	1,963	381	-91	58.5	2,447	410	-52	80.3	3,265	550	-43	120.4
Zambia	13.4	605	120	-23	18.0	705	121	-13	24.3	795	152	-11	33.8
Zimbabwe	12.7	461	131	-127	14.7	482	119	-104	17.6	606	142	-128	22.6
Total	1,037.1	41,401	10,279	-1,654	1,331.8	47,259	11,495	-746	1,717.0	54,893	15,094	-299	2,309.5

What does it all mean?

The variables considered in this chapter – specifically births, number of women of childbearing age, migration and deaths are very important as they determine the future shape (in terms of size and age profile) of the individual countries and the global population.

The following charts serve to summarise the overall pattern of population development by Country Segment. Figure 3-19 shows the absolute projected change in total population between 2019 and 2045 and Figure 3-20 shows the source of this change.

As shown in Figure 3-19, the Old Affluent is showing only marginal growth.   Figure 3-20 shows that growth is a function of immigration marginally exceeding the negative natural growth (births minus deaths).

Both China and the other Older Low-Income Countries show a marginal decline for the next 25 years, as their growth from immigration is close to zero whereas natural growth has been minus 5% and 9% respectively (relative to their 2019 population).

Figure 3-19: Change in Total Population between 2019 and 2045 by Country Segment.

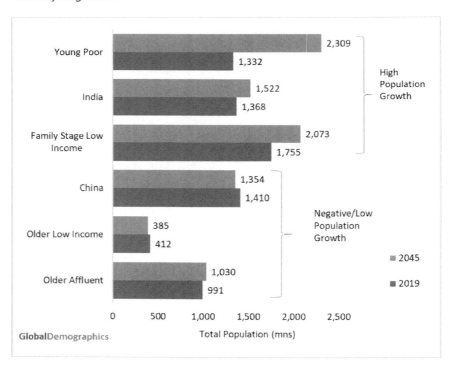

The Family Stage Low Income (excluding India) and India have population growth and as shown in Figure 3-20 this is a function of natural growth

126

(births minus deaths). The population of this Country Segment is growing at just around 0.5% per annum.

The obvious outlier is the Young Poor Country Segment. The total population of this segment is projected to grow at 2.1% per annum. Taking the total population from 1.33 billion persons in 2019 to 2.31 billion in 2045.

Figure 3-20: Sources of Change in Total Population as Percent of 2019 Population.

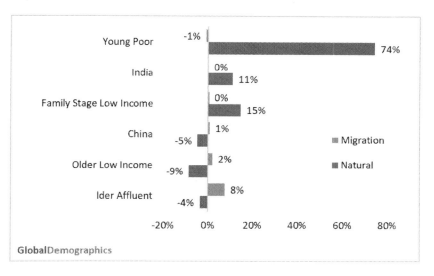

GlobalDemographics

That is an additional 1 billion persons in 25 years – and that is despite the equivalent of 1% of the 2019 population of these countries emigrating over that same period. The high birth rates overwhelm death rates (which are proportionally low due to the population bias toward young people) and are causing what can only be described as 'explosive' population growth in a governmental and sociological environment not equipped to handle it.

The total population of the Young Poor Countries is projected to grow at 2.1% per annum, taking the total population from 1.33 billion persons to 2.31 billion. That is an additional 1 billion persons in 25 years.

The key point to flow from this chapter is that the course of the change in population size (and age profile) is relatively fixed in nature. The two aspects that can be varied are migration and births.

In terms of migration, this can be changed abruptly, and it is becoming increasingly likely that it will be more constrained as awareness of the enormity of the potential number of people seeking to migrate is realized.

However, while migration levels can change abruptly, as shown in Figure 3-20, it does not play a particularly significant role in shaping the size and age profile of the population of any of the Country Segments. The most extreme case is Australia where reduced migration would slow the growth of the 'family stage' population but not significantly change the overall age profile or dependency ratio.

In terms of birth rates, it is expected that they will decline because of improving education and awareness of alternatives. But as demonstrated earlier in this chapter with Kenya, it takes a long time (10 years typically) for the decline in birth rates to be sufficient to also reduce total births per annum. The projected population growth of the poorer countries for the next 25 years is, to a very large extent, 'locked in'.

The world is going to have to prepare itself for a massive increase in the number of people who are poorly educated, have poor health due to lack of nutrition and basic sanitation, and have no real future – except to forcibly move to other countries that offer better futures.

Summary Profile – Population Change

Older Affluent

	2019	2030	2045
Total Population Mns	991	1,025	1,030
Pop Growth rate % pa	0.5%	0.3%	0.0%
Births (mns)	10	10	10
Births Growth rate % pa	-0.5%	-0.1%	-0.2%
Birth Rate per 000	47	47	49
Births-Deaths 000	808	-958	-3,310
Migration 000s	0.08	0.09	0.08
Average Age yrs.	41	43	45
Median age yrs.	42	44	46

Older Low Income

	2019	2030	2045
Total Population Mns	1,821	1,837	1,740
Pop Growth rate % pa	0.4%	0.1%	-0.4%
Births (mns)	19	17	16
Births Growth rate % pa	-0.8%	-1.2%	-0.6%
Birth Rate per 000	44	44	50
Births-Deaths 000	3,053	-2,515	-10,700
Migration 000s	-0.02	-0.01	-0.01
Average Age yrs.	39	42	45
Median age yrs.	39	43	47

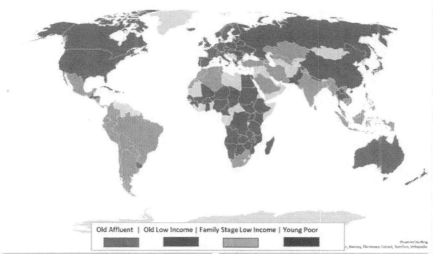

Old Affluent | Old Low Income | Family Stage Low Income | Young Poor

Family Stage Low Income

	2019	2030	2045
Total Population Mns	3,122	3,425	3,595
Pop Growth rate % pa	1.2%	0.8%	0.3%
Births (mns)	54	48	39
Births Growth rate % pa	-0.6%	-1.1%	-1.3%
Birth Rate per 000	66	54	45
Births-Deaths 000	33,034	21,260	1,935
Migraton 000s	0.00	0.00	0.00
Average Age yrs	31	34	38
Median age yrs	29	33	38

Young Poor

	2019	2030	2045
Total Population Mns	1,332	1,717	2,309
Pop Growth rate % pa	2.5%	2.3%	2.0%
Births (mns)	44	50	59
Births Growth rate % pa	1.5%	1.2%	1.1%
Birth Rate per 000	137	118	101
Births-Deaths 000	33,531	37,636	41,315
Migraton 000s	0.07	-0.02	-0.02
Average Age yrs	23	25	27
Median age yrs	19	21	23

Chapter 4
The Global Age Profile

Introduction

The previous Chapter on Births, Deaths and migration identifies the likely size of the population of each country and Country Segment. This chapter looks at the resulting dynamics of the age profile of these populations.

The age profile of a country influences the nature of society quite significantly. Its impact is most easily observable and describable in terms of consumption and lifestyle, but it must be appreciated that it does influence the overall attitudes of society. Younger (and better educated) people tend to have a more 'liberal' attitude, whereas older people tend to be more conservative. As such the changing age profile of a country will change the relative role/influence of these different views and governmental styles.

To avoid being lost in the detail, the population of the world and countries has been divided into 5 key age/life stages. These breaks reflect major changes in the individual's life, and with that, their needs, objectives, risk profiles and ultimately, consumption habits.

The age groups/life stages used are:

1) The Child Stage – typically defined as 0 to 14 years of age inclusive and this life stage is important in terms of the demands this group place on education and health care (especially in the first four years of their life). Also, their presence does impact their parents' desire for security and stability.

2) The Young Adult Stage – ages 15 to 24 years. This is typically the age range within which significant lifestyle changes take place. Either their entry into the workforce or advanced education. Also, there is an increased awareness of, and opinions about, how

130

things work in the world. This age group are increasingly the decision-maker in terms of their consumption.

3) The Family Stage – which is ages 25 to a range between 39 and 44 years of age depending on the affluence and education level of the society. Typically, less educated, and lower-income societies tend to have their children when they are quite young (e.g., 18 – 24 years) and the children are independent when their parents are reaching age 40. In contrast, older more affluent societies are increasingly having children at age 25 to 34 and as such a child is leaving the family home when this segment is around 44 years of age.

   This is the age range during which the individuals are typically in a relationship with another adult and have children in their home. As such their focus is increasingly on the home and its security. This includes the provision of the home and the essentials to the household functioning smoothly. The ability to improve the lifestyle of the family is important and that is very much a function of the availability of work for those of working age in the family.

4) The Working-age Empty Nester. While the home and security of their society continue to be important, these individuals have more time and funds to devote to their interests. Their children have grown up and are typically economically independent. As such the consumption pattern of this segment changes in predictable ways. For example, this age group is a major consumer of leisure travel, wellness, and media.

   In the older more affluent countries this life stage tends to start at around age 45 and continues through to age 69 if not further due to longer working life. However, in the less affluent countries where marriage and having children take place at a younger age, this life stage will start at around age 40 and extends to age 64.

5) The Retired/fixed income stage – this is typically starting at ages 65 through to 74 years onward. The entry age of this segment is again a function of the stage of development of the country.

Persons in the Older Affluent Countries increasingly retire later in life (as discussed in the Chapter on the workforce). In the less affluent countries, life expectancy is such that retirement occurs at age 60 to 64 years.

Not surprisingly this older segment is concerned about health and wellness and security of funds for their retirement years – will they have enough? As such they are increasingly less influential on the nature of society. Typically, the older people in most societies are less well educated than the young for obvious reasons – availability of education when they were young.

As one would expect, the proportion of the total population in a country in each life stage changes over time, and this chapter demonstrates what those changes are projected to be.

It is important to appreciate that these changes significantly impact other aspects of society. For example:

- The demand for education – this is a function of births and the number of couples of childbearing age.
- The demand for work – a function of the number of persons who have reached working age and need to acquire an income to support themselves (and their family)
- The demand for health services – the probability of a person needing health services increases with age and particularly when they pass 40 years of age.
- Younger and better-educated adults will be less willing to accept societal norms and more willing to challenge them.
- The greater the proportion of society that is in a stable family relationship with improving lifestyles the less willing they are to accept or want radical change.

An Overview of Age Dynamics by Country Segment

Figure 4-1 summarises the age profile of the four country segments as of 2020. The purpose of this chart is to highlight just how different they are (which, given that median age was used as one of the criteria for segmenting the countries, should not be surprising). However, even with that knowledge, the difference between the Young Poor Segment and the two Older Segments is quite significant. Specifically:

- 27% of the Young Poor Countries population need a school place (persons aged 5 to 14 years) compared with 11% of the Older Affluent.
- 19% of the Young Poor Country Segment are over 40 and have an increasing demand for health care. This compares with 47% of Older Affluent.
- 56% of the Young Poor population are of working age (15 to 64). This compares with 70% of Older Affluent being of working age.

Figure 4-1: Relative Age Profiles of Country Segments in 2020.

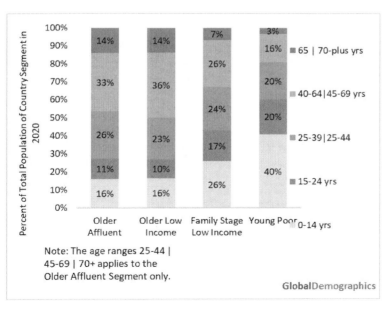

Older Affluent Country Segment

Table 4-1 shows the aggregate picture of the population for all countries in this Country Segment and reveals an important point. As detailed in Chapter Eight, these countries account for 62% of *global* household consumption expenditure. Yet the total number of persons in these countries is virtually static for the next 25 years and the number of key consumption decision-makers (ages 15 to 69 years) is in decline.

Whereas in the past. growth in total consumption expenditure was a function of both increased number of consumers and increased affluence per consumer, now it is driven by just increased affluence. This has implications for the growth rate of global consumption expenditure and hence economic activity.

Table 4-1: Trend in Total Size of Age Groups for all Countries in the Older Affluent Segment.

	2010	2020	2030	2045	2010-20	2020-30	2030-45
	Persons mns				Growth rate % pa		
0-14 yrs	162	160	153	149	-0.1%	-0.4%	-0.2%
15-24 yrs	119	114	113	106	-0.4%	-0.1%	-0.4%
25-44 yrs	262	257	254	241	-0.2%	-0.1%	-0.4%
45-69 yrs	297	324	328	321	0.9%	0.1%	-0.1%
70-plus yrs	110	141	176	213	2.5%	2.2%	1.3%
Total	950	996	1,025	1,030	0.5%	0.3%	0.0%
15-69 yrs	678	695	695	668	0.3%	0.0%	-0.3%

The group of countries that account for 62% of global consumption expenditure no longer have a growing number of consumers. This has implications for the future global demand for workers.

For this Country Segment, it is necessary to look at two subsets of countries within it due to differences in terms of immigration policy. 10 countries have relatively high inward migration. As a result, their direction of development is slightly different from the others who have very low, and in a few cases, mildly negative migration rates. The ten countries with inward migration are the first ten listed in Table 4-3.

Figure 4-2 shows the projected trend in the individual age groups for each of the two groups of countries. The one on the left is the total for countries with low or negative migration and the one on the right is the total for countries that permit migration – albeit projected to be at a marginally declining rate. As Figure 4-2 demonstrates, the non-immigrant countries reach their peak population in 2030-35 and all but the oldest age groups are in absolute decline. For the countries that allow immigration (albeit assumed at a slowing rate in this model), all age groups continue to grow.

Figure 4-2: Comparative Age Group Trends for Older Affluent Countries with and without Migration.

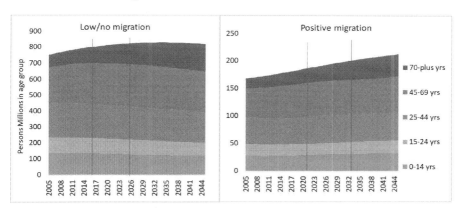

Note: Left axis is different for the two charts – otherwise the trend by age group would not be observable for the countries with positive migration.

No-immigration Countries.

Table 4-2 provides the details for the 'No Migration' set of countries. Not surprisingly in total, these countries reach peak population between 2032 and 2034. They are then projected to slowly decline in absolute population size. All age groups under 70 years of age are projected to decline in size. Overall, this means the number of school places is now stabilised, and the working-age population is projected to decline by 7% in absolute size and from 70% of the total population to 65%.

Table 4-2: Historic and Projected Total Age Profile of Countries in the Older Affluent Country Segment with Limited or Negative Migration.

	2010	2020	2030	2045	2010-20	2020-30	2030-45
	Persons mns				Growth rate % pa		
0-14 yrs	135	131	119	117	-0.3%	-1.0%	-0.1%
15-24 yrs	97	94	84	83	-0.4%	-1.1%	-0.1%
25-44 yrs	215	209	194	189	-0.3%	-0.7%	-0.2%
45-69 yrs	241	262	259	255	0.9%	-0.1%	-0.1%
70-plus yrs	89	115	168	173	2.6%	3.9%	0.2%
Total	777	811	824	819	0.4%	0.2%	0.0%
Working Age	553	565	537	528	0.2%	-0.5%	-0.1%
	Share of total population						
0-14 yrs	17%	16%	14%	14%			
15-24 yrs	13%	12%	10%	10%			
25-44 yrs	28%	26%	24%	23%			
45-69 yrs	31%	32%	31%	31%			
70-plus yrs	11%	14%	20%	21%			
Working Age	71%	70%	65%	64%			

Countries that Allow Immigration

The 10 countries that allow immigration to a measurable level, (top ten of Table 4-4) are projected to grow in absolute size for all age groups for the next 25 years – albeit very marginally (less than 0.7% per annum) for all but the oldest age group.

As for the other countries in this Country Segment, the older age group (70 years and above) is projected to increase in the share of the total population. But a comparison of the bottom section of Table 4-2 and Table 4-3 shows that the differences in overall age profile are very small.

The one significant difference is the trend in the working-age population (and the potential demand for work). For those that have immigration, it is projected to increase from 130 million to 140 million over the next 25 years. This compares with a decline for the other countries. But for both sets of countries, the working-age as a proportion of the total population declines from 70% to between 64% and 66%.

Table 4-3: Historic and Projected Age Profile of the Ten Countries with immigration in the Older Affluent Country Segment.

	2010	2020	2030	2045	2010-20	2020-30	2030-45
	Persons mns				Growth rate % pa		
0-14 yrs	26	29	30	32	0.8%	0.7%	0.3%
15-24 yrs	21	20	21	23	-0.5%	0.5%	0.6%
25-44 yrs	47	49	50	51	0.3%	0.4%	0.1%
45-69 yrs	56	61	63	66	0.9%	0.2%	0.3%
70-plus yrs	21	26	32	40	2.0%	2.2%	1.4%
Total	172	185	197	212	0.7%	0.7%	0.5%
Working Age	125	130	134	140	0.4%	0.3%	0.3%
	Share of total population						
0-14 yrs	15%	15%	15%	15%			
15-24 yrs	12%	11%	11%	11%			
25-44 yrs	27%	26%	26%	24%			
45-69 yrs	33%	33%	32%	31%			
70-plus yrs	12%	14%	16%	19%			
Working Age	72%	70%	68%	66%			

This indicates that while immigration may grow the total headcount and Gross Domestic Product it does not significantly change the age structure. The number of dependents per worker remains almost the same as will GDP per capita.

While immigration may grow the total working-age population and Gross Domestic Product the number of dependents per worker remains almost the same as does GDP per capita.

Changing Age Profile by Country

Table 4-4 shows how the age profile for individual countries in the Older Affluent Country Segment are projected to change over the next 25 years. The countries have been sorted by the extent to which the two younger age segments decline over the next decade.

Table 4-4: Projected Growth Rates by Age Group for Older Affluent Countries: 2020 to 2045.

	Average Growth Rate pa 2020-2030					Average Growth Rate pa 2030-2045				
	Age Groups					Age Groups				
	0-14 yrs	15-24 yrs	25-44 yrs	45-69 yrs	70+ yrs	0-14 yrs	15-24 yrs	25-44 yrs	45-69 yrs	70+ yrs
Hong Kong	2.2%	0.0%	-1.4%	0.2%	5.0%	-1.2%	2.3%	-1.0%	-0.3%	2.2%
Austria	0.8%	0.2%	0.6%	0.5%	1.6%	0.3%	0.8%	0.1%	0.3%	1.8%
Germany	0.8%	0.4%	0.4%	-0.1%	1.4%	0.3%	0.8%	0.3%	-0.1%	1.2%
Sweden	0.7%	1.5%	0.3%	0.4%	1.1%	0.8%	0.7%	0.3%	0.5%	1.1%
Switzerland	0.6%	0.3%	0.1%	0.8%	2.3%	0.5%	0.7%	0.1%	0.1%	2.1%
Macao	0.5%	1.4%	-1.0%	1.3%	8.4%	-1.6%	0.7%	-1.0%	0.9%	3.5%
Canada	0.4%	0.1%	0.6%	0.3%	3.5%	0.4%	0.4%	-0.1%	0.9%	1.3%
Denmark	0.4%	-0.8%	0.8%	-0.1%	1.3%	0.1%	0.4%	-0.4%	0.1%	1.1%
Australia	0.4%	1.3%	0.3%	1.0%	3.0%	0.4%	0.1%	0.2%	0.7%	1.8%
New Zealand	0.0%	0.4%	0.8%	0.2%	3.1%	0.1%	-0.1%	-0.2%	0.4%	1.7%
United Kingdom	0.0%	0.9%	0.0%	0.6%	1.5%	0.3%	-0.1%	-0.1%	0.2%	1.4%
Singapore	-0.1%	-2.9%	-0.7%	0.5%	8.5%	-2.0%	-0.1%	-2.2%	0.0%	3.3%
Norway	-0.1%	0.1%	0.9%	0.7%	2.3%	0.2%	-0.1%	0.1%	0.7%	1.7%
Belgium	-0.2%	1.0%	0.0%	0.2%	2.1%	0.4%	-0.2%	0.3%	0.0%	1.3%
Netherlands	-0.3%	-1.0%	0.2%	-0.4%	2.4%	-0.3%	-0.3%	-0.7%	-0.5%	1.3%
USA	-0.3%	-0.3%	0.6%	0.0%	3.2%	-0.4%	-0.3%	-0.4%	0.5%	1.0%
France	-0.6%	0.2%	-0.3%	0.0%	2.1%	0.0%	-0.6%	-0.1%	-0.4%	1.2%
Slovenia	-0.7%	1.5%	-2.2%	0.0%	2.8%	0.6%	-0.7%	-0.2%	-1.0%	1.1%
Iceland	-0.8%	0.6%	0.0%	0.6%	3.6%	-0.3%	-0.8%	-0.2%	0.5%	1.6%
Ireland	-1.2%	2.1%	-0.2%	2.0%	3.5%	0.8%	-1.2%	1.4%	0.3%	2.7%
Sth Korea	-1.3%	-2.2%	-1.5%	0.4%	5.0%	-0.8%	-1.3%	-2.1%	-1.0%	3.0%
Finland	-1.3%	0.4%	-0.2%	-0.3%	1.9%	-0.7%	-1.3%	-0.3%	0.2%	0.2%
Italy	-1.5%	-0.2%	-0.8%	0.0%	1.3%	-0.2%	-1.5%	-0.4%	-1.3%	1.7%
Japan	-1.6%	-0.6%	-1.6%	-0.1%	0.8%	-0.8%	-1.6%	-0.8%	-1.3%	0.6%
Spain	-2.2%	0.6%	-2.3%	0.9%	1.9%	-0.7%	-2.2%	-0.2%	-1.5%	2.2%

There is a simple story here. Those countries that allow immigration maintain their total population size whereas for the others, population declines – initially in the younger age groups (under 25 years but then by 2045 this has extended out to all but the oldest age group.

Changing Household Size and Number of Households

A direct side effect of the changing age profile is a move to a smaller household size. In more affluent societies older households have fewer dependents/children in them, and household size is smaller. That in turn means that even with a stable or reducing total population size, future demand for housing will nonetheless be positive. Table 4-5 summarises the position in terms of average household size for this set of countries.

Table 4-5: Current and Projected Number and Nature of Households by Country. Older Affluent Country Segment.

| | 2019 | | | | 2045 | | | |
	Households 000s	Avg pers per hhold	% Hholds > 4 pers	Employed Persons	Households 000s	Avg pers per hhold	% Hholds > 4 pers	Employed Persons
Australia	9,407	2.67	7.9%	1.34	11,761	2.61	7.9%	1.29
Austria	3,598	2.48	4.7%	1.23	4,243	2.47	4.7%	1.19
Belgium	4,456	2.58	6.3%	1.08	5,041	2.54	6.3%	1.05
Canada	14,721	2.54	6.3%	1.31	17,945	2.50	4.7%	1.24
Denmark	2,240	2.58	6.3%	1.27	2,397	2.57	6.3%	1.18
Finland	2,172	2.54	6.3%	1.18	2,230	2.43	4.7%	1.11
France	24,797	2.62	7.9%	1.09	26,135	2.56	6.3%	1.02
Germany	33,792	2.46	4.7%	1.25	37,582	2.48	4.7%	1.25
Hong Kong	3,114	2.40	4.0%	1.21	3,444	2.42	4.7%	1.07
Iceland	125	2.70	9.5%	1.58	147	2.54	6.3%	1.45
Ireland	1,772	2.75	9.5%	1.28	2,427	2.55	6.3%	1.20
Italy	24,792	2.44	4.7%	0.94	23,980	2.37	4.0%	0.88
Japan	52,498	2.41	4.7%	1.27	46,618	2.34	4.0%	1.15
Macao	236	2.71	9.5%	1.62	339	2.32	4.0%	1.33
Netherlands	6,675	2.56	6.3%	1.33	6,840	2.50	4.7%	1.22
New Zealand	1,747	2.74	9.5%	1.48	2,052	2.67	7.9%	1.41
Norway	2,003	2.68	7.9%	1.37	2,308	2.75	9.5%	1.36
Sth Korea	21,023	2.43	4.7%	1.28	20,946	2.33	4.0%	1.07
Singapore	1,836	3.16	16.7%	1.87	2,697	2.28	3.3%	1.21
Slovenia	835	2.48	4.7%	1.18	808	2.51	6.3%	1.09
Spain	18,843	2.48	4.7%	1.05	18,488	2.35	4.0%	0.99
Sweden	3,865	2.59	6.3%	1.29	4,495	2.63	7.9%	1.26
Switzerland	3,434	2.50	4.7%	1.38	4,081	2.48	4.7%	1.28
United Kingdom	25,517	2.64	7.9%	1.31	28,051	2.67	7.9%	1.29
USA	123,254	2.67	7.9%	1.30	138,097	2.55	6.3%	1.17
Total/Average	386,754	2.56	6.4%	1.24	413,153	2.49	5.5%	1.15

As shown at the bottom of this table, the average household size in terms of the number of people in the economic unit is projected to decline from its present relatively low value (compared to other Country Segments) of 2.57 to 2.49 by 2045. That decline is sufficient in the context of a near static total population to mean overall demand for housing can be expected to be mildly positive for the next 25 years. Increasing from 395 million households in 2019 to reach a projected 423 million in 2045.

Not surprisingly that is biased toward the countries that allow migration. In contrast, housing demand in Japan, Spain and Italy is potentially negative over the next 25 years as a result of the projected contraction of the overall population more than offsetting the decline in average household size

The changing age profile of the Older Affluent Countries will result in more 2 person households meaning demand for housing should remain positive through to 2045 for nearly all these countries, preserving an important aspect of household wealth.

The number of Workers per Household

The changing age profile of households also impacts the number of workers per household. The more workers per household the better the household income. In the case of these countries, it is 1.24 in 2019 and is projected to decline marginally to 1.15 by 2045.

This does impact the trend in the average income of households and is discussed later in this book. For now, it is perhaps useful to bear in mind that this very important group of countries in terms of overall consumption. It is of concern that their household incomes are impeded (albeit marginally) by a small decline in the average number of workers per household.

Immigration compared to no immigration.

Finally, in terms of the Older Affluent Country Segment, it is useful to look in detail at two countries. Japan because it is one of the oldest and also one that is least likely to have inward migration and the United States of America because of its more open borders, which has also made it one of the youngest countries in this Country Segment.

Japan

Japan has very low immigration levels. As such, it is an example of the effects of simultaneously declining propensity to have children and increasing life expectancy and affluence. As shown in Table 4-6 and Figure 4-3, only the oldest age group is projected to grow through to 2045. All other age/life stage segments are projected to be in slow decline (circa -1% per annum) in the absolute number of persons.

Figure 4-3: The Changing Size of Age Groups in Japan to 2045.

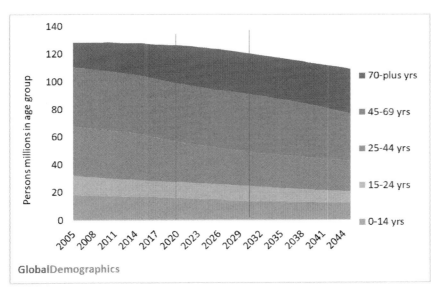

Table 4-6: Historic and Projected Age Profile of Japan.

	2010	2020	2030	2045	2010-20	2020-30	2030-45
	Persons mns				Growth rate % pa		
0-14 yrs	17	16	13	12	-0.9%	-1.6%	-0.8%
15-24 yrs	13	12	11	9	-1.0%	-0.6%	-1.6%
25-44 yrs	35	29	25	22	-1.8%	-1.6%	-0.8%
45-69 yrs	43	42	42	34	-0.1%	-0.1%	-1.3%
70-plus yrs	21	28	30	32	2.9%	0.8%	0.6%
Total	129	126	121	109	-0.2%	-0.5%	-0.7%
Working age	91	83	78	65	-0.9%	-0.7%	-1.2%
	Share of total population						
0-14 yrs	13%	12%	11%	11%			
15-24 yrs	10%	9%	9%	8%			
25-44 yrs	27%	23%	21%	20%			
45-69 yrs	33%	34%	35%	31%			
70-plus yrs	16%	22%	25%	30%			
Working age	71%	66%	64%	59%			

As a result, the total population is projected to decline from 126 million in 2020 to 109 million by 2045 and the working-age population declines from 83 million to 65 million.

Because of this combination of ageing and declining total population size, there is often concern expressed about having enough workers. This is discussed in detail in Chapter Six which is on employment. However, working-age has extended to 74 years of age (see Chapter Six). As a result, the proportion of the population within the extended working age is projected to decline less. From 66% in 2020 to 59% by 2045. Add to that a projected marginally increased participation rate (due to longer working life), the proportion of the population in work stays almost constant.

Consequently, Japan continues to have one of the lowest dependency ratios in the world (that is non-working persons per employed person).

The United States of America

This country is the largest by population in this Country Segment (Older Affluent) and allows migration at a low rate as a percentage of the population. (0.3% compared with 0.8% for Australia). Consequently, the average annual growth rate for its total population over the last decade (2009 to 2019) was 0.7% whereas for Australia it was 1.5%.

Like the other countries in this segment, the oldest age group is projected to show strong growth in the next decade. However, as detailed in Table 4-7 the growth of this older age group is projected to level off after 2030. The USA is approaching 'peak aged'.

In contrast, the under 45-year-old age group is projected to show only marginal growth to 2030 (plus 3 million) and then decline steadily thereafter. As a proportion of the total population, they are projected to decline from 58% in 2020 to 52% by 2045.

This shift in the relative importance of the older and younger age segments will have implications for the range of goods and services sought by consumers. Why is this important? Because this country accounts for 31 % of global consumption.

Overall, the outcome by 2045 is not that much different from that of Japan. The migrants were not sufficient to maintain the proportion of the population that is working-age. It declines, in this case by 3 percentage points compared with 5 for Japan.

Figure 4-4: Changing Size of Life Stage Segments in the United States of America.

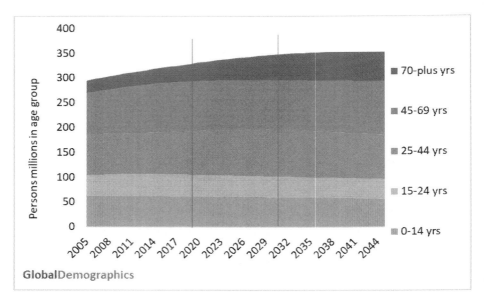

Table 4-7: Historic and Projected Age Profile of the United States of America.

	2010	2020	2030	2045	2010-20	2020-30	2030-45
0-14 yrs	62	61	59	56	-0.3%	-0.3%	-0.4%
15-24 yrs	44	44	42	40	-0.1%	-0.3%	-0.3%
25-44 yrs	82	89	94	88	0.9%	0.6%	-0.4%
45-69 yrs	93	101	100	109	0.8%	0.0%	0.5%
70-plus yrs	28	37	51	59	2.9%	3.2%	1.0%
Total	309	331	347	352	0.7%	0.5%	0.1%
Working age	219	233	237	237	0.6%	0.2%	0.0%
Share of total population							
0-14 yrs	20%	18%	17%	16%			
15-24 yrs	14%	13%	12%	11%			
25-44 yrs	26%	27%	27%	25%			
45-69 yrs	30%	30%	29%	31%			
70-plus yrs	9%	11%	15%	17%			
Working age	71%	70%	68%	67%			

The Older Low Income Country Segment

This segment includes China which, with 1.4 billion persons, dominates what happens on average for this segment. For that reason, China is considered first in this discussion.

China – there are two relevant populations.

There is a unique aspect to China. It effectively has two populations that are quite different in age profile, occupation, income, and consumption profile. That is an urban population and a rural population (in terms of actual occupation rather than historic registration – Hukou).

China effectively has two populations that are quite different in nature and consumption profile. That is Urban and Rural (based on actual occupation and not hukou).

Rural China

Over the last two decades, an average of 19 million persons each year have moved from rural to urban areas of China. Initially (1990-2010) they were biased toward persons in the 15 to 39 years age range. But in the last fifteen years, this has expanded out to under 64 years as moving to urban areas became more accepted and perceived as less risky.

This mass movement has, of course, resulted in the urban population's projected age trends being different from those of the rural population. These are shown in separate charts in Figures 4-5 (Rural) and 4-6 (Urban).

In respect of the rural population, (Figure 4-5) the story is obvious and simple –

1) All age groups under 65 years of age (and hence all consumer market segments) are in steady (and by global standards, quite rapid) decline.
2) Given current trends, the rural population in 2045 is projected to be nearly half what it is today. That is 295 million persons in 2045 versus a reported 561 million in 2020.
3) Even in just a decade (to 2030) it is projected that all the younger age segments (those under 40 years of age) will have declined by at least a third from their 2020 size.
4) Not surprisingly, the working-age population in rural areas is projected to decline significantly. From 390 million in 2020 to a projected 151 million persons in 2045.

This rural to urban migration is encouraged by the government as it means that the productivity of the average worker is increased. Rural employment has been inefficient in its present form (small plots of land per farmer and low mechanisation). Moving people off the land into industry benefits both agriculture production (larger land areas justify the use of capital equipment) and industry as it has more skilled (educated) workers.

Overall, the rural population of China is projected to experience a steep reduction in the number of persons and is ageing in profile as those leaving for the urban areas are typically younger (under 65 years of age)

The impact of ongoing urban to rural migration indicates that the rural population of China in 2045 will be nearly half what it is today.

Figure 4-5: Changing Size of RURAL Consumer Age/Life Stage Segments in China.

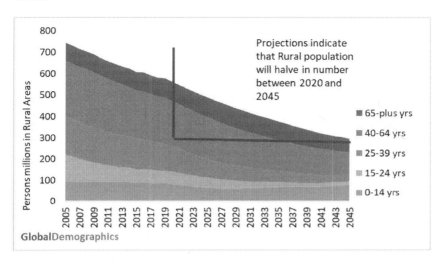

GlobalDemographics

Table 4-8: Historic and Projected Age Profile of Rural China.

	2010	2020	2030	2045	2010-20	2020-30	2030-45
0-14 yrs	89	81	60	79	-0.9%	-3.0%	1.9%
15-24 yrs	87	60	37	15	-3.7%	-4.9%	-5.6%
25-40 yrs	161	118	66	30	-3.0%	-5.6%	-5.2%
40-64 yrs	251	212	172	106	-1.7%	-2.1%	-3.2%
65 yrs Plus	83	90	93	65	0.7%	0.4%	-2.3%
Total	671	561	427	295	-1.8%	-2.7%	-2.4%
Working age	499	390	275	151	-2.4%	-3.5%	-3.9%
Share of total population							
0-14 yrs	13%	15%	14%	27%			
15-24 yrs	13%	11%	9%	5%			
25-40 yrs	24%	21%	16%	10%			
40-64 yrs	37%	38%	40%	36%			
65 yrs Plus	12%	16%	22%	22%			
Working age	74%	70%	64%	51%			

Urban China

Because of the rural to urban migration the urban population of China has been growing and has a very different projected age profile. Figure 4-6 shows the projected shape of the future population by age segment and Table 4-9 provides the detail.

In the last decade, the total urban population grew at 2.6% per annum, and with ongoing rural to urban migration, the urban population is projected to continue to show robust growth at 1.4% per annum through to 2030 despite a reduction in both the number of births and the number of rural to urban migrants (due to the reduction in the rural population). Positive population growth, albeit much slower at 0.4% per annum, continues to 2045.

The key points to note in terms of Urban China are:

1) The 'dominance and dynamics' of the 40-to-64-year age group. This is an important segment in terms of consumption power It has a higher disposable income per capita as the children have left home. In the last decade, it grew from 227 million persons to 318 million – that was 3.4% per annum and a 40% increase.

2) This age segment is projected to continue to grow at 2.0% per annum to 2030. While a robust rate of growth, it is much slower than before, and this may have implications for the future growth of consumer spending in urban China (which is 84% of all consumer spending in China). From 2030 to 2045 the number of persons in this age segment is projected to decline. This has significance for the trend in global consumption expenditure.

3) The Urban Aged (over 64 years) is projected to grow rapidly in size. From 13% of the urban population to 26%. This will have implications for the demand for health services.

4) The urban working-age population (and, as shown later, the employed population) is projected to decline quite significantly as a *proportion* of the urban population. Down from 71% to 60%. However, the absolute number of working-age increases through to 2030 and declines very marginally (-0.2% pa) to 2045.

Figure 4-6: Changing Size of URBAN Consumer Age/Life Stage Segments in China.

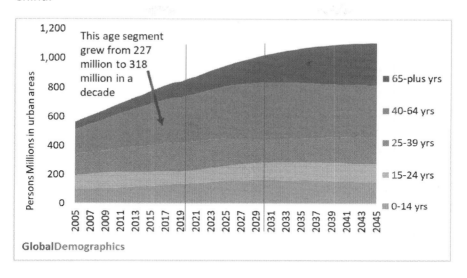

Table 4-9: Historic and Projected Age Profile of Urban China.

	2010	2020	2030	2045	2010-20	2020-30	2030-45
0-14 yrs	108	137	166	151	2.4%	1.9%	-0.6%
15-24 yrs	110	89	120	127	-2.0%	3.0%	0.4%
25-40 yrs	160	199	161	189	2.2%	-2.1%	1.1%
40-64 yrs	227	318	387	350	3.4%	2.0%	-0.7%
65 yrs Plus	66	113	185	287	5.6%	5.0%	3.0%
Total	670	857	1,018	1,105	2.5%	1.7%	0.5%
Working age	496	606	667	667	2.0%	1.0%	0.0%
Share of total population							
0-14 yrs	16%	16%	16%	14%			
15-24 yrs	16%	10%	12%	11%			
25-40 yrs	24%	23%	16%	17%			
40-64 yrs	34%	37%	38%	32%			
65 yrs Plus	10%	13%	18%	26%			
Working age	74%	71%	66%	60%			

5) The size of the three younger age groups is 'lumpy' as a result of the changes in the one-child policy from 2013 onward. This resulted in a substantial increase in births in 2014 and 2017. The inventory of people wanting a second child caught up in the

149

subsequent 4 years and by 2018 births had returned to trend. This 'short term lift in births' is now working its way through the different age groups.

In the last decade, the Urban 'Working-age Empty Nester' segment grew at 3.4% per annum adding 91 million consumers on a base in 2010 of 227 million persons. This drove strong demand for discretionary products and services. For the next decade, it is projected to grow by 69 million which is 2.0% per annum.

Overall, the urban population is projected to increase in size through to 2035 and thereafter largely stabilises at around 1 billion persons. This is important as 'urban' is where the consumption power is in China. The projected growth of the 40-to-64-year age group at 2.0% per annum for the decade to 2030 will sustain growth in the total number of consumers and expenditure. However, after 2030 total consumption expenditure will be reliant on increased individual spending power (and propensity to spend) of the (ageing) individual rather than an increased number of consumers.

The Rest of the Older Low-Income Country Segment

The profile of the *other* countries in this Country Segment is shown in Figure 4-7. And the relevant statistics are in Table 4-10. The key issues for this group of countries are seen as follows:

1. The total population is projected to decline slowly. This is a function of declining births and an increasingly ageing population with increasing deaths. This is not offset by immigration.

2. The proportion of the total population that is of working-age declines from 67% in 2020 to 60% in 2045. This ultimately has an

150

impact on the size of the workforce and economic output – as discussed in Chapter Six which is on Employment.

3. The population gets older, with 51% over 40 years of age in 2020, and is projected to reach 55% by 2045. However, this is not just a result of an increasingly older population but also the projected decline in the size of the younger population due to falling total births.

4. The relatively stable size of the 40 years and above age group means the health sector will not be under pressure to expand (see Chapter Nine on Health Care). There are 212 million persons over 40 years of age in 2020 and this is projected to be 215 million in 2045. They are at 'peak aged'. (As explained in the Chapter on Health, demand for health services increases substantially once an individual is over 40 years of age).

Figure 4-7: Average Change in Consumer Segments of the Old Low-Income Country Segment Excluding China.

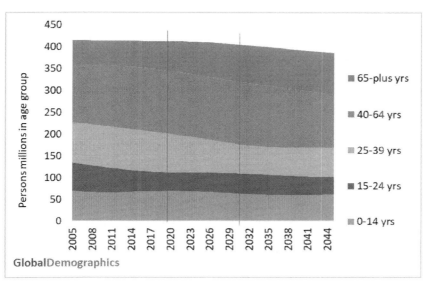

Table 4-10: Historic and Projected Age Profile of other Countries in the Older Low-Income Country Segment

	2010	2020	2030	2045	2010-20	2020-30	2030-45
0-14 yrs	65	69	63	61	0.5%	-0.8%	-0.3%
15-24 yrs	59	43	46	41	-3.1%	0.8%	-0.8%
25-39 yrs	95	89	68	68	-0.6%	-2.6%	0.0%
40-64 yrs	139	144	143	121	0.3%	0.0%	-1.1%
65-plus yrs	55	68	84	94	2.0%	2.2%	0.7%
Total	413	412	405	385	0.0%	-0.2%	-0.3%
Working age	292	276	258	230	-0.6%	-0.7%	-0.7%
	Share of total population						
0-14 yrs	16%	17%	16%	16%			
15-24 yrs	14%	10%	11%	11%			
25-39 yrs	23%	22%	17%	18%			
40-64 yrs	34%	35%	35%	31%			
65-plus yrs	13%	16%	21%	24%			
Working age	71%	67%	64%	60%			

Table 4-11 shows the projected growth rate for each Life Stage/Age segment for all countries in this Country Segment for the periods 2020 to 2030 and then from 2030 to 2045.

It strongly demonstrates how, in this set of countries, the only age group with projected future growth is that over 64 years of age. The other age segments are typically projected to have close to zero or negative growth. These countries are effectively at a 'tipping point' in terms of population dynamics.

Changing Household Size and Number of Households

With the projected ageing of the population of all countries in this Country Segment and the bias to 40-year-old and above population (empty nesters) overall household size is relatively small at 2.87 persons and is projected to decline to 2.57 by 2045. This is shown in Table 4-12.

152

Table 4-11: Changing Age Profile of Countries in the Old Low-Income Segment. 2020 to 2045.

	Average Growth Rate pa 2020-2030					Average Growth Rate pa 2030-2045				
	0-14 yrs	15-24 yrs	25-39 yrs	40-64 yrs	65+ yrs	0-14 yrs	15-24 yrs	25-39 yrs	40-64 yrs	65+ yrs
Uruguay	-0.2%	-0.7%	0.3%	0.4%	1.6%	-0.6%	-0.2%	-0.6%	0.3%	1.2%
Russia	-0.2%	2.7%	-3.8%	0.3%	2.4%	0.6%	-0.2%	1.3%	-1.0%	0.3%
Belarus	-0.3%	1.7%	-3.0%	-0.2%	2.7%	0.0%	-0.3%	0.1%	-0.8%	0.3%
Czechia	-0.4%	1.9%	-2.3%	0.4%	0.9%	0.4%	-0.4%	0.7%	-1.4%	1.3%
Georgia	-0.5%	1.6%	-2.1%	-0.4%	1.6%	0.5%	-0.5%	0.5%	-0.9%	-0.1%
Hungary	-0.6%	-0.7%	-1.3%	-0.2%	0.4%	-0.8%	-0.6%	-1.0%	-1.2%	0.7%
China	-0.7%	0.5%	-2.8%	0.6%	3.4%	-1.4%	-0.7%	-0.5%	-1.3%	2.0%
Slovakia	-0.8%	0.2%	-2.7%	0.3%	2.2%	-1.0%	-0.8%	-0.5%	-1.1%	1.0%
Estonia	-0.8%	1.8%	-2.0%	0.1%	1.4%	0.0%	-0.8%	0.4%	-0.4%	0.5%
Cuba	-1.0%	-1.0%	-1.2%	-0.5%	2.9%	-1.0%	-1.0%	-1.1%	-1.2%	1.2%
Lithuania	-1.0%	-1.6%	-4.0%	-2.4%	1.5%	-2.8%	-1.1%	-2.5%	-2.8%	-0.4%
Thailand	-1.1%	-1.5%	-0.1%	-0.5%	4.4%	-1.2%	-1.1%	-1.3%	-0.8%	2.0%
Albania	-1.2%	-3.0%	-0.4%	-0.7%	3.3%	-3.8%	-1.3%	-2.5%	0.2%	0.3%
Latvia	-1.3%	0.6%	-4.8%	-1.5%	1.1%	-2.2%	-1.3%	-1.1%	-2.5%	-0.4%
Bulgaria	-1.4%	1.3%	-3.1%	-0.4%	0.0%	-0.3%	-1.3%	-0.1%	-1.9%	0.0%
Romania	-1.4%	-0.3%	-2.7%	-0.3%	0.4%	-0.9%	-1.4%	-0.8%	-2.3%	0.9%
Poland	-1.5%	0.2%	-3.3%	0.3%	1.9%	-1.6%	-1.5%	-0.7%	-1.1%	0.6%
Mauritius	-1.5%	-2.4%	0.4%	-0.2%	3.8%	-1.8%	-1.5%	-2.1%	0.2%	1.3%
Ukraine	-1.8%	1.8%	-3.7%	0.2%	1.0%	-0.5%	-1.8%	0.2%	-1.3%	0.0%
Portugal	-1.9%	-1.4%	-1.1%	-0.8%	1.4%	-1.4%	-1.9%	-1.3%	-1.7%	0.9%
Moldova	-2.1%	-0.2%	-3.6%	1.1%	2.8%	-2.4%	-2.1%	-1.3%	-0.4%	0.2%
Greece	-2.5%	-0.6%	-2.1%	-0.5%	1.3%	-1.1%	-2.5%	-0.9%	-1.9%	1.1%

Also, except for 6 countries (Mauritius, Georgia, Albania, Uruguay, Belarus, and China) just 12% of households have more than 4 persons in them in 2019. This reflects a movement away from the extended family living together – which in turn tends to coincide with increased education and affluence.

As a result, the total number of households is projected to stabilise but not sufficient to maintain the market size. For half the countries in this Country Segment, the number of households will be less in 2030 than in 2019. By 2045 two thirds of these countries will have fewer households than in 2019. This may have implications for an individual household's financial well-being as the 'house' is generally a major family asset.

The interesting case here is China. With reducing household size, the total demand for housing grows significantly from 492 million in 2019 to reach a projected 590 million units in 2039 and then is negative to 2045 to be 579 million. But again, there is a significant difference between urban and rural China. In urban China, in 2019 there are estimated to be 297 million households with an average of 2.83 persons per household. By 2045 this is projected to have increased to 409 million households with an average of 2.7 persons per household.

That means that total urban households can be expected to increase at 1.28% per annum for the next 25 years (although most of that growth will be in the period to 2038). In contrast, the number of rural households is projected to decline from 196 million in 2019 to 170 million by 2045.

Table 4-12: Number of Households, Person per Household and Employed per Household in the Older Low-Income Segment.

| | 2019 | 94.9481 | | | 2045 | | | |
| | 132.26348 | 95.296 % Hholds | Employed | Households | Avg pers | % Hholds | Employed |
	156.95418	101.832 > 4 pers	Persons	000s	per hhold	> 4 pers	Persons
Albania	948	3.04	14.7%	1.17	1,016	2.36	4.0%	0.86
Belarus	3,363	2.81	11.1%	1.36	3,504	2.59	6.3%	1.25
Bulgaria	2,829	2.47	4.7%	1.04	2,268	2.50	6.3%	1.03
Cuba	4,424	2.56	6.3%	1.08	4,199	2.46	4.7%	0.97
Czechia	4,266	2.50	6.3%	1.17	4,233	2.52	6.3%	1.09
Estonia	522	2.53	6.3%	1.20	528	2.51	6.3%	1.17
Georgia	1,260	3.17	16.7%	1.41	1,380	2.78	9.5%	1.16
Greece	4,238	2.47	4.7%	0.86	3,716	2.34	4.0%	0.70
Hungary	3,896	2.48	4.7%	1.09	3,469	2.45	4.7%	1.06
Latvia	757	2.51	6.3%	1.14	527	2.49	4.7%	1.06
Lithuania	1,107	2.49	4.7%	1.16	714	2.48	4.7%	1.00
Mauritius	385	3.29	18.6%	1.42	493	2.40	4.7%	0.99
Poland	15,175	2.49	4.7%	1.09	13,833	2.38	4.0%	1.00
Portugal	4,116	2.48	4.7%	1.13	3,688	2.33	4.0%	0.93
Republic of Mold	1,521	2.65	7.9%	0.94	1,443	2.35	4.0%	0.81
Romania	7,669	2.52	6.3%	1.06	6,192	2.49	4.7%	0.91
Russian Federati	56,016	2.60	6.3%	1.20	54,498	2.69	7.9%	1.20
Slovakia	2,098	2.60	6.3%	1.17	2,059	2.44	4.7%	1.03
Thailand	26,702	2.61	7.9%	1.41	27,814	2.43	4.7%	1.17
Ukraine	16,606	2.64	7.9%	1.04	14,938	2.48	4.7%	0.93
Uruguay	1,230	2.81	11.1%	1.27	1,380	2.63	7.9%	1.22
China	492,588	2.86	11.6%	1.52	579,134	2.34	7.1%	1.09
Total/Average	651,718	2.79	10.4%	1.43	731,025	2.38	6.9%	1.09

In Urban China, demand for housing will continue through to 2045. For the period from 2019 to 2045, there is projected to be demand for an additional 111 million units which is a growth rate of 1.28% per annum.

154

The Number of Workers per Household

Finally, in terms of this Country Segment, the projected significant decline in the number of employed persons per household must be mentioned. In 2019 it is estimated at 1.43 employed persons per household and this is projected to reduce to 1.07 by 2045. The reduction in the number of workers means that average household income does not grow as fast as wages.

This applies as much to China as it does to the other countries in this segment. However, do note there is a significant difference between urban and rural households in China as discussed in Chapter 10 which focuses on China.

To summarise, overall, the projected trend for the consumer market in this Country Segment is one of stability rather than growth. There will be stability in the size of the 40 to 64 years age group for the decade to 2030. Then it starts to decline in size along with all the younger age groups. In contrast, the 65 years and above segment will grow at 2.2% per annum to 2030 and then at a slower rate thereafter.

Family Stage Low Income Country Segment

The reader is reminded that this Country Segment is mainly made up of countries in South America, Developing Asia, and South Asia (India, Bangladesh, and Sri Lanka). India dominates this segment. However, do also keep in mind that this segment includes some other large countries in terms of population. Specifically, Brazil and Indonesia. Figure 4-8 shows the projected changes in the age segments and Table 4-13 provides summary statistics for the same.

Figure 4-8: The Changing Size of Age Groups in Family Stage Low Income Segment to 2045.

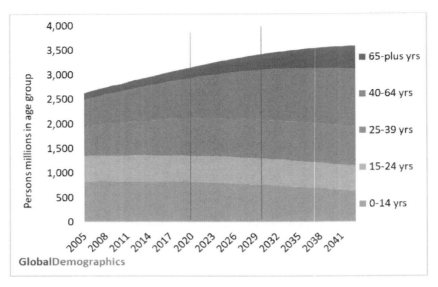

Table 4-13: Historic and Projected Age Profile of Other Countries in the Family Stage Low Income Country Segment.

	2010	2020	2030	2045	2010-20	2020-30	2030-45
	Persons mns				Growth rate % pa		
0-14 yrs	824	812	760	626	-0.1%	-0.7%	-1.3%
15-24 yrs	530	538	536	486	0.1%	0.0%	-0.7%
25-39 yrs	661	759	787	781	1.4%	0.4%	-0.1%
40-64 yrs	638	825	1,015	1,199	2.6%	2.1%	1.1%
65 plus yrs	153	220	327	504	3.7%	4.0%	2.9%
Total	2,806	3,154	3,425	3,595	1.2%	0.8%	0.3%
Working age	1,829	2,122	2,338	2,466	1.5%	1.0%	0.4%
	Share of total population						
0-14 yrs	29%	26%	22%	17%			
15-24 yrs	19%	17%	16%	14%			
25-39 yrs	24%	24%	23%	22%			
40-64 yrs	23%	26%	30%	33%			
65 plus yrs	5%	7%	10%	14%			
Working age	65%	67%	68%	69%			

156

Key points to note from this are:

1. The total population of these countries is still growing but the rate of increase is projected to slow considerably. From 1.2% per annum for the last decade to a projected 0.3% for the period 2030 to 2045. The younger age groups go negative after 2030. This reflects the significant decline in birth rates that have taken place – India particularly.
2. This means that the potential 'demographic dividend' is weakening rapidly. In the last decade, the working-age population increased by 293 million persons. For the next decade, it is projected to add 217 million and then 127 million by 2045.
3. The number of school-age children is projected to decline significantly, and this will enable budget priorities to shift from increasing the number of education seats to lifting the quality.
4. The projected rapid growth in the 40 years and above age group will have implications for the demand for health services and the overall nature of consumer demand. This age group is projected to grow from 33% of the population to 47% and at 1.9% per annum from 2020 to 2045. That is a significant change.

The Family Stage Low Income Country Segment are still large youth markets, but they are not growth youth markets.

Table 4-14 shows for each country the projected growth rate in the absolute size of the key age segments from 2020 through to 2030 and then 2030 to 2045. For the next decade, it is mainly the youngest age group that is generally reducing in size or showing virtually no growth. However, after 2030 this decline in age segment size extends out to the 15- to 24-year-old age group.

Table 4-14: Changing Age Profile of Countries in the Family Stage Low Income Country Segment. 2020 to 2045.

	Average Growth Rate pa 2020-2030					Average Growth Rate pa 2030-2045				
	0-14 yrs	15-24 yrs	25-39 yrs	40-64 yrs	65+ yrs	0-14 yrs	15-24 yrs	25-39 yrs	40-64 yrs	65+ yrs
Algeria	1.3%	3.6%	-1.5%	3.1%	4.4%	1.1%	1.3%	2.4%	0.7%	3.8%
Kazakhstan	0.7%	4.7%	-2.2%	1.5%	4.6%	2.1%	0.7%	2.6%	0.1%	1.9%
Panama	0.6%	0.9%	1.2%	2.1%	4.3%	0.5%	0.6%	0.9%	1.4%	3.4%
Ecuador	0.3%	0.2%	1.5%	2.4%	4.1%	-0.5%	0.3%	0.5%	1.9%	3.3%
South Africa	0.1%	1.5%	-0.1%	2.9%	3.2%	0.2%	0.1%	1.0%	1.3%	2.8%
Peru	0.1%	-1.4%	0.4%	4.0%	5.0%	-0.9%	0.1%	-1.2%	2.2%	4.6%
Tunisia	0.1%	1.5%	-1.3%	1.6%	4.2%	-0.3%	0.1%	0.9%	0.2%	2.4%
Indonesia	0.0%	0.2%	0.5%	1.6%	4.9%	0.1%	0.0%	0.3%	0.6%	3.4%
Iran	0.0%	1.6%	-2.9%	3.4%	4.9%	-1.0%	0.0%	0.8%	0.2%	3.9%
Argentina	-0.1%	0.4%	0.5%	1.5%	1.9%	-0.6%	-0.1%	0.3%	1.0%	1.9%
Morocco	-0.2%	0.9%	-0.1%	1.9%	5.1%	-0.5%	-0.1%	0.5%	1.0%	2.6%
Malaysia	-0.2%	-1.0%	0.1%	2.8%	4.6%	-1.9%	-0.2%	-0.6%	1.5%	3.0%
Uzbekistan	-0.2%	1.5%	-0.4%	2.7%	5.9%	-0.6%	-0.2%	0.8%	1.4%	2.7%
Dominican Rep	-0.2%	0.1%	0.5%	1.7%	4.1%	-0.9%	-0.2%	0.1%	1.1%	2.8%
Chile	-0.3%	-0.1%	0.6%	1.6%	3.8%	-0.4%	-0.3%	-0.4%	1.3%	2.3%
Viet Nam	-0.4%	0.8%	-1.5%	1.7%	5.0%	-1.0%	-0.4%	0.0%	0.1%	2.8%
Sri Lanka	-0.4%	0.3%	-0.6%	0.3%	3.5%	0.1%	-0.4%	0.1%	-0.6%	1.8%
Mexico	-0.4%	0.0%	0.8%	1.8%	3.8%	-1.0%	-0.4%	0.0%	1.1%	2.9%
Bolivia	-0.5%	0.3%	1.5%	2.5%	3.2%	-1.6%	-0.5%	0.4%	2.0%	3.1%
Nicaragua	-0.6%	0.3%	0.1%	3.0%	4.6%	-1.3%	-0.6%	0.1%	1.4%	3.6%
Turkey	-0.6%	0.4%	0.7%	2.2%	4.2%	-0.6%	-0.6%	0.4%	1.1%	3.5%
Colombia	-0.6%	-1.0%	1.3%	2.0%	4.4%	-1.3%	-0.6%	-0.6%	1.7%	2.9%
Azerbaijan	-0.7%	1.4%	-1.7%	1.5%	6.6%	-0.4%	-0.7%	0.4%	0.5%	1.9%
Cambodia	-0.7%	1.0%	-0.3%	3.8%	4.7%	-1.8%	-0.7%	0.6%	2.1%	2.1%
Paraguay	-0.7%	0.0%	0.7%	2.8%	3.4%	-2.3%	-0.7%	0.0%	1.9%	2.4%
Brazil	-0.7%	-1.3%	-0.4%	1.5%	4.1%	-1.3%	-0.7%	-1.0%	0.5%	2.7%
Myanmar	-0.8%	-0.9%	0.5%	1.3%	4.0%	-1.5%	-0.8%	-0.6%	0.6%	2.6%
Philippines	-0.9%	0.7%	1.6%	2.1%	4.7%	-1.7%	-0.9%	0.5%	1.8%	3.1%
India	-1.0%	-0.3%	0.7%	2.2%	3.7%	-1.9%	-1.0%	-0.2%	1.4%	2.7%
El Salvador	-1.1%	-1.4%	0.8%	1.3%	2.5%	-2.7%	-1.1%	-1.1%	1.2%	2.1%
Saudi Arabia	-1.1%	1.0%	0.1%	3.8%	5.3%	-3.5%	-1.2%	0.2%	1.3%	5.6%
Bangladesh	-1.3%	-0.6%	0.6%	2.6%	4.2%	-2.8%	-1.3%	-0.5%	1.3%	3.8%
Armenia	-1.4%	1.5%	-2.8%	0.7%	3.7%	-1.1%	-1.4%	0.1%	0.0%	0.1%
Venezuela RB	-2.2%	-0.5%	-3.1%	-0.3%	3.4%	-2.6%	-2.3%	-1.1%	-2.1%	1.5%

Changing Household Size and Number of Households

As shown in Table 4-15, in 2019 the average household consisted of 3.45 persons and 23% of households have more than 4 persons in them. This is high compared to the previous two (older) Country Segments.

158

But with the shift of the population bias to the 40 plus age group, there will be fewer households with dependent children and relatively few older dependents in the household (note the 65 years of age and above population is just 6.7% of the total population in 2019 and is projected to reach only 14% in 25 years). This is driving down the average household size. It is projected to decline from 3.45 persons in 2019 to 2.81 persons by 2045 - half a person less, which positively impacts household income per capita.

Two other points to note in terms of this Country Segment is that the per cent of households with more than 4 persons declines significantly (as would be expected given a smaller average household size).

Finally, the projected moderate growth in total population and reduction in average household size means the potential demand for housing is robust. There are 906 million households in 2019, and that is projected to increase to 1.28 billion by 2045. That represents a 41% absolute increase in housing units in the next 25 years.

Demand for housing will be very strong in the Family Stage Low-Income Countries. From 906 million households to 1.280 million. That is a growth rate of 1.3% per annum for 25 years.

The Number of Workers per Household

The ageing of the population does mean that an increasing number of households are older and with just one employed person in them. This is projected to result in the average number of workers per household declining from 1.32 in 2019 to 1.13 in 2045. That does mean that average household income will not increase in line with wages as there are fewer wage earners per household.

Table 4-15: Number and Size in Persons of Households in Family Stage Low-Income Country Segment.

	2019				2045			
	Households 000s	Avg pers per hhold	% Hholds GT 4 pers	Employed Pers	Households 000s	Avg pers per hhold	% Hholds GT 4 pers	Employed Pers
Algeria	7,154	6.02	80.0%	1.49	12,605	5.21	63.3%	1.35
Argentina	13,077	3.42	22.6%	1.39	16,509	3.19	16.7%	1.39
Armenia	859	3.44	22.6%	1.21	1,113	2.55	6.3%	0.88
Azerbaijan	2,260	4.44	45.3%	2.08	3,786	3.02	14.7%	1.43
Bangladesh	37,664	4.33	42.7%	1.77	56,521	3.11	16.7%	1.42
Bolivia	2,647	4.36	42.7%	2.05	4,114	3.43	22.6%	1.81
Brazil	73,254	2.88	11.1%	1.25	90,602	2.51	6.3%	1.06
Cambodia	3,654	4.51	47.6%	2.52	5,095	3.85	30.6%	2.47
Chile	5,851	3.23	18.6%	1.46	8,757	2.70	7.9%	1.25
Colombia	13,583	3.69	26.6%	1.74	17,695	3.48	22.6%	1.71
Dominican Repu	3,378	3.18	16.7%	1.37	4,561	2.76	9.5%	1.25
Ecuador	4,279	4.06	35.2%	1.88	7,608	3.09	14.7%	1.52
El Salvador	2,048	3.15	16.7%	1.29	2,414	2.60	6.3%	1.17
India	438,316	3.12	16.7%	1.05	587,811	2.59	6.3%	0.92
Indonesia	74,749	3.62	26.6%	1.69	118,720	2.81	11.1%	1.32
Iran (Islamic Rep	19,802	4.18	37.7%	1.22	37,721	2.64	7.9%	0.78
Kazakhstan	4,600	4.03	35.2%	1.83	7,813	3.36	20.6%	1.45
Malaysia	8,045	3.97	32.6%	1.84	13,435	2.82	11.1%	1.37
Mexico	34,353	3.71	28.6%	1.57	47,292	3.17	16.7%	1.42
Morocco	5,768	6.33	85.9%	1.89	10,105	4.45	45.3%	1.40
Myanmar	12,649	4.28	40.2%	1.91	17,792	3.16	16.7%	1.46
Nicaragua	1,495	4.38	42.7%	1.89	2,390	3.25	18.6%	1.63
Panama	1,107	3.84	30.6%	1.76	2,147	2.81	11.1%	1.31
Paraguay	1,688	4.17	37.7%	2.00	2,415	3.32	20.6%	1.83
Peru	8,157	3.98	32.6%	2.19	10,557	4.38	42.7%	2.65
Philippines	28,864	3.75	28.6%	1.50	48,559	2.67	7.9%	1.20
Saudi Arabia	5,993	5.70	73.9%	2.23	7,924	5.31	65.4%	2.52
South Africa	15,311	3.83	30.6%	1.07	21,886	3.48	22.6%	1.03
Sri Lanka	5,871	3.63	26.6%	1.38	8,098	2.80	11.1%	1.01
Tunisia	2,240	5.22	63.3%	1.50	3,982	3.49	22.6%	1.00
Turkey	28,080	2.96	12.7%	1.00	41,163	2.58	6.3%	0.88
Uzbekistan	7,329	4.50	45.3%	1.92	11,470	3.62	26.6%	1.71
Venezuela RB	8,069	3.58	24.6%	1.37	7,336	2.79	9.5%	1.06
Viet Nam	23,811	4.05	35.2%	2.31	41,143	2.61	7.9%	1.49
Total/Average	906,007	3.45	23.2%	1.32	1,281,139	2.81	10.8%	1.13

The Young Poor Country Segment

This Country Segment is different from the other three in that it is not dominated by any one country in terms of population size. Pakistan and Nigeria with just over 200 million population and Ethiopia and Egypt with just over 100 million population account for just under half the total population of this Country Segment. The remaining 28 countries have a total population of under 80 million each and typically under 30 million.

They are very young and very poor. The median age is 20 years and the per capita Gross Domestic Product with a few exceptions is under US$2,000 per annum (US$5.50 per day).

Figure 4-9 shows the projected trend in the size of the different age segments for the next quarter-century to 2045 and Table 4-16 summarises the key statistics.

Key points to note in respect of this set of countries are:

1. The total population is projected to increase by nearly 1 billion persons in the next 25 years. This is on a 2020 base of 1.36 billion.
2. Growth of the youngest age group is slowing due to a projected moderation in birth rates but adds 225 million school-age children.
3. In contrast to the three other Country Segments, the Working-age Population is projected to *increase* from being 56% of the total population to 61%. In absolute numbers, it is projected to grow from 764 million in 2020 to reach 1,418 million in 2045. ***Essentially, the Working-age population and those of them looking for work, almost double in number.***
4. Growth of the 40 plus age groups is very rapid (3.4% per annum for the next decade) and while a small proportion of the total population this has implications for future demands on health services (see Chapter Nine on health later)

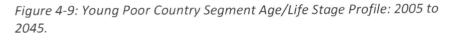

Figure 4-9: Young Poor Country Segment Age/Life Stage Profile: 2005 to 2045.

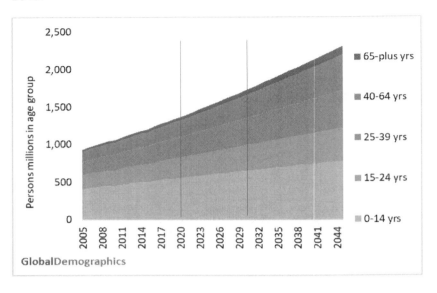

Table 4-16: Age Profile Statistics for Young Poor Segment Country Segment.

	2010	2020	2030	2045	2010-20	2020-30	2030-45
	Persons mns				Growth rate % pa		
0-14 yrs	444	551	647	776	2.2%	1.6%	1.2%
15-24 yrs	210	268	336	430	2.5%	2.3%	1.7%
25-39 yrs	206	278	362	509	3.0%	2.7%	2.3%
40-64 yrs	158	218	306	480	3.3%	3.4%	3.0%
65 plus yrs	35	46	67	115	3.0%	3.7%	3.7%
Total	1,052	1,361	1,717	2,309	2.6%	2.3%	2.0%
Working age	574	764	1,004	1,418	2.9%	2.8%	2.3%
	Share of total population						
0-14 yrs	42%	40%	38%	34%			
15-24 yrs	20%	20%	20%	19%			
25-39 yrs	20%	20%	21%	22%			
40-64 yrs	15%	16%	18%	21%			
65 plus yrs	3%	3%	4%	5%			
Working age	55%	56%	58%	61%			

5. Every age group is projected to grow in absolute size for the next 25 years. Typically, at over 2% per annum for all but the youngest age group. It is a high growth market in terms of the number of people.

In the Young Poor countries, there are estimated to be 551 million persons aged 0 to 14 years in 2020. This is projected to reach 647 million in 2030 and 776 million by 2045. That is 225 million extra consumers of children's products and services in 25 years.

Table 4-17 provides summary detail for each country included in this Country Segment. As is apparent from this table, there are very few countries in this group where even the youngest age group is projected to decline in absolute size – even between 2030 and 2045.

Changing Household Size and Number of Households

The impact of the projected changing age profile of these countries on the nature of the household is summarised by country and in total for the Country Segment in Table 4-18.

Household size is much larger than that of the other three Country Segments and reflects the younger age profile of these countries.

As a result of the projected reduction in birth rates, household size will reduce over the next 25 years from 4.69 to 4.28 persons. This will have a positive impact on per capita household income.

However, do note that a very high proportion – 51% in 2020 and a projected 42% in 2045 - of households have more than 4 persons in them.

Table 4-17: *Changing Age Profile of Countries in the Young Poor Country Segment - 2020 to 2045.*

	Average Growth Rate pa 2020-2030					Average Growth Rate pa 2030-2045				
	0-14 yrs	15-24 yrs	25-39 yrs	40-64 yrs	65+ yrs	0-14 yrs	15-24 yrs	25-39 yrs	40-64 yrs	65+ yrs
Niger	3.7%	4.2%	4.8%	3.3%	3.9%	3.7%	3.7%	4.2%	4.3%	3.3%
DR Congo	2.9%	3.6%	3.5%	3.5%	3.7%	3.0%	3.0%	3.5%	3.5%	3.8%
Angola	2.5%	3.8%	3.4%	3.9%	4.6%	2.2%	2.6%	3.6%	3.7%	4.1%
Mali	2.5%	3.5%	3.4%	3.6%	2.8%	2.4%	2.5%	3.4%	3.3%	4.3%
Tanzania	2.4%	3.1%	3.0%	3.9%	4.4%	2.3%	2.4%	3.0%	3.4%	4.6%
Mozambique	2.3%	2.8%	3.6%	3.6%	2.7%	1.9%	2.4%	2.9%	3.6%	3.4%
Nigeria	2.1%	2.9%	2.7%	3.1%	3.1%	2.0%	2.2%	2.8%	2.7%	3.5%
Chad	2.0%	2.9%	3.8%	3.8%	3.2%	1.0%	2.1%	3.0%	3.9%	3.4%
Burkina Faso	2.0%	2.9%	3.2%	3.8%	4.0%	1.6%	2.1%	2.9%	3.4%	4.2%
Uganda	2.0%	3.5%	4.4%	4.9%	5.1%	1.0%	2.0%	3.5%	4.7%	5.3%
Senegal	1.9%	3.1%	2.7%	3.9%	3.6%	1.8%	1.9%	2.9%	3.2%	4.0%
Zambia	1.8%	2.7%	3.5%	4.4%	4.5%	1.1%	1.8%	2.8%	3.9%	5.2%
Guinea	1.7%	2.1%	3.9%	3.7%	3.2%	0.7%	1.8%	2.3%	4.2%	2.9%
Sudan	1.7%	1.9%	3.2%	3.0%	3.9%	1.3%	1.7%	2.1%	3.1%	3.5%
Cameroon	1.5%	2.7%	2.5%	4.0%	3.1%	0.9%	1.6%	2.5%	3.1%	4.0%
Madagascar	1.5%	1.9%	3.3%	3.4%	4.6%	0.1%	1.5%	2.1%	3.3%	4.0%
Egypt	1.4%	2.6%	0.6%	2.9%	3.5%	1.8%	1.4%	2.2%	1.7%	2.9%
Ghana	1.2%	1.9%	2.0%	3.0%	5.2%	0.8%	1.3%	1.8%	2.4%	3.9%
Namibia	1.2%	1.8%	1.4%	3.2%	3.2%	1.0%	1.2%	1.6%	2.4%	3.4%
Malawi	1.1%	2.6%	3.3%	4.2%	3.4%	0.0%	1.2%	2.5%	3.8%	4.4%
Ethiopia	1.1%	1.5%	3.7%	3.9%	3.3%	-0.7%	1.2%	1.8%	4.0%	4.0%
Rwanda	1.0%	2.3%	2.0%	4.1%	5.9%	-0.5%	1.1%	2.3%	3.1%	3.5%
South Sudan	0.8%	0.7%	1.5%	1.6%	1.8%	0.0%	0.9%	0.9%	1.6%	1.9%
Zimbabwe	0.7%	2.7%	0.9%	3.1%	2.9%	1.7%	0.8%	2.2%	1.7%	3.9%
Pakistan	0.7%	1.2%	1.8%	3.2%	3.8%	-0.7%	0.8%	1.3%	2.6%	3.3%
Botswana	0.6%	1.8%	1.2%	3.8%	4.3%	0.7%	0.6%	1.6%	2.4%	4.4%
Kenya	0.2%	1.9%	2.6%	4.3%	5.6%	-0.9%	0.3%	1.9%	3.1%	5.3%
Guatemala	-0.4%	0.3%	2.3%	3.9%	3.8%	-1.8%	-0.3%	0.6%	3.0%	4.0%
Lao PDR	-0.8%	0.6%	1.0%	3.2%	4.2%	-2.4%	-0.8%	0.4%	2.1%	3.6%
Haiti	-0.8%	0.5%	0.7%	3.1%	3.4%	-2.4%	-0.8%	0.5%	1.9%	2.9%
Honduras	-0.9%	-0.4%	1.9%	3.5%	4.5%	-1.9%	-0.9%	0.0%	2.5%	4.2%
Nepal	-1.9%	-1.5%	3.9%	3.0%	2.8%	-3.9%	-1.9%	-0.8%	3.7%	3.4%

The Number of Workers per Household

Finally, the number of workers per household is quite high compared with the other Country Segments. It is at 1.67 in 2020 and projected to increase to 1.7 by 2045 if the existing propensity to be employed is maintained. This reflects the earlier mentioned projection of the working-age population doubling in number. This is good, as combined with a

164

reduced number of persons per household this means the dependents per worker is reduced and per capita income increases.

Table 4-18: Number and Size in Persons of Households in the Young Poor Country Segment.

	2019				2045			
	Households 000s	Avg pers per hhold	% Hholds GT 4 pers	Employed Pers	Households 000s	Avg pers per hhold	% Hholds GT 4 pers	Employed Pers
Angola	6,640	4.85	54.5%	1.84	14,664	4.68	52.2%	2.00
Botswana	486	4.76	52.2%	1.82	867	4.11	37.7%	1.83
Burkina Faso	3,473	5.91	78.1%	2.01	6,799	5.71	73.9%	2.05
Cameroon	5,387	4.85	54.5%	2.02	9,695	4.63	52.2%	2.21
Chad	3,300	4.90	56.9%	1.77	6,302	4.77	52.2%	2.05
DR Congo	18,876	4.66	52.2%	1.49	46,185	4.33	42.7%	1.40
Egypt	25,501	3.94	32.6%	1.06	48,271	3.37	20.6%	0.92
Ethiopia	24,359	4.62	52.2%	2.13	42,992	4.17	37.7%	2.40
Ghana	5,890	5.19	61.1%	2.08	10,183	4.74	52.2%	2.03
Guatemala	3,734	4.71	52.2%	1.87	3,403	6.83	92.3%	3.24
Guinea	2,693	4.79	52.2%	1.58	4,893	4.65	52.2%	1.80
Haiti	2,546	4.44	45.3%	1.72	3,471	3.67	26.6%	1.66
Honduras	2,181	4.47	45.3%	1.99	3,592	3.37	20.6%	1.70
Kenya	13,049	4.05	35.2%	1.77	23,232	3.38	20.6%	1.83
Lao PDR	1,918	3.75	28.6%	1.97	2,990	2.83	11.1%	1.77
Madagascar	5,250	5.16	61.1%	2.58	9,420	4.77	52.2%	2.87
Malawi	3,585	5.23	63.3%	2.12	6,350	4.94	56.9%	2.49
Mali	4,085	4.88	54.5%	1.66	8,684	4.78	52.2%	1.78
Mozambique	6,373	4.81	54.5%	2.00	12,747	4.74	52.2%	2.14
Namibia	540	4.64	52.2%	1.37	886	4.35	42.7%	1.43
Nepal	6,277	4.58	47.6%	2.64	9,110	3.77	28.6%	2.68
Niger	4,585	5.15	61.1%	1.82	12,483	5.06	59.0%	1.86
Nigeria	44,622	4.55	47.6%	1.23	94,398	4.02	35.2%	1.13
Pakistan	43,543	5.00	59.0%	1.61	68,419	4.50	47.6%	1.68
Rwanda	2,672	4.74	52.2%	2.34	4,695	4.25	40.2%	2.48
Senegal	3,449	4.75	52.2%	1.15	6,837	4.55	47.6%	1.16
South Sudan	2,376	4.72	52.2%	1.73	3,053	4.57	47.6%	1.83
Sudan	9,074	4.75	52.2%	1.14	16,630	4.47	45.3%	1.16
Uganda	9,021	4.93	56.9%	1.80	19,660	4.65	52.2%	2.13
United Republic	11,932	4.90	56.9%	2.22	26,106	4.61	52.2%	2.25
Zambia	3,658	4.92	56.9%	1.79	7,302	4.63	52.2%	2.00
Zimbabwe	3,066	4.80	54.5%	2.16	4,988	4.54	47.6%	2.18
Total/Average	284,140	4.69	51.2%	1.67	539,307	4.28	41.7%	1.70

Summary Comment.

What is evident from the above description of the changing size of the consumer life stages is that for all but the Young Poor Country Segment the projected population growth dimension is now almost exclusively in the 40 years of age and above segment and increasingly the 65 years and above.

This is significant for many products and services as well as the political and societal structure. Take the Old Affluent Country segment – which is the most extreme example. The under 40-year age group is projected to decline from 477 million in 2019 to 441 million in 2045 - down 30 million. In contrast, the over 40 age group is projected to increase in size from 542 million in 2020 to 612 million by 2045 – up 70 million. This means the affluent over 40-year market is a very significant growth sector, whereas the affluent under 40-year segment is not.

In 2020, 42% of the population in the countries covered in this book were over 40 years of age. By 2045 it is projected to be 50%. This age group is projected to grow at 1.5% p.a. and add 1.2 billion persons – mostly in the older affluent regions. In contrast, globally, the under 40-year age segment is projected to show virtually no growth through to 2045.

This change in age profile is also important politically. Younger voters tend to be more liberal in their orientation. So, this important influence on society is declining in significance.

In the older low-income countries, the pattern is similar except the under 40-year-olds have declined from 60% in 2005 to 50% in 2020 and are projected to decline to 40% by 2045. That is a very significant change in age profile projected to take place in those populations.

Being middle-aged (age range of 40- 64 years) is increasingly the new normal. In many countries, it is the dominant age/consumer group and in the short term to 2030, the one where there is projected growth.

It must also be noted that the very nature of the household in the world is changing. From a bias to 'family households' (Mum, Dad, and 2 children) with 1.5 wage earners to the emergence of a new dominant group of 'childless households. This new household has a very different consumption profile and a much higher per capita spending power. Over the next 25 years, the growing presence of these types of households will be felt.

Summary Profile – The Global Age Profile

Older Affluent

	2019	2030	2,045
Persons (Mns) 0-14 yrs	160	153	149
Persons (Mns) 15-24 yrs	114	113	106
Persons (Mns) 25-44yrs	257	254	241
Persons (Mns) 45-69 yrs	323	328	321
Persons (Mns) 70+ yrs	136	176	213
Household size (pers)	2.6	2.5	2.5
Households (Mns)	387	407	413
Workers per household	1.2	1.2	1.2

Older Low Income

	2019	2030	2,045
Persons (Mns) 0-14 yrs	303	279	237
Persons (Mns) 15-24 yrs	194	203	182
Persons (Mns) 25-39 yrs	418	314	297
Persons (Mns) 40-64 yrs	662	697	579
Persons (Mns) 65+ yrs	245	345	445
Household size (pers)	2.8	2.6	2.4
Households (Mns)	652	720	731
Workers per household	1.5	1.3	1.1

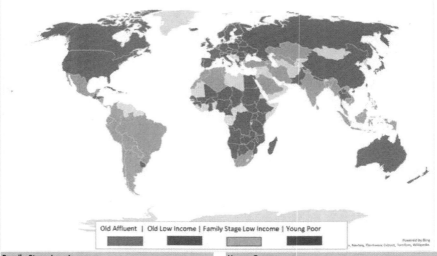

Old Affluent | Old Low Income | Family Stage Low Income | Young Poor

Family Stage Low Income

	2019	2030	2045
Persons (Mns) 0-14 yrs	817	760	626
Persons (Mns) 15-24 yrs	537	536	486
Persons (Mns) 25-39 yrs	753	787	781
Persons (Mns) 40-64 yrs	805	1,015	1,199
Persons (Mns) 65+ yrs	210	327	504
Household size (pers)	3.4	3.1	2.8
Households (Mns)	906	1,095	1,281
Workers per household	1.3	1.3	1.2

Young Poor

	2019	2030	2045
Persons (Mns) 0-14 yrs	545	647	776
Persons (Mns) 15-24 yrs	262	336	430
Persons (Mns) 25-39 yrs	270	362	509
Persons (Mns) 40-64 yrs	211	306	480
Persons (Mns) 65+ yrs	45	67	115
Household size (pers)	4.7	4.5	4.3
Households (Mns)	284	381	539
Workers per household	1.7	1.7	1.7

Chapter 5
Education

Introduction – Why Education?

As a rule, education is generally not considered a 'demographic' variable. So why include it in an analysis of demographic trends of the future? Because it is one of the most important determinants of the 'demographic profile' of a country *over time*. It impacts in multiple ways.

1. It significantly impacts the propensity to have children. Educated couples are more aware of contraception. They also understand societal attitudes towards having responsibility for, and some control over, the size of their commitment to their children.

2. It impacts employability. A person who can read and write in their language and do basic arithmetic is significantly more employable than one who cannot. Furthermore, the better the level of education the more productive (employable) the person and their ability to support themselves and their family.

3. It impacts fixed capital investment in the society and hence the creation of job opportunities. As shown in this chapter, cheap (and typically uneducated) labour pools attract some fixed capital investment but on a per capita basis, it is much lower than for countries where the labour force is educated.

4. It impacts health outcomes. The better educated a society is the more aware it is of hygiene, nutrition and wellness which leads to healthier and longer lifestyles.

However, education has a problem associated with it. *It takes time to implement.* A person is not 'educated' overnight. To create an educated person an education infrastructure must be in place which takes the child at age 5 or 6 and teaches them skills (including reading, writing and arithmetic) for at least the next 9-10 years (reaching around age 15 and completing lower secondary). The education process can continue beyond that but completing Lower Secondary is a minimum requirement for today's world.

Even then, the benefits are not immediate for society (although, for the individual, the chances of getting work are significantly improved). It takes at least another 10 years for the workforce of the country to have enough educated people in it to attract a higher level of fixed capital investment. It also takes that long to change birth rates, hygiene, wellness etc.

Unfortunately, the availability of most education funding is at the behest of politicians, few of whom take such a long term (20 years) view of what is good for society. Consequently, a slow payoff investment like education often does not get the attention it needs. Especially in a society that does not inherently value education or where the decision-makers are not held accountable to the population.

Leveraging Education

There is however an important qualifier in terms of education. There is compelling evidence that education is a necessary but not sufficient attribute for a society to achieve prosperity. If the worker is not given the equipment to leverage their skills then they are just another worker. This is thought to be why there are three groups of countries when looking at the impact of education.

1. Those poorly educated and with limited Fixed Capital Investment to support them. It is limited investment as the workers lack the skills to leverage it and end hence there is a poor return on anything but a basic investment. Unfortunately, the productivity of these workers is low as a result.
2. Those well educated but with low fixed capital investment to support them. An educated worker with limited facilities to leverage is just another worker. However, these countries are worth watching as given the two parts to the equation – education and facilities – education is the one that takes time to

implement. Getting investment can be done quickly in the right environment. Consequently, these economies can accelerate quickly.
3. Finally, there are those with education and Fixed Capital investment. These are the countries where productivity per worker is high – as are individual incomes and hence better lifestyles. As education and Fixed Capital Investment do not 'disappear' (but can weaken) these countries can 'coast' to some extent in terms of such investment and not suffer in the short term.

Education is a necessary but not sufficient attribute for a society to achieve prosperity. It must be accompanied by Fixed Capital Investment to leverage the skills given by education.

Education Index Explained

To summarize the relative level of education of the adult population of the 103 countries for which we have data, an index has been created with 0 applied to the proportion that has none or not completed primary, 1 to the proportion that has completed primary, 2 to completed lower secondary, 3 to completed upper secondary or better including Vocational and or tertiary. There is some inconsistency between countries in reporting Upper Secondary, Vocational and Tertiary – with vocational being included with upper secondary in some cases. For that reason, those three categories have been given the same weight.

This index value has then been multiplied by the percentage of the adult population that has achieved each stage. The range is zero – no one has an education level above primary – to 300 – everyone has an upper secondary or better (tertiary/vocational) qualification. A value of 200 typically means that around 50% of the population has a lower secondary or better education.

Accumulated Fixed Capital Investment per worker explained.

This is a measure of the resources available to the individual worker. The better the infrastructure (roads, power etc.), work environment (factories, offices) and equipment (machines, computers etc.) the more productive the worker will be. It is the sum of the Total Fixed Capital Investment over the last 10 years depreciated at 10% per annum. This is then divided by the number of workers.

The Relationship Between Education, Accumulated Fixed Capital Investment and Productivity

Accumulated Fixed Capital Investment is the enabler that leverages education, lifts productivity per worker and ultimately total Gross Domestic Product. A worker with no Fixed Capital Investment to use is just another worker. Figure 5-1 shows the relationship between Accumulated Fixed capital Equipment and education for the 103 countries for which such data is available.

Figure 5-1: The Relationship between Accumulated Fixed Capital Investment per worker and Education: 2019. The dots are individual countries.

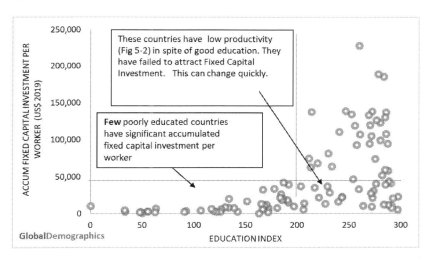

As shown in Figure 5-1, no country with a low standard of education (below an index value of 200) has attracted Fixed Capital Investment to the point where the Accumulated Fixed Capital Investment per worker is over US$43,000. Most (28 out of 42 countries) are significantly below that figure at less than US$10,000 per worker.

35 countries have an education profile/Index greater than 200 but have *failed* to attract investment to the point where accumulated Fixed Capital Investment is over US$43,000. Not surprisingly these are, with a few exceptions, the same as those listed later in Table 5-1. That is countries with a high standard of education but relatively low productivity per worker.

Fixed Capital Investment is a precursor to productivity and education is a precursor to Fixed Capital Investment. However other factors can frustrate the relationship between having a well-educated labour force and attracting investment. For example, tax.

This suggests that the countries listed in Table 5-1 could experience rapid productivity growth if they could change the investment environment and attract Fixed Capital Investment and then leverage their 'Education asset'.

Education and Prosperity

The combined impact of the level of education and amount of Fixed Capital Investment on productivity explains a lot of the differences in societal outcomes across the world.

There is reasonably good data on the highest level of educational attainment of the adult (15 years and above) population for most of the countries included in this book.   In total 103 of the 116 countries included in this book report relevant data. Those missing are generally at the lower end of the Gross Domestic Product per capita scale suggesting that the education level in those countries is also low.

Figure 5-2 shows the relationship between the level of education and Gross Domestic Product per capita and demonstrates the following important points:

1) This shows that Education is a *necessary,* but not *sufficient,* condition to achieve a high Gross Domestic Product per capita.

2) Of the 60 countries with an education index value above 200, 34 have a Gross Domestic Product per worker above US$40,000

(2019 values). These are in the top right quadrant of Figure 5-1 *and* Figure 5-2.

3) 26 countries in the bottom right quadrant have a high education profile but not a high GDP per worker. In short, they have not leveraged their education advantage. They are all at the bottom right of Figure 5-1. That is, they have low accumulated Fixed Capital per worker.

   These are 'countries of interest' as education is the hard (and slow) part of the productivity equation to get right. They probably can quickly correct the factors limiting fixed capital investment and lift their productivity and wellbeing. Table 5-1 lists these countries.

4) Finally, as also shown in Figure 5-2, only one country with an Education Index value **below** 200 has a Gross Domestic Product per capita above US$20,000 and only 3 countries are above US$10,000. As shown in Figure 5-1 they suffer from a lack of Fixed Capital Investment.

Figure 5-2: The Relationship Between Education and Gross Domestic Product per Capita. 2019.

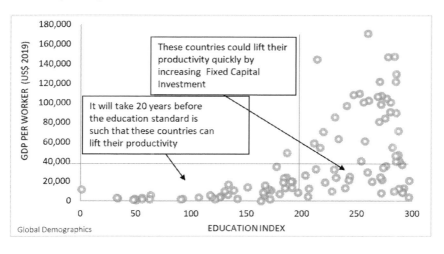

Table 5-1: Countries Whose Productivity Lags Their Standard of Education (Sorted on Basis of Education Index). The bottom Right cell of Figure 5-1.

Older Countries	GDP per worker US$	Education Index	Younger Countries	GDP per Worker US$	Education Index
Belarus	6,684	292	Kazakhstan	9,723	297
Georgia	4,448	291	Uzbekistan	1,757	297
Ukraine	3,505	291	Armenia	4,635	288
Latvia	17,982	291	Azerbaijan	4,792	284
Hungary	16,641	276	South Africa	5,996	243
Poland	15,658	274	Malaysia	11,422	231
Bulgaria	9,715	273	Chile	14,950	229
Moldova	2,838	272	Sri Lanka	3,940	227
Russia	11,689	271	Iran	5,686	221
Cuba	8,815	264	Panama	15,259	213
Romania	12,925	260	Peru	6,984	207
Mauritius	11,169	243	Viet Nam	2,718	206
Albania	5,305	239	Turkey	9,075	203

The countries listed in Table 5-1 are all ones with potential rapid economic growth. They have done 'the hard part' – getting education in place.

Education and the Propensity to have Children.

The other relationship that warrants attention is that between education and the propensity to have children. As explained at the beginning of this chapter, education appears to change not only people's awareness of contraception options but also reduces their willingness to have more than 2 children.

This is demonstrated in Figure 5-3. What is interesting is that the index value of 175 appears to be the key point in terms of this change of behaviour. No country with an Education Index value of 175 or above has a birth rate over 100 per thousand women of childbearing age. Most countries in this education index range (175 and above) have a birth rate below 60 which is less than 2 children per woman.

Figure 5-3: The Relationship Between Education and Birth rates: 2019.

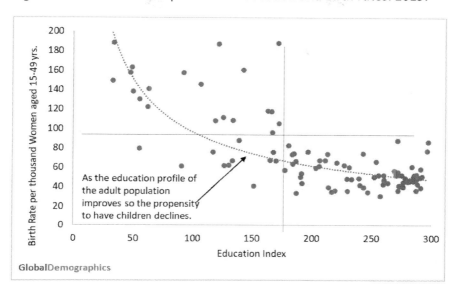

GlobalDemographics

Conversely, all countries with a birth rate of over 100 per thousand women of childbearing age have an education index score below 175. While this does not prove causality, it does nonetheless suggest that education is a contributor to lower birth rates.

So how do the countries compare in terms of their attitude towards, and achievement of, education and how rapidly is it changing? There is a wide variation across countries in terms of their allocation of resources to this important public need and the next section of this chapter describes that.

Propensity to spend on Education.

A good indicator of how seriously a country values education is the proportion of the total Gross Domestic Product that is allocated to education after considering the proportion of the population that is school age. It is a crude measure but is a good statement about the importance given to it. It is better to use 'proportion' of Gross Domestic

Product rather than absolute amount per young person as the latter measure would be biased toward more affluent countries. By looking at the *proportion* of Gross Domestic Product spent on education we can see which countries are *'trying, given available resources'*, versus those that are not.

However, there is a need to make some adjustments for the age profile of each country. Two countries of the same affluence but with different proportions of their population being children should be allocating government expenditure differently to reflect the level of demand for education (number of children) in each population.

To make that adjustment the absolute amount of Gross Domestic Product spent on education is expressed as a proportion of the Gross Domestic Product that theoretically is the 'school-age child' share. If 20% of the population is school age, then theoretically 20% of the Gross Domestic Product relates to them and the total expenditure on education is expressed as a percentage of that share of total Gross Domestic Product due to them. A worked example for two countries is given below.

It is a crude but reasonably robust indicator and assumes all expenditure on education is spent on school-age children (5 to 14 years inclusive) and none on adults, which is not strictly the case.

The average rate for the countries in which we have data is 29.4%. Except for Cuba and Venezuela – where we have concerns about the relevant data – the highest value for the countries covered is 56% and the lowest is 5.7%.

Figure 5-4 shows the distribution of countries by 'Adjusted Percent of Gross Domestic Product Spent on Education' and their Education Index score (the higher the better). The horizontal line at the value of 200 for the education index axis reflects the preceding section of this chapter which demonstrates that a value of 200 coincides with increased Fixed Capital Investment and productivity and a reduction in birth rates.

The vertical line is at 29% being the average *relative* spend (as explained above) on education for the 98 countries for which this data was available and could be included in this analysis.

Relative Education Spend calculation

Country A:
- *35% of the population is 5-14 years of age.*
- *Total GDP is US$100 BN*
- *Student share of GDP is US$35 Bn. (US$100 *35%)*
- *Total spend on education is US$10 Bn.*
- *Spend per student as a share of GDP is*
  *US$10/(US$100 * 35%) = 10/35 = 28%*

Country B
- *10% of the population is 5-14 years of age.*
- *Total GDP is US$100 Bn*
- *Student share of GDP is US$10 Bn. (US$100 * 10%)*
- *Total spend on education is US$5 Bn.*
- *Spend per student share of GDP is*
  *US$5/(US$100 * 10%) = 5/10 = 50%*
-

Result – Country B values education more than Country A

There is an unfortunate propensity for countries with the lowest education index values to be also spending a below-average share on education.

Figure 5-4: Distribution of Countries by Share of Gross Domestic Product Spent on Education (Adjusted for Size of Student Population) and Current Education Index Value.

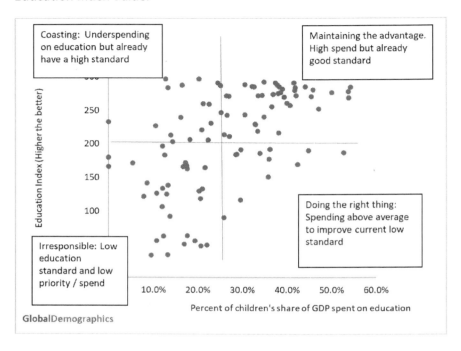

GlobalDemographics

As shown, the countries divide into four groups – the nature of each is described below.

Countries Increasing their Advantage (top right segment in Fig 5-4)

These 35 countries, as listed in Table 5-2, already have a high standard of education (Education Index value over 200) and wish to remain strong on that dimension. Therefore, they are spending an above-average proportion of Gross Domestic Product on education. That is, over 29% after adjusting for the proportion of the population that is of student age.

Table 5-2: List of Countries with a High Education Standard and High Education Spend in 2019 (By Country Segment) Sorted on Basis of Education Index Within Country Segments.

Country Segment	Country	Education Index	% GDP spent on education	Adj GDP % per student	Expenditure (US$ pa) per student age person	School Age as % total population	Teachers Salary as % Class funding
Older Affluent	USA	285	5.1%	32.2%	20,372	15.8%	10.6%
Older Affluent	Canada	285	5.1%	38.3%	17,796	13.2%	7.8%
Older Affluent	Denmark	285	7.7%	54.4%	32,792	14.1%	5.7%
Older Affluent	Switzerland	284	5.1%	41.8%	34,311	12.2%	6.1%
Older Affluent	Slovenia	282	4.8%	39.0%	10,094	12.3%	9.0%
Older Affluent	Austria	280	5.5%	45.9%	22,932	12.0%	6.8%
Older Affluent	Germany	280	4.8%	41.8%	19,308	11.5%	7.4%
Older Affluent	Norway	278	8.0%	53.8%	40,415	14.8%	5.2%
Older Affluent	Finland	276	6.9%	50.1%	24,394	13.8%	6.7%
Older Affluent	United Kingdom	275	5.6%	38.1%	15,971	14.6%	8.5%
Older Affluent	Australia	272	5.3%	33.6%	18,077	15.7%	8.9%
Older Affluent	Iceland	270	7.6%	45.4%	32,415	16.7%	5.5%
Older Affluent	New Zealand	270	6.5%	39.4%	17,126	16.4%	7.3%
Older Affluent	Sweden	269	7.7%	53.9%	28,526	14.3%	5.6%
Older Affluent	Netherlands	260	5.5%	40.0%	21,286	13.8%	7.5%
Older Affluent	Sth Korea	257	4.7%	40.7%	13,064	11.5%	7.4%
Older Affluent	France	256	5.6%	36.7%	15,310	15.1%	10.5%
Older Affluent	Belgium	252	6.7%	47.1%	21,670	14.3%	7.9%
Older Affluent	Hong Kong	240	3.3%	34.8%	17,099	9.6%	9.5%
Older Affluent	Italy	230	3.8%	32.8%	10,886	11.6%	13.2%
Older Affluent	Spain	219	4.2%	33.4%	9,986	12.6%	11.9%
Older Low Income	Belarus	292	4.7%	34.9%	2,333	13.5%	9.5%
Older Low Income	Ukraine	291	5.5%	41.6%	1,458	13.2%	10.7%
Older Low Income	Latvia	291	4.7%	37.4%	6,727	12.6%	9.2%
Older Low Income	Slovakia	288	3.9%	30.6%	5,912	12.7%	11.5%
Older Low Income	Estonia	288	5.1%	37.8%	8,985	13.5%	8.5%
Older Low Income	Lithuania	285	4.0%	32.7%	6,416	12.2%	10.7%
Older Low Income	Czechia	285	5.6%	44.2%	10,191	12.7%	7.4%
Older Low Income	Hungary	276	4.7%	38.6%	6,420	12.2%	9.3%
Older Low Income	Poland	274	4.6%	36.9%	5,785	12.5%	9.9%
Older Low Income	Bulgaria	273	4.3%	34.5%	3,352	12.3%	11.0%
Older Low Income	Moldova	272	5.6%	42.0%	1,193	13.3%	13.9%
Older Low Income	Mauritius	243	4.9%	30.5%	3,412	15.9%	13.4%
Older Low Income	Greece	217	4.7%	38.1%	7,659	12.4%	12.5%
Family Stage Low Inc	Chile	229	5.5%	32.9%	4,923	16.6%	10.9%

The less affluent countries in this segment are spending a lower absolute amount because of their smaller Gross Domestic Product but without exception are spending at least over US$1,000 per student. The average is a very impressive US$5,340 per student aged person in the countries not considered affluent (i.e., not in the top part of Table 5-2).

If teachers get the equivalent of the average wage for workers in each of these countries and assuming a class size of 30 (probably too high in this instance) then wages account for an average of 12% of total funds devoted to education in these countries. That leaves ample funds for facilities including the provision of labs, computers, and of course books (physical or digital) which enhance the education process.

Coasting (Top Left Segment in Figure 5-4)

This is made up of countries that have a high standard of education (over 200 on the education index and an average of 248) but are spending a below-average proportion of Gross Domestic Product on education (after adjusting for the number of student-age persons). That is, below 29%. The average for this group of countries is 20% and the lowest is 13%

Countries can 'coast' in terms of expenditure on education if they already have a good standard of education in their adult population. To have achieved that they must already have a good education infrastructure in place and in the absence of a growing number of students, only need maintenance expenditure to *maintain* a good competitive standard.

The diversity of countries in this group is considerable. From Japan with a relatively low proportion of the population in school-age through to many countries in the Family Stage Low Income Segment where the proportion of the population that is school age is quite high.

This does, however, have one important characteristic. Assuming an average class size of 40 (given most countries in this group are lower-income and more constrained in terms of facilities available) then the average share of the spend on education that goes to the teacher is 21% (compared with 12% for the previous group with a class size of

30). This does mean there are fewer funds available for the provision of education facilities. But it is still a significant proportion at 79%.

Table 5-3: Listing of Countries with High Education and Below Average Spend Per Student Age Person on Education. (2019). Sorted on the Basis of Education Index Within Country Segment.

Country Segment	Country	Education Index	% GDP spent on education	Adj GDP % per student	Expenditure (US$ pa) per student age person	School Age as % total population	Teachers Salary as % Class funding
Older Affluent	Japan	287	2.8%	25.1%	9,477	11.0%	11.9%
Older Affluent	Ireland	260	3.7%	21.2%	16,909	17.7%	14.1%
Older Affluent	Singapore	247	2.6%	25.3%	16,233	10.5%	9.9%
Older Affluent	Macao	214	2.7%	25.9%	22,369	10.3%	9.7%
Older Low Income	Georgia	291	3.9%	24.6%	1,092	15.9%	14.8%
Older Low Income	Russian Federatio	271	3.8%	27.0%	3,157	14.1%	12.9%
Older Low Income	Romania	260	3.0%	22.5%	2,911	13.3%	17.1%
Older Low Income	Albania	239	2.5%	16.2%	860	15.2%	29.9%
Family Stage Low Inc	Kazakhstan	297	2.7%	12.8%	1,247	21.3%	27.5%
Family Stage Low Inc	Uzbekistan	297	4.5%	20.3%	356	22.3%	19.2%
Family Stage Low Inc	Armenia	288	2.7%	16.5%	766	16.6%	34.1%
Family Stage Low Inc	Azerbaijan	284	2.4%	13.3%	639	18.3%	26.2%
Family Stage Low Inc	Malaysia	231	4.5%	22.9%	2,618	19.8%	15.4%
Family Stage Low Inc	Sri Lanka	227	2.1%	10.5%	414	19.9%	42.4%
Family Stage Low Inc	Iran (Islamic Repu	221	3.9%	20.9%	1,191	18.8%	28.9%
Family Stage Low Inc	Panama	213	3.0%	13.9%	2,127	21.8%	25.0%
Family Stage Low Inc	Saudi Arabia	211	5.2%	27.0%	6,273	19.4%	15.6%
Family Stage Low Inc	Peru	207	3.7%	18.2%	1,274	20.4%	16.1%
Family Stage Low Inc	Viet Nam	206	4.1%	22.4%	608	18.4%	12.8%
Family Stage Low Inc	Turkey	203	2.9%	14.4%	1,303	20.4%	35.1%

Doing the Right Thing (Countries on the Lower Right of Fig 5-4)

These are countries that currently have a poor education index score (less than 200) but are spending above average on education – presumably to improve their competitiveness and, ultimately, the wellbeing of their populations.

The bad news is that out of the 39 countries that score below 200 on the education index (and for whom expenditure data is available), only 9 are in this category, as listed below in Table 5-4

Table 5-4: Listing of Countries with Low Education but are above Average in Spending Per Student on Education.

Region	Country	Education Index	% GDP spent on education	Adj GDP % per student	Expenditure (US$ pa) per student age person	School Age as % total population	Teachers Salary as % Class funding
Older Low Income	China	192	4.0%	36.2%	3,311	11.0%	8.8%
Older Low Income	Portugal	187	4.9%	52.7%	12,272	9.3%	6.8%
Older Low Income	Uruguay	177	4.9%	36.1%	5,842	13.6%	10.1%
Older Low Income	Thailand	151	4.1%	35.8%	2,796	11.6%	8.6%
Family Stage Low Inc	Colombia	191	4.5%	29.7%	1,914	15.2%	12.0%
Family Stage Low Inc	Brazil	190	6.3%	44.9%	3,912	14.1%	8.7%
Family Stage Low Inc	Argentina	186	5.5%	34.0%	3,416	16.3%	12.1%
Family Stage Low Inc	Tunisia	170	6.6%	42.4%	1,508	15.6%	14.7%
Young Poor	Honduras	117	6.1%	29.5%	760	20.8%	14.8%

The presence of China in this group is not surprising and do note that at an Education Index value of 192 it is close to being a member of the first segment – 'Increasing Their Advantage'.

China has been relentlessly improving its education standard ever since it introduced compulsory education for all 6 to 12 years olds in 1984 – irrespective of whether the child was male or female, urban or rural. That investment has paid off, as demonstrated by the growth of the country's productivity and household incomes and consumer wellbeing.

Of the 39 countries that are below 200 on the education index, only 9 are spending a higher than average (for all countries) share of GDP on education.

The useful point to note from this table is that the average proportion of total Gross Domestic Product spent on education is 5.2% which is close to the proportion spent by the group in the top right of Figure 5-4. That is, countries increasing their advantage. The lower spending per student is more a function of the per capita Gross Domestic Product than it is a lack of concern for education.

The Losers (Countries on the lower left of Fig 5-4)

Finally, and sadly, there are those countries that score less than 200 on the education index and who are also below average in terms of propensity to spend on education.

The problem is exacerbated further by the fact that they are all relatively poor economies, so the low spending rate, applied to a low Gross Domestic Product per capita means that, for all but nine of the 30 countries in this table, the spending is below US$500 per student per annum.

It also raises real concern about the universality of education in these countries. Assuming a class size of 40 students (which is higher than what is generally considered desirable) the cost per teacher (assuming they are on at least the average wage of the country) is over 30% of the total funds per class. This compares with 12% for the countries spending above average on education.

As such, in this group of countries, the student is under-resourced in all other aspects of education such as room, books/computer access etc. For the worst of these (for example Uganda) there is no credibility to their claim that all children are being (effectively) educated. The problem here is poor governance and miss allocation of national funds. This is unfortunate as these are the countries that need education if they are ever to get out of the poverty trap.

The situation does in part stem from the reality that currently the school-age population is a very significant proportion of the total population, so a greater proportion of the overall Gross Domestic

Product must be devoted to education than in countries with an older population.

Table 5-5: Listing of Countries with Low Education and Below Average Spend on Education.

Region	Country	Education Index	% GDP spent on education	Adj GDP % per student	Expenditure (US$ pa) per student age person	School Age as % total population	Teachers Salary as % Class funding
Family Stage Low Inc	Philippines	197	2.5%	12.1%	420	20.5%	36.6%
Family Stage Low Inc	Ecuador	185	5.2%	28.8%	1,779	18.2%	12.5%
Family Stage Low Inc	Mexico	184	5.0%	28.5%	2,810	17.5%	13.9%
Family Stage Low Inc	Dominican Repub	183	2.3%	12.6%	1,045	18.3%	31.0%
Family Stage Low Inc	Paraguay	168	3.4%	17.5%	948	19.3%	19.9%
Family Stage Low Inc	Indonesia	165	3.8%	21.6%	892	17.4%	16.7%
Family Stage Low Inc	India	133	3.8%	21.0%	444	18.0%	25.3%
Family Stage Low Inc	El Salvador	130	3.6%	20.3%	849	17.9%	24.1%
Family Stage Low Inc	Bangladesh	127	2.0%	10.8%	199	18.4%	39.9%
Family Stage Low Inc	Cambodia	55	2.2%	10.7%	176	20.3%	28.1%
Young Poor	Egypt	172	3.6%	17.2%	504	21.1%	44.3%
Young Poor	DR Congo	172	1.5%	5.4%	29	27.9%	99.4%
Young Poor	Ghana	166	4.0%	16.7%	367	23.7%	25.4%
Young Poor	Uganda	142	2.5%	8.5%	67	29.0%	55.2%
Young Poor	Guatemala	139	2.9%	13.3%	580	22.2%	38.8%
Young Poor	Namibia	134	2.8%	12.0%	594	23.4%	49.9%
Young Poor	Pakistan	126	2.9%	13.0%	151	22.2%	47.9%
Young Poor	Chad	122	2.2%	7.9%	55	28.5%	64.8%
Young Poor	Kenya	119	5.3%	20.6%	373	25.7%	22.2%
Young Poor	Cameroon	107	3.2%	11.9%	177	26.5%	35.1%
Young Poor	United Republic o	92	3.7%	13.7%	151	27.2%	26.7%
Young Poor	Nepal	91	5.2%	25.9%	276	20.1%	11.3%
Young Poor	Senegal	63	4.7%	17.6%	253	26.9%	43.5%
Young Poor	Rwanda	63	3.1%	12.3%	97	25.1%	29.2%
Young Poor	Ethiopia	55	4.9%	19.4%	159	25.5%	19.0%
Young Poor	Malawi	50	4.7%	16.9%	69	27.8%	28.1%
Young Poor	Burkina Faso	49	6.1%	22.0%	169	27.7%	23.6%
Young Poor	Mozambique	48	5.7%	20.7%	101	27.5%	19.9%
Young Poor	Mali	33	3.8%	13.2%	116	29.0%	39.2%
Young Poor	Guinea	33	2.6%	9.5%	100	27.1%	57.2%

It is a major concern that most countries with an existing poor adult education profile are still underspending per child (relative to other countries) on education

The problem is probably going to get worse, not better. For example, Uganda is under significant pressure. From 13.2 million school-age in 2020 to 16.4 million by 2030 and 20 million by 2045. That is a 50% lift in demand for school places in 25 years. This country's expenditure on education must increase by 50% just to 'stand still' let alone improve the education profile of its children. This, if nothing else demonstrates the importance of getting birth rates down – quickly.

The Demand Side of the Equation

Funding education is difficult if the number of people needing to be educated is increasing at a rapid rate. This of course is the typical scenario of the Young Poor Country Segment. Table 5-6 shows the total demand for school places for each of the Country Segments.

Table 5-6: Historic and Projected Number of School-Age Children by Country Segment.

	School Age Population 000s (5 to 14 yrs)				Growth Rate per annum		
	2,010	2,020	2,030	2,045	2010-20	2020-30	2030-45
Older Affluent	108,023	108,370	102,912	100,197	0.0%	-0.5%	-0.2%
Older Low Income	188,385	203,115	183,173	151,884	0.8%	-1.0%	-1.2%
Family Stage Low Inc	547,148	543,607	518,947	429,110	-0.1%	-0.5%	-1.3%
Young Poor	275,686	343,922	411,324	497,757	2.2%	1.8%	1.3%

What is apparent is that there is only one Country Segment where this is an issue – the Young Poor. For those countries, the number of school-age children (defined as 5 to 14 years inclusive) is projected to grow quite rapidly at 1.8% per annum by 2030 and then 1.3% per annum by 2045.

This adds another 154 million children over and above those being educated in 2020. To maintain accessibility and facilities the average country in this Country Segment needs to increase its education spending by 45% over the next 25 years.

187

Table 5-7 lists the countries in this segment and the projected growth rate in terms of the number of students.

Table 5-7: Historic and Projected Number of School-Age Children by Country. Young Poor Country Segment.

	School Age Population 000s (5 to 14 yrs)				Growth Rate per annum		
	2,010	2,020	2,030	2,045	2010-20	2020-30	2030-45
Angola	6,515	9,453	12,292	17,267	3.8%	2.7%	2.3%
Botswana	442	514	548	606	1.5%	0.6%	0.7%
Burkina Faso	4,370	5,802	7,170	9,275	2.9%	2.1%	1.7%
Cameroon	5,425	7,051	8,366	9,809	2.7%	1.7%	1.1%
Chad	3,505	4,706	5,894	7,173	3.0%	2.3%	1.3%
DR Congo	17,656	25,187	33,538	52,978	3.6%	2.9%	3.1%
Egypt	17,199	22,016	26,155	33,017	2.5%	1.7%	1.6%
Ethiopia	25,133	29,099	33,948	31,570	1.5%	1.6%	-0.5%
Ghana	6,148	7,368	8,479	9,642	1.8%	1.4%	0.9%
Guatemala	3,811	3,908	3,985	2,969	0.3%	0.2%	-1.9%
Guinea	2,935	3,553	4,297	4,972	1.9%	1.9%	1.0%
Haiti	2,345	2,440	2,361	1,638	0.4%	-0.3%	-2.4%
Honduras	2,090	2,013	1,932	1,422	-0.4%	-0.4%	-2.0%
Kenya	11,406	13,706	14,172	12,874	1.9%	0.3%	-0.6%
Lao PDR	1,492	1,527	1,498	1,057	0.2%	-0.2%	-2.3%
Madagascar	5,796	6,984	8,369	8,815	1.9%	1.8%	0.3%
Malawi	4,107	5,300	6,018	6,317	2.6%	1.3%	0.3%
Mali	4,219	5,914	7,533	10,982	3.4%	2.4%	2.5%
Mozambique	6,585	8,615	10,940	14,843	2.7%	2.4%	2.1%
Namibia	505	600	689	796	1.7%	1.4%	1.0%
Nepal	6,780	5,687	5,028	2,686	-1.7%	-1.2%	-4.1%
Niger	4,814	7,236	10,394	18,156	4.2%	3.7%	3.8%
Nigeria	42,102	55,706	69,086	94,558	2.8%	2.2%	2.1%
Pakistan	43,612	48,951	55,394	51,222	1.2%	1.2%	-0.5%
Rwanda	2,592	3,228	3,757	3,604	2.2%	1.5%	-0.3%
Senegal	3,369	4,516	5,493	7,239	3.0%	2.0%	1.9%
South Sudan	2,555	2,919	3,252	3,281	1.3%	1.1%	0.1%
Sudan	9,294	11,113	13,122	16,396	1.8%	1.7%	1.5%
Uganda	9,653	13,252	16,404	20,009	3.2%	2.2%	1.3%
Tanzania	12,000	16,278	20,678	29,447	3.1%	2.4%	2.4%
Zambia	3,948	5,146	6,190	7,535	2.7%	1.9%	1.3%
Zimbabwe	3,286	4,132	4,344	5,601	2.3%	0.5%	1.7%
Total/Average CAGR	275,686	343,922	411,324	497,757	2.2%	1.8%	1.3%

The obvious issue here is the considerable range in outcomes by individual countries. For the next decade to 2030, there are some countries in this segment where the projected growth rate of the school-age population is projected to exceed 2% per annum. This means that the total number of school places must increase by 22% by 2030. Yet these are all countries where, based on the current spend per student, the existing facilities are probably not very good. Niger and the Democratic Republic of Congo are of particular concern, followed by Angola, Mozambique, Mali, Uganda, and Nigeria.

As such the probability of the education profile of these countries improving over the next 25 years is very. This is of concern as the evidence is that education is probably the best route out of endemic poverty and the ability of these countries to deliver on that is at risk simply because of unalterable population trends. Many of these children are already alive.

To Summarize

Using current spending behaviour, the prognosis in terms of education for the next 25 years is not good. The 'educated' will continue to be educated. This will apply even to those countries that are 'coasting' at present as education and the education infrastructure do not go away.

There is a positive picture in that some of the less educated countries are making a serious effort to improve, but the sad point is that that applies to just nine countries (out of the 40 countries that are below 200 on the education index). They are not affluent countries so the average expenditure per student at US$3,916 is not as high as that of the affluent countries (US$14,321) – but it is approaching that of the 'Coasting' countries (US$4,853 per student) and is probably sufficient to have an impact over time.

The prognosis for education in many of the countries which are below standard on education is not good. It is concerning that 30 of the 42 countries below 200 on the education index are underspending on education relative to the global norm. Only four are spending more than US$1,000 per student per annum.

The failure to deal with this issue does not portend well for their future. The well-being of their citizens will not improve, and the future economic development of these countries is at risk. A poorly educated labour force is less able to attract Fixed Capital Investment which would create employment and lift the productivity of the labour force and hence the overall wellbeing of society.

Similarly, being poorly educated, society will not understand the value of limiting population growth (births), good nutrition, wellness etc.

Education is probably one of the best methods to end endemic poverty over time. However, for some countries the inevitable rapid growth in the number of persons needing to be educated means that the availability and improvement in education facilities/opportunities will not happen to a degree to make a significant difference in outcomes.

The Current Educational Profile of the Adult Population

This section looks at the existing and projected 'education profile of adults' in the countries covered in this book. Figure 5-5 shows the proportion of the 25 years of age and above population in each segment by the highest level of education achieved in 2019.

For the Young Poor country segment, only 29% of its adult population has more than lower secondary education. For the Family Stage Low Income segment, the figure is 37%. This would suggest that these economies will have difficulty attracting Fixed Capital Investment and hence lifting labour productivity and incomes. Fixing this education deficiency should be a priority. However, as shown in Table 5.5 earlier, most of these countries are the ones that are under-investing in education.

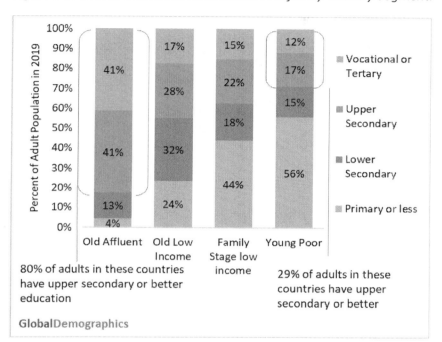

Figure 5-5: Overall Education Achievement Profile by Country Segment.

This does, however, lead to the question of just how rapidly can this profile change? Figure 5-6 shows the change over the last decade and projected change for the next twenty-five years to 2045. This is restricted to those countries in each segment for which such data is available for the time period. As such, due to the change in the underlying sample base, there is a minor change in the profile for 2019 from Figure 5-5.

Also, the forecast uses the trend in the proportions by education level for the last decade. This is used to estimate the future adult education profile because historically there is *not* a good relationship for many countries between *claimed* enrolments (and hence the potential education level of those departing the education system) and change in the educational profile of the workforce. One suspects it is easier to overstate the number of enrolled students than the education outcome amongst adults.

What is good to see in Figure 5-6 is that for all the less well-educated regions a significant improvement is expected. This should help improve the economic prospects of the next generation who increasingly will have lower secondary education or better.

Figure 5-6: Historical and Projected Education Profile of Adult Population by Country Segments.

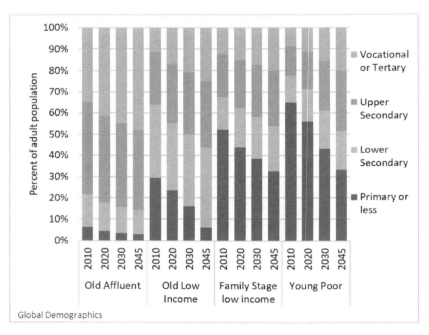

The reader is reminded that changing the *overall* education profile of the adult population in a country takes time. It is not just a case of the years it takes to educate someone and get them into the labour force. There is also a hysteresis effect of those (less well educated) already in the labour force. It can take forty years for them to leave the labour force.

192

Therefore, it is so important that governments address education as quickly as possible.

It is this which explains why even countries such as China, with an aggressive education program in place, will not catch up with the older affluent countries in the next 25 years. It has a residual of a large, older, workforce who did not benefit from the education reforms of 1984 onward.

Figure 5-7 shows the absolute numbers behind Figure 5-6. And here the picture is not quite so good. While there is a clear improvement in the number of persons with a lower secondary or better education in the two youngest Country Segments the reality remains that because of the above-mentioned hysteresis effect, particularly in the Family Stage Low Income segment, the absolute number of adults with primary or less education declines only marginally.

Figure 5-7: Long Term Forecast of Adult Education Profile – person Millions.

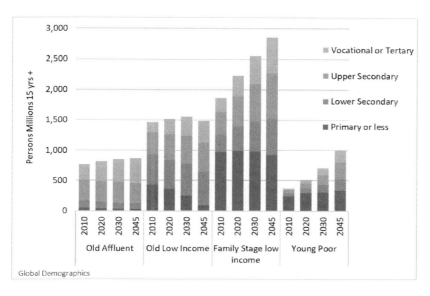

Note: In Figure 5-7 the Young Poor segment profile is estimated by applying the average rate for different education levels as reported by some countries in that

segment to all countries in that region to adjust for non-reporting. It is believed those countries reporting (and setting the average) are the better performing on education, so this picture is probably more positive than reality.

Worse, in the Young Poor Segment as a proportion of adults, the number with Primary or less increases slightly as there is still a proportion of children getting primary or less education in those countries. But they do decline as a proportion of all adults.

The standout segment is, of course, the Old Low Income Country Segment with a substantial decline in the absolute number of adults with primary or less education. This is China, which numerically dominates this segment. By 2045 virtually all adults in China will have lower secondary or better education.

In Summary

Education is very important because it so significantly influences the development of a society. It helps bring about a better social environment where wellness and hygiene are understood, where the capabilities of individuals are increased and most importantly the rule of law and democracy can exist. The failure of so many countries to give education the priority it deserves is very worrying.

The forecasts included in this Chapter and the overall population model tend to be positive in terms of improvement in the availability of education. There is growing affluence in the poorer countries and that in turn gives them access to media and realization of the role of education. So, the pressure for improvement may well come from the citizens rather than the politicians.

The worrying aspect is, however, that in the Young Poor countries the almost inevitable growth in the number of young people/children is so large that the education system becomes overwhelmed. Between 2020 and 2045 the number of 'school age' children is projected to increase by 45% - which means a significant increase in the education budget is required to simply 'stand still' in terms of availability. Let alone improve both availability and quality. For some countries, such as Nigeria, the per cent increase required is over 80%. Nigeria currently has 55.7 million school-age children and projections indicate that this will increase to 94.6 million by 2045. Can it keep up with demand? Let alone improve it.

But to end on a positive note – technology may make a significant difference in this regard. We cannot include its impact in our forecasts (or even estimate it) but the ability to deliver lessons by properly trained teachers in the relevant language or dialect to remote classrooms should become more affordable using existing technology. It is just the cost of a decent sized TV per class and an internet connection (perhaps from a satellite in remote areas). A little more expenditure per child would provide them with a tablet loaded with the appropriate textbooks/learning material in the relevant language.

Summary Profile – Education

Older Affluent

	2019	2030	2045
Education index	272	277	280
% adults with Upper Sec +	80%	83%	85%
School age population Mns	108	103	100
Growth of School age pop.	0.0%	-0.5%	-0.2%
School age as % population	11%	10%	10%
% GDP spent on education	4.7%	4.9%	5.0%
Educ Exp per school age pers (US$)	21,163	28,335	35,878

Older Low Income

	2019	2030	2045
Education index	205	222	239
% adults with Upper Sec +	44%	50%	56%
School age population Mns	202	191	160
Growth of School age pop.	0.5%	-0.5%	-1.2%
School age as % population	11%	10%	9%
% GDP spent on education	4.0%	3.7%	3.3%
Educ Exp per school age pers (US$)	3,860	5,968	9,289

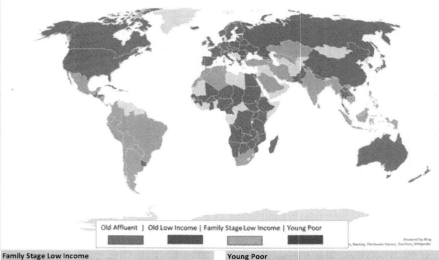

Old Affluent | Old Low Income | Family Stage Low Income | Young Poor

Family Stage Low Income

	2019	2030	2045
Education index	159	178	195
% adults with Upper Sec +	35%	40%	45%
School age population Mns	545	519	429
Growth of School age pop.	0.0%	-0.4%	-1.3%
School age as % population	17%	15%	12%
% GDP spent on education	5.1%	5.3%	5.1%
Educ Exp per school age pers (US$)	1,276	1,850	3,189

Young Poor

	2019	2030	2045
Education index	82	111	131
% adults with Upper Sec +	18%	26%	32%
School age population Mns	338	411	498
Growth of School age pop.	2.2%	1.8%	1.3%
School age as % population	25%	24%	22%
% GDP spent on education	3.8%	3.8%	4.0%
Educ Exp per school age pers (US$)	224	313	572

Chapter 6
Working-age and Employment

Today, around 300,000 people will be turning 15 years of age, leaving education (if they are fortunate) and looking for a job. It is estimated that 56% of them will at best have primary education.

This continues for the next 25 years – and to provide them with employment there is a need for a net increase of 725 million jobs in the world by 2045. That is a 30% increase on the 2019 employed population of 2,365 million. Will there be enough employment opportunities for these people?

*This chapter looks at the jobs required to **maintain present** levels of employment. Please note that is very different from the employment that may or may not be achieved.*

The trends in consumption (see Chapter 8) and productivity indicate that there will not be enough employment opportunities. That is of concern.

Why is employment important?

The employed labour force of a country is effectively the *'engine'* of its economy. The greater the proportion of the population in employment and the more productive the average worker the better off will be the society.

Figure 6-1 shows the average proportion of the *total* population employed in 2019 for each of the four Country Segments. (Note the emphasis here is on 'total population' and not the working-age population).

The two younger segments have a lower percentage because a significant proportion of their population is under the age of 15 years. It shows how these economies are stressed because a significant proportion of their population cannot be in work because of age. In these younger countries, the typical wage earner is supporting themselves and 1.8 *other* persons (dependents). This compares with the average wage earner having just 1 dependent in the older countries.

Figure 6-1: Percent of the Total Population that is Employed in 2019.

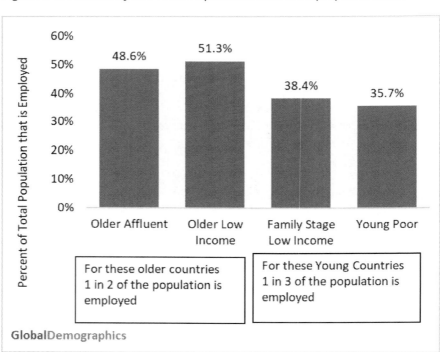

However, to get a reading of the ability of the population to *find* work, it is necessary to look at the proportion of the population of *working age* that is employed. But even here care must be exercised. 'Working-age' does vary by country.

The widely used definition of 'Working-age' is 15 to 64 years, but the reality is different. In many countries child labour is widespread, and in others the propensity to be employed after age 64 years is high. For reasons explained later in this Chapter, working-age is defined as 15 to 64 years for all countries except those in the Older Affluent Country Segment where working age is 15 to 74 years.

Figure 6-2 shows the proportion of the working-age *population* in each Country Segment that is employed. As can be seen, the differences between the four segments are less than when based on the total population (Fig 6-1).

Figure 6-2: Propensity of the Working-age Population to be Employed. 2019.

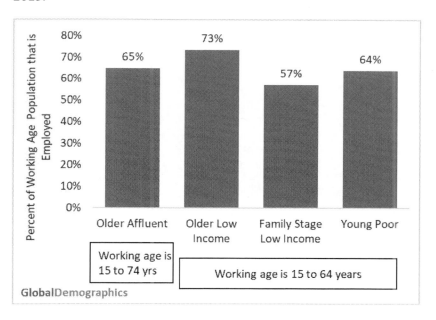

The Family Stage Low Income Country Segment has the lowest level of employment, reflecting that these economies are more traditional in terms of the role of women in the workforce. In the case of the Young Poor Country Segment, it is high because the countries in this Segment are biased toward being rural economies and the entire family is more likely to be engaged in the production process. This serves to offset the traditional attitudes towards female participation in the workforce in those countries.

The other key issue in terms of employment that needs to be quantified at the outset is the productivity of the worker. There are many esoteric measures of worker productivity, but they are not available across all countries. As such the productivity measure used in this analysis is Gross Domestic Product per worker. The two components (Gross Domestic Product and the number of workers) are relatively easy to measure, widely understood and subject to multiple cross-checks. As shown earlier this measure of productivity also has a logical relationship with education and Accumulated Fixed Capital Investment.

Wages multiplied by the number of workers per household determine the average household income and hence lifestyle. Figure 6-3 shows the average Gross Domestic Product per worker for each of the four Country Segments in 2009 and 2019 expressed in 2019 US$ values.

Figure 6-3: GDP Per Worker (US Dollars 2019 values) for 2009 and 2019.

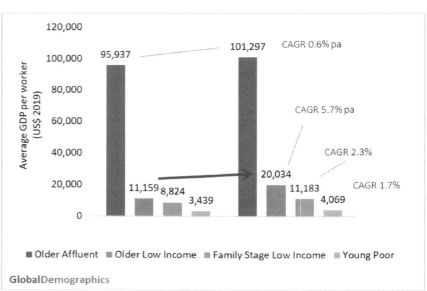

GlobalDemographics

The dichotomy between the Old Affluent Segment of countries and the others is extreme but to a very large extent reflects differences in education and accumulated Fixed Capital Investment as explained in the previous chapter on education. Ideally, the difference should reduce over time as the less productive regions improve the education standard of their workforce and the fixed capital investment made annually. But this (education) takes time and as all countries are improving on one or both variables the gap does not reduce a lot, as demonstrated in Figure 6-3.

While the productivity per worker of the Older Affluent Countries was the slowest growing at 0.6% per annum, the *absolute* increase in productivity exceeds the total productivity of the youngest segments. Also, it must be noted that in the case of the Older Lower Income segment, the relatively high growth rate of GDP per worker of 5.7% per annum is particularly a function of China.

The Potential to be Employed.

The propensity of someone to be in work is a function of multiple factors which vary significantly in their applicability to individual countries and segments. These are as follows:

1) Working-age – the definition of this varies across societies at different stages of development. The wider the *accepted* age range over which to be working the greater the proportion of the total population that will be employed.
2) The age profile of the population – this is the proportion of the population that falls within the band considered 'working-age'.
3) Societal and religious factors. The obvious one is the acceptance of females in the workforce and the ability of females to be in the workforce when there is a large family. It also encompasses the acceptance of child labour which typically is not measured.
4) Education. This is covered in detail in the previous chapter, but the point needs to be remade – the better educated a person is, the more likely it is that they will be in employment. Note that gender differences in terms of education achievement impact gender differences in employment.

Working-age and the Age Profile of Countries

It is necessary to define what is meant by working-age as that effectively determines the upper limit for the size of the labour force. Theoretically, persons outside that age range are not (or should not in the case of younger ages) be in employment.

The traditional definition has been 15 to 64 years of age. The younger age limit of 15 years is defensible, in that most countries now define compulsory school age as 6 to 14 years inclusive. Some start a year earlier but generally, the upper end of the range is 14 years of age. As such the ability to enter the full-time workforce before then is (legally, if not factually) constrained.

However, in the more developed countries over 50% of persons aged 15 to 22 continue in education to complete upper secondary typically by age 18 and then some (circa 25%) continue in education for a vocational or tertiary degree. As such the effective average 'start of working age' in those countries is 18 or 19 years.

The older age limit of 64 years is also changing. The belief that all people stop work and become dependent at age 65 is irrational. Consider the ages of the Presidential Candidates in the United States of America for the 2020 elections?? Even in the early stages of the selection process few of the candidates were under 70 years of age!

In the United States of America – which is one of the wealthiest countries on a per capita basis and *not* the oldest by any means – 24% of males aged 70 to 74 years are still in full-time employment. This same statistic is 25% in Japan, and for many of the other countries in the Older Affluent Country Segment, it is approaching those levels.

In short, the *growth* area in the labour market of the Older Affluent countries is workers *staying in work* beyond the age of 64 years. As the 65 years plus age group is the fastest-growing age segment in these older countries that means their workforce is receiving a significant boost.

*The growth area in the labour market of the Older Affluent
countries is workers staying in work beyond the age of 64 years.*

It should be noted that in the countries where this phenomenon is
happening, life expectancy is into the early 80s and therefore a high
proportion of them are still physically fit in their mid-70s. They are also
well educated by global standards and have gained good work experience.
This makes them valuable employees.

Why do they keep working? There are three main reasons.
1) Pension insecurity. There are very few people in the world who,
   when they reach age 64, are secure in the knowledge that they
   have an adequate pension/funds to finance themselves for the
   rest of their life. There are some lucky ones – but they are the
   exception. This delayed exit from the workforce is also a plus for
   the pension industry. The older worker means people pay into
   their pension fund longer than expected and delay/reduce the
   drawdown. This provides some relief to the obvious funding crisis
   in that sector.
2) Extended life expectancy. In the more affluent countries with a
   history of good nutrition, healthcare, and awareness of wellness
   and hygiene, life expectancy has steadily increased over time. In
   most of these countries, it is now normal for males to live to their
   late 70s or early 80s and women 2-4 years longer than that. As
   such, they can continue in work past age 64. This is facilitated by
   how the nature of work is changing. An increasing proportion of
   work is 'non-physical' (or, with the use of machinery, less
   physically demanding) and hence available to the older, less
   physically strong individual.
3) Education. Educated people tend to do something for their
   remaining 15+ years of life and being gainfully employed is an
   attractive option. It gives a reason to get up in the morning. It is
   better than being 'entertained' for the next 15 years and living
   with a lower income.

For all these reasons it is better to define working age for these Older
Affluent countries as 15 to 74 years – recognizing that the participation

rates are lower at the two extremes of this range. That is 15 to 19 years and 65 to 74 years.

It might be noted that this 'Older' labour pool is only available to the countries in the Older Affluent Segment as they have a history of education, wellness, and the necessary life expectancy. It will extend to the Older Less Affluent Country Segment over time but for many, that is not an option yet. The old (as compared to the younger generations in those countries) have a life expectancy of low to mid-70s and are, in some cases, less well educated.

China is a good example of this. Many of those over 45 years of age did not benefit from either the education reforms or a good nutritional intake in their childhood years. As such they simply never got the chance to understand or live a healthy lifestyle – at least not in time to make a difference. This will change over the next two decades as the current younger and healthier population ages.

Given this definition of working age, the next section of this chapter examines how the size of the working-age population is projected to change over time in each of the country segments.

The Older Affluent Countries

To be clear, the working-age definition applied to all countries in this Country Segment is 15 to 74 years. Figure 6-4 shows on the left the overall age profile of the total population of this Country Segment in 2019 and its projected shape in 2045 given projected trends in birth rates (stable), death rates (declining within age groups but increasing overall as more of the population is older) and immigration (declining).

As a result, even though this Country Segment is generally ageing and the working-age population declines in absolute number, as a proportion of the population the decline is not as dramatic as might have been expected. The 15-to-74-year age group is projected to decline from 75% of the total population in 2019 to an estimated 71% of the population in 2045.

The traditional working-age group of 15 to 64-year age is projected to decline by 32 million persons between 2019 and 2045. In contrast, the 65 to 74-year age group grows by 17 million offsetting nearly half the decline in the younger working-age group.

Figure 6-4: Overall Age Profile and Working-age Population of the Older Affluent Country Segment.

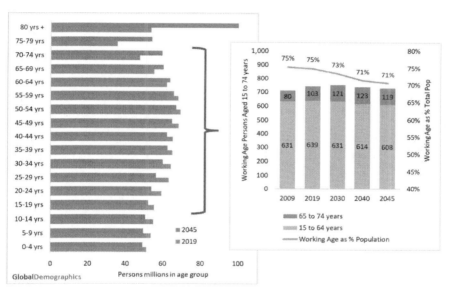

This means that the total working-age population in this Country Segment is projected to decline from 742 million in 2019 to 727 million by 2045 which is not a significant reduction (an absolute reduction of 2.0% over 25 years or 0.13% per annum). This is in the context of societies that are the most likely to embrace robotics and Artificial Intelligence early and thereby enhance the productivity per worker by at least 0.13% per annum and probably more.

This suggests that the decline in the 'working-age population' is probably not an impending crisis. Table 6-1 shows the size and trend of the working-age population for each of the countries included in this segment.

Table 6-1: Current and Projected Size of the Working-age Population of Countries in the Old Affluent Country Segment.

Older Affluent				Working age as %	
Country	Working age (15-74 yrs) Mns			Total Pop	
	2019	2030	2045	2019	2045
Australia	18.6	20.4	21.7	74%	71%
Austria	6.8	7.3	7.6	76%	73%
Belgium	8.5	8.9	9.0	74%	71%
Canada	28.7	30.6	32.2	77%	72%
Denmark	4.3	4.3	4.3	75%	70%
Finland	4.1	4.0	3.9	75%	71%
France	47.3	47.3	45.4	73%	68%
Germany	62.3	64.9	66.2	75%	71%
Hong Kong	6.0	6.0	5.8	80%	70%
Iceland	0.3	0.3	0.3	74%	72%
Ireland	3.6	4.1	4.5	73%	72%
Italy	45.4	44.5	39.3	75%	69%
Japan	92.9	84.7	74.0	73%	68%
Macao	0.5	0.6	0.6	83%	76%
Netherlands	12.9	12.7	11.8	76%	69%
New Zealand	3.5	3.8	3.8	74%	70%
Norway	4.0	4.4	4.6	75%	73%
South Korea	41.4	40.6	33.9	81%	70%
Singapore	4.9	4.9	4.5	84%	73%
Slovenia	1.6	1.5	1.4	76%	68%
Spain	35.3	35.0	30.5	76%	70%
Sweden	7.3	7.7	8.3	73%	70%
Switzerland	6.5	6.9	7.1	76%	71%
United Kingdom	49.7	52.2	52.8	74%	70%
USA	245.6	254.7	253.4	75%	72%
Total	742.0	752.2	727.1	75%	71%

Two key points flow from this table. First, for all these countries, the working-age population – even with the extension into the older age range – is declining as a *proportion* of the total population. But by just 3-4 percentage points over 25 years for *most* countries.

This relatively small projected reduction in the absolute number of working-age persons as a proportion of the total population means that these countries would only need to lift employment participation rates (proportion of working-age population employed) and/or worker productivity by a total of 2.6% over the next 25 years (0.14% per annum) to maintain their current level of affluence per capita.

For those countries where immigration is projected to be positive, for example, Australia, the working-age population is projected to increase in absolute number. But even then, the working-age population as a percentage of the total population declines marginally. This is because most long-term migrants bring dependents. So, while the number of workers is increased the net improvement on a per capita basis is minimal.

The Older Low-Income Countries

It should be noted that this segment is dominated by China and for that reason, China is listed separately at the bottom of Table 6-2. However, while the *absolute* numbers change a lot with the removal of China from the analysis of this segment, the trends and overall pattern are little changed. As such China is included in Figure 6-5.

Figure 6-5 shows how the projected age profile, and the working-age population, are projected to change over the next 25 years. For this Country Segment, the projected degree of change is quite dramatic, from 'late stage' pyramid countries to a 'square' population profile albeit with a bulge in the 50-to-74-year age range. But there is also a significantly smaller young population, even in 2019.

The total working-age population in this Country Segment excluding China is projected to decline by 17%, which is 47 million persons. This results in working-age reducing from 67% to 60% of the total population (see Table 6-2).

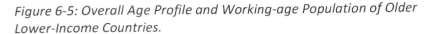

Figure 6-5: Overall Age Profile and Working-age Population of Older Lower-Income Countries.

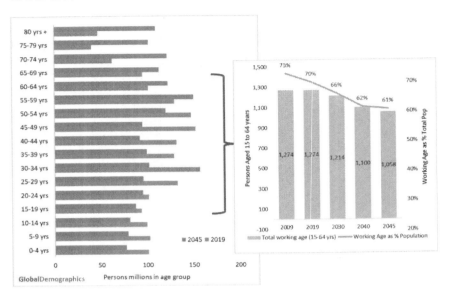

Table 6-2 shows the details for individual countries in this segment. The significant point to observe here is (a) the proportion of the population that is working age (70% in 2019) is lower than the previous (Older Affluent) segment in the same year and (b) without exception it is projected to decline further over the next 25 years to an unweighted average of 61% (compared with 71% for the Older Affluent countries).

This potentially constrains the economic development of these (largely Eastern European) countries. We revisit this later in this chapter when discussing the propensity to be employed and the trend in the size of the employed labour force.

208

Table 6-2: Current and Projected Size of the Working-age Population of Countries in the Old Affluent Country Segment.

Older Low Income				Working age as %	
Country	Working age (15-64 yrs) Mns			Total Pop	
	2019	2030	2045	2019	2045
Albania	2.0	1.8	1.5	68%	65%
Belarus	6.4	5.9	5.5	68%	60%
Bulgaria	4.5	4.1	3.3	64%	59%
Cuba	7.8	7.1	6.0	68%	58%
Czechia	6.9	6.8	6.1	65%	57%
Estonia	0.8	0.8	0.8	64%	59%
Georgia	2.6	2.4	2.3	65%	60%
Greece	6.7	6.1	4.7	64%	54%
Hungary	6.4	6.0	5.1	66%	60%
Latvia	1.2	1.0	0.7	64%	54%
Lithuania	1.8	1.3	0.9	65%	51%
Mauritius	0.9	0.9	0.8	71%	64%
Poland	25.3	23.1	19.7	67%	60%
Portugal	6.6	5.9	4.6	64%	54%
Moldova	2.9	2.7	2.3	72%	69%
Romania	12.7	11.4	8.8	66%	57%
Russia	97.3	91.3	88.4	67%	60%
Slovakia	3.7	3.5	3.0	68%	61%
Thailand	49.3	46.6	40.1	71%	59%
Ukraine	29.6	27.2	23.4	68%	63%
Uruguay	2.2	2.3	2.3	65%	62%
Total excl China	277.6	257.9	230.5	67%	60%
China	996.4	955.7	827.3	71%	61%
Total	1,274.0	1,213.7	1,057.7	70%	61%
Urban China	595.8	667.2	666.7	72%	80%
Rural China	400.6	288.5	160.5	70%	50%

China – Two Labour Forces

It is important to look specifically at China. The overall working-age population as shown in Table 6-2 (line labelled China) is projected to decline from 996 million in 2019 to 827 million by 2045. This is very much in line with the other countries in this Country Segment. On that basis, some commentators are suggesting that China's economic growth rate will slow in future as there are fewer people to be employed.

However, this overlooks the impact of the ongoing rural to urban migration that is taking place at around 19 million persons per year – mainly of working age. The Rural to Urban migration means that the working-age population in rural China has experienced a steep decline in size and this is projected to continue – as shown at the bottom of Table 6-2. Between 2019 and 2045 given current trends in rural to urban migration rates, the working-age population in rural China is projected to reduce by 60% in absolute terms. This, however, is not such an issue as might be expected. The rural labour force is much less productive than the urban one which is where the migrants are going.

China has two labour forces. The decline in the working-age population in China is a rural phenomenon. The Urban Working-age population continues to increase through to 2033.

Not surprisingly, and as also shown in Table 6-2, the Urban China working-age population is projected to increase. Most of the growth is achieved by 2035 after which the growth continues but at a much slower rate. Given that urban employment is estimated (based on wages paid) to be 3 to 4 times more productive than rural employment this means the overall productivity of the total workforce increases even though the number of working-age persons (and employed persons) declines. This is looked at in more detail in Chapter Ten.

The Family Stage Low Income Segment

As shown in Figure 6-6, this Country Segment currently (2019) has a 'pyramid' population profile (the orange bars in Figure 6-6) which means it has a strong bias toward the younger age groups. However, it is projected to begin to rebalance *towards* a population 'square' with a limited increase in population size. All age groups above 30 years are projected to grow significantly in size, whereas below 30 years of age they are projected to decline in absolute size.

Figure 6-6: Overall Age Profile and Working-age Population of the Family Stage Low Income Segment of Countries.

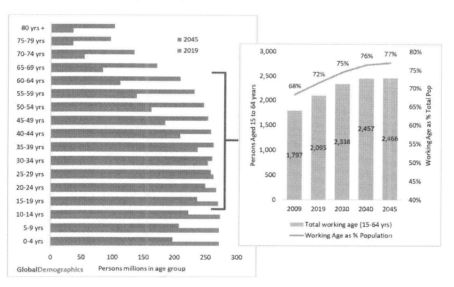

Consequently, it is expected that this Country Segment will grow its working-age population (15 to 64 years in this case) from 2.1 billion in 2019 to 2.5 billion in the next 25 years – that is an 18% increase. It also means that, unlike the previous two older segments, the working-age population is expected to increase marginally as a percentage of the total population – from 67% to 69%.

Table 6-3: Current and Projected Size of the Working-age Population of Countries in the Family Stage Low Income Country Segment.

Family Stage Low Income				Working age as %	
Country	Working age (15-64 yrs) Mns			Total Pop	
	2,019	2,030	2,045	2019	2045
Algeria	27.1	32.2	39.5	63%	60%
Argentina	28.7	31.8	34.3	64%	65%
Armenia	2.0	1.9	1.9	68%	66%
Azerbaijan	7.0	7.4	7.6	70%	66%
Bangladesh	110.2	124.5	127.5	68%	73%
Bolivia	7.1	8.5	9.6	62%	68%
Brazil	147.1	152.8	148.6	70%	65%
Cambodia	10.6	12.4	14.2	64%	72%
Chile	13.0	14.4	15.5	69%	66%
Colombia	34.5	38.9	42.0	69%	68%
Dominican Rep	7.0	7.7	8.2	65%	65%
Ecuador	11.3	13.4	15.6	65%	66%
El Salvador	4.2	4.4	4.3	65%	68%
India	915.6	1,029.3	1,082.8	67%	71%
Indonesia	183.2	203.0	215.6	68%	65%
Iran	57.2	62.9	66.1	69%	66%
Kazakhstan	11.8	13.0	15.2	64%	58%
Malaysia	22.2	24.7	26.6	69%	70%
Mexico	84.7	94.8	100.4	66%	67%
Morocco	24.0	26.7	29.1	66%	65%
Myanmar	36.8	39.1	38.6	68%	69%
Nicaragua	4.2	4.8	5.2	65%	67%
Panama	2.8	3.3	3.8	65%	63%
Paraguay	4.5	5.2	5.7	64%	71%
Peru	21.6	25.9	29.8	66%	64%
Philippines	69.4	82.2	91.2	64%	70%
Saudi Arabia	24.5	30.3	33.0	72%	78%
South Africa	38.4	44.9	51.5	66%	68%
Sri Lanka	13.9	14.0	13.3	65%	59%
Tunisia	7.9	8.4	8.9	67%	64%
Turkey	55.7	64.2	69.5	67%	66%
Uzbekistan	22.0	25.2	28.6	67%	69%
Venezuela RB	18.7	16.3	12.3	65%	60%
Viet Nam	66.8	69.9	69.8	69%	65%
Total	2,095.5	2,338.3	2,465.7	67%	69%

Table 6-3 shows the detail by country for this segment of countries. India dominates in terms of the share of the population in this segment, but its profile is pretty much 'average' and does not create a skew in the summary profile of the segment. The key point to appreciate from this table is that except for three countries (Sri Lanka, Venezuela, and Armenia) the rest are projected to experience an increase in the absolute size of the working-age population.

212

The Young Poor Segment

The dramatic aspect of this segment is the projected lack of change in age profile despite a significant increase in the absolute number of persons. As shown in Figure 6-7, the population profile – a pyramid – is projected to move to the right as the population increases – across all age groups.

The working-age population in this Segment of Countries is projected to double in size in the next 25 years, from 742 million to 1.42 billion. As a proportion of the total population, it is projected to grow from 56% in 2019 to 65% by 2045.

Figure 6-7: Overall Age Profile and Working-age Population of the Young Poor Country Segment.

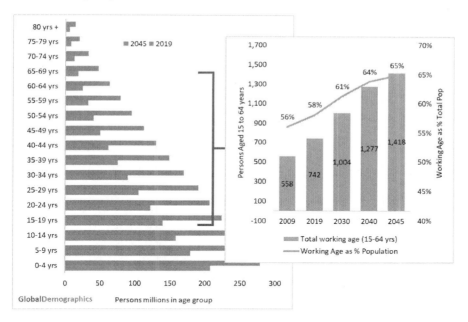

This is low compared with the other Country Segments and reflects the extreme age bias of these countries toward young (under 15 years) dependent persons. Nonetheless, the projected increase in the size of the working-age population could boost the size of these economies if the propensity to be in work is maintained.

Table 6-4 shows for the individual countries the existing and projected size of the working-age population – which, to remind you, for these countries is ages 15 to 64 years. The projected significant increase in the absolute number of working-age persons has potentially positive implications in terms of actual workforce growth and prosperity of the countries shown.

Table 6-4: Current and Projected Size of the Working-age Population of Countries in the Young Poor Country Segment

Young Poor				Working age as %	
Country	Working age (15-64 yrs) Mns			Total Pop	
	2,019	2,030	2,045	2019	2045
Angola	16.3	24.3	39.3	51%	57%
Botswana	1.4	1.8	2.3	62%	66%
Burkina Faso	10.8	15.3	22.9	52%	59%
Cameroon	14.2	19.7	28.1	54%	63%
Chad	8.1	11.7	18.0	50%	60%
DR Congo	44.3	65.0	106.3	50%	53%
Egypt	61.1	75.8	98.7	61%	61%
Ethiopia	62.9	87.1	122.8	56%	69%
Ghana	18.1	23.3	30.6	59%	63%
Guatemala	10.8	13.6	16.5	61%	71%
Guinea	6.9	9.7	14.4	53%	63%
Haiti	7.0	8.2	9.1	62%	71%
Honduras	6.2	7.6	8.6	64%	71%
Kenya	30.7	41.9	55.0	58%	70%
Lao PDR	4.6	5.5	6.2	63%	73%
Madagascar	15.3	20.8	29.4	56%	65%
Malawi	10.0	14.4	20.8	54%	66%
Mali	9.9	14.4	22.6	50%	54%
Mozambique	16.0	22.9	35.2	52%	58%
Namibia	1.5	1.9	2.4	59%	63%
Nepal	18.6	23.2	26.9	65%	78%
Niger	11.1	17.4	31.4	47%	50%
Nigeria	107.7	147.0	214.9	53%	57%
Pakistan	131.3	165.2	209.9	60%	68%
Rwanda	7.2	9.7	13.5	57%	67%
Senegal	8.8	12.4	18.4	54%	59%
South Sudan	6.1	7.0	8.3	54%	59%
Sudan	24.1	32.2	45.0	56%	61%
Uganda	22.8	35.8	58.2	51%	64%
Tanzania	31.1	44.5	68.7	53%	57%
Zambia	9.5	13.9	21.0	53%	62%
Zimbabwe	8.0	10.2	12.8	55%	57%
Total	742.2	1,003.7	1,418.2	56%	61%

*The working-age population of the Young Poor Segment of
countries is projected to double in size in the next 25 years, from
742 million to 1.42 billion.*

Summary of the Trend in Working-age Populations

The above section identifies that the projected *demand for work* is rapidly
expanding in the Young Poor Country Segment. The projection indicates
an additional 725 million persons of working age for this Country
Segment. The working-age population is also growing in the Family Stage
Low Income segment. But at a much slower rate and it effectively peaks
in 2038. That Country Segment is nonetheless projected to add a total of
370 million persons to the working-age population by 2045, of which
(based on historical norms) around 58% will be looking for employment.

This compares with the two older segments where the working-age
population is initially stable and then declining. Both in absolute number
as well as a proportion of the total population. Furthermore, for most of
these countries, the proportion of working-age that are employed is high
and their ability to expand (maintain) the size of the total labour force by
increasing participation rates is limited. This indicates that the future
growth of these economies will be almost entirely a function of increased
productivity of the existing (or reducing) labour pool.

Whether this is an issue for the future is examined in the next section of
this chapter – conversion of the working-age population to workers.

*Growth of the Older and more affluent economies will be entirely a
function of increased productivity of the existing (or reducing)
labour pool. Due to the changing age profile of the population, the
number of persons of working age is unlikely to increase
significantly, if at all.*

Conversion of Working-age Persons into Employed Persons

Having a large and or growing *working-age* population is a necessary, but not sufficient, condition for having a growing workforce. The size of the workforce is also a function of the ability of society to convert those working-age persons into workers.

As belaboured throughout this book that is, to a very significant extent, a function of education and the (typically) subsequent fixed capital investment behind each employee. Figure 6-8 shows the average proportion of the working-age population of each of the Country Segments that are in work in each of 2009 and 2019.

Figure 6-8: Average Propensity of the Working-age Population to be in Work by Country Segment. 2009 and 2019.

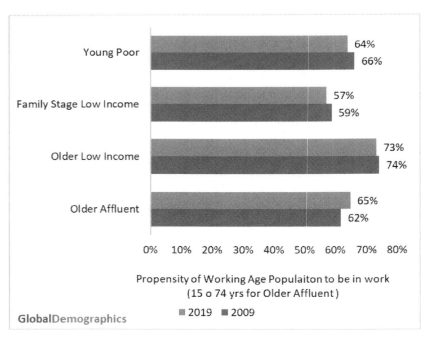

Within each of the four Country Segments, this statistic does vary by individual country. Some of the difference in employment levels is explained by female participation rates. Figure 6-9 shows the countries where female participation rates are below 50%. These countries account for 54% of all women of working age in the 116 countries covered, but 24% of women in employment.

Figure 6-9: Countries with Below 50% Female Participation Rates in Their Labour Force (Employed Females as a Percent of Females Aged 15 To 64 Years). 2019.

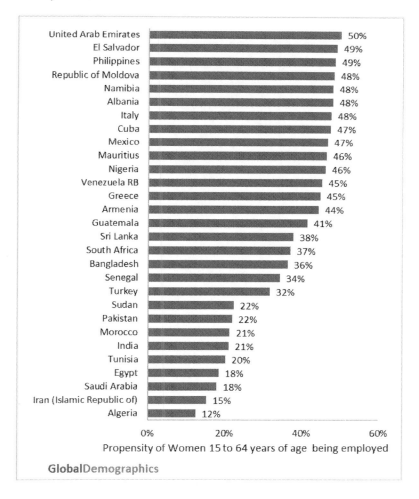

In theory, to estimate the size of the workforce for future years one can multiply….

1. the number of persons of working age, which can be forecast with reasonable reliability (certainly for the next 15 years as all those participants are already alive)
2. by the propensity of the working-age population to be employed which tends to be a reasonably stable trend over time (it may vary year on year due to specific economic shocks but typically reverts to trend quite quickly)
3. to obtain the total expected number of employed persons.

This indicates that the projected overall number of people that would be employed would increase from 3.09 billion in 2019 to 3.64 billion by 2045. That is a **net** addition of 549 million jobs over the next 26 years – or 21 million extra jobs a year. However, that is provided **countries can maintain their propensity to find employment** for the working-aged. This projection is summarised in Figure 6-10.

Figure 6-10: Expected Number of Employed Persons Given Trend in Working-age Population and Trend in Propensity to be Employed. 2019,2030 and 2045

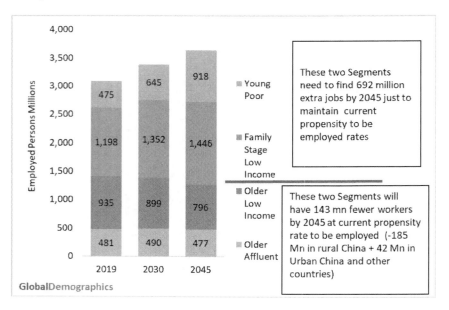

The emphasis on the word 'net' in the previous paragraph is deliberate and important. While the two older segments show an overall reduction in projected employed persons of 133 million, *most of this relates to rural China and will not create job vacancies for persons from other countries*. This is explained in more detail below.

If historic trends in the propensity to be employed are maintained, the number of people that will be employed in the younger countries is projected to increase from 1.67 billion in 2019 to 2.36 billion by 2045. An additional 692 million jobs need to be created over the next 26 years.

The real demand for work is in the Young Family Low Income Segment and Young Poor Segment, and the projected requirement is an additional 692 million jobs by 2045 to maintain the current levels of employment rate.

Number of Employed in Older Countries

In the two older Country Segments the number of employed people is projected to decline. This is primarily due to the aforementioned decline in the working-age population in rural China (see a separate discussion on this in Chapter Ten which focuses on China). The aggregate decline of employed persons in the two older Country Segments is 133 million persons by 2045. However, this does require some breakdown by type.

Maintaining the current propensity to be employed through to 2045 would mean that China would have 187 million fewer rural workers but 70 million more urban workers – which logically will come from the decline in work opportunities in the rural areas. In total China is projected to have 117 million fewer workers. The other countries in the Older Low-Income segment will have 22 million fewer workers given the decline in working age and the Older Affluent segment would lose 4.3 million workers.

If the decline in employment in Rural China is excluded, then the Older Country Segments only lose 26 million workers over the next 25 years as a result of a declining working-age population. This is not significant in the context of 681 million employed persons in 2019 and the growth of robotics.

This means that for the two older segments excluding China the net loss of workers due to the changing age profile but maintaining the propensity to be employed would be 26 million jobs, on a 2019 base of 681 million employed persons. This loss of workers is compensated for by a mere 4% lift in productivity in total over the next 26 years. It also means that there is little variation in the dependency ratios and there is not a significant need for an immigrant workforce to maintain the economy.

The reality is that the potential 26 million jobs available in the older countries does little to address the need for 692 million additional jobs in the two younger Country Segments.

Number of Employed in Younger Countries

To leverage the 'demographic dividend' of projected increases in the working-age populations, these countries must at least maintain the current levels of worker participation rates between 2019 and 2045. That means the Young Poor Segment is going to need to create an additional 443 million additional jobs and the Family Stage Low Income Segment requires an additional 248 million jobs by 2045.

In total, 692 million additional employment opportunities must be created by 2045.

That is a 41% increase in the number of employed persons in these Countries in 2019. That is a growth rate of 1.3% per annum. To achieve that there must be growth in global consumer demand and investment in productive capacity in these countries.

The issue is that the total population of the older countries which account for 78% of global household consumption is not growing (refer to Chapter Four) and real growth in their incomes is also slowing from 2.3% pa to 1.9% pa (refer to Chapter Seven). In total, the growth rate of household consumption expenditure in the two older Country Segments is projected to decline from 2.3% per annum for the last decade to 1.9% per annum to 2030 and then to 1.1% per annum to 2045.

Slowing global demand growth combined with robotics, automation and Artificial Intelligence creates a real concern about the availability of work for these relatively poorly educated populations. That has serious social implications. This is demonstrated in numbers in the last Chapter.

Slowing global demand combined with robotics, automation and AI creates a real concern about the availability of work. That has serious implications.

Required Employment to Maintain Existing Propensity to be Employed

The following sections of this Chapter look at the required employment levels for each of the four Country Segments by multiplying the number of persons of working age by the trend in the propensity to be employed considering improvements in education profile and accumulated Fixed Capital Investment per worker. It also examines the implications of that for the overall dependency ratio.

Dependency Ratio Defined

This term is used throughout this Chapter. It is the number of non-working persons per working person.

It is calculated by subtracting the number of employed persons from the total population – which gives the number of non-employed (dependents) and that is divided by the number who are employed. Typically, the resulting number is between 1 and 2. That means that the worker is supporting between 1 and 2 other persons in addition to themselves. The lower the figure the better.

The Old Affluent

Table 6-5 shows the projected number of working-age persons based on the changing age profile of the relevant populations, their projected propensity to be employed based on the historic level and trend of that, and the resulting number that would be employed under those projections

The forecast of employed persons is significantly driven by the projections in terms of propensity to be employed as shown in columns 5 to 8 in this Table. This in turn is based on trends in the education profile of the adult population (by gender) and Accumulated Fixed Capital Investment per worker.

Overall, for this set of countries, the propensity to be employed is static at 65% reflecting the fact that these countries already have a high standard of education and accumulated Fixed Capital Investment per worker. In addition, because of universal education, these countries also have high female participation rates.

The collective impact of the share of the population that is working age and their propensity to be employed means that most of the countries in this Segment would have sufficient workers to maintain low dependency ratios as compared to the other three Country Segments.

But there are some countries in this Country Segment where the dependency ratio is over 1.2. Most of them are in Western Europe and two are countries whose labour force has been decimated by the European Union. The European Union allows free movement of labour between member countries and not surprisingly there has been a movement from the less affluent (lower-paying) countries to the more affluent (higher paying) ones- particularly of the more skilled workers. As such Italy and Spain (and Greece in the next Country Segment) have declining workforces.

But those countries with a high dependency ratio in this Country Segment are the exception. The average is a very low 1.06 in 2019 and only 4 countries in this segment have a ratio over 1.2 which is low relative to the other Country Segments.

Table 6-5: Working-age, Employed, Dependency Ratio - Older Affluent Country Segment. 2019 to 2045.

	Working Age mns 15-74 yrs.			Propensity to be employed			Expected number to be employed			Dependency Ratio	
	2019	2030	2045	2019	2030	2045	2019	2030	2045	2019	2045
Australia	18.6	20.4	21.7	68%	69%	70%	12.6	14.0	15.1	0.99	1.03
Austria	6.8	7.3	7.6	65%	66%	66%	4.4	4.8	5.0	1.02	1.08
Belgium	8.5	8.9	9.0	57%	58%	59%	4.8	5.1	5.3	1.38	1.41
Canada	28.7	30.6	32.2	67%	68%	69%	19.3	20.9	22.2	0.93	1.02
Denmark	4.3	4.3	4.3	66%	65%	65%	2.9	2.8	2.8	1.02	1.18
Finland	4.1	4.0	3.9	62%	63%	64%	2.6	2.6	2.5	1.16	1.18
France	47.3	47.3	45.4	57%	58%	58%	27.0	27.3	26.5	1.41	1.52
Germany	62.3	64.9	66.2	68%	69%	71%	42.3	44.9	46.8	0.97	0.99
Hong Kong	6.0	6.0	5.8	63%	63%	64%	3.8	3.8	3.7	0.98	1.25
Iceland	0.3	0.3	0.3	79%	79%	79%	0.2	0.2	0.2	0.71	0.76
Ireland	3.6	4.1	4.5	64%	65%	65%	2.3	2.6	2.9	1.15	1.12
Italy	45.4	44.5	39.3	52%	53%	53%	23.4	23.4	21.0	1.58	1.70
Japan	92.9	84.7	74.0	72%	72%	73%	66.8	61.3	53.8	0.90	1.03
Macao	0.5	0.6	0.6	72%	74%	76%	0.4	0.4	0.5	0.68	0.74
Netherlands	12.9	12.7	11.8	68%	69%	71%	8.8	8.8	8.3	0.93	1.05
New Zealand	3.5	3.8	3.8	73%	74%	75%	2.6	2.8	2.9	0.85	0.89
Norway	4.0	4.4	4.6	68%	68%	68%	2.7	3.0	3.1	0.96	1.02
Sth Korea	41.4	40.6	33.9	65%	66%	66%	26.9	26.6	22.4	0.90	1.18
Singapore	4.9	4.9	4.5	71%	72%	72%	3.4	3.5	3.3	0.69	0.88
Slovenia	1.6	1.5	1.4	63%	63%	64%	1.0	1.0	0.9	1.11	1.31
Spain	35.3	35.0	30.5	56%	58%	60%	19.7	20.3	18.4	1.36	1.37
Sweden	7.3	7.7	8.3	68%	68%	69%	5.0	5.3	5.7	1.01	1.09
Switzerland	6.5	6.9	7.1	73%	73%	73%	4.8	5.1	5.2	0.80	0.94
United Kingdom	49.7	52.2	52.8	67%	68%	69%	33.5	35.4	36.2	1.01	1.07
USA	245.6	254.7	253.4	65%	65%	64%	160.0	164.4	162.1	1.05	1.17
Total	742.0	752.2	727.1	65%	65%	66%	481.3	490.3	476.9	1.06	1.16

Overall, the total 'required' employed labour force of the countries in this Country Segment is stable (down 1% over 25 years) and except for the few countries mentioned above with a high dependency ratio, there is relatively little threat of them not having enough workers to support the dependent age groups.

Japan: Out of Step or the New Way?

Japan is of relevance here as it represents a combination of factors that are potential indicators of the new norm.

First, as a country, it has a history of limited immigration. As such the existing and future age and gender profile of its population is almost totally a function of internal factors – specifically births and deaths.

Second, it is one of the oldest countries in the world. They have a good education standard and good health services and as a result, have a longer life expectancy than most other countries. This means they can, and have, extended their working-age to 74 years.

Third, it is one of the few countries to already be experiencing a decline in total population. (But note that it will be joined by others in the next decade).

Figure 6-11 shows the historic and projected age profile of Japan's population. In total, the population has been declining since 2010 when it was at 129 million persons, and it is projected to continue to decline slowly to 109 million by 2045. The projected decline is in the under 65-year age groups – all down 25% on the 2019 base by 2045. The 65 to 74 age group is stable in absolute size, and growth (24%) is in the oldest group. That is persons aged 75 and above.

This in turn means that the working-age population of Japan declines as a proportion of the total population. In aggregate the 15-to-74-year age range is 73% of the total population in 2019 and by 2045 it is expected to be 68%. The decline is moderated by the increasing proportion of the population aged 65 to 74 – extended working age.

Given the trend in the propensity to be employed, this means that the total employed as a percentage of the population is 53% in 2019 and is projected to drop to 49% by 2045.

Figure 6-11: Changing Age Profile of Japan 2019 to 2045.

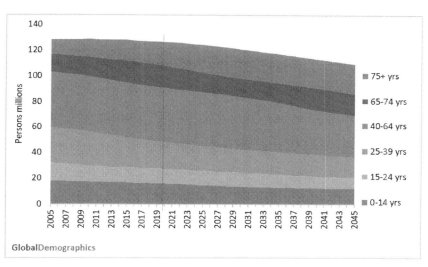

GlobalDemographics

This is a relatively small change and means that Japan's dependency ratio, which is already low by global norms at 0.9 dependents per worker, increases marginally to 1.03 by 2045. Very few countries have a dependency ratio lower than that even in 2019.

A different picture would exist if the working age had not increased to include 65 to 74 years.

The Older Low-Income Countries

The employment profile of these countries is given in Table 6-6. This group of countries is quite different from the previous segment. Except for one country (Uruguay) the total employed labour force is projected to decline in absolute size – in some cases quite significantly. For example, Portugal is projected to have 26% fewer workers by 2045 than it had in 2019. For Greece, it is 28% less.

Table 6-6: Projected Change in the Working-age Population, Labour Force Size and Dependency Ratios for the Old Low-Income Countries.

	Working Age mns 15-64 yrs.			Propensity to be employed			Employed Mns			Dependency Ratio	
	2019	2030	2045	2019	2030	2045	2019	2030	2045	2019	2045
Albania	2.0	1.8	1.5	56%	58%	56%	1.1	1.0	0.9	1.60	1.75
Belarus	6.4	5.9	5.5	71%	78%	80%	4.6	4.6	4.4	1.07	1.06
Bulgaria	4.5	4.1	3.3	66%	67%	70%	3.0	2.7	2.3	1.37	1.44
Cuba	7.8	7.1	6.0	62%	65%	67%	4.8	4.6	4.1	1.37	1.55
Czechia	6.9	6.8	6.1	73%	72%	76%	5.0	4.9	4.6	1.14	1.31
Estonia	0.8	0.8	0.8	75%	78%	79%	0.6	0.6	0.6	1.11	1.13
Georgia	2.6	2.4	2.3	69%	70%	69%	1.8	1.7	1.6	1.24	1.40
Greece	6.7	6.1	4.7	54%	55%	56%	3.6	3.3	2.6	1.87	2.33
Hungary	6.4	6.0	5.1	66%	68%	72%	4.2	4.1	3.7	1.28	1.32
Latvia	1.2	1.0	0.7	71%	76%	79%	0.9	0.7	0.6	1.19	1.35
Lithuania	1.8	1.3	0.9	72%	77%	78%	1.3	1.0	0.7	1.16	1.47
Mauritius	0.9	0.9	0.8	61%	63%	64%	0.5	0.5	0.5	1.31	1.42
Poland	25.3	23.1	19.7	65%	68%	70%	16.5	15.6	13.8	1.29	1.39
Portugal	6.6	5.9	4.6	70%	71%	74%	4.6	4.2	3.4	1.20	1.50
Moldova	2.9	2.7	2.3	49%	51%	50%	1.4	1.4	1.2	1.82	1.89
Romania	12.7	11.4	8.8	64%	63%	64%	8.1	7.1	5.6	1.39	1.75
Russia	97.3	91.3	88.4	69%	73%	74%	67.0	66.4	65.2	1.17	1.25
Slovakia	3.7	3.5	3.0	66%	67%	69%	2.4	2.3	2.1	1.23	1.38
Thailand	49.3	46.6	40.1	77%	80%	81%	37.7	37.2	32.6	0.84	1.07
Ukraine	29.6	27.2	23.4	58%	59%	59%	17.2	16.0	13.9	1.55	1.67
Uruguay	2.2	2.3	2.3	70%	73%	75%	1.6	1.6	1.7	1.21	1.15
China	996.4	955.7	827.3	75%	75%	76%	746.7	717.3	630.0	0.89	1.15
Total	1,274.0	1,213.7	1,057.1	73%	74%	75%	934.8	899.1	796.1	0.95	1.19
Total Excl China	277.6	257.9	230.5	68%	70%	72%	188.1	181.8	166.1	1.19	1.32
Urban China	595.8	667.2	666.7	75%	77%	78%	447.8	511.1	518.1	0.87	1.13
Rural China	400.6	288.5	160.5	75%	71%	70%	298.9	206.2	111.9	0.91	1.23

The principal reason for this decline in the size of the workforce is the projected decline in the number of persons of working age (which for these countries is ages 15 to 64 years). That is a function of reduced births, ageing and emigration.

Some of these countries are in the EU and their skilled labour can easily move to other countries that have higher pay rates (such as Germany and France) and there is no evidence to date that they will return to their native country. See an earlier discussion on the impact of emigration on Greece in Chapter 3.

In addition, many of these countries have a declining total number of births as a result of a reducing birth rate and, because of emigration, fewer women of childbearing age. Consequently, the number of new entrants into working age is in rapid decline.

This means that the Dependency Ratio increases for these countries. Excluding China, it is projected to increase from 1.19 in 2019 to reach 1.32 by 2045. Some of these may need immigration to protect their lifestyle.

China – Two Scenarios in One Country

China is shown at the bottom of Table 6-6 and is an interesting 'labour market' going forward. As shown in this Table the total employed labour force of China declines by 16% over the next 25 years. However, the labour force situation in China is more complex. There are two labour forces – urban and rural, with quite different dynamics. **The dynamics of each of the two labour forces of China are shown at the bottom of Table 6-6.**

As shown, the decline in employed persons is exclusively within the rural labour force. The urban labour force, which is 3 times more productive than the rural one (based on wages), is still expanding in absolute size through to 2045 although most of the growth is before 2033.

This dynamic of a declining rural working-age population and a growing urban one is due to the ongoing rural to urban migration facilitated by the availability of education to everyone including rural persons. While the rate of rural to urban migration is projected to slow, it continues at a sufficient level to sustain the growth of the productive (urban) sector of the workforce to 2045. As such the ongoing growth of the Chinese economy is not threatened by the decline in the absolute number of workers. It is the number of more productive Urban based workers that is of relevance here.

While the total labour force of China is projected to decline by 16%
by 2045, all this decline is in the rural labour force (down 62%). In
contrast, the Urban (and much more productive) labour force is
projected to grow by 16% in absolute size between 2019 and 2045.

The Family Stage Low Income Segment

The changing employment profile for this segment is shown in Table 6-7.
Overall, this segment of countries is characterised by steady growth in
both the working-age population and employed population. The total
working-age population of these countries is projected to grow from 2.1
billion persons in 2019 to reach 2.47 billion in 2045.

That is an additional 370 million working-age persons by 2045, and if they
can increase their propensity to be employed from the average for 2019
of 57% to the projected 59% for 2045 (reflecting improvements in
education), then this group of countries would need to place an additional
248 million people in work over the next 26 years. That is an additional
9.6 million employed persons a year. Failure to achieve this would mean
lower household incomes and slower growth of the consumer market in
these countries and potential political tension.

The forecasts assume a marginal increase in the propensity to be
employed from its 2019 levels, but this is frail. India for example has held
its level at just over 50% for the last 5 years but is well down on its 2005
rate of 58.6% and 2009 rate of 55.3%.

This is a concern, as during that same period education and fixed capital
investment (the two drivers of employment) increased. This is discussed
in more detail in Chapter Eleven which focuses on India, but it does mean
that between 2009 and 2019 India was *unable* to find enough jobs for the
new entrants to the working-age population. It is short by 45 million jobs
– or an average of 4.5 million per annum. That means there were around
4.5 million households each year that expected an additional wage earner
and did not get it. (Note, it may be the new younger entrant into working

age and employment has displaced an older less educated employed person. Either way, a job has been lost.)

Table 6-7: Projected Change in the Working-age Population, Labour Force Size and Dependency Ratios for the Family Stage Low Income Countries.

	Working Age mns 15-64 yrs.			Propensity to be employed			Employed Mns			Dependency Ratio	
	2019	2030	2045	2019	2030	2045	2019	2030	2045	2019	2045
Algeria	27.1	32.2	39.5	39%	41%	43%	10.6	13.2	17.1	3.05	2.85
Argentina	28.7	31.8	34.3	63%	65%	67%	18.2	20.5	22.9	1.46	1.30
Armenia	2.0	1.9	1.9	52%	54%	53%	1.0	1.0	1.0	1.85	1.89
Azerbaijan	7.0	7.4	7.6	67%	71%	71%	4.7	5.2	5.4	1.13	1.11
Bangladesh	110.2	124.5	127.5	60%	61%	63%	66.5	76.3	80.4	1.45	1.18
Bolivia	7.1	8.5	9.6	76%	76%	78%	5.4	6.5	7.4	1.13	0.90
Brazil	147.1	152.8	148.6	62%	64%	65%	91.4	97.1	96.3	1.31	1.36
Cambodia	10.6	12.4	14.2	87%	89%	89%	9.2	11.0	12.6	0.79	0.56
Chile	13.0	14.4	15.5	66%	69%	71%	8.6	9.9	10.9	1.21	1.16
Colombia	34.5	38.9	42.0	68%	70%	72%	23.6	27.3	30.2	1.13	1.03
Dominican Rep	7.0	7.7	8.2	66%	68%	69%	4.6	5.2	5.7	1.33	1.21
Ecuador	11.3	13.4	15.6	72%	73%	74%	8.1	9.7	11.6	1.15	1.03
El Salvador	4.2	4.4	4.3	63%	64%	66%	2.6	2.8	2.8	1.45	1.22
India	915.6	1,029.3	1,082.8	50%	50%	50%	461.4	515.4	541.1	1.96	1.81
Indonesia	183.2	203.0	215.6	69%	71%	73%	126.5	144.0	157.0	1.14	1.12
Iran	57.2	62.9	66.1	42%	43%	45%	24.2	27.3	29.6	2.42	2.36
Kazakhstan	11.8	13.0	15.2	71%	74%	75%	8.4	9.7	11.4	1.21	1.31
Malaysia	22.2	24.7	26.6	67%	68%	69%	14.8	16.8	18.5	1.16	1.05
Mexico	84.7	94.8	100.4	64%	65%	67%	54.1	61.9	67.3	1.36	1.23
Morocco	24.0	26.7	29.1	45%	47%	49%	10.9	12.7	14.2	2.35	2.18
Myanmar	36.8	39.1	38.6	66%	66%	67%	24.2	25.9	26.0	1.24	1.16
Nicaragua	4.2	4.8	5.2	67%	70%	74%	2.8	3.4	3.9	1.31	0.99
Panama	2.8	3.3	3.8	71%	72%	74%	1.9	2.4	2.8	1.18	1.14
Paraguay	4.5	5.2	5.7	75%	76%	78%	3.4	3.9	4.4	1.09	0.81
Peru	21.6	25.9	29.8	83%	87%	94%	17.8	22.6	28.0	0.82	0.65
Philippines	69.4	82.2	91.2	62%	63%	64%	43.2	51.8	58.2	1.51	1.23
Saudi Arabia	24.5	30.3	33.0	54%	57%	60%	13.4	17.3	19.9	1.56	1.11
South Africa	38.4	44.9	51.5	43%	43%	44%	16.4	19.4	22.6	2.58	2.37
Sri Lanka	13.9	14.0	13.3	58%	60%	62%	8.1	8.4	8.2	1.63	1.77
Tunisia	7.9	8.4	8.9	43%	44%	45%	3.4	3.7	4.0	2.48	2.49
Turkey	55.7	64.2	69.5	50%	51%	52%	28.1	32.6	36.1	1.96	1.94
Uzbekistan	22.0	25.2	28.6	64%	67%	69%	14.1	16.8	19.6	1.34	1.12
Venezuela RB	18.7	16.3	12.3	59%	61%	63%	11.1	10.0	7.8	1.61	1.63
Viet Nam	66.8	69.9	69.8	83%	86%	88%	55.1	59.9	61.3	0.75	0.75
Total	2,095.5	2,338.3	2,465.7	57%	58%	59%	1,197.7	1,351.7	1,446.2	1.61	1.49
Total Excl India	1,179.9	1,308.9	1,382.9	62%	64%	65%	736.3	836.3	905.1	1.38	1.29

However, this concern is not unique to India in this Country Segment. Under the assumptions made in terms of propensity of working-aged people to be employed with each country on average increasing from 57%

to 59%, the total number of employed persons would need to increase by 21% over the next 26 years from 1.2 billion to 1.45 billion. Can that be achieved?

India has been unable to find enough jobs for the new entrants to the working-age population in the last decade. It fell short by 45 million jobs – or an average of 4.5 million per annum with the proportion of working-age in work declining from 58% in 2005 to 50% in 2019.

The worry in terms of the smaller countries is the absolute increase in employment that needs to be achieved. This is driven mostly by the projected rapid increase in the number of persons of working age which is inevitable given the existing age profile of the population.

Finally, the Dependency Ratio. Relative to the preceding two Country Segments, this Country Segment in 2019 is quite high at 1.61. This means that each worker is supporting themselves and 1.61 other persons – a total of 2.61 persons. This does mean the per capita spending power of the household is more constrained.

The good news is that this ratio is projected to decline by 2045 under the assumptions made about the propensity to be employed. However, if the individual countries cannot maintain or achieve the projected level of propensity to be employed then the dependency ratio will increase with a consequent lowering of per capita incomes.

The Young Poor Segment of Countries

This is the problem area in terms of future employment. The amount of change expected to take place within this Country Segment is considerable. Table 6-8 provides details by country. In total, the number of persons of working age is projected to increase from 742 million in 2019 to reach 1,418 million by 2045. That is a 91% increase and 26 million persons a year. This forecast has a high level of confidence.

Based on the 2019 propensity to be employed and assuming that it will improve because of the marginal improvements in the education profile of the workforce, it is expected that the total employed labour force would grow from 475 million persons to 918 million in 2045 – a 93% increase in workers. As shown in Table 6-8, in some countries, under the assumption that work can be found, the employed workforce would more than double in size.

Uganda, for example, is projected to increase its labour force from 16.2 million to 41.8 million by 2045. This increase is mainly driven by the increasing number of persons reaching working age and a very marginal increase in propensity to be employed because of improvements in education and fixed capital investment. If the forecast of a stable propensity to be employed is wrong, then the implications would be considerable. The risk of the forecast being wrong is considered high for reasons discussed in Chapter Eight.

Will Uganda be able to find an additional 25.6 million jobs? This requires that total employment grows at 3.9% per annum for 25 years. What competitive advantage does this country have over the other countries in this segment (as well as many in the preceding segment) such that it can create this amount of additional employment? Even if the propensity to be employed dropped to the Country Segment average of 65% in 2045 it would still need to double its employed workforce by 2045.

Of course, the answer to this question is unknown. One hopes that such employment will happen because of increased affluence in the world and a resulting increase in demand for products (particularly) and services. This is discussed in a later chapter. However, the indications are that perhaps the work opportunity is not actually there and that will create a sociological disaster.

Table 6-8: Projected Change in the Working-age Population, Labour Force Size and Dependency Ratios for the Young Poor Countries.

	Working Age mns 15-64 yrs.			Propensity to be employed			Employed Mns			Dependency Ratio	
	2019	2030	2045	2019	2030	2045	2019	2030	2045	2019	2045
Angola	16.3	24.3	39.3	75%	75%	75%	12.2	18.2	29.4	1.63	1.34
Botswana	1.4	1.8	2.3	62%	64%	68%	0.9	1.2	1.6	1.62	1.24
Burkina Faso	10.8	15.3	22.9	65%	63%	61%	7.0	9.6	13.9	1.94	1.79
Cameroon	14.2	19.7	28.1	77%	76%	76%	10.9	15.0	21.4	1.40	1.10
Chad	8.1	11.7	18.0	72%	72%	72%	5.8	8.4	12.9	1.77	1.33
DR Congo	44.3	65.0	106.3	64%	62%	61%	28.2	40.4	64.7	2.12	2.09
Egypt	61.1	75.8	98.7	44%	45%	45%	27.1	33.9	44.5	2.71	2.66
Ethiopia	62.9	87.1	122.8	82%	83%	84%	51.8	72.1	103.1	1.18	0.74
Ghana	18.1	23.3	30.6	68%	68%	67%	12.2	15.7	20.7	1.50	1.34
Guatemala	10.8	13.6	16.5	65%	66%	67%	7.0	8.9	11.0	1.52	1.11
Guinea	6.9	9.7	14.4	62%	62%	61%	4.2	6.0	8.8	2.04	1.58
Haiti	7.0	8.2	9.1	62%	63%	63%	4.4	5.1	5.8	1.59	1.21
Honduras	6.2	7.6	8.6	69%	70%	71%	4.3	5.3	6.1	1.25	0.98
Kenya	30.7	41.9	55.0	75%	76%	77%	23.1	31.8	42.5	1.29	0.85
Lao PDR	4.6	5.5	6.2	83%	84%	86%	3.8	4.6	5.3	0.90	0.60
Madagascar	15.3	20.8	29.4	89%	90%	92%	13.6	18.8	27.0	1.00	0.66
Malawi	10.0	14.4	20.8	76%	75%	76%	7.6	10.9	15.8	1.47	0.99
Mali	9.9	14.4	22.6	69%	68%	68%	6.8	9.9	15.5	1.93	1.68
Mozambique	16.0	22.9	35.2	79%	78%	78%	12.7	17.9	27.3	1.41	1.21
Namibia	1.5	1.9	2.4	50%	51%	52%	0.7	1.0	1.3	2.38	2.04
Nepal	18.6	23.2	26.9	89%	89%	91%	16.5	20.7	24.4	0.74	0.41
Niger	11.1	17.4	31.4	75%	75%	74%	8.4	13.0	23.2	1.83	1.72
Nigeria	107.7	147.0	214.9	51%	50%	50%	55.1	73.9	106.6	2.69	2.56
Pakistan	131.3	165.2	209.9	53%	54%	55%	70.0	89.3	115.1	2.11	1.68
Rwanda	7.2	9.7	13.5	87%	87%	87%	6.3	8.4	11.6	1.02	0.71
Senegal	8.8	12.4	18.4	45%	44%	43%	4.0	5.5	7.9	3.14	2.93
South Sudan	6.1	7.0	8.3	67%	67%	67%	4.1	4.7	5.6	1.73	1.50
Sudan	24.1	32.2	45.0	43%	43%	43%	10.4	13.8	19.3	3.16	2.86
Uganda	22.8	35.8	58.2	71%	71%	72%	16.2	25.5	41.8	1.74	1.19
Tanzania	31.1	44.5	68.7	85%	85%	85%	26.5	37.9	58.7	1.21	1.05
Zambia	9.5	13.9	21.0	69%	69%	70%	6.5	9.6	14.6	1.75	1.31
Zimbabwe	8.0	10.2	12.8	83%	83%	85%	6.6	8.5	10.9	1.22	1.08
Total	742.2	1,003.7	1,418.2	64%	64%	65%	474.9	645.5	918.4	1.80	1.51

The number of persons of working age in the Young Poor countries is projected to increase from 742 million in 2019 to reach 1,418 million by 2045. That is a 91% increase and 26 million persons a year. To maintain current employment rates a total of 443 million extra jobs need to be created by 2045. Failure to do so would be catastrophic for these countries.

To Conclude

Three key issues emerge from the analysis in this Chapter.

First, there is a very substantial number of additional persons reaching working age in the next 25 years and the world will need to find 692 million extra jobs (half of that in the next decade) just to maintain existing levels of employment relative to the total population.

The demand for these extra jobs is almost exclusively in the young countries which generally have inadequate education systems. As such the type of work being sought is low skilled and that is most easily replaced by robots and automation – and in factories located near the market rather than where the labour is.

The inability of countries in these regions to find work for their young populations would inevitably lead to social unrest and illegal migration (which is already the case). If you have poor education, no job and no obvious opportunities then moving to where there is some work is an inevitable drive.

Second, the problem of finding enough employment is exacerbated by the changing nature of the labour force in the older countries. In the older affluent countries, the change is already in process. That is the extension of working age. Working to age 74 is quite rapidly becoming the norm rather than the exception and these skilled, well-educated and in good health, workers are playing a significant role in maintaining the 'dependent to worker' ratio which is already low.

As shown in this Chapter, the dependency ratio in Japan is not increasing rapidly and is low by global standards. This of course shuts off the opportunity for people from young countries to find work there – even assuming they have the requisite skill level.

Third, the risk of there not being enough employment opportunities is high. Not only because of the rapid increase in the number of people looking for work but also as shown earlier in Chapter Four, the number of consumers in the affluent regions which account for 78% of global consumption expenditure is not expected to grow as rapidly in future as it did in the past. That may reduce the demand for goods to be made in remote factories (thereby reducing employment opportunities in the young countries).

The 'Demographic Dividend ', so often touted for India and Africa, is at risk. It only pays out if the increased working-age population can find work.

This combination of events, rapid increase in the number seeking work, the extended working life of those in countries which account for most consumption, and the reduced growth rate in the number of key consumers (and potential demand for goods and services) is potentially a major sociological risk. A large unemployed population is not a good scenario.

Summary Profile – Employment

Older Affluent [Note: Working age is 15 to 74 yrs]	2019	2030	2045
Working Age Pop. (mns)	742	752	727
As % Population	74.9%	73.4%	70.6%
Growth pa of working age	0.4%	0.1%	-0.2%
Propensity to be employed	64.9%	65.2%	65.6%
Total Employed (mns)	481	490	477
Growth pa of Employed pers.	0.9%	0.2%	-0.2%
Dependency Ratio	1.06	1.09	1.16
GDP per worker (US$)	101,297	120,058	149,205
Growth of GDP per worker	0.5%	1.6%	1.5%
Avg Wage per worker (US$)	65,155	76,812	91,206
Avg wage as % GDP pw	64%	64%	61%

Older Low Income [Note: Working age is 15 to 64 yrs]	2019	2030	2045
Working Age Pop. (mns)	1,274	1,214	1,058
As % Population	69.9%	66.1%	60.8%
Growth pa of working age	0.0%	-0.4%	-0.9%
Propensity to be employed	73.4%	74.1%	75.3%
Total Employed (mns)	935	899	796
Growth pa of Employed pers.	-0.1%	-0.4%	-0.8%
Dependency Ratio	0.95	1.04	1.19
GDP per worker (US$)	20,034	33,119	55,200
Growth of GDP per worker	6.0%	4.7%	3.5%
Avg Wage per worker (US$)	12,837	21,039	34,188
Avg wage as % GDP pw	64%	64%	62%

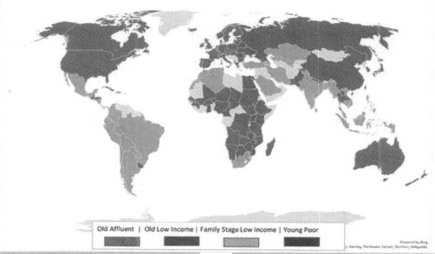

Old Affluent | Old Low Income | Family Stage Low Income | Young Poor

Family Stage Low Income [Note: Working age is 15 to 64 yrs]	2019	2030	2045
Working Age Pop. (mns)	2,095	2,338	2,466
As % Population	67.1%	68.3%	68.6%
Growth pa of working age	1.6%	1.0%	0.4%
Propensity to be employed	57.2%	57.8%	58.7%
Total Employed (mns)	1,198	1,352	1,446
Growth pa of Employed pers.	1.3%	1.1%	0.5%
Dependency Ratio	1.61	1.53	1.49
GDP per worker (US$)	11,183	13,182	17,980
Growth of GDP per worker	2.4%	1.5%	2.1%
Avg Wage per worker (US$)	8,019	9,439	12,820
Avg wage as % GDP pw	72%	72%	71%

Young Poor [Note: Working age is 15 to 64 yrs]	2019	2030	2045
Working Age Pop. (mns)	742	1,004	1,418
As % Population	55.7%	58.5%	61.4%
Growth pa of working age	2.9%	2.8%	2.3%
Propensity to be employed	64.0%	64.3%	64.8%
Total Employed (mns)	475	645	918
Growth pa of Employed pers.	2.5%	2.8%	2.4%
Dependency Ratio	1.80	1.66	1.51
GDP per worker (US$)	4,069	4,954	7,321
Growth of GDP per worker	1.7%	1.8%	2.6%
Avg Wage per worker (US$)	3,176	3,898	5,651
Avg wage as % GDP pw	78%	79%	77%

Chapter 7
Incomes

Note: All financial data in this and the next chapter is expressed in United States Dollars in 2019 real values. That is, the effect of inflation has been removed from historic data and all trends identified exclude the impact of inflation. The conversion rate used is the average exchange rate of the local currency to US Dollars for the 2019 year as published by the World Bank. 2019 has been used as 2020 has been 'disturbed' by the pandemic.

What this Chapter is About

This chapter is going to be contentious! First, there is the issue of "what is household income?" Second, there are the glaring inequalities that exist between, and within, countries.

In terms of *what is household income*, the definition and methodology used for this book are explained in the next section of this chapter. It is not intended as a definitive definition. Rather, it is just the measurement method used in this book. It is sufficient to say that it is a method that the Author found could be applied relatively consistently across multiple countries and which produces figures which were defensible in the context of the wider economy.

That is to say, total incomes (number of households multiplied by the average household income) do not *exceed* total GDP and are not *below* the amount spent in the economy as measured by the Private Consumption Expenditure component of GDP. Thus, it is in the 'right ballpark'.

The distribution of households around that average is more problematic. We accept there is a possible discrepancy here, but we have used the best available data (specifically Household Income and Expenditure Surveys for each country that it is available) to indicate what it is probably like. If the reader has better data on this which is available across a broad section of countries including those with less than adequate standards of measurement of the national economy and society, we would like to hear about it and explore using it.

Given these caveats, this chapter is about the enabler of lifestyles. The more money (income) one has the better the quality of lifestyle in terms of access to food, shelter, health care, education and ultimately self-actualisation and leisure. Classic Maslow's Need Hierarchy.

In an ideal world, everyone has the same income and can afford an idyllic lifestyle. But the reality is far, far away from that. This chapter reveals how significant the differences are. Sadly, there will in the near future (to 2045 at least) be a continuing wide difference in terms of income both between individual countries as well as within countries. This chapter reveals just how wide that is.

Claims of a growing middle class in the Young Poor Countries hide an unfortunate truth – the lowest income segment is growing even faster. The lowest income segment (under US$5,000 pa) increased by 74 million households in the last decade. The middle income (US$15,000) and above increased by 54 million households.

But on the plus side, for most countries, it does show how the median income is improving. But - and this is important to note – this does not mean that the number of poor households (and persons) is declining. It has not been and is not projected to. In the Young Poor Country Segment, the *number* (if not proportion) of households in the lowest income segment is projected to increase in all but 4 of the 32 countries in that segment. That is of concern as such growing inequality ultimately destabilizes a country – and these countries are not particularly stable anyhow.

But First, The Issue of Measurement

The problem with reporting incomes for a country – let alone multiple countries – is one of measurement. There is first the issue of self-reporting. Most people – unless they are doing well – do not like to tell strangers (interviewers) what they earn – including the tax department, where there is one.

There are government data collection agencies such as tax and social security departments but generally, that information is very confidential.

There is also the question of what is income? Earned income only? What about capital gains? Social security payments?

In short, it is very hard to get a real figure that is comparable to spending power, without even considering the issue of relative purchasing power.

For that reason, we have taken a somewhat different approach to measure what the average household gets as income. It has some defensible parameters and, more importantly, can be applied consistently across all countries with at least a basic national statistical reporting system.

The constraints we look at are:

Determining the *maximum* wage per average worker:

This is Gross Domestic Product per worker. Typically, people do not get paid more than they contribute – at least not over the medium and long term - so hence it is the effective maximum average wage for the country.

Gross Domestic Product per worker is made up of two variables, total Gross Domestic Product, and the number of workers. It can be reliably measured in that total Gross Domestic Product is a well-understood aggregate statistic and has a reasonably clear method behind its collection and aggregation. Countries can fudge it, but they generally get caught out as other statistics do not 'add up'.

The other variable in this equation is the size of the workforce (number of workers) and this is also generally reasonably well measured. It is subject to constraints such as the number of persons of working age (ignoring for the moment child labour). Again, it is a gross statistic that can be validated to some extent.

Dividing the total Gross Domestic Product by the number of workers determines what the maximum *average* wage per worker can be.

Determining the minimum average wage per worker

Private Consumption expenditure, after adjusting for the 'charity' component (typically 5-7%), is a measure of the total consumption expenditure of all households. It is measured at the wholesale level, so it has the added advantage of catching all expenditures of households. Irrespective of whether the income used for that expenditure has been reported to the appropriate authorities (Tax) or not. The subjective issue with this measure is the impact of tourism – inward and outward. Generally, the net position is not enough to significantly move the total.

Dividing Private Consumption Expenditure (discounted by 5% to allow for charities) by the number of households (which is also a reasonably reliable statistic at the gross level) gives a defensible *average* expenditure per household of all households in the country.

To this must be added the average Income tax take per household – this is available for many countries in gross terms. This is the aggregate tax on earned income and is the same as expenditure – it must be paid.

This is then divided by the average number of workers per household. Again, there is some reliability in the reported number of workers and the number of households, so there is a reasonably accurate measure of the number of workers per household

Dividing average expenditure (including tax) per household by the number of workers per household provides the average *minimum* wage per worker because over the medium-term people can only spend what they earn. This estimated wage is the minimum. Wages can, and typically will be higher than this minimum, the difference being Savings that are not in the Private Consumption Expenditure total.

Possible average wage range

The residual between the maximum average wage and the minimum average wage is then a combination of average household savings and the share of GDP per worker that is retained by the employer to pay for the capital employed.

The range can be further reduced if two other assumptions are applied.

- Factors determining the share of GDP per worker paid in wages

  No business would pay out all its earnings in wages. Some – at least 10% - would be retained for payment for capital (equipment or cash flow) used in production including depreciation and savings for a 'rainy day'. The highest proportion of GDP per worker paid out in wages is almost certainly less than 100% and probably closer to 70%.

  To refine this further we have sought to understand the relationship between GDP per worker (gross productivity) and wages per worker. For many countries, it is possible to get the estimated average income per worker from the Household Income and Expenditure survey (that is, where the country reports gross income as well as expenditure) and use that as a base to develop a function of the relationship between GDP per worker and the proportion that is paid out in wages. It has been found that:

- the greater the level of education of the worker,
- the greater the accumulated Fixed Capital Investment per worker and
- the higher the proportion of the population employed.

the lower will be the wage paid as a percentage of GDP.

This data set, using 65 countries and a 12-year period has an explained variance of 57% which, while not overwhelming, is at a sufficiently high level to not be random. We use this function to derive the wage per worker given GDP per worker.

- Propensity to save. An average household would save some of its income. It is recognised that the very poor do not – but even in those countries the dictator is a good saver – look at the homes they own in other (democratic) countries – and that affects the average. It is assumed that a minimum of 10% is saved each year by the average household.

As a result of this process, the gap between the two constraints (maximum and minimum average household income) typically drops to plus or minus 11% of the midpoint between gross income and gross expenditure plus tax and savings per household. That is an acceptable range. We then use the centre point of that range.

Determining the Distribution around the Average Household Income

Finally, the Household Income and Expenditure Survey for as many counties as possible (94) is used to get estimates of the distribution of households by income or expenditure segment. That gives a measure of income distribution which is held mathematically as a log-normal distribution. This is back-checked to ensure the sum of expenditure by income segments is in line with the total value of Private Consumption Expenditure less allowance for charities.

The justification for this approach is that it ensures that the average household income of individual countries falls within reasonable constraints. That is, the incomes do not exceed productivity and they are greater than the amount spent plus taxes. In short, the estimates are defensible in terms of basic logic.

While there are obvious flaws in this system – starting with the question of how accurately Gross Domestic Product is measured in some countries – it does have the advantage of 'reasonableness'. Assuming Gross Domestic Product and Private Consumption Expenditure are measured reasonably accurately by the relevant government departments, then the maximum and minimum average wage are hard constraints. The average income must fall between them – and the range is quite small.

How Different are Incomes?

As is to be expected, average household income varies significantly between countries as does the distribution (variance) within countries. As the Country Segments used in this book are in part defined by GDP per capita it is not surprising that there is greater consistency of income within the Country Segments than between them.

To start, we will look at the averages and median as these are simple statistics to use. Averages are the most popular, but the reader is reminded that 'averages' hide a lot of information as well. Some of the hidden information is revealed by comparing the median with the average (mean).

The median is the level of income at which half the households have an income above that level and the other half of households have an income below that level.

This is a better measure in situations where the distribution is not 'normal' – that is, not evenly balanced on each side of the mean. Such is the case for incomes – there is always a bias to the lower end of the range, so the median is below the mean. A few very rich households offset a lot of poor households when calculating the average (mean).

Figure 7-1 shows the mean and median income per household for each of the four segments in 2019. As shown in Figure 7-1 the differences between the segments are quite considerable and later parts of this Chapter will venture to explain why these differences exist.

Figure 7-1: Average and Median Household Income in 2019 by Country Segment (US$ pa).

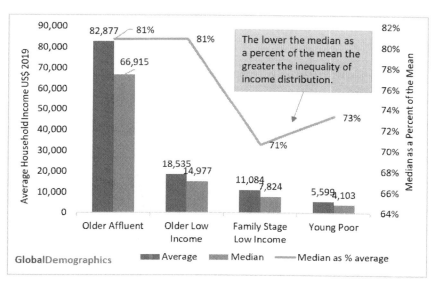

Figure 7-2 shows the same variables on a ***per capita*** basis. This is useful because, as shown in Chapter Four, there is a significant difference in household size across the four Country Segments. In 2019 it is 2.56 persons per household for the Old Affluent Segment and 4.69 per household for the Young Poor. So per capita is a better measure of the relative ability to spend on an individual in the household.

The low-income population in the Young Poor countries are suffering from two levels of income disparity – both between countries as well as within their own country.

The per capita calculation increases the differences between the four country segments. A person in a median income household in the Young Poor segment is living on US$875 per annum – or to put it more starkly, on US$2.40 per day. This compares with US$71.57 per day for the median Older Affluent resident.

Figure 7-2: Average and Median Household Income Per Capita in 2019 by Country Segment (US$ pa).

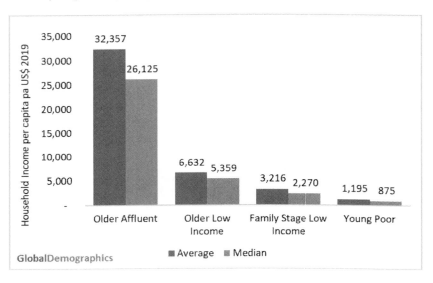

This disparity in incomes between the four Country Segments more than offsets the differences in population size. As shown in Figure 7-3, the Old Affluent Segment of Countries account for 14% of the total population in the 116 countries included in this analysis, but 57% of total household incomes (That is the product of the average household income in each country multiplied by the number of households in each country). In contrast, the Young Poor Country Segment, with 18% of the global population, accounts for just 3% of all household income.

But also note that the disparity of incomes is also significant *within* the lower income countries. This is shown in Figure 7-1 earlier. For both the Family Stage Low Income and Young Poor Country Segments, the median income is 71% - 73% of the mean. Compared with 81% - 82% for the two older segments. The low-income population in the Young Poor countries are suffering from two levels of disparity – both between countries as well as within their own country.

Figure 7-3: Share of Total Household Incomes (Average Multiplied by Number of Households) and Total Population by Country Segments. 2019.

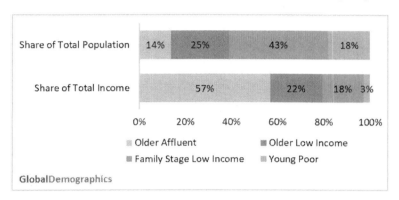

GlobalDemographics

The Old Affluent Segment of Countries accounts for 14% of the total population but 58% of total household incomes. In contrast, the Young Poor Countries, with 18% of the global population account for just 3% of all household income.

This leads to the issue of the distribution of households by income. Figure 7-4 compares the four Country Segments and the urban and rural households of China in terms of their 2019 distribution of households by income. It is necessary to have a detailed number of income breaks as the different country segments have quite different ranges.

As clearly shown and not unexpected, the older affluent dominate the income segment from US$50,000 and above. Urban China and the Older Low-Income Segment are increasingly important, in the range of US$50,000 to US$15,000.

245

Then Family Stage Low income grows in importance (share of households within the Income range) from US$15,000 to US$1,250 - the range is so wide as India (which dominates this Country Segment) has a huge range because of the dichotomy between its rural population and affluent urban population. Finally, the Young Poor Country Segment starts to become significant in share of income segment below US$15,000 and particularly below US$5,000

Figure 7-4: Share of Income Segment by Country Segment 2019.

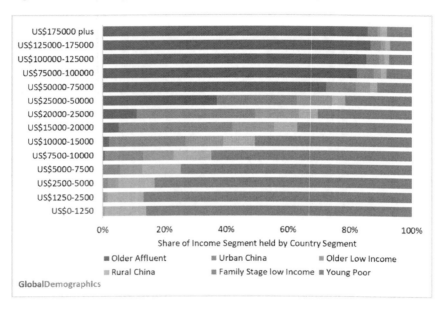

Why is there such a difference in Household Incomes?

It is useful to try and understand why some countries have high household incomes and others have very low ones. Unless that is understood it is difficult to make forecasts on earnings and, ultimately, household incomes.

Education is considered to be the key. As shown in Figure 7-5, **all** but one of the countries with a GDP per worker over US$40,000 pa have an education Index value over 200.

Figure 7-5: The Relationship Between Education and Productivity (GDP Per Worker). 104 Countries In 2019

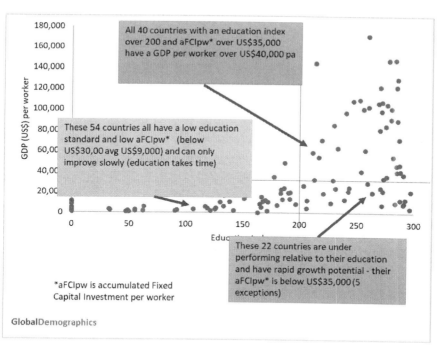

As also shown in Figure 7-5 there are 22 countries with an Education Index value of over 200 but their productivity (GDP per worker) is below US$40,000. With just 5 (typically small) exceptions, they all have low accumulated Fixed Capital Investment per worker. That is less than US$35,000 per worker. This reinforces the point that education is a *necessary, but not sufficient*, requirement to lift the productivity of workers and hence incomes.

Education gives the worker the potential to be more productive by enabling them to be more flexible in their work and to use equipment that facilitates their work. This advantage cannot happen if there is limited capital equipment to 'leverage' the skill set that education provides.

China is the prime example of this, with Fixed Capital Investment running at 47% of GDP and Productivity per (educated) worker growing at over 7% per annum for the last decade. India has been copying this level of Fixed Capital Investment in recent years and while it has not increased the demand for workers sufficiently to absorb a large number of new entrants to 'working age' it has had a positive effect on the productivity of those employed.

Finally, the 54 countries at the bottom left of Figure 7-5 are the ones of concern. Their productivity issue is a lack of education (low education index score). The data suggests that attracting fixed capital investment is inhibited if the overall education standard is low. Until these countries can lift their education standard there will not be sufficient investment to lift productivity. Hence, incomes suffer.

Also, as mentioned in the Chapter on Education – raising the education standard of a society takes at least 10 years if not longer. So do not expect a significant improvement in incomes in the short term for these countries. The picture shown in Figure 7-5 is, unfortunately, enduring.

The conclusion must be that there is no 'quick fix' to this diversity of incomes between countries in the lower left quadrant and those in the top right quadrant. It will take time for education to improve in the countries where it is inadequate. Only then will they attract Fixed Capital Investment. But it is up to the individual countries to initiate this. The provision of an adequate education infrastructure and an attractive investment environment is not something that is uniquely owned by one culture or another – they can be provided anywhere. It just requires the will.

There is no 'quick fix' to this diversity of incomes between countries. It will take years, or more specifically a generation before the educational difference is reduced.

Until the education environment changes – and that is a matter for the residents - the sociological issues are not expected to improve. Nonetheless, it should be recognised that some improvement is taking place and hence while the poor countries will remain relatively poor, they are nonetheless increasing in affluence.

The Changing Distribution of Households by Income

In this section, we examine how the income of households has changed over the last decade and can be expected to change through to 2045. Forecasts of household income are a function of GDP, which in turn makes assumptions about education trends (reasonably reliable), fixed capital investment (stable but subject to random variance due to government policy), the working-age population (reliable) and then participation rates (stable trends).

Appendix B gives our GDP forecasts for each country under our most likely scenario, and please refer to that for context.

The Old Affluent Countries

Note: The income groups used for this Country Segment are different from that used for the other three Country Segments. This is necessary due to the difference in the distribution.

Over the last decade, the average household income in these countries has increased at a relatively modest rate of 0.94% per annum. In 2009 the unweighted average household income for all countries in this segment was US$76,412 and by 2019 it is estimated at US$83,917 using the methodology described earlier in this Chapter. *(Note that all financial data is expressed in 2019 real values).* Some countries have done better than others but except for Ireland and Italy, most countries achieved circa 1% growth.

The economic and hence household income forecast for the next 25 years for this set of countries is positive, albeit muted. These countries are not going to be showing stellar economic growth rates in the future because they are already well developed in terms of the key drivers of productivity – specifically education and accumulated Fixed Capital Investment per worker (aFCIpw).

The gains achievable on these key drivers of economic growth become more marginal as the countries get more developed. Adding an extra factory is a small gain for these countries, whereas it is a significant gain for less developed countries.

In the case of these countries considering:
- the expected improvements in their education profile and
- increase in accumulated Fixed Capital Investment per worker,
- the changing (reducing) number of workers per household, and
- change in the share of GDP paid in wages.

The projected average increase in real household incomes for the period 2019 to 2045 is 1.03% per annum. This lifts the average for all households in this Country Segment from US$83,937 in 2019 to US$109,554 by 2045 in real 2019 values.

While it might be a small percentage gain per annum, it is nonetheless a significant absolute amount. That is US$25,617 per household over the next 26 years (from 2019) or just under an additional US$1,000 per annum per household.

This does, of course, impact the distribution of households by gross household income quite significantly over time. At the same time, the number and nature of households are changing. As explained earlier in Chapter Four, with the ageing of the population there is a move to smaller households (in terms of the number of persons), and this means more individual households. Total households are projected to grow from 387 million in 2019 to 413 million by 2045.

The resulting cumulative impact of these two changes (increasing affluence per household and an increasing number of households) on the distribution of households by income is shown in Figure 7-6.

Figure 7-6: Distribution of Households (mns) by Income Segment for 2009, 2019,2030 and 2045 for the Older Affluent Country Segment.

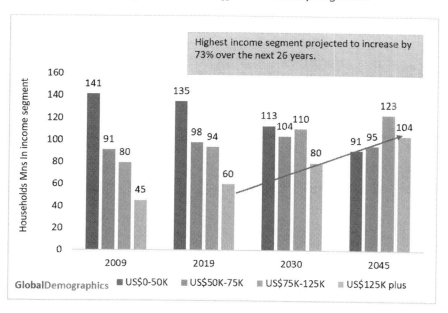

The upper-middle-income segment (US$75,000 to US$125,000 per household) is projected to add 29 million households. The high-income segment (households with an income over US$125,000) is projected to increase by 44 million households by 2045 on a base of 60 million in 2019.

This, combined with a smaller household size because of fewer dependents, means the total purchasing power per capita of this Country Segment increases by 34% in absolute terms over the next twenty-five years. That is 1.12% per annum.

Perhaps equally important is the absolute total household income of this segment. That is, average household income multiplied by the number of households. Here there is both good and bad news.

For the last decade, the estimated total household income of this segment grew at 1.73% per annum. While not a spectacular growth rate compared with the other Country Segments, it nonetheless means the market increased by 19% in absolute real terms. The good news is that this rate of growth is projected to continue through to 2030 at 1.87% per annum. Resulting in a 20% absolute increase in total spending power over a decade.

The bad news is that the growth rate is then projected to slow to 0.98% per annum from 2030 to 2045. This is of concern as in 2030 this Country Segment is projected to account for 58% of global household consumption expenditure. This slower growth in incomes (and therefore expenditure – see the next Chapter) will surely have implications for the demand for labour in future years.

Table 7-1 summarises the projected distribution of households in each of the countries in this segment for each of 2019 and 2045 to show the amount of change that is expected to take place by country.

For most countries in this Country Segment, the highest income group shown in this table (US$125,000 and above) is projected to increase by over 50% in terms of the number of households over the next 25 years. In absolute terms, the total value of this income segment is projected to *increase* by US$11.5 Trillion.

Table 7-1: Distribution of Households (mns) by US$ Income Segments. 2019 and 2045. Old Affluent Countries.

	Households (Mns) Within Income Segment								Average Income	
	2019				2045					
	US$0-50K	US$50K-75K	US$75K-125K	US$125K plus	US$0-50K	US$50K-75K	US$75K-125K	US$125K plus	2019	2045
Australia	2.5	2.3	2.7	1.9	2.1	2.1	3.4	4.1	92,796	129,126
Austria	0.8	1.2	1.2	0.4	0.6	1.1	1.7	0.8	80,682	95,264
Belgium	1.1	1.5	1.4	0.5	1.1	1.6	1.7	0.6	78,639	81,144
Canada	4.7	4.5	3.9	1.6	5.6	5.5	4.9	2.0	74,902	75,871
Denmark	0.3	0.5	0.8	0.5	0.3	0.5	0.8	0.7	100,001	113,371
Finland	0.5	0.7	0.7	0.3	0.4	0.6	0.8	0.4	80,935	92,709
France	8.4	7.5	6.3	2.6	7.8	7.9	7.3	3.1	73,509	77,446
Germany	10.2	10.6	9.3	3.6	8.5	11.4	12.4	5.2	75,496	83,509
Hong Kong	1.1	0.8	0.8	0.4	0.6	0.8	1.1	0.9	78,700	106,215
Iceland	0.0	0.0	0.0	0.0	0.0	0.0	0.0	0.1	128,071	183,873
Ireland	0.2	0.3	0.6	0.6	0.1	0.2	0.6	1.4	126,449	178,301
Italy	13.4	6.5	3.7	1.2	9.2	7.2	5.5	2.1	56,239	69,198
Japan	28.1	13.4	8.1	2.9	12.1	13.0	14.1	7.4	57,432	85,552
Macao	0.0	0.0	0.1	0.1	0.0	0.1	0.1	0.1	140,694	135,078
Netherlands	1.2	2.0	2.4	1.0	0.6	1.4	2.9	1.9	87,666	108,044
New Zealand	0.7	0.5	0.4	0.2	0.5	0.5	0.6	0.4	73,903	97,010
Norway	0.1	0.3	0.8	0.8	0.2	0.4	1.0	0.8	123,710	118,362
South Korea	12.1	5.7	2.6	0.6	1.2	3.0	8.5	8.3	52,320	126,023
Singapore	0.2	0.3	0.6	0.6	0.1	0.3	0.8	1.6	122,386	169,224
Slovenia	0.6	0.2	0.1	0.0	0.1	0.2	0.3	0.1	44,055	91,076
Spain	11.3	4.6	2.3	0.7	2.2	4.5	7.6	4.1	51,505	99,712
Sweden	0.6	1.1	1.5	0.7	0.7	1.3	1.7	0.8	90,380	91,695
Switzerland	0.4	0.7	1.2	1.1	0.5	0.7	1.3	1.6	118,564	134,232
United Kingdom	9.4	7.0	6.1	3.0	9.2	7.3	7.2	4.3	74,402	82,671
USA	26.7	25.7	36.1	34.8	26.9	23.5	36.7	51.0	111,853	138,764
Total	134.7	98.0	93.8	60.2	90.9	95.0	123.2	104.1	82,877	107,756
Total Excl USA	108.0	72.3	57.7	25.4	63.9	71.5	86.5	53.1	69,959	93,067

Accounting for 23% of global household incomes in 2019, what the US$125,000 plus household want and do is going to be significant in terms of future product and service demand as well as overall lifestyle trends.

The Older Low-Income Segment

Note: This and the subsequent two Country Segments use different income breaks from the preceding Country Segment.

This segment is dominated by China – which, in turn, confuses things by having two economically diverse populations – urban and rural. In China, the average urban household earns over 3 times as much as the average rural household. This income differential is expected to continue, albeit declining, at least for the next 25 years.

For that reason, the analysis first looks at the countries in this segment *other than China*. A total of 159 million households are in countries other than China, with the largest country in the remaining set being Russia at 56 million households.

Excluding China

With the projected real GDP growth through to 2045 as shown in Appendix B, the distribution of households by gross income is expected to improve over time, with the highest income segment (over US$25,000 pa) projected to be the growth segment. All lower-income segments are projected to decline in size.

Sociologically this is a good trend. Fewer poor households. As shown in Figure 7-7, the top income segment increases from 42.7 million to 66.9 million households. The lowest income segment (US$5,000 or less) is projected to decline from 15 million households in 2019 to 6 million households by 2045. Thailand and Ukraine are projected to perform particularly well regarding this shift to higher-income segments. Followed by Russia.

For obvious reasons (given the movement shown in Figure 7-7) all expected growth in spending power of this Segment of Countries in the next 25 years is in this highest income segment. Again, an older demographic, well-educated by global standards, with increased spending power. The upper-middle-class segment (US$15,000 to

US$25,000) remains relatively static in size and happily, the lowest income segments decrease significantly in the number of households.

Figure 7-7: Distribution of Households (Mns) by Income Segment for the Older Low-Income Country Segment – Excluding China.

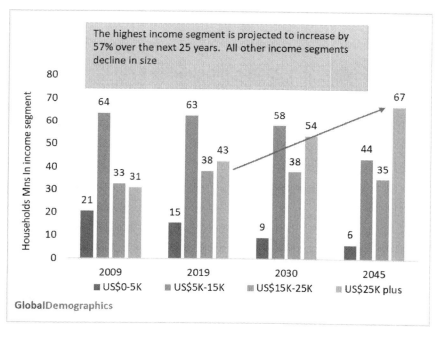

GlobalDemographics

Overall gross income (average income multiplied by the number of households) of this Country Segment (excluding China) is projected to increase at 1.7% per annum through to 2030 and then at 1.5% per annum to 2045. Lifting it from US$3.3 trillion to US$5.0 trillion in 2019 values.

Such a significant change in the distribution of households by income, as demonstrated by comparing 2019 with 2045, does drive change in consumption habits and the type of retail environment that people want – so expect wider changes to flow from this.

As shown in Chapter Two these countries are mainly in Eastern Europe, plus Russia and Thailand. Perhaps more importantly a significant number of these countries were identified earlier as having a high standard of education but low accumulated Fixed Capital Investment per worker and hence lower productivity per worker.

Table 7-2 provides a summary profile of the projected distribution of households by income in the countries included in this segment. *Note that the total shows both including and excluding China.*

Table 7-2: Distribution of Households (mns) by US$ Income Segments. 2019 and 2045. Older Lower Income Countries.

	Households (Mns) Within Income Segment								Average Income	
	2019				2045					
	US$0-5K	US$5K-15K	US$15K-25K	US$25K plus	US$0-5K	US$5K-15K	US$15K-25K	US$25K plus	2019	2045
Albania	0.1	0.6	0.2	0.1	0.0	0.1	0.2	0.8	12,851	50,119
Belarus	0.2	2.3	0.7	0.2	0.0	1.1	1.5	0.9	12,894	20,971
Bulgaria	0.2	1.4	0.7	0.5	0.0	0.4	0.7	1.1	17,431	31,130
Cuba	0.5	2.3	1.0	0.6	0.4	2.1	1.0	0.7	15,733	16,286
Czechia	0.0	0.2	0.8	3.3	0.0	0.0	0.1	4.2	39,686	91,286
Estonia	0.0	0.0	0.1	0.4	0.0	0.0	0.0	0.5	40,414	118,370
Georgia	0.2	0.8	0.2	0.1	0.1	0.6	0.4	0.3	10,655	19,259
Greece	0.0	0.4	1.0	2.9	0.0	0.1	0.3	3.4	36,837	64,785
Hungary	0.0	0.5	1.3	2.1	0.0	0.0	0.2	3.2	29,845	56,064
Latvia	0.0	0.1	0.2	0.4	0.0	0.0	0.0	0.5	31,866	92,739
Lithuania	0.2	0.7	0.2	0.1	0.0	0.2	0.2	0.2	11,482	23,005
Mauritius	0.0	0.1	0.1	0.2	0.0	0.1	0.1	0.3	28,284	46,569
Poland	0.1	2.2	5.5	7.5	0.0	0.3	1.5	12.0	28,115	48,604
Portugal	0.0	0.4	0.9	2.8	0.1	0.4	0.5	2.8	40,759	88,713
Moldovia	0.8	0.7	0.0	0.0	0.2	1.1	0.2	0.0	5,660	10,390
Romania	0.0	1.7	3.2	2.7	0.0	0.1	0.4	5.7	23,921	55,993
Russia	3.2	22.6	16.0	14.3	2.9	21.6	15.7	14.3	21,133	21,445
Slovakia	0.0	0.2	0.5	1.4	0.0	0.0	0.1	2.0	34,585	75,675
Thailand	3.5	15.6	5.0	2.6	0.1	4.2	10.4	13.1	13,325	27,435
Ukraine	6.4	9.7	0.4	0.1	2.1	11.2	1.3	0.3	6,469	9,410
Uruguay	0.0	0.2	0.3	0.7	0.0	0.3	0.4	0.7	35,615	35,150
China	92.0	165.3	121.9	113.4	42.5	109.7	101.7	325.2	17,929	38,741
Total	107.5	227.9	160.3	156.1	48.6	153.7	136.7	392.1	18,535	37,395
Total Excl China	15.5	62.6	38.4	42.7	6.1	43.9	35.0	66.9	20,665	32,698

Given that these countries have the educational advantage in place, they may show accelerated growth (over that shown here) if they can lift their fixed capital investment more rapidly than forecast in this analysis. A change in the investment environment could have significant positive implications for these markets.

Countries in Eastern Europe, as well as Thailand, have the potential for much more rapid economic growth and a lift in household incomes. Their education standard is already high. They simply need to attract more investment which can be achieved in a short time frame.

China.

China must be treated separately in this analysis as it dominates this Country Segment in the share of households and is also quite dichotomous in its income profile because of the quite different socio-economic profiles of the urban and rural populations.

In 2019 the average urban household's gross income was 2.8 times that of the average rural household. That is, US$25,264 compared to US$8,924, and it is expected that this difference will reduce marginally to 2.6 overtime.

Figure 7-8 shows how different the two populations of households are in 2019 and as projected to 2045. With continued rural to urban migrations (19 million per annum in 2019 declining to an expected 11 million per annum by 2045), the number of households in each of urban and rural areas changes significantly.

Urban households are the most important segment as they already account for 81% of all household income in China, and this increases to an estimated 86% by 2045. By 2045 there are expected to be 148 million urban households with an income over US$50,000 per annum (2019 values). That is 36% of urban households. That compares with 26 million (8%) urban households above that level of income in 2019.

Figure 7-8 also shows the data for rural households and the difference in the shape of the distribution as well as the pattern of change is evident. Because of the ongoing rural to urban migration, the total number of rural households declines significantly over time. However, the average household income of rural households does increase – from US$8,924 in 2019 to a projected US$18,819 in 2045. This reflects the growing productivity of the rural worker as the increase of land area to work with justifies the use of capital equipment.

The key issue in terms of rural households is the projected reduction in the number of poor rural households as shown in this chart. The number of rural households with an income below US$10,000 reduces significantly. That is a desirable outcome.

Figure 7-8: Changing Distribution of Urban and Rural Households by Income in China 2019-2045.

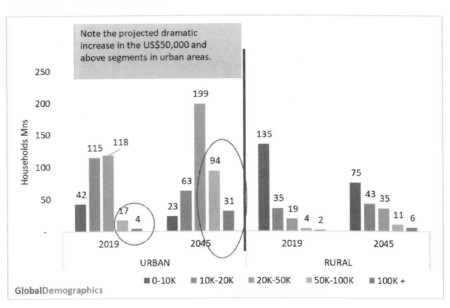

As a result of changing demographics, the retail sector of China is still a growth market – even with conservative GDP growth

*forecasts – and will result in a very significant increase in the
number of affluent households and purchasing power.*

The Family Stage Low Income Segment

This set of countries includes India – which again needs to be considered
separately as it does account for a significant number of households and
proportion (44%) of the total population of this Country Segment.

India

Figure 7-9 shows the projected changing distribution of households
for India only. The good news is that whereas India did not perform
well in terms of reducing the number of low-income households in
the last decade, it is projected to stop this deterioration in the future.
This is assuming the education improvements and the fixed capital
investment continues as projected. For the period 2019 to 2030, the
number of households with an income below US$5,000 per annum in
2019 values is projected to stabilise and then decline from 2030
through to 2045. That is from 297 million households in 2019 to 216
million in 2045. Still a lot of poor households but at least, potentially,
no longer an increasing number.

That change is projected to result in very significant growth of the
US$5,000 to US$15,000 income segment in India. From 125 million
households in 2019 to a projected 291 million in 2045. That is the
new and rapidly growing middle class of India.

Finally, while the numbers are, and remain, small relative to all
households, the number of households with an income over
US$15,000 in 2019 values is projected to grow from 16 million to 80
million by 2045.

If that happens, then retail in India will both grow, and change dramatically, over the next 25 years. To some extent, this replicates the China experience.

Figure 7-9: Distribution of Households (Mns) By Income Segment For 2009, 2019, 2030 And 2045 For India.

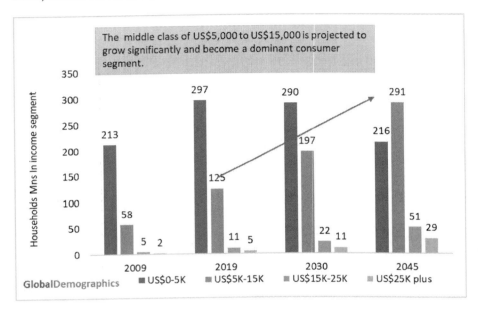

The emerging Middle Class of India is households with an income between US$5,000 and US$15,000. It is projected to grow from 125 million households to 291 million in the next 25 years. That is a growth rate of 3.3% per annum.

Countries in the Young Family Low Income Segment other than India

Like India, the other countries included in this Country Segment also have a rapid increase in the number and *proportion* of their households that have an income over US$15,000. From a total of 152 million households in 2019 to a projected 298 million in 2045. In terms of the number of people (living in those households), it means an increase from 524 million persons to 932 million. This is a rapidly growing upper-middle-class and consumer market (as discussed in the next Chapter on Expenditure).

Figure 7-10: Distribution of Households (Mns) By Income Segment For 2009, 2019,2030 and 2045 For the Family Stage Low Income Country Segment Excluding India.

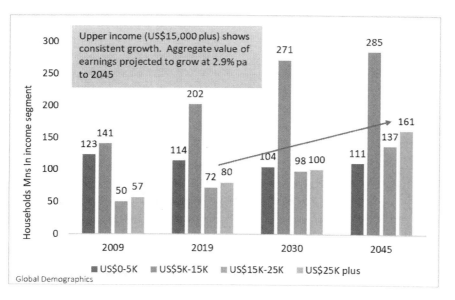

As discussed in the next chapter, these households are in the 'family' stage and their expenditure is biased to necessities rather than discretionary (setting up and running a family household is expensive)

but that nonetheless is a wide range of products and some services including health and education. The aggregate income earned by this segment of households is projected to grow at 2.9% per annum through to 2045.

The upper-middle class in the Family Stage Low Income Countries will nearly double in size in the next decade. That is half a billion more consumers (and 146 million households) with a projected household income of over US$15,000 pa.

Table 7-3 shows for each country in this Country Segment the projected change in the distribution of households by income between 2019 and 2045 as well as the projected change in average household income.

However, there is some dichotomy in that 20 of the 34 countries in this segment are achieving a decline in the number of low-income households and 14 are projected to increase the number of low-income households (7 countries by over 1 million) over the same time period to 2045. The worst is Indonesia where the number of low-income households is projected to increase from 21 million to 34 million. The second is the Philippines with an increase of 8.1 million low-income households. The rate of expansion of the population overwhelms the increase in affluence.

Table 7-3: Distribution of Households (Mns) By US$ Income Segments for Family Stage Low Income Country Segment. 2020 and 2045.

	Households (Mns) Within Income Segment								Average Income	
	2019				2045					
	US$0-5K	US$5K-15K	US$15K-25K	US$25K plus	US$0-5K	US$5K-15K	US$15K-25K	US$25K plus	2019	2045
Algeria	0.2	3.3	2.6	1.2	1.6	6.9	2.6	1.6	17,670	14,618
Argentina	0.2	1.8	3.0	8.1	0.1	1.3	3.0	12.2	40,576	45,795
Armenia	0.1	0.5	0.2	0.1	0.0	0.0	0.1	0.9	13,071	46,661
Azerbaijan	0.2	1.3	0.5	0.2	0.0	0.5	0.9	2.4	14,309	38,053
Bangladesh	20.6	15.6	1.0	0.3	3.7	36.7	12.1	4.0	5,734	13,143
Bolivia	0.6	1.5	0.3	0.2	1.8	1.8	0.3	0.2	10,471	8,775
Brazil	14.1	31.6	13.2	14.4	14.8	38.1	17.6	20.1	18,990	20,599
Cambodia	2.4	1.1	0.1	0.1	2.9	1.9	0.2	0.1	5,055	6,169
Chile	0.2	1.4	1.4	2.8	0.2	1.7	2.1	4.8	35,749	38,818
Colombia	2.4	6.1	2.6	2.6	3.0	7.9	3.4	3.4	18,232	18,495
Dominican Rep	0.4	1.5	0.8	0.7	0.0	0.2	0.9	3.4	18,748	38,243
Ecuador	0.6	2.0	0.9	0.7	3.2	2.9	0.8	0.8	17,097	12,394
El Salvador	0.5	1.2	0.3	0.1	0.3	1.5	0.4	0.2	10,715	12,048
India	296.7	124.8	11.4	5.4	215.9	291.5	51.2	29.2	4,945	9,050
Indonesia	20.8	41.3	8.3	4.4	33.8	65.5	12.7	6.7	10,213	10,014
Iran	3.2	10.8	3.6	2.3	0.4	7.0	11.8	18.5	13,997	30,099
Kazakhstan	0.0	0.7	1.6	2.2	0.0	0.4	1.6	5.8	28,627	38,449
Malaysia	0.2	1.7	2.3	3.8	0.0	0.6	2.3	10.6	31,295	41,752
Mexico	2.7	12.4	8.5	10.8	4.3	17.9	11.3	13.8	25,290	24,177
Morocco	0.7	3.0	1.2	0.9	0.6	4.1	2.8	2.6	15,824	21,294
Myanmar	8.5	4.0	0.1	0.0	0.7	11.3	4.5	1.3	4,615	13,852
Nicaragua	0.9	0.5	0.1	0.0	1.5	0.8	0.1	0.1	6,316	5,782
Panama	0.0	0.2	0.3	0.6	0.2	0.7	0.5	0.8	38,380	29,852
Paraguay	0.3	0.8	0.3	0.3	0.4	1.2	0.5	0.4	16,744	16,690
Peru	0.7	3.8	2.0	1.6	0.3	3.2	3.5	3.6	18,643	24,442
Philippines	11.2	13.6	2.5	1.6	19.3	22.5	4.1	2.6	9,224	9,060
Saudi Arabia	0.0	0.1	0.2	5.7	0.0	0.1	0.3	7.5	88,310	90,340
South Africa	5.8	5.3	1.7	2.5	9.0	7.3	2.3	3.2	18,465	17,163
Sri Lanka	1.5	3.2	0.7	0.4	1.3	4.3	1.5	1.0	11,055	14,296
Tunisia	0.2	1.3	0.5	0.2	0.2	2.1	1.2	0.5	13,616	16,134
Turkey	1.8	11.0	7.7	7.6	2.7	18.1	11.3	9.0	22,102	19,497
Uzbekistan	4.3	2.6	0.3	0.1	4.0	5.9	1.0	0.5	5,884	8,956
Venezuela RB	0.4	2.6	2.2	2.9	0.1	1.4	2.0	3.7	26,665	33,054
Viet Nam	8.0	14.2	1.2	0.4	0.2	8.9	17.0	15.0	7,467	24,286
Total	410.5	326.9	83.4	85.2	326.4	576.2	187.9	190.6	11,084	14,927
Total Excl India	113.8	202.1	72.0	79.7	110.6	284.7	136.7	161.3	17,358	20,419

The Young Poor

This is an area of concern when looking at household incomes. The lack of education is limiting the ability to lift the productivity of workers and hence incomes and lifestyle. Rather, the opportunities are to some extent selective to a small group (to date) that get educated to an upper secondary and above level. This is resulting in a more dichotomous (or less equitable) distribution of households by income.

A middle class is indeed growing in these parts of the world - middle class being defined here as households with an income over US$5,000. However, as shown in Figure 7-11 the lowest income segment, that is households with an income less than US$5,000 per annum, is also projected to grow – from 183 million households (approximately 820 million persons) in 2019 to 268 million households (approximately 1.2 billion persons) by 2045.

While affluence is expected to improve in this group of countries it is not improving sufficiently fast to offset the growth in the number of persons and households. Until population growth can be constrained this problem will not go away.

However, as explained earlier in Chapter Three, it takes at least 10 years for a change in birth rates or education policy to take effect. As such the picture shown in Figure 7-11 is 'locked in'.

The number of households with an income less than US$5,000 per annum, is growing rapidly – from 183 million households (approximately 820 million persons) to 268 million households (approximately 1.2 billion persons) between 2019 and 2045.

Figure 7-11: Distribution of Households (Mns) By Income Segment For 2009, 2019, 2030 And 2045 For the Young Poor Country Segment.

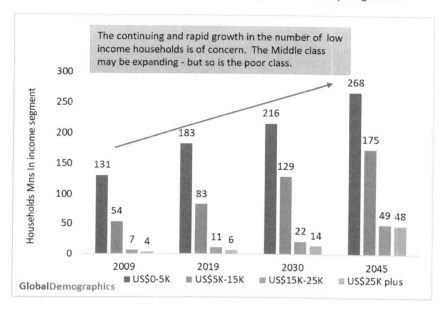

Table 7-4 lists the countries in this segment and shows the current and expected size of each of the household income segments for each of 2019 and 2045. With very few exceptions the lowest income segment increases in the absolute number of households (and hence persons).

A significant part of this issue is that population growth overwhelms the growth in the overall economy. To explain, the lowest income segment (less than US$5,000 pa) is projected to decline as a proportion of all households. From 64% in 2019 to a projected 50% in 2045. But the absolute number of households during that period is projected to increase from 284 million to 539 million. Fifty per cent of 539 million households is 268 million which is greater than 64% of the 284 million households in 2019. While the declining proportion of households that are poor looks good, it hides the reality that the absolute number of poor households is increasing.

Table 7-4: Distribution of Households (Mns) By US$ Income Segments for the Young Poor Country Segment. 2020 and 2045.

	Households (Mns) Within Income Segment								Average Income	
	2019				2045					
	US$0-5K	US$5K-15K	US$15K-25K	US$25K plus	US$0-5K	US$5K-15K	US$15K-25K	US$25K plus	2019	2045
Angola	1.6	3.1	1.0	0.9	1.8	6.7	3.2	3.0	14,938	18,851
Botswana	0.1	0.2	0.1	0.2	0.1	0.3	0.2	0.2	28,469	26,200
Burkina Faso	2.9	0.5	0.0	0.0	5.6	1.1	0.1	0.0	3,399	3,478
Cameroon	3.6	1.5	0.2	0.1	5.5	3.3	0.5	0.3	5,367	6,847
Chad	2.9	0.3	0.0	0.0	4.4	1.7	0.1	0.1	2,694	4,703
DR Congo	18.0	0.8	0.1	0.0	44.7	1.4	0.1	0.0	1,780	1,494
Egypt	5.8	16.1	2.6	1.0	6.7	30.8	7.6	3.1	9,626	11,771
Ethiopia	22.0	2.2	0.1	0.0	0.6	10.0	14.2	18.1	2,741	27,395
Ghana	2.0	3.1	0.5	0.3	2.2	5.7	1.4	0.8	8,916	11,642
Guatemala	0.5	1.8	0.8	0.7	0.0	0.1	0.5	2.7	17,493	42,286
Guinea	2.2	0.5	0.0	0.0	3.8	1.1	0.0	0.0	3,688	3,984
Haiti	1.9	0.5	0.0	0.0	2.8	0.6	0.0	0.0	4,110	3,529
Honduras	0.9	0.9	0.2	0.1	0.1	1.8	1.3	0.5	9,323	16,690
Kenya	7.3	5.0	0.5	0.2	7.8	13.7	1.3	0.4	5,947	7,650
Lao PDR	0.9	0.9	0.1	0.0	0.1	1.0	0.9	1.0	6,934	24,409
Madagascar	4.9	0.3	0.0	0.0	8.4	0.9	0.1	0.0	2,014	2,634
Malawi	3.4	0.2	0.0	0.0	5.7	0.6	0.1	0.0	1,696	2,483
Mali	3.6	0.5	0.0	0.0	6.5	2.1	0.0	0.0	3,203	4,181
Mozambique	6.0	0.3	0.0	0.0	12.0	0.6	0.1	0.1	1,689	1,694
Namibia	0.2	0.2	0.1	0.1	0.3	0.3	0.1	0.2	18,306	18,924
Nepal	5.4	0.9	0.0	0.0	7.1	2.0	0.0	0.0	3,430	4,003
Niger	4.4	0.2	0.0	0.0	12.0	0.5	0.0	0.0	2,077	1,974
Nigeria	21.0	18.9	3.0	1.8	30.6	36.6	12.2	15.0	7,857	17,111
Pakistan	24.3	17.3	1.4	0.5	27.7	35.8	3.6	1.3	5,798	7,209
Rwanda	2.4	0.3	0.0	0.0	4.0	0.6	0.0	0.0	2,705	3,089
Senegal	2.2	1.2	0.1	0.0	3.6	2.8	0.3	0.1	5,366	6,293
South Sudan	2.4	0.0	0.0	0.0	3.1	0.0	0.0	0.0	106	99
Sudan	7.1	1.9	0.1	0.0	12.5	3.8	0.2	0.1	3,921	4,118
Uganda	8.0	0.9	0.1	0.0	17.1	2.3	0.2	0.1	2,657	2,915
United Republic	9.7	2.0	0.2	0.1	20.7	4.7	0.4	0.2	3,566	3,785
Zambia	2.6	0.8	0.1	0.1	5.1	1.7	0.3	0.2	5,574	5,595
Zimbabwe	3.1	0.0	0.0	0.0	5.0	0.0	0.0	0.0		
Total	183.2	83.1	11.4	6.4	267.9	174.5	49.2	47.7	5,599	10,100

What can be done about it? Unfortunately, the problem harks back to the issue of education. Without exception these countries score poorly on this dimension, and that in turn leaves them with high population growth and a consequent lack of improvement in education and health. This leads to a rapidly growing low skilled workforce that is increasingly irrelevant to the modern world. This is a sociological catastrophe that is going to have global implications.

Without exception, the Young Poor countries score poorly on education and that in turn has left them with high population growth, and a growing low skilled workforce that is increasingly irrelevant to the modern world. Hence low incomes.

To Summarise

Generally, the expectation is that average household incomes will increase. This is predicated on the assumption that the education profile of the labour force will improve in quality in the future (as it has in the past) and that there will be a steady increase in the fixed capital investment underlying the individual worker. If either of these assumptions proves to be invalid for a country, then the growth in incomes will not take place – largely because of lack of employment.

It should be emphasized that the risk of these assumptions not being met is high. This is explained in the Conclusion Chapter and the Chapter on Consumption. There is a very high probability that there will not be sufficient additional employment opportunities to create demand for low skilled workers. That means reduced employment and lower household incomes.

In terms of the Older Affluent countries, it should also be appreciated that the slower growth rate in average household income is a function of them already having high levels of education and fixed capital investment per worker. As such the marginal impact of improvements is lower. In addition, the number of households (and therefore consumers) is relatively static – growing from 387 million in 2019 to a projected 413 million by 2045 – largely because of smaller household size rather than more people. The aggregate income earned by all households is therefore expected to grow at a relatively sedate rate of 1.29% per annum which is lower than that of the other Country Segments.

The older Low Income County segment does see a significant increase in the number and proportion of households that are more affluent – that is with an income over US$25,000 per annum. This is driven by (Urban) China. On average for this Country Segment household income (for all households) lifts from US$18,532 to US$36,092 which represents a growth rate of 2.6 % per annum.   That combined with a marginal increase in the total number of households means total incomes earned by households in this Country Segment are projected to grow at 1.6% per annum through to 2045 excluding China and at 3.4% per annum for China. (Note for the decade to 2019 China's total earned household incomes grew at 9.98% per annum).

The Family Stage Low Income Segment is moving into positive territory. Average Incomes are expected to increase (at 1.2% per annum, 2.4% per annum for India) and the number of low-income households is in (marginal) decline. The total earnings (as measured by average household income multiplied by the total number of households) are expected to increase at the rate of 1.3% per annum. This is driven in part by the projected significant increase in the absolute number of households in this Country Segment. From 906 million in 2019 to a projected 1,281 million by 2045. That is a lift of 33%.

Perhaps even more important though, is that the number of households with an income below US$5,000 is expected to decline after 2030. This is a very important sociological trend. But there remains a lot of such households. In 2019 it is estimated at 410 million and is projected to drop to 326 million by 2045.

The Young Poor Segment is the one with extremes. In terms of the number of households, it is projected to grow at 4.8% per annum between 2019 and 2045. The absolute number of households is projected to increase from 284 million to 539 million.   In short, they almost double in number.

At the same time, the average household income of this Country Segment is projected to increase at 2.3% per annum, from US$5,599 to US$10,100 – again it nearly doubles.

Combined (increased number of households and increased average income per household) this means total household income is projected to grow at 4.9% per annum. This is, of course, good to see. It means that the consumer market will grow substantially, and hopefully with that, employment.

However, this is not without a 'cost'. The number of low-income households (less than US$5,000) still increases. From 183 million in 2019 to a projected 268 million by 2045. This compares with the highest income segment (US$25,000 and above) increasing from 6.4 million to 47.7 million in the same period. Inequality of distribution of incomes is a real issue for this segment.

Summary Profile – Household Incomes

Older Affluent [Note: Different Income Breaks from other segments]	2019	2030	2045
Households (Mns) 0-US$50K	135	113	91
Households (Mns) US$50K-75K	98	104	95
Households (Mns) US$75K-125K	94	110	123
Households (Mns) US$ 125K +	60	80	104
Average Household Inc (US$)	82,877	94,593	107,756
Growth rate pa	0.9%	1.2%	0.9%
Median Household Inc (US$)	66,915	74,753	84,130
Average Household inc per cap	32,357	37,582	43,205
Median Household inc per cap	26,125	29,699	33,732

Older Low Income	2019	2030	2045
Households (Mns) 0-US$5K	107	77	49
Households (Mns) US$5K-15K	228	195	154
Households (Mns) US$15K-25K	160	162	137
Households (Mns) US$ 25K +	156	286	392
Average Household Inc (US$)	18,535	26,422	37,395
Growth rate pa	5.7%	3.3%	2.3%
Median Household Inc (US$)	14,977	20,973	29,166
Average Household inc per cap	6,632	10,349	15,713
Median Household inc per cap	5,359	8,215	12,256

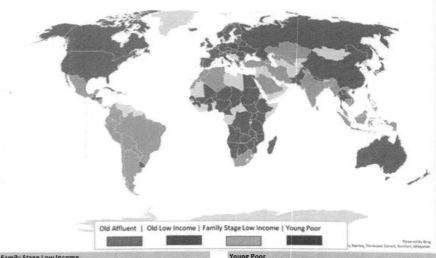

Old Affluent | Old Low Income | Family Stage Low Income | Young Poor

Family Stage Low Income	2019	2030	2045
Households (Mns) 0-US$5K	410	394	326
Households (Mns) US$5K-15K	327	469	576
Households (Mns) US$15K-25K	83	120	188
Households (Mns) US$ 25K +	85	111	191
Average Household Inc (US$)	11,084	12,113	14,927
Growth rate pa	0.7%	0.8%	1.4%
Median Household Inc (US$)	7,824	8,663	10,975
Average Household inc per cap	3,216	3,871	5,319
Median Household inc per cap	2,270	2,769	3,911

Young Poor	2019	2030	2045
Households (Mns) 0-US$5K	183	216	268
Households (Mns) US$5K-15K	83	129	175
Households (Mns) US$15K-25K	11	22	49
Households (Mns) US$ 25K +	6	14	48
Average Household Inc (US$)	5,599	6,927	10,100
Growth rate pa	1.9%	2.0%	2.5%
Median Household Inc (US$)	4,103	4,922	7,003
Average Household inc per cap	1,195	1,539	2,358
Median Household inc per cap	875	1,094	1,635

Chapter 8
Consumption – The Route to Employment

Introduction

The consumption of goods and services plays a very important role in the global economy. By purchasing a new shirt, pair of shoes, cosmetics, cars, or going on holiday we obviously (but not always) gain satisfaction from the new goods. But just as importantly, it creates jobs. Someone must make the shirt. Also, someone must grow the cotton or make the artificial materials used in it. As shown earlier in Chapter 6 on Employment, the demand for additional jobs in the future is considerable. Specifically, in the younger countries/regions an estimated 692 million people will be looking for a job *in addition to* those that already have a job. (1.67 billion). If these people cannot find work the social consequences would be considerable. Consumption is important.

In terms of consumption, the world performed very well over the last decade. Total household expenditure (consumption) for the 116 countries included in this book grew at 2.64% per annum. In real 2019 values, it grew from US$35 trillion in 2009 to US$45 trillion in 2019 which is an absolute increase of 30% in value.

This consumption growth grew faster than the growth in the number of persons (or households). In short, the world consumed more per person as well as increasing in population. Per capita expenditure on consumption grew in real terms at 1.48% per annum for the period 2009 to 2019. That is, from US$5,332 per capita to US$ 6,196 (in 2019 values) in 2019.

At the same time, the world got more efficient at producing what was consumed. The global average in terms of consumption per worker increased from US$12,3342 to US$14,577. An absolute increase in productivity of 14% in a decade, or 1.68% per annum. If the productivity gains had not been made, then another 559 million persons would have needed to be employed, an increase of 18% over actual.

Given the relatively high participation rates (propensity of those of working age to be employed) as shown in Chapter Six, with most countries running at close to 65% it would suggest that at the moment (2019) the world is at equilibrium – the demand for workers largely meets the supply of workers. Will that continue?

Historic trend and Location of Consumption

Overall Trend

Figure 8-1 shows the trend in total consumption expenditure by households (as measured by the Private Consumption Expenditure Component of Gross Domestic Product and therefore captures all expenditure including any undeclared economy) by each of the four Country Segments. Again, all values are in 2019 US$ values, removing the impact of inflation and showing the real growth in total household expenditure.

Figure 8-1: Trend in Global Consumption Expenditure by Country Segment from 2009 To 2019. US$ Bn Pa 2019 Values.

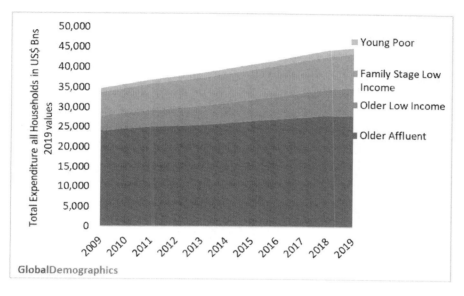

As is apparent from Figure 8-1, starting in 2009, consumption expenditure grew steadily through to 2019. A very high proportion of that expenditure took place in the Older Affluent Country Segment. That segment accounted for 62% of total expenditure in 2019 – down from 69% in 2009. Nonetheless, the 'Older Affluent' group of countries accounted for 40% of the total increase in consumption in the last decade and its expenditure grew at 1.6% per annum.

The Older Less Affluent (which is dominated by China) grew at a more robust 5.8% per annum for the last decade and the other two segments at 3.7% and 4.7% per annum.

When global total consumption expenditure is divided by the total number of persons it translates into an average expenditure on consumption of US$5,332 per person in 2009 increasing to US$6,196 per person by 2019. But if this is done by Country Segment the differences are considerable as shown in Figure 8-2 for each of 2009 and 2019.

Figure 8-2: Average Expenditure Per Person Per Annum by Country Segments. 2009 And 2019.

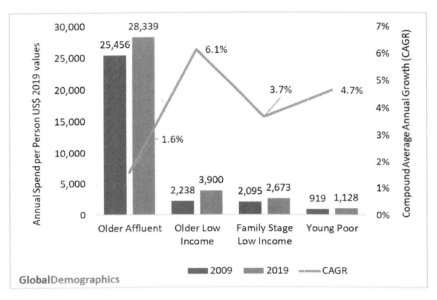

As is to be expected, the Older Affluent spend considerably more per capita with an average per annum spend of US$28,339 in 2019 – or US$78 per day per person. This compares with US$3 per person per day for the Young Poor countries.

The difference in consumption capability and lifestyle that this enables is considerable. The Older Affluent are clearly at the higher levels of Maslow's Need hierarchy, whereas the Young Poor is still at the basic 'security' level.

Where was the growth?

Several different factors caused this growth, and it is useful to examine the specific income segments and locations where the historic growth in consumption expenditure took place.

To do this India and China (Urban and Rural) have been separated from their base Country Segments because they are important markets. That is, they are very large.

Figure 8-3 summarises the relative importance of each Country Segment by Income segment. (Note the income breaks for the Older Affluent are different from that of the other segments). It shows the relative share of total expenditure in 2019 and also the per cent by which each country's income segment contributed to the total change in the last decade.

In terms of market share, (the orange bars in Figure 8-3) the obvious important country/income segments are the four income segments within the Older Affluent Country Segment. Collectively they are 62%. Followed by the US$25,000 plus segment in the Family Stage Segment (excluding India) and then Urban China with income over US$25,000. Collectively these six country/income segments account for 74% of all consumption expenditure in the world.

In terms of absolute growth, the picture changes slightly. Just six country/income segments accounted for 68% of all expenditure growth in the last decade. That is the over US$75,000 households in the Older Affluent Segment, Urban China with income over US$15,000 and then the over US$25,000 for Family Stage (excluding India).

Figure 8-3: Historic Percent Share of Market and Share of Growth of Total Consumption Expenditure by Country Segment and Income Group For 2009 To 2019.

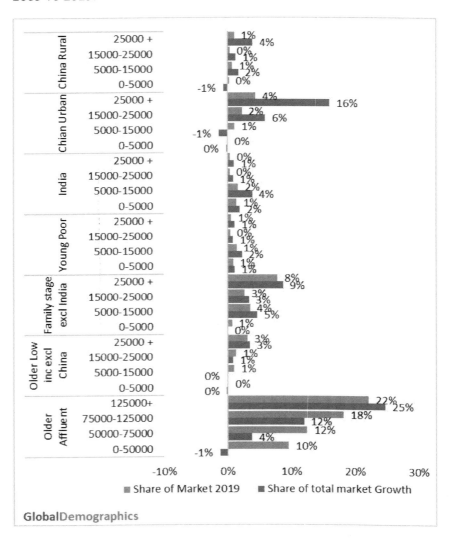

Propensity to spend.

The top category in Figure 8-4 shows the average propensity to save and pay tax on gross household income. There is a significant difference between the Country Segments (and between individual countries within Country Segments) in terms of their propensity to spend. This difference in behaviour is a function of many things.

The standout country is China, where the propensity to save/pay tax is very high compared to the rest of the world. Do note that the average urban tax rate in China is 16% (it is progressive) which is not out of line with the averages for other countries. This means that the real difference between China and other countries is in terms of propensity to save – which is very high in China. It may also be a reduction of debt incurred by buying speculative properties.

and What is it Spent on?

Figure 8-4 also shows the average allocation of gross income by expenditure category for each Country Segment as well as India and China (urban and rural). To a large extent, the differences reflect the differences in average incomes.

Analysis of this data by income level by *individual* country shows that changes in consumption habits are more a function of the changing *distribution* of households by income rather than there being changes in consumption patterns *within* an income segment.

Thus, at a country level, changes in average household incomes indicate potential changes in consumption patterns. Typically, the higher the income the greater the importance of discretionary items.

Figure 8-4: Share of Gross Income Saved or Spent by Category 2019.

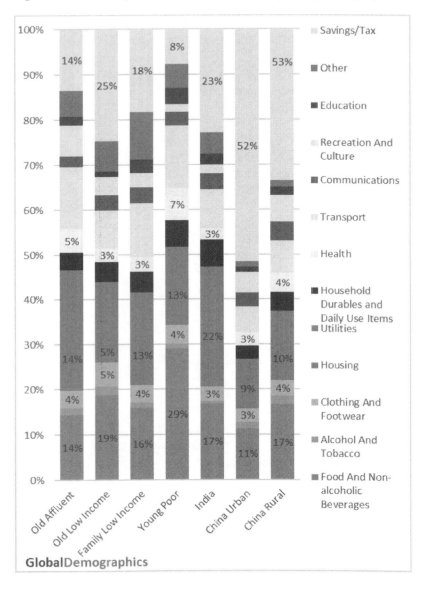

Table 8-1 shows the absolute amount in US Dollars that is spent by the average household in each of the four Country Segments as well as India and China. Here the differences between Country segments are particularly clear.

Even though food and non-alcoholic beverages are 14% of the Older Affluent Segment's gross income, the absolute amount spent on food and non-alcoholic beverages is 7 times greater than that of the average Young Poor household that is spending 29% of its gross income on the same.

Table 8-1: Average Absolute Amount Spent per household by Category In 2019

	Country Segments excl India and China				Specific Countries		
	Old Affluent	Old Low Income	Family Low Income	Young Poor	India	China Urban	China Rural
Gross Income	83,938	20,666	17,360	5,730	5,054	24,449	8,522
Savings/Tax	11,353	5,103	3,167	443	1,152	12,602	4,486
Total Expenditure	72,585	15,563	14,192	5,287	3,902	11,847	4,036
Food And Non-alcoholic	12,110	3,852	2,755	1,669	853	2,782	1,408
Alcohol And Tobacco	1,208	408	216	50	21	346	165
Clothing And Footwear	3,288	1,117	670	251	164	709	302
Housing	12,109	988	2,292	743	1,133	2,126	810
Utilities	10,359	2,706	1,276	253	220	560	503
Durables and Daily Use	3,309	929	824	338	300	706	342
Health	4,474	642	533	407	130	758	377
Transport	11,647	1,750	2,110	801	438	1,376	612
Communications	1,951	706	622	174	177	741	367
Recreation And Culture	5,756	826	544	97	103	1,167	505
Education	1,666	238	519	208	117	300	154
Other	4,707	1,400	1,830	297	245	278	123

Future Demand Trends

The future demand for products and services is very important because, as argued earlier, unless consumption spending can be grown in line with the number of persons seeking work there will be a significant social disaster developing. Specifically, many unemployed persons who cannot support themselves or their families live in countries where there are low levels of social support.

Previous Chapters have provided projections in terms of the key components of this ongoing demand taking place. These are.

- Number of consumers (Chapter Four),
- The level of Education and Fixed Capital Investment and their impact on the ability to earn income and overall productivity,
- Share of productivity paid in wages,
- The propensity of working age to be employed and hence workers per household.

Collectively these enable projections of the total income and spending through to 2045 under stable political and social environments. Figure 8-5 shows this graphically.

The expectation is that total consumption expenditure will continue to grow in the future for all four Country Segments. In the case of the two older Country Segments, it is driven more by the increase in real incomes than by an increase in the number of consumers. In contrast, for the Young Poor Segment, both the number of consumers and real incomes are playing a dramatic role with the number of consumers (population) increasing by 73% and real average household incomes by 82% over the next 25 years.

However, as is apparent from Figure 8-5, the relative importance of the four Country Segments does change over time. The three less affluent Country Segments all increase in share – but by only 2 to 3 percentage points. This lowers the share held by the Older Affluent Segment from 62% in 2019 to 52% by 2045. A wider distribution of spending is therefore happening.

Figure 8-5: Trend in Global Consumption Expenditure (By Households) from 2006 To 2045 US$ mns p.a. 2019 Values.

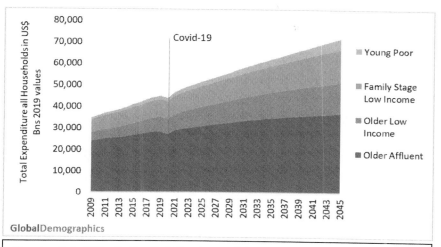

GlobalDemographics

There is a dip in 2020 reflecting the IMF estimates of the impact of the Corvus-19 pandemic on consumer spending in that year and then the recovery in years 2021 and 2022. At the time of writing these are estimates and may well change.

This change in share of total expenditure is, of course, a reflection of different projected growth rates relative to the past decade. In particular, the slower growth of expenditure in China. This is shown in Figure 8-6.

Urban China's share of total consumption expenditure is 7% in 2019 up from 5.4% in 2009. The expectation is that the rate of growth of consumption expenditure will slow from 9.6% per annum from 2009 to 2019 to 2.7% per annum from 2030 to 2045. This is projected to happen because of the shift in the age profile of the population. It moves more people (and households) into the retirement stage who have a lower propensity to spend. At the same time, the growth rate of the urban workforce goes to almost zero after 2035 and hence the growth of household incomes slows as the number of workers per household stabilises.

In a similar vein, the Older Affluent is projected to experience slower growth as the populations stabilise and age. The total workforce is stable, and the number of persons (consumers) is also stable. In the previous decade, there was still some growth in *both* consumers and income. Now consumer spending growth is dependent on increased incomes alone.

Figure 8-6: Historic and Projected Growth Rate Per Annum of Household Expenditure by Country Segment.

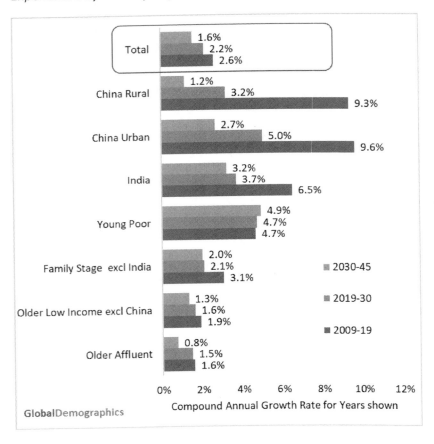

China's Urban Household Expenditure growth is projected to slow dramatically. From 9.5% per annum from 2009 to 2019 to 2.2% per annum from 2030 to 2045.

In contrast to the other three Country Segments, as shown in Figure 8-6 the Young Poor Segment is projected to grow in consumption power at the very high rate of 4.7% per annum for the next decade and then at 4.9% to 2045. This is driven by the combination of the two earlier discussed projected trends and a key assumption. That is:

First, a projected growing working-age population can be employed because of the age profile of the population. The growth of the working-age population is extremely likely to happen given the present age profile and births.

Second, a projected improved productivity per worker because of expected improvements in education and then fixed capital investment.

The assumption is that the number of persons of working age seeking work can find work at the same rate as in the past. The subsequent section assumes that is the case. But for reasons discussed later in this Chapter, that probably will not be the case and hence earnings and expenditure in the Younger Country Segments will probably be lower than that shown in the next section of this Chapter.

The Young Poor countries are collectively projected to grow in consumption power at a very high rate of 4.7% per annum for the next decade. But they are just 3% of global consumption.

Which Country and Income Segments are Important?

The Older Affluent

As mentioned earlier in this Chapter this Country Segment accounts for 62% of global consumption expenditure in 2019 and while increasing in absolute amount through to 2045 it is projected to decline in the share of total consumption expenditure to 52%. Table 8-2 shows how the profile of expenditure of this Country Segment is projected to change over the next 25 years by income segment.

The outstanding statistic for this Country Segment is that the highest income segment which is 16% of the persons in this segment accounted for 22% of the global market in 2019 and their share is projected to increase to 24.5% by 2045. These people are very important to the global economy and employment.

Table 8-2: Older Affluent Segments Share of Global Expenditure 2019 to 2045.

US$ Income Segment	Total Exp by segment				CAGR			Share of Global Market		Growth	
	2009	2019	2030	2045	2009-19	2019-30	2030-45	2019	2045	2030	2045
0-5000	4,436	4,311	3,791	3,154	-0.3%	-1.2%	-1.2%	9.6%	4.4%	-4.4%	-4.2%
5000-15000	5,221	5,617	5,965	5,591	0.7%	0.5%	-0.4%	12.5%	7.8%	2.9%	-2.5%
15000-25000	6,957	8,196	9,593	10,654	1.7%	1.4%	0.7%	18.2%	14.8%	11.7%	7.1%
25000 +	7,384	9,949	13,669	17,650	3.0%	2.9%	1.7%	22.1%	24.5%	31.2%	26.5%
Total	23,999	28,073	33,018	37,049	1.6%	1.5%	0.8%	62.3%	51.5%	41.4%	26.8%

US$ Income Segment	Persons (mns) in segment				CAGR		
	2009	2019	2030	2045	2009-19	2019-30	2030-45
0-5000	368	340	282	227	-0.8%	-1.7%	-1.4%
5000-15000	240	250	259	236	0.4%	0.3%	-0.6%
15000-25000	212	243	279	306	1.3%	1.3%	0.6%
25000 +	123	158	204	261	2.5%	2.4%	1.6%
Total	943	991	1,025	1,030	0.5%	0.3%	0.0%

While this concentration of spending power is interesting, the more important issue is perhaps the change in growth rate. For the decade to 2019 total consumption expenditure by this Country Segment grew at 1.6% per annum. In part that was driven by the growth in population in the segment as well as increased affluence. For the period to 2045, the population growth is close to zero and hence growth in spending is now totally a function of increased incomes (productivity). This results in a projected growth rate of consumption expenditure of 1.5% per annum to 2030 and then 0.8% per annum to 2045 as shown in Table 8-2.

Figure 8-7 shows the dynamics in terms of the individual income segments for this Country Segment. In total, the number of persons in this segment is projected to increase by only 3% between 2019 and 2045 (basically a stable total population) whereas total consumption expenditure is projected to increase by 32%. This means the market in future is a stable number of customers spending more per customer.

Figure 8-7: Projected Shift in Distribution of Persons and Spending Power by Income Segment. Older Affluent Country Segment.

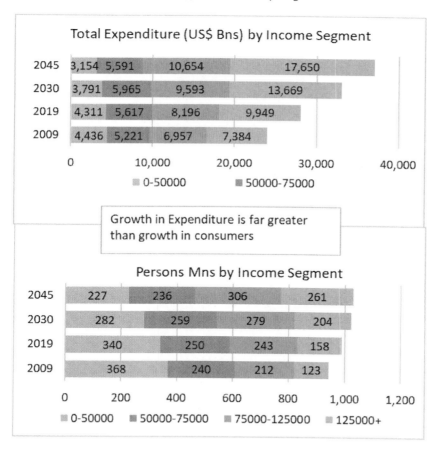

The Older less Affluent Segment (Excluding China)

Please note that the income segments used for this Country Segment are US$0 to US$5,000, US$5,000 to US$15,000, US$15,000 to US$25,000, and US$25,000 and above.

China is not included in this Segment's analysis due to its much higher propensity to save. It is covered separately later in this section.

A key characteristic of this Country Segment is that the number of consumers (and households) is projected to decline from 412 million in 2019 to 385 million in 2045. However, their income is expected to increase. As a result, this Country Segment is relatively static in its global share of consumption expenditure. Specifically, it is circa 5.5% of the global market and 4% share of global growth through to 2030 and then 5% and 4.3% respectively through to 2045. Overall, the total expenditure of this Country Segment (excluding China) grows at a slowing pace – from 1.9% per annum to 2019 to 1.3% for 2030 to 2045.

Table 8-3: Older Low Income Segment's Share of Global Expenditure 2019 to 2045. (Excludes China)

US$ Income Segment	Total Exp by segment				CAGR			Share of Global Market		Growth	
	2009	2019	2030	2045	2009-19	2019-30	2030-45	2019	2045	2030	2045
0-5000	59	45	27	18	-2.6%	-4.5%	-2.8%	0.1%	0.0%	-0.2%	-0.1%
5000-15000	472	466	447	347	-0.1%	-0.4%	-1.7%	1.0%	0.5%	-0.2%	-0.7%
15000-25000	486	572	555	508	1.6%	-0.3%	-0.6%	1.3%	0.7%	-0.1%	-0.3%
25000 +	1,034	1,392	1,929	2,728	3.0%	3.0%	2.3%	3.1%	3.8%	4.5%	5.3%
Total	2,052	2,476	2,957	3,601	1.9%	1.6%	1.3%	5.5%	5.0%	4.0%	4.3%

US$ Income Segment	Persons (mns) in segment				CAGR		
	2009	2019	2030	2045	2009-19	2019-30	2030-45
0-5000	59	41	23	16	-3.6%	-5.0%	-2.5%
5000-15000	180	164	149	113	-1.0%	-0.8%	-1.8%
15000-25000	90	99	98	90	0.9%	-0.1%	-0.6%
25000 +	84	109	136	167	2.6%	2.0%	1.4%
Total	413	412	405	385	0.0%	-0.1%	-0.3%

Within this Country Segment, the growth in household incomes is projected to create a 50% increase in the number of persons in the US$25,000 plus Household Income range. With that, expect significant growth in the total expenditure of that income segment (See Figure 8-8).

Figure 8-8: Projected Shift in Distribution of Persons and Spending Power by Income Segment – Family Stage Low Income (Excluding China).

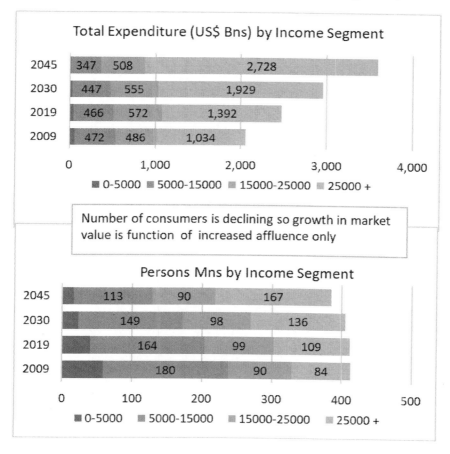

China - Urban

While China has very similar characteristics to the other countries in the Old Low-Income segment in terms of age, birth rates, household size and education it is very different in terms of growth of affluence and propensity to spend. It is also a very large number of people.

The focus here is on the urban population which has been expanding rapidly due to the previously discussed ongoing rural to urban migration, and its higher affluence compared to the rural population. Table 8-4 summarises the relative importance of this specific population to global consumption expenditure.

Table 8-4: **Urban** China's Share of Global Expenditure 2019 to 2045.

US$ Income Segment	Total Exp by segment				CAGR			Share of Global Market		Growth	
	2009	2019	2030	2045	2009-19	2019-30	2030-45	2019	2045	2030	2045
0-5000	289	403	489	562	3.4%	1.8%	0.9%	0.9%	0.8%	0.7%	0.5%
5000-15000	406	639	1,008	1,414	4.6%	4.2%	2.3%	1.4%	2.0%	3.1%	2.7%
15000-25000	113	198	377	865	5.8%	6.0%	5.7%	0.4%	1.2%	1.5%	3.2%
25000 +	145	262	626	2,306	6.1%	8.2%	9.1%	0.6%	3.2%	3.1%	11.2%
Total	953	1,502	2,501	5,146	4.7%	4.7%	4.9%	3.3%	7.1%	8.4%	17.6%

US$ Income Segment	Persons (mns) in segment				CAGR		
	2009	2019	2030	2045	2009-19	2019-30	2030-45
0-5000	630	871	1,000	1,191	3.3%	1.3%	1.2%
5000-15000	252	380	564	717	4.2%	3.6%	1.6%
15000-25000	31	52	93	200	5.4%	5.5%	5.3%
25000 +	17	29	61	203	5.8%	6.9%	8.3%
Total	930	1,332	1,718	2,310	3.7%	2.3%	2.0%

As a group, they account for 8% of global consumption expenditure in 2019 and this is projected to increase to 12% by 2045. However, while increasing in relative importance do note that like the Older Affluent Country Segment their rate of growth (in total expenditure) is slowing – and quite dramatically. From 9.6% in the last decade to a projected 5% per annum to 2030 and 2.4% per annum to 2045. This is significant in the context of creating demand for workers globally and particularly in the Young Poor Countries.

The reason for this projected slowdown is that China's total population is projected to stop growing in 2028 and the urban population levels out around 2035. As such one of the key drivers of the historic increase in consumption spending no longer exists.

Figure 8-9 shows how the size of the different income segments changes in terms of total expenditure as well as persons. The dominance of the US$25,000 plus households/consumers in terms of share of spend is evident in 2019 and is projected to increase through to 2045.

Figure 8-9: Projected Shift in Distribution of Persons and Spending Power by Income Segment in Urban China 2009 to 2045.

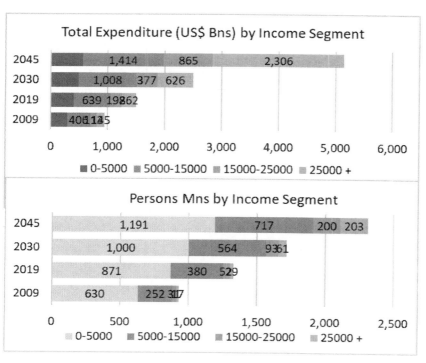

The growth rate of Urban China Consumer spending is projected to slow dramatically from 9.6% per annum in the last decade to a projected 2.4% per annum from 2030 to 2045. This may be averted if they lower their high rates of saving.

The Family Stage Low Income Segment – Excluding India

Please note that the income segments used for this Country Segment are US$0 to US$5,000, US$5,000 to US$15,000, US$15,000 to US$25,000, and US$25,000 and above.

In this instance, India because of its absolute size relative to other countries in this segment, has been presented separately (below) in this Chapter. Table 8-5 summarises the importance of this Country Segment (excluding India). As a share of the global market, it is projected to be relatively static at circa 15% even though it is projected to have both a growing number of consumers and growing affluence/income. It is not sufficient to change its relative position globally.

*Table 8-5: Family Stage Low Income Segment's Share of Global Expenditure and Expenditure Growth 2019 to 2045 (**excluding India**).*

US$ Income Segment	Total Exp by segment				CAGR			Share of Global			
								Market		Growth	
	2009	2019	2030	2045	2009-19	2019-30	2030-45	2019	2045	2030	2045
0-5000	312	312	288	296	0.0%	-0.7%	0.2%	0.7%	0.4%	-0.2%	0.1%
5000-15000	1,109	1,592	2,162	2,286	3.7%	2.8%	0.4%	3.5%	3.2%	4.8%	0.8%
15000-25000	844	1,190	1,591	2,205	3.5%	2.7%	2.2%	2.6%	3.1%	3.4%	4.1%
25000 +	2,643	3,544	4,289	6,448	3.0%	1.7%	2.8%	7.9%	9.0%	6.2%	14.3%
Total	4,907	6,638	8,330	11,235	3.1%	2.1%	2.0%	14.7%	15.6%	14.2%	19.3%

US$ Income Segment	Persons (mns) in segment				CAGR		
	2009	2019	2030	2045	2009-19	2019-30	2030-45
0-5000	511	439	346	328	-1.5%	-2.1%	-0.4%
5000-15000	567	757	919	850	2.9%	1.8%	-0.5%
15000-25000	202	264	329	405	2.7%	2.0%	1.4%
25000 +	227	295	345	491	2.6%	1.4%	2.4%
Total	1,507	1,755	1,939	2,074	1.5%	0.9%	0.4%

As shown in Figure 8-10 (and Table 8-5) the main dynamic in this group of countries for the next 25 years is the growth of the number of persons (and households) with a household income over US$15,000 per annum. They are projected to double in number in the next 25 years and that will lift consumption expenditure to over 2% per annum.

Figure 8-10: Projected Shift in Distribution of Persons and Spending Power by Income Segment – Family Stage Low Income. (Excluding India)

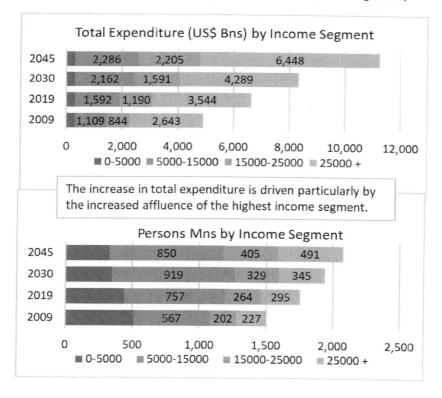

India

This country is being treated separately as it is very large in terms of population at 1.4 billion persons in 2019. However, it accounts for just 3.8% of global expenditure in 2019 because its incomes are lower than the other countries in the Family Stage Low Income Country Segment (detailed above). In addition, as explained earlier in this book, India's birth rate is reducing and after 2030 so are the number of births. Whereas the population grew at 1.1% for the last decade, for the period 2030 to 2045 it is projected to grow at 0.2% per annum – a significant change.

Because of its lower incomes and then slowing growth rate, it accounts for 3.8% of global expenditure in 2019 and is projected to increase to just 5.7% by 2045 even though it then has a projected population of 1.52 billion persons and is, by then, the largest country by population.

Table 8-6: India's Share of Global Expenditure and Expenditure Growth 2019 to 2045.

US$ Income Segment	Total Exp by segment				CAGR			Share of Global Market		Growth	
	2009	2019	2030	2045	2009-19	2019-30	2030-45	2019	2045	2030	2045
0-5000	419	618	642	505	4.0%	0.3%	-1.6%	1.4%	0.7%	0.2%	-0.9%
5000-15000	351	753	1,224	1,912	7.9%	4.5%	3.0%	1.7%	2.7%	3.9%	4.6%
15000-25000	67	159	313	714	9.0%	6.3%	5.6%	0.4%	1.0%	1.3%	2.7%
25000 +	75	179	375	990	9.1%	6.9%	6.7%	0.4%	1.4%	1.6%	4.1%
Total	913	1,710	2,554	4,121	6.5%	3.7%	3.2%	3.8%	5.7%	7.1%	10.4%

US$ Income Segment	Persons (mns) in segment				CAGR		
	2009	2019	2030	2045	2009-19	2019-30	2030-45
0-5000	937	926	828	559	-0.1%	-1.0%	-2.6%
5000-15000	253	390	563	755	4.4%	3.4%	2.0%
15000-25000	21	36	64	133	5.6%	5.5%	5.0%
25000 +	10	17	32	76	5.7%	6.0%	5.8%
Total	1,221	1,369	1,487	1,522	1.1%	0.8%	0.2%

However, its increasing real household incomes mean that while it may be an unexpectedly small share of global consumption expenditure, it is more important in terms of growth of expenditure and hence future demand for goods and services. For the period to 2030, it is projected to account for 7.1% of global consumption growth and for the period 2030 to 2045 it is projected to be 10.4%. A country of increasing importance.

Figure 8-11 shows the projected changes in the number of persons by income segment and total expenditure by income segment. This market is driven more by the increase in growing incomes than the number of persons.

Figure 8-11: Projected Shift in Distribution of Persons and Spending Power by Income Segment – India.

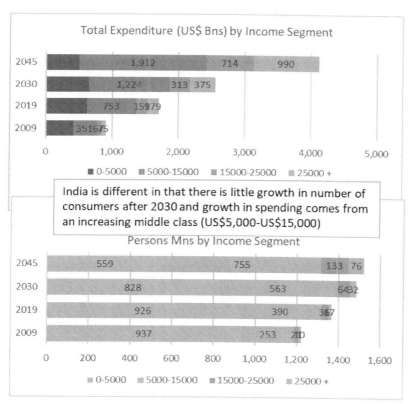

It also differs from the other countries in the Family Stage segment in that the projected growth is in the US$5,000 to US$15,000 income segment rather than being almost exclusively in the highest income group. The segments above US$15,000 pa household income are relatively small in terms of persons (and households).

The Young Poor Country Segment

Please note that the income segments used for this Country Segment are US$0 to US$5,000, US$5,000 to US$15,000, US$15,000 to US$25,000, and US$25,000 and above.

With a GDP per capita mostly below US$10,000, these economies are biased to the lower household income segment of US$0 to US$5,000 per annum. It is estimated that only 6% of households in these countries have an income of more than US$15,000 in 2019. In contrast, 65% live in a household with an income of less than US$5,000 and that is with an average household size of more than 4 persons.

As shown in Table 8-7, even though this Country Segment has a large and rapidly growing population low incomes mean that it is a small share of global expenditure. It is 3.3% in 2019 and is projected to increase to 7.1% by 2045 if the rate of propensity to be employed is maintained. In terms of the share of the population, it is 18% in 2019 and projected to be 26% in 2045.

Table 8-7: Young Poor Country Segment's Share of Global Expenditure and Expenditure Growth 2019 to 2045.

US$ Income Segment	Total Exp by segment				CAGR			Share of Global Market		Growth	
	2009	2019	2030	2045	2009-19	2019-30	2030-45	2019	2045	2030	2045
0-5000	289	403	489	562	3.4%	1.8%	0.9%	0.9%	0.8%	0.7%	0.5%
5000-15000	406	639	1,008	1,414	4.6%	4.2%	2.3%	1.4%	2.0%	3.1%	2.7%
15000-25000	113	198	377	865	5.8%	6.0%	5.7%	0.4%	1.2%	1.5%	3.2%
25000 +	145	262	626	2,306	6.1%	8.2%	9.1%	0.6%	3.2%	3.1%	11.2%
Total	953	1,502	2,501	5,146	4.7%	4.7%	4.9%	3.3%	7.1%	8.4%	17.6%

US$ Income Segment	Persons (mns) in segment				CAGR		
	2009	2019	2030	2045	2009-19	2019-30	2030-45
0-5000	630	871	1,000	1,191	3.3%	1.3%	1.2%
5000-15000	252	380	564	717	4.2%	3.6%	1.6%
15000-25000	31	52	93	200	5.4%	5.5%	5.3%
25000 +	17	29	61	203	5.8%	6.9%	8.3%
Total	930	1,332	1,718	2,310	3.7%	2.3%	2.0%

Figure 8-12 shows the relative change in the size of the different income segments and their total consumption expenditure from 2009 as projected to 2045. While all income segments grow in size (in terms of people and spending) the more affluent segment makes the biggest gain in terms of spend.

As shown in Table 8-7 in real 2019 US$ terms this affluent segment's consumption expenditure is projected to grow at 8.2% per annum to 2030. However, it is a small share of the global market at 0.6% in 2019. But do note the change after 2030 when the growth rate of this income segment is projected to increase to 9.1% per annum and reach 3.2% of global expenditure *if employment rates are achieved*.

Figure 8-12: Projected Shift in Distribution of Persons and Spending Power by Income Segment – Young Poor Country Segment.

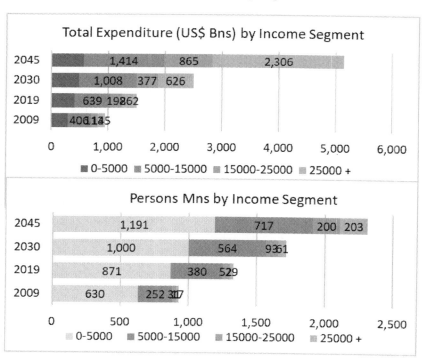

Summary

This has been quite a complex Chapter. There are several forces at play in terms of expenditure patterns. Changes in the number of households, changes in the income of those households, change in the distribution of that income across households and finally, changes and differences in terms of the propensity of households to spend that money.

Probably the most important point to flow from this Chapter is that total consumption expenditure is projected to increase because of increases in the total earned incomes of the households/population and an increasing population and number of households.

There are, however, big differences in how that plays out. For the dominant Country Segment in terms of spending power – the Older Affluent – the increase in total spending is a function of more money per customer rather than more customers. A similar story applies to the next most important Country Segment (in terms of spending power) – that is the Older Low Income – where there is a decline in the number of customers but a growth in spending per customer which more than offsets that.

For both these Country Segments, the focus is on whether this relatively stable number of consumers will spend more given their increased income. The danger is that with their changing age profile – increasingly over 40 years of age - spending patterns change and there will perhaps be a greater propensity to save.

The projection is that total spending will continue to increase but at a slowing rate. Whereas it grew at 1.6% per annum for the Older Affluent from 2009 to 2019, with the now stable population size the growth rate is projected to slow, such that it is 0.8% per annum from 2030 to 2045.

In the case of the Older Low-Income segment excluding China, total consumer spending growth slows from 1.9% per annum in 2019 to 1.6% per annum to 2030 and then 1.3% per annum to 2045. Not a significant change, but slower growth.

In the case of China, urban households are the area to focus on. They accounted for an estimated 81% of incomes in China in 2019 and a projected 86% by 2045. The issue here is that while the income of urban households is projected to continue to increase as a result of increased productivity per worker, the number of urban households and consumers is projected to stabilise after 2034. This has a significant impact on the growth of consumer spending in China. Whereas it grew at 9.6% per annum to 2019 it is projected to slow to 5% per annum to 2030 and 2.7% per annum from 2030 to 2045.

For the other two Country Segments, the story is more positive. The Family Stage Low Income Country Segment will experience a significant increase in the number of households in the next 25 years – up 41% in absolute terms (plus 375 million households) and an increase in total spending (up 84% in absolute terms by 2045 and 2.0% per annum in annual growth terms.

The Young Poor Country Segment may not have much to spend individually but the inescapable forecast is that the number of households will double in the next 25 years and their total spending (aided by a modest increase in income per household) would lift by 242% (4.8% per annum) if the employment rate can be maintained. Basically, from a retailer's point of view, it is an increased volume of customers rather than a significant spend per customer.

Summary Profile – Consumption Expenditure

Older Affluent

	2019	2030	2045
Avg Household Exp US$	72,585	81,118	89,674
Avg Household Exp per cap	28,339	32,228	35,955
Growth pa in Exp per cap	1.1%	1.2%	0.7%
Total Exp all Households (US$ Bn)	28,073	33,018	37,049
Growth pa in total exp	1.6%	1.5%	0.8%
Expenditure as % Income	86.5%	84.5%	81.9%

Older Low Income

	2019	2030	2045
Avg Household Exp US$	10,900	14,677	19,777
Avg Household Exp per cap	3,899	5,749	8,310
Growth pa in Exp per cap	5.7%	3.6%	2.5%
Total Exp all Households (US$ Bn)	7,104	10,561	14,457
Growth pa in total exp	6.1%	3.7%	2.1%
Expenditure as % Income	55.1%	52.3%	49.8%

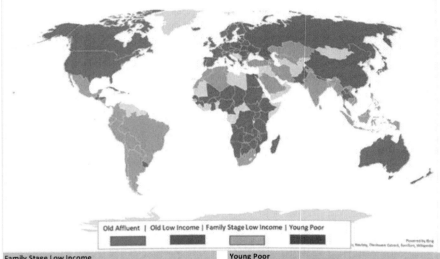

Old Affluent | Old Low Income | Family Stage Low Income | Young Poor

Family Stage Low Income

	2019	2030	2045
Avg Household Exp US$	9,214	9,943	11,987
Avg Household Exp per cap	2,673	3,178	4,272
Growth pa in Exp per cap	2.3%	1.6%	2.0%
Total Exp all Households (US$ Bn)	8,348	10,884	15,357
Growth pa in total exp	3.7%	2.4%	2.3%
Expenditure as % Income	80.8%	79.9%	78.3%

Young Poor

	2019	2030	2045
Avg Household Exp US$	5,287	6,556	9,542
Avg Household Exp per cap	1,128	1,457	2,228
Growth pa in Exp per cap	1.0%	2.4%	2.9%
Total Exp all Households (US$ Bn)	1,502	2,501	5,146
Growth pa in total exp	4.7%	4.7%	4.9%
Expenditure as % Income	92.3%	91.9%	91.0%

Chapter 9
Implications for Future Demand and Employment

One of the key issues (as is apparent from the preceding discussion) is the ability of persons of working age to find employment. Up to this stage, It has been assumed that all countries will be able to maintain the trend in the propensity of their working-age population to find employment.

That assumption has implications for the total productivity of the country (GDP), household incomes and, consumption expenditure.

But there is compelling evidence that such employment rates will not be achieved, and this chapter looks at the implications of that assuming the worst case. That is, there will be a shortfall of 400 million jobs.

As it is impossible to say where this shortfall will take place the subsequent analysis is reported at a Country Segment level rather than at a county level.

The subsequent analysis starts with demonstrating the issues concerning levels of employment that can be achieved. This is followed by an estimate of the number that can (and cannot) find work. That is then applied to the size of the workforce and then GDP, household incomes and consumption.

The result is a worrying picture.

Why is maintaining employment levels under threat?

Table 9-1 shows the projected total expenditure of households on consumer goods through to 2045. Major points to note in terms of these projections are:

1. The Older Affluent Country Segment will dominate total consumer spending through to 2045 at which time it will be 52% of all such spending.
2. Excluding China, the Older Low-Income Segment will grow at a much more sedate pace of circa 1.4% per annum from 2019 to 2045.
3. China's consumption expenditure is also expected to slow dramatically, a reflection of population reduction and ageing and slower real GDP growth. Whereas urban consumption expenditure grew at 9.6% per annum for the decade to 2019, from 2030 to 2045 it is projected to be 2.7% per annum.
4. The Young Poor Country Segment is expected to be the fastest growing after 2020. But at 3% of total spending, the impact of this fast growth on the total market is minimal through to 2045.

However, these forecasts are based on some assumptions which need to be kept in mind. They are:

1. Trends in the number of persons of working-age continue. That is considered to be a reliable forecast.
2. Trends in education and accumulated Fixed Capital investment per worker continue. Again, reasonably reliable forecasts as both variables change slowly over 10 years and have quite steady trends.
3. Trends in productivity per worker continue as a result of the trends in education and accumulated Fixed Capital Investment. Again, historically this has been a steady trend.

4. That the income earned gets spent at the rates projected from historic wage and spending rates. Given the historic stability of these variables, this projection is reliable.

5. Finally. that the working-age population can obtain employment in line with the trend in the propensity to be employed which in itself is a function of trends in education and accumulated Fixed Capital Investment. *This has low confidence*. This chapter tests the likely impact of that not being achieved.

The important question is, 'will the number of persons needed to work to satisfy the demand of consumption spending match the growth in the number of persons seeking to be in work?'

Figure 9-1 shows the historic global trend in consumption expenditure and the number of employed persons. Some relevant statistics are:

1. Global consumption expenditure grew in real terms at 2.64% per annum from 2009 to 2019. Year on year the historic rate of growth has been relatively consistent around the range of 2.6% per annum until 2019 when it slowed suddenly.
2. Employment has been growing consistently at around 1.0% per annum which is 1.6 points slower than total consumption expenditure.
3. As a result, consumption per employed person has risen by an average of 1.67% per annum for the last decade. Production has gotten more efficient. That is, it has needed fewer workers to produce the same value of consumption.

Fortunately, the growth in demand has been such that this has nonetheless effective absorbed all the available labour force of the countries included in this study. As shown at the start of Chapter 6, circa two-thirds of those of working age were employed which would suggest that this is most of those seeking work. (Not all persons of working age are seeking work).

Figure 9-1: Historic Trend in Key Variables for Consumption and Employment.

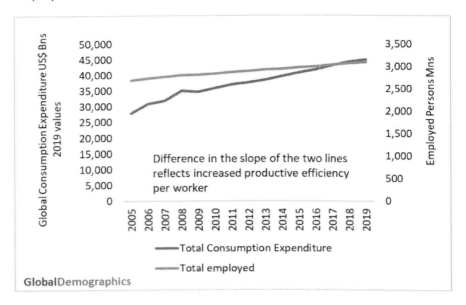

The Trend in Total Consumption Expenditure

Most consumption expenditure takes place in countries where the total number of consumers is projected to stabilise or decline. That is the Older Affluent and The Older Low Income Country Segments. Together they account for 78% of global consumption in 2020. If full employment was maintained globally this would reduce to 71% by 2045.

However, as mentioned in earlier chapters, the number of such consumers is now stable in number and their incomes are growing at a slower rate than before. This indicates that growth in the consumption expenditure will slow. The projected reduction is shown in Figure 9-2. It grows through to 2030 (mainly because of the urban working-aged empty nester in China) and then declines steeply. Form 2.5% per annum to 0.8% in 2040 to 2045.

Figure 9-2: Historic and Projected Average Growth Rate per annum in Total Household Consumption Expenditure in the Older Country Segments (Older Affluent and Older Low Income).

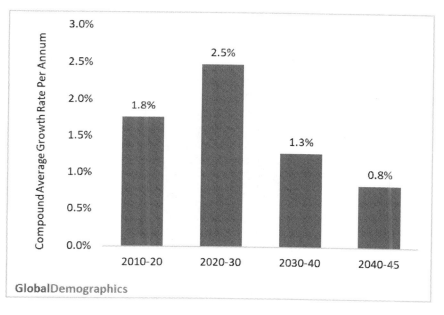

The two younger Country Segments are expected to show faster growth in consumption expenditure provided they could maintain employment rates. However, at 22% of global consumption expenditure in 2019, their faster growth is not sufficient to offset the slower growth in the older country segments even if they were able to maintain historic levels of employment.

The efficiency of creating consumer goods and services.

This is the projected trend in total consumption expenditure divided by the number of employed persons. It provides an estimate of the required number of workers (globally) to service consumption expenditure.

Over the last decade, this has been growing at 1.63% per annum. That is, production has been getting more efficient - and the number of workers required to produce the same amount of consumption goods and services has been declining at 1.63% per annum.

In 2019, each worker produced (either directly or indirectly) US$14,578 of consumption goods and services. Assuming the trend in increased efficiency/productivity continues at 1.63% per annum then by 2030 the average worker will be producing US$17,415 in consumption goods and services. This is projected to reach US$22,195 by 2045.

Implication for the number of workers required.

To determine this, it is necessary to revise two variables. The first is the number of workers required each year and then the lagged (by 1 year) effect of that on consumption as a result of fewer persons in the Younger Country Segments not being able to obtain employment.

The assumption was made that for every reduced employment opportunity because of increased productivity per worker 25% went to the Young Family Country Segment and 75% to the Young Poor. The basis for this is the difference in education profile and accumulated Fixed Capital Investment per worker.

This then applied to consumption – the total consumption in those segments was reduced proportionately to reflect the lower earnings per household because of having fewer workers (on average).

There are 3.063 billion persons employed in 2019 to satisfy (either directly or indirectly) existing consumption demand. After allowing for increased efficiency of the worker and continued, but slower, growth in consumption expenditure, by 2030 the total workforce required would increase to 3.271 billion persons and by 2045 there would be a marginal decline in the required number of workers to 3.244 billion. This compares with a projected number of persons wanting to be in work in 2045 of 3.638 billion. *A shortfall of employment of 394 million persons*.

This is summarised in Figure 9-3. What is also apparent from this Figure is that not only is there a shortfall in terms of the number of employees needed relative to the number seeking work after 2024, but in addition peak demand for workers is reached in 2034. After that year the projected demand for workers declines (lower line in Figure 9-3). The problem is imminent – not in 25 years.

Figure 9-3: Comparison of Workers needed with Persons wanting work.

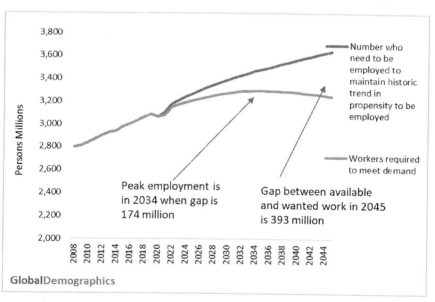

The combination of slower growth in total global consumption and increased efficiency of production means that there is potentially no demand for additional workers after 2034.

This is of major concern. While it is impossible to say where the shortfall in employment opportunities will be, it is not unreasonable to assume it will be biased toward the countries that score lowest on education and accumulated Fixed Capital Investment. They are simply less efficient producers. They may be cheap but that does not help in this scenario.

The potential gap between the number of people that need to be in work to maintain a country's economy (the employment rate) and the number of workers required given trends in total consumption expenditure and productivity per worker grows to 393 million persons. This is a major concern.

Impact on Employment Levels

As stated at the start of this chapter it is not possible to determine which individual countries would suffer the shortfall in employment opportunities, so the following has to be done at a Country Segment level.

Arbitrarily it has been assumed that 25% of the shortfall in work is borne by the Young Family Country Segment and 75% by the Young Poor Country Segment. This allocation is based on relative levels of education and accumulated Fixed Capital Investment per worker.

Figure 9-4 shows the impact of this on the propensity to be employed. For the Young Family Country Segment, the impact is small. This reflects the large number of persons already employed (1.45 billion). The reduction of 100 million is not significant in that context. As shown subsequently it also means the impact on total GDP is small.

However, for the Young Poor Country Segment, the effect is very significant. The reduction of 300 million workers is significant relative to the expected size of the employed labour force in 2045 – that is 918 million. The reduction would mean that the propensity to be employed for a person of working age in 2045 would drop from 64% to 44%. A substantial drop with serious implications for social stability. There would, by definition, be a significant unemployed population.

Figure 9-4: Impact of Slower Consumption Growth on Propensity to be Employed.

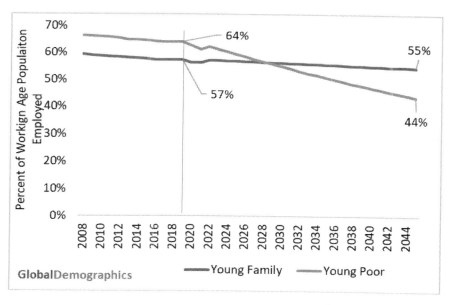

In Summary

This chapter demonstrates the significant risk the world is facing in the next 25 years. The slowdown in the rate of growth in consumption expenditure combined with ongoing rapid growth in the number of persons of working age and potentially looking for work has created a disequilibrium that is not easily avoided.

The slower consumption growth would seem to be inevitable as it is a function of slower population growth in the countries that account for most of the consumption. It is exacerbated by potentially more conservative spending patterns as this same group gets older.

The rapid growth in the number of persons of working age in the Young Poor Country Segment, particularly, is also inevitable. Many of them are already alive – just not yet working age.

In addition to it constraining incomes in those younger countries, it also impacts total GDP and the ability of the governments to spend on the development of social services so desperately needed in those countries.

The problem is real and needs to be confronted.

Chapter 10
The Health Tsunami

Introduction

The purpose of this chapter is to demonstrate, as best possible, the potential growth in demand for health care globally (and by the individual Country and Country Segments) and then secondly, examine the potential issues regarding the funding of this demand.

There are two trends taking place that, combined, potentially have a significant impact on the demand for healthcare and the consequent impact on the finances of governments and households. One is inevitable and the other is extremely likely.

Consequently, this chapter is divided into two parts. The first looks at estimating the trend in demand for healthcare and the second looks at present funding, both overall as well as by source (Government or Private), and the potential adequacy of it now and in the future.

Note: The terms 'incidence' and 'prevalence' are used in this chapter. Incidence applies to Cancers – Oncology - and is expressed as cases per 100,000 and refers to those diagnosed with cancer in that year. Prevalence, expressed as cases per 100, refers to the number of non-cancer chronic conditions (for example diabetes) that exist within that year whether newly diagnosed in that year or previously diagnosed but still requiring treatment.

The Methodology Used to Forecast Demand

The availability and adequacy of health care *data* are both good and bad. For many countries, there is good reporting via the World Health Organisation on the incidence or prevalence of a wide range of health conditions. In addition, many counties have their only public organisations reporting on health issues in some detail. The CDC in the United States is a good example.

However, there is a significant part of the world where the appropriate data is not reported in sufficient detail (if at all) to allow a global picture to be obtained.

Accordingly, the incidence or prevalence of a set of more frequently reported cancers and chronic or common conditions (detailed subsequently in this Chapter) are used to create an index of the 'overall healthiness' of a country. The assumption is that this overall healthiness index is a good proxy for overall demand for health services. We have termed this the *'Cases Index'*. Do remember it is an index and not the absolute number.

The weakness of this approach is that for some poor countries where the health system is inadequate the required data is non-existent. For those countries, the model has used the rates for surrogate countries that are reporting the data and are of a similar level of affluence (Gross Domestic Product per capita). The assumption is that incidence and prevalence to some extent are a function of the quality of life and environment associated with that level of affluence. Specifically, nutrition, education, understanding of hygiene and wellness and the environment (pollution etc) are reflected in GDP per capita.

The Likely Trend in Demand for HealthCare to 2045

The likely demand for health services in the future is a function of:

1. the changing age/gender profile of the population

2. the trend in incidence/prevalence of health conditions by age and gender over time.

The combination of these two inputs provides an estimate of the overall trend in demand for health services in the future by individual countries as well as a summary for each of the four Country Segments. This is the cases index.

The Changing Age Profile of Populations

As demonstrated graphically later in this Chapter (Figures 10-4 and 10-5) the incidence/prevalence rates of many health conditions are particularly (but not exclusively) a function of gender and age, and especially age 40 years and above. As such it is useful to examine the global trend in the number of persons over the age of 40 years.

The overall demand for health services is particularly driven by the number of persons over 40 years of age.

Due to the significant increase in the number of births starting 60 years ago, the number of persons over the age of 40 has been increasing rapidly for the last two decades and this is projected to continue to do so for the next 25 years. It will vary by the Country Segments defined in this book, but it will increase for all. In part, it is increasing as a result of improving lifestyles and health-related environments and hence a longer life expectancy.

Figure 10-1 shows the projected total number of persons in the 116 countries included in this analysis that are either 40-64 years of age or 65 years of age and older from the ear 2005 to 2045. The forecast of the population over 40 years of age tends to be quite reliable as these people are already alive today and the only issue is death rates which are normally quite stable. Even the Covid-19 Pandemic, whose death impact is biased to older persons, has not been sufficient to meaningfully change the death rates even in the year of the pandemic, let alone in future years.

Figure 10-1: Historic and Projected Number of Persons Over 40 Years of Age. 2005 to 2045.

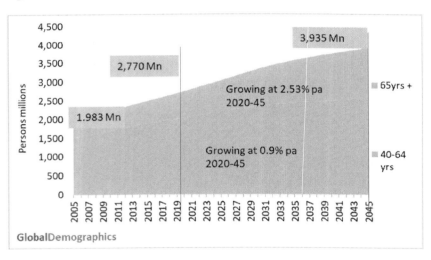

GlobalDemographics

As shown in Figure 10-1, the total number of persons over the age of 40 is projected to increase by 42% between 2019 and 2045. From 2.8 billion to 3.9 billion. That is an average growth rate of 1.4% per annum for the next 25 years but note how the 40 to 64 year age group is growing at a much slower rate which in time permeates into the 65 plus age group.

Figure 10-2 shows the total number of persons over 40 years of age in each of the four Country Segments. Table 10-1 provides details on the growth rates by Country Segment. Given that median age is one of the criteria for defining the Country Segments it is not surprising that the picture differs significantly between them.

Figure 10-2: Total Persons Over 40 Years of Age by Country Segment

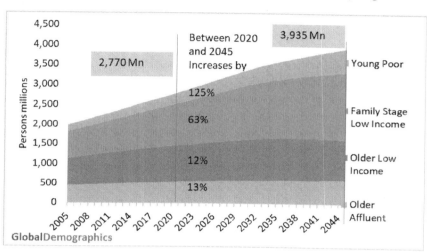

GlobalDemographics

Table 10-1: Projected Trend in Number of Persons over 40 Years of Age by Country Segment and in Total: 2009 to 2045

	Persons mns 40yrs +				Absolute Change		
	2009	2020	2030	2045	2009-20	2020-30	2030-45
Older Affluent	481	544	587	613	63	43	26
Older Low Income	756	917	1,042	1,025	161	125	-17
Family Stage Low Income	768	1,045	1,342	1,703	276	298	360
Young Poor	186	264	373	595	78	108	222
Total	2,192	2,770	3,344	3,935	579	573	591

	Absolute % increase for period shown				Growth Rate per annum		
	2020-45	2009-20	2020-30	2030-45	2009-20	2020-30	2030-45
Older Affluent	13%	13%	8%	4%	1.1%	0.8%	0.3%
Older Low Income	12%	21%	14%	-2%	1.8%	1.3%	-0.1%
Family Stage Low Income	63%	36%	29%	27%	2.8%	2.5%	1.6%
Young Poor	125%	42%	41%	60%	3.2%	3.5%	3.2%
Total	42%	26%	21%	18%	2.2%	1.9%	1.1%

313

The number of persons over 40 years of age in the Old Affluent Country Segment is projected to increase by just 69 million persons in the next 25 years – on a base of 544 million in 2020. That is a 13% lift or growth rate of 0.5% per annum. However, do note that for the period 2030 to 2045 the increase is 26 million and a growth rate of 0.3% per annum. This means the Older Affluent countries are close to 'peak aged'.

This represents a significant slowdown from the decade 2009 to 2020. For that decade, the 40 years and above population grew by 63 million persons or 1.1% per annum.

It might also be noted that even for the 65 years and above segment, the growth rate after 2030 slows dramatically to 0.9% per annum and adds 35 million persons on a base of 246 million in 2030.

A very similar scenario is taking place in the Old Low Income Country Segment. It is projected to add 107 million persons over 40 years of age in 25 years on a base of 917 million in 2020. It peaks in number in the year 2035 having risen at 1.2% per annum from 2020 and then it declines at 0.1% through to 2045. Again, a segment of countries that are reaching 'peak aged'.

In total the two older Country Segments show continued growth in the 40 plus age groups– but as shown in Table 10-1, at a relatively modest and slowing rate. They are now 'old' in that for many countries in these two Country Segments over half their population is already over the age of 40 years.

This is quite different from the two younger Country Segments. These are experiencing rapid growth in the older population age groups. While in the Family Stage Low Income segment the 40 plus age group is a small proportion of the total population, for the period 2020 to 2045 it grows by 63% (2.8% pa). In the Young Poor segment, the 40 years and above age group which is just 3% of their total population in 2020 grows by a very high 125% (3.2% per annum). Of the projected additional number of persons over 40 years of age between 2020 and 2045, 86% will be in the two young Country Segments.

Of the projected additional number of persons over 40 years of age between 2020 and 2045, 86% will be in the two young Country Segments.

Given the very definite relationship between age and the need for health services, the growth of the 40 plus age segment in what is traditionally referred to as 'Young' countries mean that that is where there will be the largest upsurge in demand for health services in future.

As is evident from Table 10-2 the Family Stage Low Income Country Segment (which contains India, Brazil, and Indonesia – all countries with large populations) is particularly important. By 2045 it is projected to account for nearly half of all persons in the world over the age of 40 and 37% of those over 64 years of age.

Trends in Incidence and Prevalence of Common Health Conditions

The second factor to consider when trying to estimate future demand for health services is the incidence and prevalence of chronic conditions.

As mentioned in the introduction to this Chapter, good epidemiology data on prevalent chronic conditions are not available for all countries and particularly not for the countries in the Young Poor Country Segment.

The issue for the Young Poor Countries is one of diagnostics. It is not that these chronic conditions do not exist in these populations, they do. However, most of these countries have inadequate health services and, in many cases, health conditions are under diagnosed and the cause of death is uncertain. For countries that are not reporting or under-reporting data, the model uses the average rates that are available for other low-income countries with a better functioning health system to indicate what the rate might be like if widespread diagnostics existed. But to be interpreted with care.

Projected Trend in Cancer Incidence Rates by Age

Figure 10-3 shows the aggregate incidence rate per 100,000 persons by age for 12 cancers for which data is available for a large number of countries in 2019. While there is a difference by country in the aggregate pattern, probably attributable to a combination of differences in lifestyle, diet, and availability of diagnostics, the overall pattern by age is quite consistent. That is, the incidence rate is generally very low (under 100 per 100,000 persons per annum) for a person under the age of 40 years.

Figure 10-3: Total Incidence by age for 13 More Common Cancers by age. 2019

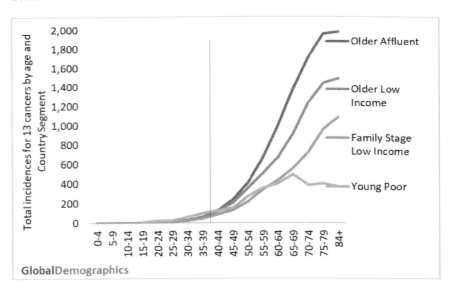

The Cancers used for this index are as follows:
Breast, Colon, Rectum and Anus, Lung, Prostate, Liver, Gastric, Oesophageal, Bladder, Uterine, Ovarian and Cervical

316

However, once that age is past, the incidence climbs – and quite steeply. Given the foregoing discussion on the growth of the population over 40 years of age from 2.8 billion persons in 2020 to a projected 3.9 billion persons in 2045, there is cause for some concern for the ability of health systems to cope with the potential future growth in incidence.

The variance in behaviour for the Young Poor after age 69 is probably a function of poor diagnostics and availability of healthcare for the older population as well as perhaps reduced exposure to causative environmental factors.

Note: The incidence rates increase over the forecast period as a result of improved diagnostics and increased access to health care as well as age. However, in terms of cases, the relative position of the four Country Segments does not change significantly.

Projected Trend in the Number of Cancer Cases.

The projected incidence rate by age and gender by year for each of the 12 cancers is applied to the age and gender profile of each country to give the expected trend in the number of cases by Country Segment. This is shown in Figure 10-4.

This is then expressed as an Index, with the year 2020 set to a value of 100. Previous and subsequent years are expressed as a proportion of that as shown in Table 10-2. It indicates that total incidence will grow by 28% by 2030 (at an annual average rate of 2.5% per annum) and then by a further 28% by 2045 (1.7% per annum 2030-45). It is projected that the total annual number of cases of Cancers will increase by 64% in the next 25 years. This is important because, at present, it is an expensive and frequently complicated condition to treat.

It is projected that between 2020 and 2045 the total annual incidence (cases) for Cancers will increase by 64% in 25 years.

317

Figure 10-4: Historic and Projected Trend in the Index Value of Incidence of Cancers by Country Segment. 2005 to 2045

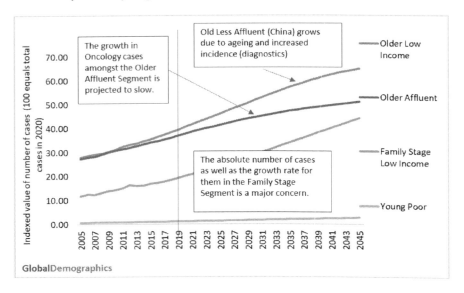

GlobalDemographics

Table 10-2: Projected trend in Incidence of Cancers by Country Segment. 2020-45

	Indexed value of Cases			% Absolute Projected increase			Growth rate p.a.	
	2020	2030	2045	2020-30	2030-45	2020-45	2020-30	2030-45
Older Affluent	38.4	45.6	52.4	2%	2%	36%	1.7%	0.9%
Older Low Income	40.3	51.5	64.5	28%	25%	60%	2.5%	1.5%
Family Stage Low Inc	20.0	28.8	44.0	44%	53%	120%	3.7%	2.9%
Young Poor	1.3	1.8	2.8	41%	56%	120%	3.5%	3.0%
Total	100.0	127.7	163.7	28%	28%	64%	2.5%	1.7%

As is to be expected from the foregoing discussion on age profile, the growth in the total number of oncology cases in the older Country Segments, is slower than it is for the two young segments. But they still have more cases in total – particularly the older Low Income Country Segment – and that is reflecting the presence of China in that segment. . In 2000 the two younger Country Segments accounted for just 21% of all cases, increasing to 29% (46.8 on a base of 163.7) by 2045.

As summarised in Table 10-2, the Old Affluent segment is projected to experience a 36% increase in total oncology cases over the next 25 years (1.2% per annum). This compares with 120% for the Family Stage Low Income Segment and the Young Poor Country Segment – albeit on a much smaller absolute number in this case. This rapid growth of cases in the young segments is a significant issue in terms of future budget requirements as discussed in detail later in this Chapter.

The projected trend in the 'Prevalence of Chronic and Other Conditions'

Figure 10-5 shows the average aggregate prevalence rate in 2019 for the selected chronic and other conditions for each of the four Country Segments. That is, the probability of a person having one or more of those conditions.

As for Cancer, the rate of prevalence increases rapidly after age 40. However, do note that it also increases, albeit at a more modest rate compared to Cancers, for all ages from age 1 onward. This is important as it means even young countries have an issue to deal with.

This wider age range in terms of prevalence rates has implications for the growth in total cases for the individual Country Segments. Again, the faster *growth* of the over 40 years of age population in the younger Country Segments translates into much faster growth in the total number of cases.

Projected Trend in the Number of Chronic Conditions

In this instance the index value for the number of chronic conditions increases by 72% for the Family Stage Low Income segment and 127% for the Young Poor where the number of cases will more than double in the next 25 years with significant implications for the need for health facilities and budget. Table 10-3 provides the detail by Country Segment.

As for Oncology, while the absolute levels may be higher, the growth rate of chronic conditions in the older countries is much slower and as such, the *share* of total cases declines marginally from 80% to 77% between 2020 and 2045. It also means their health infrastructure is under less pressure from the growth of cases than in the past.

Figure 10-5: Total Prevalence by age for 5 Selected Chronic Conditions. 2019

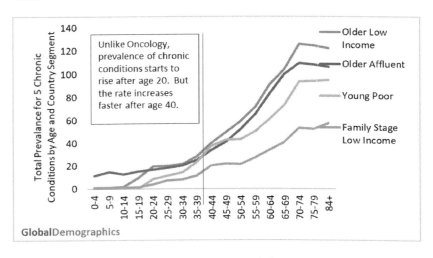

GlobalDemographics

The Conditions used for this index are as follows: Diagnosed Diabetes, Diagnosed Hypertension, TB, Diagnosed Asthma, COPD

Table 10-3: Projected Trend in Prevalence of Chronic Conditions by Country Segment. 2020-45

	Indexed Value of Cases			% Absolute Projected Increase			Growth Rate p.a.	
	2020	2030	2045	2020-30	2030-45	2020-45	2020-30	2030-45
Older Affluent	29.3	33.2	37.3	13%	12%	27%	1.3%	0.8%
Older Low Income	50.4	64.3	78.3	27%	22%	55%	2.5%	1.3%
Family Stage Low Inc	18.0	23.1	30.3	28%	31%	68%	2.5%	1.8%
Young Poor	2.3	3.1	4.7	38%	51%	107%	3.3%	2.8%
Total	100.0	123.7	150.5	24%	22%	50%	2.2%	1.3%

Figure 10-6 shows the trend in the chronic conditions index value for each of the Four Country Segments from 2010 to 2045. The Older Low Income (particularly in China) as well as having the largest number of cases also have the greatest increase in the absolute number of cases.

This is a potential cause for concern – can they increase capacity to meet demand? It is not just a matter of money there is also the issue of trained staff. That is the subject of the next section of this Chapter.

Figure 10-6: Historic and Projected Trend in The Index Value of Prevalence of Chronic Conditions by Country Segment. 2005 To 2045.

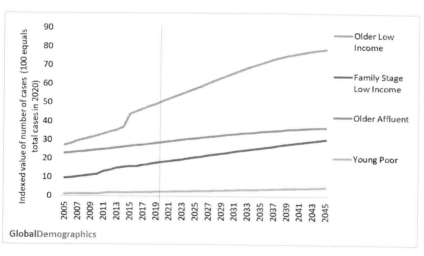

To Summarise Demand Forecasts

Assuming there is a consistent relationship between the number of cases for Oncology and Chronic conditions included in the above analysis with all other demands on the health system it is possible to estimate the likely trend in total demand for health services.

Obviously in the next 25 years, and perhaps even the next 10 years there will be advances in medical science that will provide less expensive and perhaps more effective treatment for these conditions. However, while it is likely, we cannot forecast the rate at which this will happen. For that reason, the forecasts here are worst-case – but probably are valid for the next 10 years in terms of the number of cases.

The purpose of this section was to reinforce to the reader the fact that demand for health services is likely to increase significantly - globally. It is perhaps important to also emphasise that this is not a problem unique to the older countries. To some extent, they are past the worst in terms of growth in demand – moving to a stable number of older persons. Also, in the older countries the health system appears to be better funded (see later in this Chapter) and hence diagnostic rates are probably closer to reality and there is no hidden, unknown, demand potential.

It is the younger countries where health services potentially will be under greater stress trying to keep up with rapidly increasing demand. It must be reinforced here that the above analysis reflects the changing age profile and the trend in improving diagnostics as well as changing exposure to causal agents as well as ageing of the population. As indicated in Table 10-3, the number of chronic conditions in Young Poor countries could well double in the next 25 years.

Market Value and Trend

Note: All financial data in this section are expressed in US$s and 2019 values.

Note: To estimate relative indexed caseload Oncology cases have been multiplied by 3 as a surrogate for years requiring treatment after the first diagnosis.

In terms of health expenditure, data is available for most countries from the World Health Organisation and World Bank, and these are the sources used for historic years. As shown later in this chapter, the difference between countries in terms of expenditure per capita on health is considerable – both in the absolute amount spent per capita as well as the proportion of total government expenditure that is devoted to health care. That 'proportion' reflects the extent to which 'health' is regarded as an important social (or political) issue.

In looking at potential trends in spending on healthcare it is useful to begin by looking at the last decade, as shown in Figure 10-7. During this period (2009 to 2019) total expenditure on health by all countries included in this analysis grew at 2.6% per annum.

What is also evident in Figure 10-7, is that health sector expenditure (as compared to cases) is dominated by what happens in the Older Affluent Country Segment. In 2019 these countries accounted for 77% of all health expenditure and 21% of the demand ('indexed cases') by the 116 countries included in this analysis.

The Young Poor segment is badly under-served, being currently just 1% of total health expenditure but having 9% of index cases and containing 18% of the total population in the 116 countries included in this analysis. However, it has been the fastest growing Country Segment in terms of the total value of health expenditure – at 3.7% per annum.

Table 10-4 provides an overview by Country Segment of the historic nature and trend in demand for health care (as represented by the indexed cases), expenditure per indexed case and share of Gross Domestic Product spent on healthcare for the period 2009 to 2019.

Figure 10-7: Historic Trend in Total Health Expenditure 2009-19 US$ Billion 2019 Values.

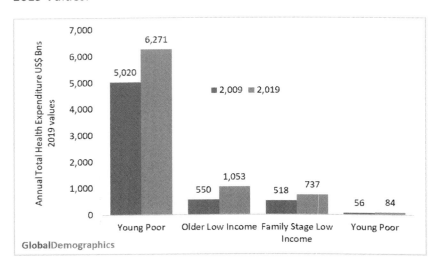

Table 10-4: Summary Profile of Historic Demand for Health Care and Associated Cost: 2009 and 2019

	Total Index cases (000s)		CAGR	Cost per indexed case (US$)	
	2009	2019	2009-19	2009	2019
Older Affluent	405	476	1.6%	12,867	11,885
Older Low Incom	525	822	4.6%	2,056	2,618
Family Stage Low	468	728	4.5%	1,193	1,492
Young Poor	120	202	5.3%	266	209
Total/Averages	1,519	2,227	3.9%	4,054	3,665

	Total Expenditure US$ Bn		As % GDP		Growth Rate
	2009	2019	2009	2019	2009-19
Older Affluent	5,020	6,271	12%	13%	2.0%
Older Low Incom	561	1,070	5%	5%	6.0%
Family Stage Low	518	737	6%	5%	3.2%
Young Poor	56	84	4%	4%	3.7%
Total/Averages	6,156	8,162	10%	10%	2.6%

Important points to take from the top part of this Table are:

- For the last decade (2009 to 2019) overall demand for health care increased by 3.9% pa. This growth rate is projected to slow to 2% pa over the next 25 years (see Table 10-5) as the growth in the number of persons over 40 years of age moderates. Particularly for the two older segments.
- However, most of the historic growth in demand was in the three less affluent Country Segments. China dominates the Older Low-Income Segment and the growth in demand in that country to 2019 is a function of the rapid increase in expenditure on health (by the Government particularly) which in turn has increased diagnostic capability and hence demand.
- In terms of the two youngest Country Segments, the growth in demand reflects improved diagnostics but also the fact that they have the most rapid growth in terms of the over 40 years of age population (along with a growing 0- to 4-year-old child population) where demand for health care is highest.

Future Trends in Healthcare Expenditure

It would be nice if funds for health care were unlimited, and everyone could have the care they need. But the reality is cruel. There is a point where the individual, the household, and the society simply cannot afford more health services. Even in affluent countries there comes a point where the individual (and the public health service) cannot afford more treatment.

For that reason, there is no point in forecasting expenditure on health care based on 'funds needed' as that has no upper bound. Rather the question must be "by how much can the expenditure per treatment or person increase and still stay affordable for the country?"

There must be a limit set in terms of the share of a country's total GDP that is eventually devoted to healthcare by 2045. This is arbitrary and there are arguments for higher and lower limits. However, the ones selected here are:

- 15% of GDP for the Older Affluent Countries. This segment currently averages 13%
- 10% of GDP for the three other Country Segments which currently average
    - 6% for Older Affluent
    - 5% for the Young Family Stage and
    - 4% for the Young Poor

There is no point in forecasting expenditure on health care based on 'funds needed' as that has no upper bound. Rather the question has to be "by how much the expenditure per treatment/person can increase and still stay affordable for the country?"

The critical issue here is the impact on 'cost per treatment'. If a country has a low growth GDP and high growth in indexed cases, then the cost per treatment probably cannot increase (improve) much. The growth in demand offsets growth in quality (assuming expenditure equates to quality).

Conversely, a country with a high growth GDP and slow increase in indexed cases can afford to increase its funds per treatment significantly.

These are scenarios, but the process serves to identify which countries can increase expenditure per case and hence overall health care.

The indexed number of oncology and chronic conditions detailed in the previous section of this Chapter is used to provide an estimate of demand trends. The index is the Chronic Conditions plus the Oncology conditions with Oncology Conditions multiplied by 3 to address the fact that Oncology Incidence is the count of when it is diagnosed, and not the period of treatment, whereas Chronic Condition Prevalence is the count of cases each year. This calculation is arbitrary but does reflect the likely demand for the health service in total.

The second required variable is the projected Gross Domestic Product in 2045 multiplied by the percentage of it that is to be allocated to health care. The GDP forecasts used are in Appendix A.

This then allows the determination of what the expenditure per condition can be for each country given the assumed maximum share of GDP by 2045 and compared to 2019.

This analysis is applied to each of the four Country Segments, and Table 10-5 provides the summary statistics for the Country Segments. Indications are that health expenditure in total would grow by 3.8% for the period 2020 to 2030 and then at 3.7% per annum to 2045.

Table 10-5: Summary Profile of Projected Demand for Health Care and Associated Cost: 2019 and 2045

	Total Index cases (000s)				CAGR		Cost per case (US$)				CAGR
	2009	2019	2030	2045	2009-19	2020-45	2009	2019	2030	2045	2020-45
Older Affluent	405	476	549	617	1.6%	1.0%	12,386	13,187	14,575	17,317	1.1%
Older Low Income	525	822	1,077	1,313	4.6%	1.8%	1,070	1,302	2,264	4,948	5.3%
Family Stage	468	728	977	1,299	4.5%	2.3%	1,107	1,012	1,294	2,054	2.8%
Young Poor	120	202	295	475	5.3%	3.3%	469	417	662	1,498	5.0%
Total/Averages	1,519	2,227	2,898	3,703	3.9%	2.0%	4,054	3,665	4,105	5,551	1.6%

	Total Expenditure US$ Bn in cost per case				As % GDP			Growth rate		
	2009	2019	2030	2045	2019	2030	2045	2009-19	2020-30	2030-45
Older Affluent	5,020	6,271	8,000	10,685	12%	13%	14%	2.0%	2.5%	1.9%
Older Low Income	561	1,070	2,439	6,494	5%	8%	15%	6.0%	8.6%	6.7%
Family Stage	518	737	1,264	2,668	5%	7%	10%	3.2%	5.5%	5.1%
Young Poor	56	84	196	711	4%	6%	10%	3.7%	8.8%	9.0%
Total/Averages	6,156	8,162	11,899	20,557	7%	7%	8%	2.6%	3.8%	3.7%

The highest growth is expected in the Young Poor Countries as they have potentially faster growing economies, and they currently have a relatively low proportion allocated to health care. Assuming they move to the position where 10% of the economy is devoted to health care by 2045 then health expenditure would grow at 8.8% per annum to 2030 and then at 9% per annum to 2045. While it might be argued that these countries can spend less as they are younger, the issue here is the growth in demand – which, as shown, more than doubles from 202 indexed cases in

2019 to an estimated 475 by 2045. This reflects both ageing of the population and increased incidence/prevalence rates.

The following pages provide the detail for the individual Country Segments. Given that they are grouped by age profile (which impacts the projected number of cases needing treatment) and GDP per capita (which impacts affordability) it is not surprising that there is quite high consistency in terms of outcomes within the individual Country Segments – but as explained above there are significant differences between the segments.

Older Affluent Country Segment

For the last decade for most countries in this Country Segment, expenditure per indexed case increased only marginally (0.6% per annum) whereas the number of cases grew by 1.6% per annum.

For the next 25 years, if health expenditure is to reach 15% of GDP for all countries in this segment, then expenditure per indexed case would grow at 1.1% per annum. Which is almost double the historic rate.

Table 10-6 shows the projected impact in terms of total health expenditure for each country and this segment of countries if they all move to 15% of GDP being spent on health by 2045. As shown in Table 10-7, this would result in total health expenditure for this segment growing at an average rate of 2.5% per annum to 2030 and then 1.9% per annum to 2045.

This is a more moderate rate of growth than that of the other Country Segments and means that the Older Affluent country's share of total (Global) health expenditure drops from 77% in 2019 to 52% by 2045.

But it does mean that cost per treatment (and presumably quality of care) would increase at 1.1% per annum for the next 25 years which results in a projected absolute real increase of 31%.

Table 10-6: Historic and Projected Trend in Cases, Cost Per Case. Older Affluent Country Segment.

	Total Index cases (000s)						Cost per case (US$)				CAGR
	2009	2019	2030	2045	2009-19	2020-45	2009	2019	2030	2045	2020-45
Australia	10,016	13,946	17,276	21,019	3.4%	1.6%	8,978	8,884	12,059	18,294	2.8%
Austria	4,650	5,492	6,334	7,411	1.7%	1.2%	8,401	8,417	10,111	12,984	1.7%
Belgium	4,122	5,262	6,353	7,579	2.5%	1.4%	11,155	10,316	11,140	12,372	0.7%
Canada	8,845	12,425	15,486	18,642	3.5%	1.6%	16,976	14,662	15,705	17,248	0.6%
Denmark	2,022	2,619	3,155	3,721	2.6%	1.4%	15,320	13,332	14,984	17,572	1.1%
Finland	3,048	3,724	4,314	4,797	2.0%	1.0%	6,957	6,575	7,909	10,176	1.7%
France	34,647	37,544	42,281	46,428	0.8%	0.8%	7,727	8,134	8,836	9,892	0.8%
Germany	43,772	46,647	51,936	58,552	0.6%	0.9%	8,060	9,237	10,428	12,304	1.1%
Hong Kong	2,819	3,718	4,533	5,296	2.8%	1.4%					0.0%
Iceland	84	106	132	156	2.4%	1.5%	19,535	19,014	27,373	44,990	3.4%
Ireland	1,755	2,312	2,984	3,797	2.8%	1.9%	12,867	11,885	19,745	39,453	4.7%
Italy	25,208	32,931	38,895	43,485	2.7%	1.1%	6,964	5,343	6,509	8,519	1.8%
Japan	50,551	52,648	55,403	57,016	0.4%	0.3%	8,021	9,894	12,574	17,435	2.2%
Macao	145	226	323	424	4.6%	2.5%					0.0%
Netherlands	6,022	6,978	7,974	8,735	1.5%	0.9%	13,057	13,040	15,824	20,605	1.8%
New Zealand	2,185	2,799	3,392	3,991	2.5%	1.4%	6,862	6,430	8,484	12,383	2.6%
Norway	2,257	2,976	3,693	4,531	2.8%	1.6%	13,930	14,078	14,181	14,322	0.1%
Sth Korea	16,719	21,744	26,686	30,475	2.7%	1.3%	4,332	5,636	10,337	23,635	5.7%
Singapore	1,247	1,888	2,494	3,020	4.2%	1.8%	6,384	8,698	18,202	49,828	6.9%
Slovenia	902	1,039	1,175	1,270	1.4%	0.8%	4,277	4,221	6,988	13,895	4.7%
Spain	21,069	21,061	23,402	25,412	0.0%	0.7%	5,372	5,810	9,249	17,434	4.3%
Sweden	5,337	6,784	8,101	9,787	2.4%	1.4%	6,975	8,514	8,968	9,628	0.5%
Switzerland	1,773	2,295	2,949	3,638	2.6%	1.8%	35,679	37,657	38,972	40,841	0.3%
United Kingdom	32,495	36,206	39,652	43,351	1.1%	0.7%	6,136	7,402	9,086	12,017	1.9%
USA	123,616	152,194	179,947	204,454	2.1%	1.1%	22,607	23,087	22,803	22,420	-0.1%
Total	405,306	475,564	548,873	616,988	1.6%	1.0%	12,386	13,187	14,575	17,317	1.1%

329

Table 10-7: Impact of Growth in Number of Cases and Cost per Case on Total Health spend and share of GDP Spent on Health. Older Affluent Country Segment.

	Total Expenditure US$ Bn				As % GDP			Growth rate		
	2009	2019	2030	2045	2019	2030	2045	2009-19	2020-30	2030-45
Australia	90	124	208	385	7.7%	8.3%	15.0%	3.0%	5.3%	4.2%
Austria	39	46	64	96	8.8%	10.1%	15.0%	1.5%	3.3%	2.8%
Belgium	46	54	71	94	9.3%	11.4%	15.0%	1.5%	2.7%	1.9%
Canada	150	182	243	322	9.8%	11.4%	15.0%	1.8%	2.9%	1.9%
Denmark	31	35	47	65	8.6%	10.9%	15.0%	1.1%	3.1%	2.2%
Finland	21	24	34	49	8.2%	10.5%	15.0%	1.3%	3.4%	2.4%
France	268	305	374	459	10.2%	12.2%	15.0%	1.2%	2.0%	1.4%
Germany	353	431	542	720	9.9%	11.3%	15.0%	1.8%	2.3%	1.9%
Hong Kong										
Iceland	2	2	4	7	6.2%	7.9%	15.0%	1.9%	6.0%	4.5%
Ireland	23	27	59	150	3.2%	5.9%	15.0%	1.8%	7.9%	6.4%
Italy	176	176	253	370	7.9%	10.3%	15.0%	0.0%	3.7%	2.6%
Japan	405	521	697	994	9.2%	10.6%	15.0%	2.3%	2.9%	2.4%
Macao										
Netherlands	79	91	126	180	8.6%	10.6%	15.0%	1.3%	3.3%	2.4%
New Zealand	15	18	29	49	6.5%	8.8%	15.0%	1.7%	4.8%	3.7%
Norway	31	42	52	65	9.5%	12.1%	15.0%	2.6%	2.3%	1.4%
Sth Korea	72	123	276	720	5.4%	6.0%	15.0%	4.9%	8.5%	6.6%
Singapore	8	16	45	150	3.4%	4.7%	15.0%	6.8%	10.7%	8.3%
Slovenia	4	4	8	18	5.9%	7.1%	15.0%	1.2%	6.5%	5.2%
Spain	113	122	216	443	6.4%	7.5%	15.0%	0.7%	5.9%	4.9%
Sweden	37	58	73	94	9.9%	11.6%	15.0%	4.1%	2.3%	1.7%
Switzerland	63	86	115	149	10.8%	11.7%	15.0%	2.9%	2.9%	1.7%
United Kingdom	199	268	360	521	8.5%	10.4%	15.0%	2.7%	3.0%	2.5%
USA	2,795	3,514	4,103	4,584	13.6%	13.5%	15.0%	2.1%	1.6%	0.7%
Total	5,020	6,271	8,000	10,685	12.4%	12.9%	14.5%	2.0%	2.5%	1.9%

The Older Low Income

This Country Segment has quite a different profile from the previous 'older' Country Segment. Also, note that it includes China which is placed at the bottom of each table so it can be easily compared with the totals/averages for the segment.

Historically there has been quite rapid growth in the demand for healthcare as indicated by the index of cases. This is driven particularly by China where there has been considerable investment in healthcare by the Government and with that, improved diagnostics and increased incidence and prevalence rates. As shown in the second to last row of Table 10-8 the demand for health care in China increased by 5.1% per annum for the last decade and that together with a 4.2% growth per annum in

330

expenditure per case means total healthcare expenditure in China grew at 8.6% per annum (see Table 10-9). A full 7% points higher than the average for the other countries in this segment.

Table 10-8: Historic Trend in Cases, Cost Per Case and Total Health Spend as Percent Of GDP. Older Low Income Country Segment.

	Total Index cases (000s)				CAGR		Cost per case (US$)				CAGR
	2009	2019	2030	2045	2009-19	2020-45	2009	2019	2030	2045	2020-45
Albania	676	1,078	1,197	1,234	4.8%	0.5%					
Belarus	3,055	4,244	4,807	5,081	3.3%	0.7%	934	882	1,523	3,212	5.1%
Bulgaria	73	920	968	1,011	28.8%	0.4%	48,709	5,937	8,727	14,759	3.6%
Cuba	3,510	5,388	6,811	7,956	4.4%	1.5%	2,880	2,137	2,007	1,841	-0.6%
Czechia	4,367	5,852	6,518	7,055	3.0%	0.7%	3,284	3,022	5,616	13,074	5.8%
Estonia	696	763	826	875	0.9%	0.5%	2,056	2,618	6,012	18,677	7.9%
Georgia	1,356	1,600	1,795	1,882	1.7%	0.6%	799	840	1,403	2,823	4.8%
Greece	4,660	5,448	5,857	6,025	1.6%	0.4%	5,246	3,104	4,789	8,652	4.0%
Hungary	3,453	3,644	3,921	4,013	0.5%	0.4%	2,579	3,040	5,141	10,527	4.9%
Latvia	961	1,108	1,069	932	1.4%	-0.7%	1,705	1,834	4,113	12,377	7.6%
Lithuania	1,105	1,309	1,318	1,169	1.7%	-0.4%	2,566	2,667	4,467	9,028	4.8%
Mauritius	373	463	556	626	2.2%	1.2%	1,113	1,713	3,175	7,364	5.8%
Poland	12,901	17,846	20,467	21,669	3.3%	0.7%	2,119	2,160	3,465	6,600	4.4%
Portugal	6,869	7,476	8,003	7,905	0.9%	0.2%	3,166	2,845	4,730	9,459	4.7%
Republic of Moldov	1,275	1,346	1,495	1,592	0.5%	0.6%	595	583	956	1,876	4.6%
Romania	7,885	9,852	10,108	9,695	2.3%	-0.1%	1,233	1,305	2,763	7,681	7.1%
Russian Federation	34,266	48,809	56,549	61,787	3.6%	0.9%	2,320	1,860	2,585	4,048	3.0%
Slovakia	1,728	2,609	3,253	3,843	4.2%	1.5%	3,651	2,715	4,618	9,530	4.9%
Thailand	13,096	19,508	25,641	32,085	4.1%	1.9%	1,053	1,038	2,103	5,507	6.6%
Ukraine	20,489	21,625	22,679	22,532	0.5%	0.2%	479	494	754	1,341	3.9%
Uruguay	1,015	1,484	1,851	2,357	3.9%	1.8%	3,568	3,555	3,713	3,941	0.4%
China	400,848	659,543	891,610	1,111,175	5.1%	2.0%	791	1,192	2,163	4,873	5.6%
Total/Averages	524,659	821,919	1,077,297	1,312,500	4.6%	1.8%	1,070	1,302	2,264	4,948	5.3%
Excluding China	123,810	162,376	185,687	201,325	2.7%	0.8%	1,973	1,747	2,752	5,360	4.4%

The other countries in this segment have had much lower growth in terms of the number of cases (2.7% pa), cost per treatment (-1.2% pa) and overall healthcare expenditure increase over the period 2009 to 2019 at 1.5% per annum. As such they are more in line with the Older Affluent Segment detailed above.

As the countries in this segment have a faster projected GDP growth rate than the Older Affluent countries and are starting from a lower percentage of GDP in 2019, the assumed increase of total health expenditure to 10% of total GDP by 2045 results in a more rapid increase in expenditure per case – specifically at an average of 4.4% per annum through to 2045.

Table 10-9: Impact of Growth in Number of Cases and Cost per Case on Share of GDP Spent on Health. Older Low Income Country Segment.

	Total Expenditure US$ Bn				As % GDP			Growth rate		
	2009	2019	2030	2045	2019	2030	2045	2009-19	2020-30	2030-45
Albania	0.0	0.0	0.0	0.0						
Belarus	2.9	3.7	7.3	16.3	5.6%	7.0%	15.0%	2.5%	6.9%	5.5%
Bulgaria	3.6	5.5	8.4	14.9	6.8%	8.5%	15.0%	3.9%	4.5%	3.9%
Cuba	10.0	11.4	13.6	14.6	10.3%	13.8%	15.0%	1.2%	1.8%	0.5%
Czechia	14.3	17.7	36.6	92.2	5.3%	6.2%	15.0%	1.9%	7.5%	6.4%
Estonia	1.4	2.0	5.0	16.3	4.0%	4.8%	15.0%	3.1%	9.5%	8.3%
Georgia	1.1	1.3	2.5	5.3	5.6%	7.3%	15.0%	2.0%	6.5%	5.1%
Greece	24.4	16.9	28.0	52.1	6.5%	8.1%	15.0%	-3.3%	5.2%	4.2%
Hungary	8.9	11.1	20.2	42.2	4.5%	7.2%	15.0%	2.0%	6.2%	5.1%
Latvia	1.6	2.0	4.4	11.5	4.4%	5.9%	15.0%	2.0%	8.0%	6.6%
Lithuania	2.8	3.5	5.9	10.6	5.3%	8.3%	15.0%	1.9%	5.4%	4.0%
Mauritius	0.4	0.8	1.8	4.6	3.9%	5.8%	15.0%	6.1%	8.3%	6.6%
Poland	27.3	38.5	70.9	143.0	5.1%	7.5%	15.0%	3.2%	6.3%	4.8%
Portugal	21.7	21.3	37.9	74.8	6.5%	7.7%	15.0%	-0.2%	5.9%	4.6%
Rep Moldovia	0.8	0.8	1.4	3.0	5.2%	7.3%	15.0%	0.3%	6.2%	5.0%
Romania	9.7	12.9	27.9	74.5	3.8%	5.7%	15.0%	2.6%	8.1%	6.8%
Russia	79.5	90.8	146.2	250.1	5.3%	8.8%	15.0%	1.2%	4.9%	3.6%
Slovakia	6.2	7.0	15.0	36.6	4.9%	6.3%	15.0%	1.1%	7.9%	6.2%
Thailand	13.8	20.2	53.9	176.7	2.9%	4.7%	15.0%	3.6%	10.3%	8.2%
Ukraine	9.8	10.7	17.1	30.2	5.9%	8.5%	15.0%	0.8%	4.8%	3.9%
Uruguay	3.6	5.2	6.8	9.3	9.0%	11.1%	15.0%	3.5%	2.7%	2.1%
China	305.7	769.6	1,627.6	3,725.8	3.6%	6.5%	15.0%	8.8%	7.8%	5.7%
Total/ Averages	549.7	1,053.1	2,138.4	4,804.8	5.4%	7.7%	15.0%	6.1%	7.3%	5.5%
Excluding China	244	283	511	1,079				1.5%	5.5%	5.1%

That combined with an expected 1.8% per annum growth in cases means that the total health expenditure of countries in this segment other than China is projected to grow at 5.5% per annum to 2030 and then 5.1% for the period to 2045.

The Family Stage Low Income Country Segment

The reader is reminded that India is significant in this Country Segment and for that reason is shown at the bottom of the subsequent tables to enable easy comparison with the totals/averages.

As shown in Table 10-10 and Table 10-11 on the subsequent pages, in the last decade, this Country Segment generally experienced quite rapid growth in demand for healthcare. This in part will be a function of improved diagnostics as well as the rather rapid increase in the over 40 years age group in which the disease rates are higher. The average rate of increase in cases was 4.5% per annum.

Table 10-10: Historic trend in Cases, Cost per case. Family Stage Low Income Country Segment.

	Total Index cases (000s)				CAGR		Cost per case (US$)				CAGR
	2009	2019	2030	2045	2009-19	2020-45	2009	2019	2030	2045	2020-45
Algeria	5,761	10,150	14,418	21,438	5.8%	2.9%	1,213	1,042	1,088	1,153	0.4%
Argentina	11,501	18,774	23,349	25,793	5.0%	1.2%	3,099	2,180	2,314	2,509	0.5%
Armenia	1,034	1,363	1,560	1,692	2.8%	0.8%	723	1,012	1,799	3,940	5.4%
Azerbaijan	1,658	2,772	3,931	5,262	5.3%	2.5%	1,292	1,143	1,980	4,190	5.1%
Bangladesh	34,166	47,412	62,848	81,840	3.3%	2.1%	110	143	362	1,277	8.8%
Bolivia	830	1,335	1,822	2,617	4.9%	2.6%	1,694	1,955	1,984	2,025	0.1%
Brazil	55,290	87,441	112,728	143,481	4.7%	1.9%	2,447	1,990	1,878	1,734	-0.5%
Cambodia	1,530	2,444	3,547	5,016	4.8%	2.8%	681	657	767	946	1.4%
Chile	5,889	9,238	11,908	15,672	4.6%	2.1%	2,495	2,734	2,831	2,968	0.3%
Colombia	10,846	18,634	25,804	35,557	5.6%	2.5%	1,516	1,245	1,232	1,216	-0.1%
Dominican Rep	852	1,341	1,787	2,401	4.6%	2.3%	3,072	4,033	6,071	10,607	3.8%
Ecuador	1,314	2,156	3,039	4,416	5.1%	2.8%	3,994	3,980	3,581	3,100	-1.0%
El Salvador	559	825	1,022	1,276	4.0%	1.7%	3,181	2,381	2,551	2,803	0.6%
Indonesia	41,701	70,507	96,772	134,438	5.4%	2.5%	425	467	719	1,297	4.0%
Iran	28,198	40,676	58,634	83,121	3.7%	2.8%	696	781	1,260	2,419	4.4%
Kazakhstan	2,581	4,371	6,000	8,717	5.4%	2.7%	1,580	1,299	2,258	4,799	5.2%
Malaysia	6,048	9,318	13,392	18,978	4.4%	2.8%	1,193	1,492	2,351	4,370	4.2%
Mexico	29,633	52,690	68,693	89,704	5.9%	2.1%	1,998	1,310	1,518	1,856	1.3%
Morocco	8,681	9,981	12,965	16,608	1.4%	2.0%	570	617	946	1,694	4.0%
Myanmar	12,343	18,479	23,230	28,124	4.1%	1.6%	66	189	416	1,220	7.4%
Nicaragua	440	720	1,006	1,426	5.0%	2.7%	1,553	1,481	1,396	1,288	-0.5%
Panama	345	570	799	1,166	5.1%	2.8%	7,453	8,333	8,333	8,333	0.0%
Paraguay	503	801	1,083	1,467	4.8%	2.4%	2,214	3,134	3,379	3,744	0.7%
Peru	4,633	7,744	11,829	18,280	5.3%	3.4%	1,567	1,462	1,717	2,136	1.5%
Philippines	14,821	22,103	31,036	44,274	4.1%	2.7%	595	747	975	1,403	2.5%
Saudi Arabia	6,869	12,089	19,022	27,621	5.8%	3.2%	3,538	3,407	3,616	3,922	0.5%
South Africa	8,834	14,007	18,630	24,866	4.7%	2.2%	2,397	2,027	1,967	1,888	-0.3%
Sri Lanka	4,973	6,200	7,718	9,105	2.2%	1.5%	425	518	846	1,651	4.6%
Tunisia	1,101	1,680	2,206	2,804	4.3%	2.0%	1,650	1,597	2,131	3,157	2.7%
Turkey	37,744	52,455	71,300	95,724	3.3%	2.3%	629	609	757	1,018	2.0%
Uzbekistan	2,328	3,691	5,152	6,935	4.7%	2.5%	697	1,002	1,343	2,003	2.7%
Venezuela RB	9,732	10,676	11,354	10,657	0.9%	0.0%	2,231	350	1,074	4,962	10.7%
Viet Nam	11,322	21,768	31,703	44,546	6.8%	2.8%	664.2	661.1	1,314	3,354	6.4%
India	104,305	163,785	216,343	283,990	4.6%	2.1%	504	628	1,130	2,513	5.5%
Total/Averages	468,364	728,193	976,632	1,299,012	4.5%	2.3%	1,107	1,012	1,294	2,054	2.8%
Excl India	364,059	564,408	760,289	1,015,022	4.5%	2.3%	1,280	1,123	1,341	1,925	2.1%

During the same period (2009 to 2019) the average expenditure per indexed case changed only marginally and for some countries, it decreased suggesting that demand outstripped supply. Fortunately, the rate of growth in the number of cases is projected to slow for the period 2020 to 2045 – and be at 2.3% per annum – and most countries are close to this average. That potentially will enable these countries to invest in quality as well as quantity of health care.

Assuming they move to 10% of GDP being spent on health care, then cost per case could grow at 2.8% per annum and total expenditure on health is then projected to grow at just over 5% per annum – compared with 3.2% per annum for the last decade. But do note that India is projected to grow at a faster rate than other countries in this Country Segment reflecting its lower spending (as a per cent of GDP) in the past. That is 2.4% compared with 5.4% for the other countries in this segment.

Table 10-11: Impact of Growth in Number of Cases and Cost per Case on Share of GDP Spent on Health. Family Stage Country Segment.

	Total Expenditure US$ Bn				As % GDP			Growth rate		
	2009	2019	2030	2045	2019	2030	2045	2009-19	2020-30	2030-45
Albania	7.0	10.6	15.7	24.7	5.3%	6.4%	10.0%	3.8%	4.0%	3.1%
Belarus	35.6	40.9	54.0	64.7	8.4%	8.4%	10.0%	1.3%	2.8%	1.2%
Bulgaria	0.7	1.4	2.8	6.7	6.0%	4.4%	10.0%	5.7%	7.4%	5.9%
Cuba	2.1	3.2	7.8	22.0	4.8%	3.8%	10.0%	3.6%	9.4%	7.2%
Czechia	3.8	6.8	22.7	104.5	1.2%	2.3%	10.0%	5.5%	12.8%	10.7%
Bolivia	1.4	2.6	3.6	5.3	5.6%	6.9%	10.0%	5.8%	3.3%	2.6%
Brazil	135.3	174.0	211.7	248.9	8.8%	8.6%	10.0%	2.3%	2.0%	1.1%
Cambodia	1.0	1.6	2.7	4.7	4.0%	5.8%	10.0%	4.0%	5.4%	3.8%
Chile	14.7	25.3	33.7	46.5	7.5%	7.4%	10.0%	5.0%	2.9%	2.2%
Colombia	16.4	23.2	31.8	43.2	6.2%	7.4%	10.0%	3.2%	3.2%	2.1%
Dominican Rep	2.6	5.4	10.8	25.5	3.6%	4.4%	10.0%	6.8%	7.2%	5.9%
Ecuador	5.2	8.6	10.9	13.7	7.1%	8.0%	10.0%	4.6%	2.4%	1.5%
El Salvador	1.8	2.0	2.6	3.6	6.1%	7.3%	10.0%	0.9%	2.9%	2.1%
Indonesia	17.7	32.9	69.6	174.3	2.2%	4.0%	10.0%	5.8%	7.8%	6.3%
Iran	19.6	31.8	73.9	201.1	4.3%	3.9%	10.0%	4.5%	8.8%	6.9%
Kazakhstan	4.1	5.7	13.5	41.8	2.2%	3.3%	10.0%	3.1%	9.1%	7.8%
Malaysia	7.2	13.9	31.5	82.9	2.8%	3.9%	10.0%	6.1%	8.5%	6.7%
Mexico	59.2	69.0	104.3	166.5	5.1%	6.3%	10.0%	1.4%	4.2%	3.2%
Morocco	4.9	6.2	12.3	28.1	4.1%	4.6%	10.0%	2.0%	7.1%	5.7%
Myanmar	0.8	3.5	9.7	34.3	2.4%	3.0%	10.0%	14.1%	10.7%	8.8%
Nicaragua	0.7	1.1	1.4	1.8	7.9%	7.8%	10.0%	4.1%	2.8%	1.8%
Panama	2.6	4.7	6.7	9.7	5.5%	6.9%	10.0%	5.7%	3.4%	2.5%
Paraguay	1.1	2.5	3.7	5.5	5.7%	6.7%	10.0%	7.7%	3.8%	2.7%
Peru	7.3	11.3	20.3	39.0	4.0%	5.3%	10.0%	4.1%	6.0%	4.5%
Philippines	8.8	16.5	30.3	62.1	2.9%	4.9%	10.0%	5.9%	6.2%	4.9%
Saudi Arabia	24.3	41.2	68.8	108.3	4.2%	6.3%	10.0%	4.9%	5.3%	3.1%
South Africa	21.2	28.4	36.7	47.0	7.2%	7.9%	10.0%	2.7%	2.6%	1.7%
Sri Lanka	2.1	3.2	6.5	15.0	2.9%	4.4%	10.0%	3.9%	7.3%	5.7%
Tunisia	1.8	2.7	4.7	8.9	4.9%	5.4%	10.0%	3.6%	5.8%	4.3%
Turkey	23.7	32.0	54.0	97.5	3.8%	5.6%	10.0%	2.7%	5.4%	4.0%
Uzbekistan	1.6	3.7	6.9	13.9	3.1%	5.0%	10.0%	7.8%	6.5%	4.8%
Venezuela RB	21.7	3.7	12.2	52.9	0.7%	2.3%	10.0%	-14.8%	12.6%	10.3%
Viet Nam	7.5	14.4	41.7	149.4	2.8%	3.0%	10.0%	6.1%	11.2%	8.9%
India	52.6	102.9	244.4	713.8	2.4%	3.5%	10.0%	6.3%	9.0%	7.4%
Total/Unweighted A	518.5	736.8	1,263.7	2,667.9	5.4%	6.9%	10.0%	3.2%	5.5%	5.1%
Total Excl India	466	634	1,019	1,954				2.8%	4.9%	4.4%

Young Poor Country Segment

In this Country Segment, the over 40-year age group, while still not a large segment proportionately, is now a rapidly growing one in terms of the number of people. At the same time, the number of births continues at a high level, meaning the 0 to 4-year-old age segment is also sustained. As a result, the demand for health care services grew very dramatically over the last decade – at an average rate of 5.3% per annum, as shown in Table 10-12. The number of (indexed) cases nearly doubled in a decade.

Not surprisingly, with that rate of growth in demand, cost per treatment declined to reflect some inability to keep up with expenditure levels required to maintain current standards. They are also below the other two lower income Country Segments in terms of proportion of GDP spent on health – specifically with an average of 4.2% in 2019 (see Table 10-13) compared with 5.4% for the others.

But as these economies are projected to show more rapid GDP growth, they have room to expand the expenditure on healthcare and still not place overwhelming demands on the total GDP. As shown in Table 10-13 if these countries target total health expenditure to be 10% of GDP by 2045 – up from 4.2% now, then cost per case can increase by 5% per annum which is a significant rate of improvement.

It is also a necessary improvement as even allowing for lower labour costs, these countries are currently spending much less than others per case – at US$417.

If these countries can move to 10% of GDP being spent on health care by 2045 this will create a very significant growth market. Total health expenditure under this scenario is projected to grow at 9% per annum for the period 2020 to 2045. That is, from US$84 billion in 2019 to reach US$710 Bn in 2045.

Table 10-12: Historic Trend in Cases, Cost Per Case and Total Health Spend as Percent Of GDP. Young Poor Country Segment.

	Total Index cases (000s)				CAGR		Cost per case (US$)				CAGR
	2009	2019	2030	2045	2009-19	2020-45	2009	2019	2030	2045	2020-45
Angola	1,899	3,651	5,699	10,199	6.8%	4.0%	1,550	757	1,514	3,894	6.5%
Botswana	215	397	590	932	6.3%	3.3%	3,510	2,838	3,001	3,238	0.5%
Burkina Faso	1,295	2,434	3,714	6,324	6.5%	3.7%	388	437	468	512	0.6%
Cameroon	1,818	3,314	4,941	8,109	6.2%	3.5%	593	545	733	1,099	2.7%
Chad	949	1,777	2,706	4,679	6.5%	3.8%	383	288	446	806	4.0%
DR Congo	5,798	10,794	16,346	28,593	6.4%	3.8%	208	171	230	345	2.7%
Egypt	25,798	41,056	58,301	88,059	4.8%	3.0%	371	403	533	783	2.6%
Ethiopia	8,022	15,236	23,279	39,893	6.6%	3.8%	212	214	754	4,185	12.1%
Ghana	2,485	4,642	6,752	10,304	6.4%	3.1%	648	463	755	1,472	4.6%
Guatemala	1,542	2,916	4,370	6,934	6.6%	3.4%	2,251	1,532	1,878	2,480	1.9%
Guinea	900	1,573	2,382	4,051	5.7%	3.7%	249	353	459	657	2.4%
Haiti	1,147	1,984	2,720	3,794	5.6%	2.5%	368	322	288	247	-1.0%
Honduras	896	1,719	2,560	3,934	6.7%	3.2%	1,751	1,135	1,420	1,927	2.1%
Kenya	3,790	5,052	7,831	12,770	2.9%	3.6%	861	905	1,189	1,725	2.5%
Lao PDR	12	145	179	214	28.4%	1.5%	27,148	3,325	10,649	52,088	11.2%
Madagascar	1,949	3,721	5,652	9,363	6.7%	3.6%	266	209	261	354	2.1%
Malawi	1,215	2,254	3,489	6,085	6.4%	3.9%	348	313	319	326	0.2%
Mali	1,249	2,243	3,349	5,772	6.0%	3.7%	465	300	466	851	4.1%
Mozambique	2,114	3,708	5,497	9,279	5.8%	3.6%	204	199	244	323	1.9%
Namibia	227	380	527	787	5.3%	2.8%	3,645	2,790	2,748	2,693	-0.1%
Nepal	3,325	5,421	7,786	12,166	5.0%	3.2%	255	311	356	427	1.2%
Niger	1,351	2,562	3,984	7,432	6.6%	4.2%	420	392	415	448	0.5%
Nigeria	17,465	21,063	29,457	45,585	1.9%	3.0%	682	829	1,723	4,671	6.9%
Pakistan	19,980	35,937	51,265	77,216	6.0%	3.0%	225	204	335	659	4.6%
Rwanda	925	1,769	2,749	4,507	6.7%	3.7%	458	364	399	451	0.8%
Senegal	1,166	2,139	3,227	5,425	6.3%	3.6%	467	454	646	1,046	3.3%
South Sudan	889	1,514	1,852	2,391	5.5%	1.8%	35	12	64	638	16.5%
Sudan	3,380	6,158	8,987	14,328	6.2%	3.3%	393	248	280	331	1.1%
Uganda	2,356	4,749	8,120	15,986	7.3%	4.8%	848	457	484	525	0.5%
Tanzania	3,835	7,286	11,310	19,730	6.6%	3.9%	462	316	459	763	3.5%
Zambia	1,048	2,043	3,285	5,967	6.9%	4.2%	605	513	610	773	1.6%
Zimbabwe	1,149	1,913	2,596	3,816	5.2%	2.7%		72	19	3	-11.5%
Total/Averages	120,189	201,550	295,500	474,625	5.3%	3.3%	469	417	662	1,498	5.0%

It is probably wishful thinking that that will happen, but if it did then the expenditure per case would almost triple and almost certainly result in a significantly better standard of health care in these countries. That, in turn, provides a healthier population, workforce and life.

Table 10-13: Impact of Growth in Number of Cases and Cost Per Case on Share of GDP Spent on Health. Young Poor Country Segment.

	Total Expenditure US$ Bn				As % GDP			Growth rate		
	2009	2019	2030	2045	2019	2030	2045	2009-19	2020-30	2030-45
Angola	2.9	2.8	8.6	39.7	1.4%	2.3%	10.0%	-0.6%	12.1%	10.7%
Botswana	0.8	1.1	1.8	3.0	4.9%	6.0%	10.0%	3.7%	4.6%	3.6%
Burkina Faso	0.5	1.1	1.7	3.2	4.6%	5.5%	10.0%	7.1%	5.0%	4.2%
Cameroon	1.1	1.8	3.6	8.9	3.2%	4.2%	10.0%	4.8%	7.2%	6.2%
Chad	0.4	0.5	1.2	3.8	3.3%	3.4%	10.0%	3.2%	8.9%	7.9%
DR Congo	1.2	1.9	3.8	9.9	2.9%	3.9%	10.0%	4.0%	7.4%	6.6%
Egypt	9.6	16.5	31.1	68.9	3.7%	4.6%	10.0%	5.1%	6.5%	5.4%
Ethiopia	1.7	3.3	17.5	167.0	1.4%	1.2%	10.0%	6.1%	18.3%	16.2%
Ghana	1.6	2.1	5.1	15.2	2.4%	3.5%	10.0%	2.7%	9.0%	7.5%
Guatemala	3.5	4.5	8.2	17.2	4.1%	4.9%	10.0%	2.3%	6.3%	5.1%
Guinea	0.2	0.6	1.1	2.7	2.9%	4.2%	10.0%	8.6%	7.0%	6.1%
Haiti	0.4	0.6	0.8	0.9	7.2%	8.3%	10.0%	3.8%	2.0%	1.2%
Honduras	1.6	2.0	3.6	7.6	5.4%	5.0%	10.0%	2.0%	6.4%	5.0%
Kenya	3.3	4.6	9.3	22.0	3.4%	4.3%	10.0%	3.1%	7.4%	5.9%
Lao PDR	0.3	0.5	1.9	11.1	1.3%	1.8%	10.0%	3.7%	14.7%	12.5%
Madagascar	0.5	0.8	1.5	3.3	3.7%	4.6%	10.0%	3.7%	6.6%	5.5%
Malawi	0.4	0.7	1.1	2.0	6.0%	5.7%	10.0%	4.8%	4.6%	3.9%
Mali	0.6	0.7	1.6	4.9	2.4%	3.3%	10.0%	1.3%	8.8%	7.9%
Mozambique	0.4	0.7	1.3	3.0	3.6%	4.6%	10.0%	5.0%	6.2%	5.5%
Namibia	0.8	1.1	1.4	2.1	7.0%	7.0%	10.0%	2.3%	3.2%	2.6%
Nepal	0.8	1.7	2.8	5.2	3.6%	5.3%	10.0%	6.4%	5.1%	4.3%
Niger	0.6	1.0	1.7	3.3	5.2%	5.1%	10.0%	5.3%	5.1%	4.8%
Nigeria	11.9	17.5	50.7	212.9	1.9%	2.5%	10.0%	3.5%	11.3%	10.0%
Pakistan	4.5	7.3	17.2	50.9	2.1%	3.4%	10.0%	4.6%	8.9%	7.5%
Rwanda	0.4	0.6	1.1	2.0	4.2%	5.5%	10.0%	3.9%	5.5%	4.2%
Senegal	0.5	1.0	2.1	5.7	2.4%	3.8%	10.0%	5.4%	7.9%	6.9%
South Sudan	0.0	0.0	0.1	1.5	0.1%	0.8%	10.0%	-4.8%	20.7%	18.5%
Sudan	1.3	1.5	2.5	4.7	5.0%	5.4%	10.0%	1.3%	5.1%	4.3%
Uganda	2.0	2.2	3.9	8.4	4.1%	4.8%	10.0%	0.7%	6.1%	5.2%
Tanzania	1.8	2.3	5.2	15.1	2.3%	3.5%	10.0%	2.4%	8.5%	7.4%
Zambia	0.6	1.0	2.0	4.6	3.3%	4.4%	10.0%	4.7%	6.7%	5.7%
Zimbabwe		0.1	0.0	0.0						
Total/Unweighted A	56.3	84.0	195.7	710.8	4.2%	5.8%	10.0%	3.7%	8.8%	9.0%

Who Pays for Healthcare?

The previous section of this Chapter has explained the likely level of total spending on healthcare in individual countries as well as for the Country Segments overall. However, there is one other level of analysis required in terms of funding – that is "who pays for it, the Government or the individual?"

Here there is quite a dichotomy as shown in Table 10-14. Those most able to afford to pay for their health care (i.e., the more affluent) have the greatest government support. Specifically, the Older Affluent and the Older Low Income Country Segments. In both cases, the government is funding just over 60% of total health expenditure in 2019. It is worth noting that the Older Less Affluent Country Segment predominantly comprises ex-communist/socialist countries from which there is a legacy of state provided healthcare.

Table 10-14: Summary of Funding Profile by Country Segment. 2009 and 2019.

Country Segment	Total Health Expenditure per household US$ pa						% HHold Exp		% of Govt		Govt Health Exp as % Total	
	Per Household		Paid by		Paid by							
	2009	2019	2009	2019	2009	2019	2009	2019	2009	2019	2009	2019
Older Affluent	14,130	16,356	8,535	10,024	5,595	6,332	8%	9%	17%	20%	60%	61%
Older Low Income	967	1,618	566	995	401	624	6%	6%	10%	11%	59%	61%
Family Stage Low I	786	813	369	396	417	417	5%	5%	11%	12%	47%	49%
Young Poor	262	298	75	86	187	212	4%	4%	7%	7%	29%	29%

In contrast, those least able to pay for anything other than basic health care, that is countries where the average household income is below US$10,000, get the least government support. This is demonstrated in the last two columns of Table 10-14, which summarise the funding profile for each of the four Country Segments. Again, detail by country is given subsequently.

Do note that in this and subsequent tables in this section, 'Government Expenditure on Health' is the proportion of total health care paid by the

Government and is different (and smaller) than the share of GDP spent on health (which is government and private expenditure on health combined).

Those most able to afford to pay for their health care have the greatest government support. In contrast, those least able, that is, countries where the average household income is below US$10,000, get the least government support.

Older Affluent Countries

Table 10-15 shows the pattern of financing health expenditure for the Older Affluent Segment of countries. The degree of consistency in terms of the share of Government spending allocated to health is interesting given that there are significant differences in terms of political orientations. Just, Singapore and the United States are substantially lower than the others in terms of the share of total health expenditure that is government-funded.

The really important point to take from this table is that in 2019 households in these countries could expect their governments to contribute on average US$10,024 towards healthcare expenditure if required. Furthermore, that accounts for 61% of the typical amount a household must spend on healthcare a year. So, a significant safety blanket.

Table 10-15: Health Funding Profile for Older Affluent Countries. 2009 and 2019.

| | Total Health Expenditure US$ pa | | | | | | | | | | Govt Health exp as % Total Health Exp | |
| | Per Household | | Paid by Goverment | | Paid by Household | | % HHold Exp | | % of Govt Exp | | | |
Country	2009	2019	2009	2019	2009	2019	2009	2017	2009	2017	2009	2017
Australia	11,192	13,170	7,755	9,076	3,436	4,094	5%	5%	16%	18%	69%	69%
Austria	11,817	12,848	8,608	9,290	3,209	3,558	5%	6%	14%	15%	73%	72%
Belgium	11,003	12,181	8,556	9,432	2,447	2,749	4%	5%	15%	15%	78%	77%
Canada	11,619	12,375	8,608	9,137	3,011	3,238	5%	5%	18%	19%	74%	74%
Denmark	14,852	15,588	12,543	13,106	2,308	2,483	4%	4%	16%	17%	84%	84%
Finland	10,307	11,272	8,022	8,670	2,284	2,602	4%	4%	13%	13%	78%	77%
France	11,366	12,315	8,702	9,467	2,664	2,847	5%	5%	15%	15%	77%	77%
Germany	10,769	12,751	8,159	9,891	2,610	2,859	5%	5%	18%	20%	76%	78%
Iceland	15,621	16,121	12,807	13,189	2,815	2,931	3%	3%	15%	16%	82%	82%
Ireland	14,097	15,509	10,865	11,277	3,232	4,232	7%	7%	17%	20%	77%	73%
Italy	7,433	7,098	5,821	5,249	1,613	1,848	3%	4%	14%	13%	78%	74%
Japan	7,735	9,922	6,288	8,370	1,447	1,553	3%	3%	18%	24%	81%	84%
Netherlands	12,429	13,630	8,289	8,733	4,141	4,897	8%	9%	14%	15%	67%	64%
New Zealand	9,659	10,300	7,507	7,785	2,152	2,515	4%	4%	19%	19%	78%	76%
Norway	17,516	20,916	14,790	17,920	2,726	2,996	3%	3%	17%	18%	84%	86%
Sth Korea	3,974	5,829	2,337	3,359	1,637	2,470	5%	7%	10%	13%	59%	58%
Singapore	5,629	8,943	1,963	4,389	3,666	4,553	6%	7%	7%	13%	35%	49%
Slovenia	4,837	5,250	3,483	3,770	1,354	1,480	5%	5%	13%	14%	72%	72%
Spain	6,548	6,494	4,937	4,588	1,612	1,906	4%	5%	15%	15%	75%	71%
Sweden	10,466	14,944	8,578	12,515	1,888	2,429	3%	4%	14%	19%	82%	84%
Switzerland	20,805	25,170	6,444	7,703	14,361	17,466	14%	17%	10%	11%	31%	31%
United Kingdom	8,363	10,502	7,123	8,332	1,240	2,170	2%	3%	15%	19%	85%	79%
USA	25,225	28,508	12,183	14,410	13,042	14,098	13%	13%	18%	23%	48%	51%
Average	14,130	16,356	8,535	10,024	5,595	6,332	8%	9%	17%	20%	60%	61%

Older Low Income Country Segment

This is shown in Table 10-16, and it must be noted that China does dominate the averages for this segment.   The key difference between this and the previous Country Segment is that the percentage of Government Expenditure that is allocated to health is much lower at 11% compared to 20% for the Older Affluent Countries. However, despite having similar age profiles the households themselves allocate less of their expenditure to health care (6% compared to 9%) suggesting a somewhat different attitude to this aspect of life or the cost of delivery is significantly lower (see later).

Table 10-16: Health Funding Profile for Older Low-Income Countries. 2009 and 2019.

Country	Total Health Expenditure US$ pa						% HHold Exp		% of Govt Exp		Govt Health exp as % Total Health Exp	
	Per Household		Paid by Goverment		Paid by Household							
	2009	2019	2009	2019	2009	2019	2009	2017	2009	2017	2009	2017
Belarus	896	1,113	578	766	317	346	4%	3%	7%	11%	65%	69%
Bulgaria	1,826	1,931	983	988	844	942	5%	7%	9%	12%	54%	51%
Cuba	2,555	2,581	2,345	2,319	209	261	2%	2%	15%	16%	92%	90%
Czechia	3,434	4,145	2,846	3,364	588	781	3%	3%	14%	15%	83%	81%
Estonia	2,721	3,829	2,100	2,857	621	972	3%	3%	11%	12%	77%	75%
Georgia	862	1,067	185	407	678	660	8%	6%	6%	10%	21%	38%
Greece	5,726	3,989	3,877	2,400	1,850	1,589	5%	5%	12%	10%	68%	60%
Hungary	2,274	2,844	1,546	1,950	728	893	5%	4%	10%	10%	68%	69%
Latvia	1,960	2,684	1,169	1,549	791	1,135	4%	4%	8%	9%	60%	58%
Lithuania	3,522	3,155	2,531	2,059	990	1,096	10%	11%	12%	13%	72%	65%
Mauritius	1,341	2,060	508	865	833	1,195	4%	4%	6%	10%	38%	42%
Poland	1,998	2,540	1,433	1,754	564	787	3%	4%	10%	11%	72%	69%
Portugal	5,550	5,168	3,878	3,402	1,672	1,765	5%	5%	14%	13%	70%	66%
Moldova	543	516	262	262	281	254	6%	5%	13%	12%	48%	51%
Romania	1,329	1,677	1,045	1,315	283	361	2%	2%	11%	12%	79%	78%
Russia	1,451	1,621	901	927	550	694	4%	5%	9%	9%	62%	57%
Slovakia	3,234	3,349	2,363	2,606	870	744	4%	3%	13%	13%	73%	78%
Thailand	672	758	492	584	181	174	2%	2%	14%	15%	73%	77%
Ukraine	573	643	334	281	239	362	4%	6%	8%	7%	58%	44%
Uruguay	3,216	4,253	1,908	3,070	1,308	1,183	5%	4%	17%	20%	59%	72%
China	725	1,562	369	936	357	626	8%	7%	9%	10%	51%	60%
Average	967	1,618	566	995	401	624	6%	6%	10%	11%	59%	61%

The other point to note in terms of the Country Segment is the significant real growth in expenditure on health. It reflects the change in China particularly where there has been a significant increase in government expenditure on health. The amount paid by the government per household almost doubled in the last decade, and private increased by 81%.

Family Stage Low Income Country Segment

This Country Segment differs from the preceding two in that the share of total health expenditure paid for by the governments of these countries is much lower at 49% in 2019. However, it does vary substantially by country as shown in the last two columns of Table 10-17.

341

Table 10-17: Health Funding Profile for Family Stage Low Income Countries. 2009 and 2019.

| Country | Total Health Expenditure US$ pa | | | | | | % HHold Exp | | % of Govt Exp | | Govt Health exp as % Total Health Exp | |
| | Per Household | | Paid by Goverment | | Paid by Household | | | | | | | |
	2009	2019	2009	2019	2009	2019	2009	2017	2009	2017	2009	2017
Algeria	1,243	1,478	881	969	362	509	4%	5%	9%	11%	71%	66%
Argentina	3,097	3,130	1,949	2,304	1,148	825	3%	2%	16%	16%	63%	74%
Armenia	897	1,606	192	186	705	1,420	8%	11%	6%	5%	21%	12%
Azerbaijan	1,073	1,401	233	212	840	1,189	8%	11%	3%	3%	22%	15%
Bangladesh	114	181	23	29	91	152	3%	3%	4%	3%	20%	16%
Bolivia	648	986	396	679	253	306	3%	3%	9%	12%	61%	69%
Brazil	2,336	2,376	1,032	998	1,304	1,378	7%	8%	10%	10%	44%	42%
Cambodia	344	440	55	108	289	331	9%	7%	6%	6%	16%	25%
Chile	3,071	4,317	1,439	2,198	1,632	2,119	6%	7%	14%	18%	47%	51%
Colombia	1,425	1,707	1,027	1,148	398	560	3%	3%	18%	17%	72%	67%
Dominican Rep	1,005	1,601	460	751	545	849	4%	5%	14%	16%	46%	47%
Ecuador	1,524	2,006	628	1,085	896	920	6%	6%	8%	12%	41%	54%
El Salvador	1,013	959	503	622	510	337	4%	3%	17%	19%	50%	65%
India	190	235	49	65	141	170	4%	4%	3%	3%	26%	28%
Indonesia	281	440	97	215	185	226	3%	3%	5%	9%	34%	49%
Iran	1,176	1,604	431	832	745	772	9%	9%	12%	23%	37%	52%
Kazakhstan	1,046	1,234	794	775	252	460	2%	2%	11%	8%	76%	63%
Malaysia	1,131	1,728	627	879	504	849	2%	3%	6%	9%	55%	51%
Mexico	2,061	2,009	962	1,049	1,099	961	5%	4%	10%	11%	47%	52%
Morocco	1,008	1,068	435	470	573	598	6%	5%	8%	7%	43%	44%
Myanmar	73	277	6	43	66	234		7%	1%	3%	9%	16%
Nicaragua	539	713	253	419	286	294	5%	5%	16%	19%	47%	59%
Panama	2,967	4,285	2,013	2,556	955	1,730	4%	6%	20%	20%	68%	60%
Paraguay	799	1,487	380	684	419	804	3%	5%	8%	10%	48%	46%
Peru	985	1,388	495	886	490	502	4%	3%	12%	15%	50%	64%
Philippines	447	572	137	176	310	396	4%	4%	7%	7%	31%	31%
Saudi Arabia	5,328	6,872	3,463	4,538	1,866	2,335	4%	5%	8%	10%	65%	66%
South Africa	1,627	1,855	822	1,017	805	837	5%	5%	11%	13%	51%	55%
Sri Lanka	439	547	178	230	261	318	3%	3%	8%	8%	41%	42%
Tunisia	943	1,198	519	690	424	508	3%	4%	12%	14%	55%	58%
Turkey	1,314	1,138	1,058	893	256	245	2%	1%	12%	10%	80%	78%
Uzbekistan	260	504	122	220	138	285	5%	6%	7%	10%	47%	44%
Venezuela RB	3,094	462	1,064	67	2,030	396	7%	1%	8%	1%	34%	14%
Viet Nam	363	604	132	298	232	306	5%	4%	6%	9%	36%	49%
Average	786	813	369	396	417	417	5%	5%	11%	12%	47%	49%

Young Poor Country Segment

As is to be expected the absolute amount spent by countries in this segment per household on health is significantly lower than for the other Country Segments.

Table 10-18: Health Funding Profile for Young Poor Countries. 2009 and 2019.

Country	Total Health Expenditure US$ pa								% of Govt Exp		Govt Health exp as % Total Health Exp	
	Per Household		Paid by Govermen		Paid by Household		% HHold Exp					
	2009	2019	2009	2019	2009	2019	2009	2017	2009	2017	2009	2017
Angola	619	416	419	195	200	221	2%	2%	6%	5%	68%	47%
Botswana	1,908	2,317	983	1,760	925	556	5%	3%	6%	14%	52%	76%
Burkina Faso	193	306	62	133	131	173	6%	6%	8%	10%	32%	43%
Cameroon	260	335	44	46	215	289	5%	5%	5%	3%	17%	14%
Chad	156	155	33	24	124	131	5%	5%	4%	5%	21%	15%
DR Congo	88	98	6	12	82	86	5%	5%	3%	3%	7%	12%
Egypt	532	648	186	213	346	436	4%	5%	5%	5%	35%	33%
Ethiopia	92	134	18	32	74	102		4%	5%	5%	20%	24%
Ghana	347	365	164	125	183	240	3%	3%	12%	6%	47%	34%
Guatemala	1,079	1,196	385	431	695	765	5%	4%	16%	17%	36%	36%
Guinea	107	206	9	33	97	174	3%	5%	2%	4%	9%	16%
Haiti	194	251	43	32	151	219	4%	5%	7%	5%	22%	13%
Honduras	890	895	395	359	495	536	6%	6%	14%	12%	44%	40%
Kenya	350	350	98	153	252	197	6%	5%	7%	8%	28%	44%
Lao PDR	208	252	69	90	139	162	4%	3%	6%	4%	33%	36%
Madagascar	130	148	36	70	94	78	5%	4%	10%	15%	28%	47%
Malawi	155	197	28	61	127	136	10%	8%	5%	10%	18%	31%
Mali	189	164	24	60	165	105	6%	3%	3%	6%	13%	36%
Mozambique	89	115	13	35	77	81	6%	5%	2%	5%	14%	30%
Namibia	1,807	1,965	691	893	1,116	1,072	7%	6%	11%	11%	38%	45%
Nepal	150	268	31	58	120	211	5%	6%	5%	5%	20%	21%
Niger	179	219	47	75	132	144	8%	7%	9%	10%	26%	34%
Nigeria	337	391	54	53	284	339	4%	4%	4%	5%	16%	13%
Pakistan	128	169	28	53	100	116	2%	2%	3%	4%	22%	31%
Rwanda	206	241	48	85	158	156	8%	6%	8%	9%	23%	35%
Senegal	207	282	76	59	131	223	3%	5%	7%	4%	37%	21%
South Sudan	16	8	7	1	9	6		6%	14%	8%	41%	17%
Sudan	187	168	77	29	110	139	3%	4%	14%	8%	41%	17%
Uganda	321	240	68	40	253	200	10%	8%	14%	5%	21%	17%
Tanzania	200	193	59	85	141	108	6%	4%	7%	10%	29%	44%
Zambia	233	287	23	115	210	172	7%	5%	2%	7%	10%	40%
Zimbabwe												
Average	262	298	75	86	187	212	4%	4%	7%	7%	29%	29%

In part, this can be explained by the fact that the GDP per capita of these countries is also very low. Also, some of this difference can be accounted for by the fact that these countries have a smaller proportion of their population in the crucial age range of 40 years above.

However, these countries are underfunded in terms of health care, and the governments contribute relatively little to the individual household's health spending needs. This means a household with 4 or more persons in it and with an average income of US$5,000 per annum must fund most of its health needs.

To Conclude.

The expectation that in the future, economies and health systems will be overloaded with health-related demands and costs is not borne out by current trends.

Projections based on trends in epidemiological data applied to the projected age and gender profiles of the populations of the same country indicate that the overall demand for the health system increases but at reasonably moderate rates. That is 1% per annum for the Older Affluent up to 3% per annum for the Young Poor. These projections include improving diagnostics as a result of ongoing investment in the provision of health services in each country.

There is no country where there is a significant difference between the growth of GDP and the growth of expected demand for health services. In fact, for nearly every country the GDP grows at a faster rate than the projected case demand meaning that the individual countries can increase expenditure per demand unit and maintain healthcare at its present share of GDP.

For most countries, the assumption that health care expenditure in total increases to 10% of GDP by 2045 will mean expenditure per case will also increase. At 1.1% per annum for the Older Affluent and 5% per annum for the Young Poor Country Segment.

However, some interesting sub-trends need to be understood.

First, the growth in the number of people in what might be termed the 'health vulnerable age range' (ages 0-4 and 45 years plus) is ongoing – but the rate of increase in the older (more affluent countries) is not as fast as it has been, and the real growth of the health service demand is in the less affluent and younger countries. They are transiting *into* older middle-age and hence their faster growth in demand for health care.

Second, there is a huge differential in terms of the quality of healthcare provided – as measured by expenditure per case. Even if adjusted for labour costs the dichotomy is significant. The Older Affluent is spending more than ten times as much per person (in the relevant age range). While differences in local delivery costs exist, they are not considered sufficient to offset this difference.

Third, many Young Poor Countries need to be held to account. They are under-spending on health care, and it is not a function of their low incomes alone (although that is a significant factor). The evidence is that the 'governments' of these countries are somewhat irresponsible on this issue.

Many spend less than 5% of GDP on health care and this is significantly a function of the fact that they are spending less than 5% of total *Government* expenditure on health (for most countries it is over 10%). In these poor countries, the governments must provide the funding as the individual households simply cannot pay privately.

Summary Profile – Health Expenditure and Demand

Older Affluent

	2019	2030	2045
% Population 40 yrs +	52.9%	55.7%	57.9%
Persons (Mns) > 40 yrs	524	571	597
Indexed demand	476	549	617
Cost per index item	13,187	13,311	13,389
Total Exp on Health (Bns)	6,271	7,306	8,261
As % of GDP	12.9%	12.2%	11.5%
Annual Growth rate %	2.3%	1.4%	0.8%

Older Low Income

	2019	2030	2045
% Population 40 yrs +	49.8%	56.7%	58.9%
Persons (Mns) > 40 yrs	907	1,042	1,025
Indexed demand	822	1,077	1,313
Cost per index item	1,281	1,266	1,255
Total Exp on Health (Bns)	1,053	1,364	1,647
As % of GDP	5.4%	4.4%	3.7%
Annual Growth rate %	6.7%	2.4%	1.3%

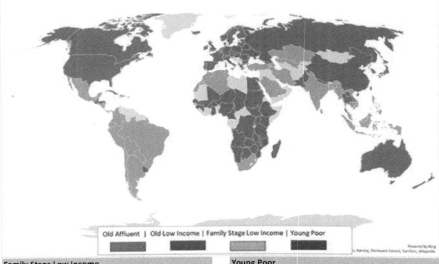

Old Affluent | Old Low Income | Family Stage Low Income | Young Poor

Family Stage Low Income

	2019	2030	2045
% Population 40 yrs +	32.5%	39.2%	47.4%
Persons (Mns) > 40 yrs	1,016	1,342	1,703
Indexed demand	728	977	1,299
Cost per index item	1,012	1,014	1,014
Total Exp on Health (Bns)	737	990	1,317
As % of GDP	5.4%	5.4%	4.9%
Annual Growth rate %	3.6%	2.7%	1.9%

Young Poor

	2019	2030	2045
% Population 40 yrs +	19.2%	21.7%	25.8%
Persons (Mns) > 40 yrs	255	373	595
Indexed demand	202	295	475
Cost per index item	417	416	415
Total Exp on Health (Bns)	84	123	197
As % of GDP	4.2%	3.7%	2.8%
Annual Growth rate %	4.1%	3.5%	3.2%

Chapter 11 The Future Demographics of China

Introduction

China and India have an estimated combined population in 2020 of 2.78 billion persons. This represents 38% of the total population of the countries covered in this book and 34% of the global population as estimated by the United Nations (at 8.3 billion). As such it is important to look at the potential demographic profile of these countries in the future.

However, demographically the two countries are quite different from each other. As such, they are covered separately in this and the next Chapter.

> *Three major policies – birth control, education, and employment/location - have significantly changed the course of China and will continue to do so for the next 25 years.*

China had three historic events that have, and will continue to, influence the future shape of its population.

1. The most publicised of these is, of course, the ***One-Child Policy*** introduced in 1979. This policy has significantly influenced the age and social structure of that society in subsequent years to 2020 and even if removed now (it has recently been changed to what is a three-child policy), it will continue to do so into the future. Certainly, to the horizon of this book in 2045.
2. The second significant change was compulsory ***universal education***. With the number of children needing education stabilised by the one-child policy, it was possible to introduce universal education. From 1984 onward every child aged 6 to 12

years inclusive has been going to school for a (largely) free education. As the reader will have gathered from earlier chapters, this is regarded as a positive attribute for a society.

Please note that this education was available as much for a girl in a remote rural village as it was for a boy in central Beijing. There was no gender or regional bias in availability.

3. The third change that influenced the existing and future nature of China was **urbanisation**. Educating every child meant that when they reached working age (typically 15 to 20 years at the start of this process) they found they could move to an urban area and work in a factory or office where their productivity (and hence incomes) was much higher than working in agriculture.

   It should be emphasized that this shift in employment could not have happened without the increased availability of education. Persons who cannot read or write are of little value to tertiary industries.

It is important to recognise the 'order' of these events. First birth control to make it feasible to educate every child. Second, once births were under control, they introduced compulsory (free) education so that every child could be more productive when they entered the workforce. Third, allow (encourage) the movement of the population from rural to urban employment given their improved skill set.

It is also useful to digress marginally here in terms of reinforcing how one must think about China (and India). The numbers are huge. People understand that there has been a significant movement of the Chinese population from a rural environment to an urban one. But not all understand that this has been at the rate of around 19 million persons a year.

Every year for the last 10 years around 20 million persons a year have moved from rural to urban locations and employment. That is the equivalent of nearly the entire population of Australia moving location (residence and environment) each year!

The One-Child Policy

The Initial Concept

To some extent, this has not been well understood by those outside China. One suspects that most people outside China see it as a 'one child *only* policy' when it was not. The One-Child Policy only limited couples to one child if they were born in, and whose family was registered as living in, an urban area. That is a person with an *Urban* Hukou. Note this is *not* the same as where a person lives currently — which is now predominantly urban irrespective of their Hukou. The important point to note is that from the start of the 'One Child Policy' those with what is called a *Rural* Hukou could have a second child if the first is a female and those with a rural hukou were the majority of the population in 1979 and remain so even in 2020 despite moving to urban areas.

This registration certificate (called Hukou) in theory determines where a person can live and where they can have access to social services such as health and education. As such it is a powerful influence on people's behaviour.

Be that as it may, the Government decided that allowing educated people to move to urban areas and engage in more productive jobs (that is manufacturing and tertiary) was desirable and the freedom of movement away from their designated Hukou area was allowed. But no access to social services in their new location. Individuals must register with the Public Security Bureau if they move to a new location for more than six months and that is the best measure of where the population is located.

Note that the reported urban and rural populations in this publication are based on registration with the Public Security Bureau and are not the Hukou urban-rural designations. This reflects the reality of where the population lives.

Consequently, the situation now exists where approximately one-third of Shanghai's population has a Shanghai Hukou and the rest have a Hukou from outside the city and typically a rural one.

This is important because, as mentioned, those with a rural Hukou can have a second child if the first is a girl. This option is typically exercised and given that it impacts gender selection for the second child, it is a key reason why there is a male bias in births. Overall, in the last decade, the average number of children a woman has had by age of 49 years has been around 1.4. That, interestingly, is not out of line with the birth rate of other countries of a similar level of affluence and education without any policies regarding birth control.

The Birth Policy Changes – Determinants of the Birth Rate

The following subsections describe how the birth policy has changed since 2005 and is expected to change for the period 2021 to 2023. Note that the 'One Child' Policy was first introduced in 1979.

2005-2012 –Steady birth rate

As shown in Figure 11-1, for the period 1998 to 2012 the propensity to have a child declined from a high of 55 when the policy was still not fully enforced to a stable level at around 44 per thousand women aged 15 to 49 years in 2005. From 2005 to 2012 it stayed at around 44 per thousand

It is important to appreciate that this means that many women were having more than one child. Available data indicates that until 1998 the average number a woman had was 1.7 children. Many of the women in 1998 had had children before the introduction of the policy. The available data indicates that by 2012 the average number of children per woman had settled back to 1.46 children for women aged 40 years of age.

2013 to 2014 – Initial change in One-Child Policy

In 2012 the first of two changes happened. The number of women aged 15 to 49 years had started to decline, initially slowly and then at a faster rate through to 2020 (See Figure 11-2). This meant the number fell from 371 million to 334 million. A 10% decline in absolute number and the start of an increasing trend. This is discussed in greater detail later.

Figure 11-1: Long Term Historic Trend in Births per Thousand Women Aged 15 to 49 Years

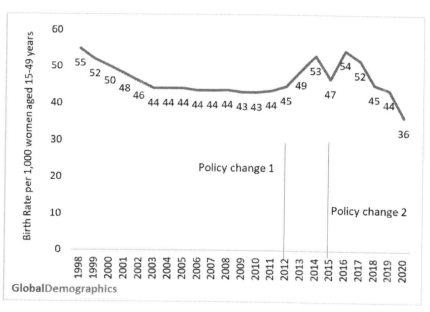

GlobalDemographics

At the same time, and perhaps as a result of this decline in the number of females aged 15 to 49 years, the Government introduced changes to the one-child policy which allowed couples with an *urban* Hukou to have a second child. As shown in Figure 11-1, this caused a significant increase in the birth rate – but for 2013 and 2014 only.

There was an 'inventory' of urban couples who wanted a second child but could not under the old regulations. When the legislation changed, they took advantage of it. The birth rate climbed from 44 per thousand in 2012 to peak at 53 in 2014 – and then it plummeted back to 47 in 2015. The 'inventory' was largely depleted. As a result, total births dropped from a peak of 19.2 million in 2014 to 16.9 in 2015. However, using 2012 as a base year, this meant that 3.9 million 'additional' children were born in 2013 and 2014 than would have otherwise been the case. That is an 8% to 10% increase.

It is considered that the limited effect of this change in the policy was a function of it only affecting a small number of couples. That is, those with an Urban Hukou and who were not themselves both from one-child families (and therefore could have a second child if they wanted to). Probably less than 20% of all couples in that year.

2015 to 2019 – further changes to the One-Child Policy

In 2015 a further change was made. All couples, irrespective of their Hukou and whether or not they were from one-child families, could have up to two children. It was now effectively a 'Two-Child Policy'.

Again the 'inventory effect' came into play and for 2016 total births lifted to 19.2 million and then remained high at 18.2 million for 2017.

However, this increase cleared the backlog and for 2018 total births returned to trend (15.6 million) and a birth rate per thousand of 45.

In 2019 – which is still pre-pandemic – the historic trend of circa 44 per thousand women aged 15 to 49 years continued. Consequently, total births in that year declined to 14.9 million.

2020 – The Pandemic

It is not surprising that total births reduced substantially in 2020. The risks associated with Covid-19 inhibited any activity that potentially would require medical attention/care. As a result, a significant proportion of couples delayed having a child and total births declined to 12.0 million which is a birth rate per thousand of 36.

In short, the period 2013 to 2020 was quite a roller coaster ride for the maternity industry.

Figure 11-2 summarises the dynamics of births and women of childbearing age for the period 2005 to 2020. This is actual data.

Figure 11-2: Historic trend in Total Births and Number of Women aged 15 to 49 yrs.

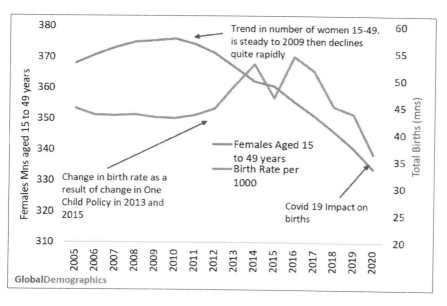

GlobalDemographics

2021 – Up to Three Child Policy

In 2021 the Birth Policies changed again and now any couple can have up to three children. This opens up a whole series of questions about the extent to which this will be taken advantage of and the implications of that for the overall population? There is no real data available for this.

As explained subsequently in this section, there appears to have been a high propensity of those allowed to have a second child to actually have a second child. This may be a function of the constraint. At present, it would appear that nearly all that were able to do so (rural Hukou and the first child is a girl) took advantage of this. International experience is that couples with the level of education and income of those in China, average out at around 1.5 children - which coincidentally, is where China was in 2020.

Does this mean that 'third child' take-up may be quite low?

2021 to 2023 – Uncertainty but net-zero impact over 4 years.

No one knows what will happen to the birth rate in these years. The delayed births because of Covid-19 combined with allowing more children per couple does create some potential scenarios. Given Covid-19 is still present in parts of China in 2022 the birth rate has likely continued to be suppressed for that year. But by how much?

Assuming that vaccines prove to be effective, how much will the birth rate bounce back in 2023?

For forecasting purposes, the view has been taken that the wish to have a child (whether it is the first child or subsequent child) probably has not changed – it has simply been delayed until safe to do so. As such the expectation is that by 2023 the average birth *rate* for the whole period of 2020 to 2023 will match the projected trend for 2020 to 2023. That is 43 births per thousand women aged 15 to 49 *if there had been no change* in the birth policy.

However, as explained later in this section, scenarios have been tested to identify the sensitivity of the future population size and age profile to different trends in the propensity to have a child given the changes in the one-child policy. But first, it is important to examine the trend in the other key determinant of the number of births. That is the number of women of childbearing age.

The Number of Women Aged 15 to 49 years

This is the other key determinant of the number of births per annum. In many respects, its impact is much greater than that of the birth rate.

First, the number of women in this age range *for the next 15 years* is already predetermined by the number of births in the last 15 years. That is, the age cohort of 15 to 49 year-olds in 2035 are aged 0 to 34 years in 2020 and are already alive. The only uncertainty in terms of this variable is the number of such women after 2035. That is a function of the number of births in the next 15 years.

Second, the change in the number of women aged 15 to 49 years is significant and is shown in Figure 11-3. Between 2020 and 2035 (the period where there is certainty about the number – that is, they are already alive) the number of such women declines by 50 million.

Furthermore, under the central forecast of the trend in birth rates (taking into account the change in policy to three children), it would decline by a further 50 million by 2045. In total under the central scenario, it is projected that the number of women aged 15 to 49 years will decline by 100 million persons in the next 25 years on a base of 334 million in 2020. That is a significant decline.

Figure 11-3: Historic and Projected (passive forecast) trend in the absolute number of women in Millions aged 15 to 49 years.

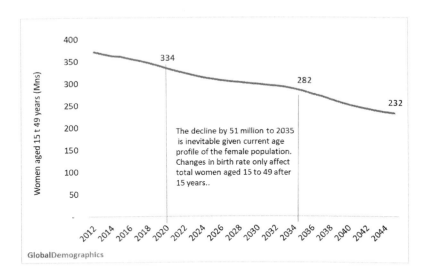

To further complicate the analysis, it needs to be noted that the *age profile* of women aged 15 to 49 also changes dramatically over the same time period. This is important as it does impact the average birth rate. Older women have a much lower propensity to have a child than young women.

Figure 11-4 shows how the absolute importance of different age groups has, and will, change. Again, the data for this is reliable through to 2035 given the existing age profile of females currently aged 0 to 35 years. The fluctuations are considerable. It is the age groups under 35 years that are important in this respect as in total they account for just on 90% of all births in any one year.

As shown in Figure 11-4 the youngest age group (15 to 24 years) declined significantly in number from 2012 to 2020 – and then shows marginal growth to 2035. For the period 2036 to 2045 the trend depends on assumptions about the birth rate over the next 10 years. Even if it increases substantially then the decline in the number of 15 to 24 years olds after 2036 will still happen, albeit more muted.

The key age group though is the 25 to 34 years (which accounts for 60% of all births). It is projected to decline over the period 2020 to 2030 and then stay at a lower level to at least 2045 (note, this age group is 0 years of age or older in 2020 so its number can be projected with some certainty to 2045).

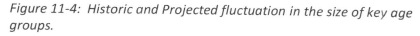

Figure 11-4: Historic and Projected fluctuation in the size of key age groups.

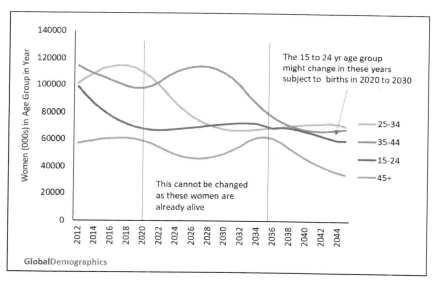

Thus, in aggregate the key age groups for having children (15 to 34 years) are quite reliably projected to decline from 177 million in 2020 to 138 million in 2035 and with some confidence to remain at that level or lower through to 2045 even under the most optimistic scenario in terms of birth rates and propensity to have two or three children.

This is a dramatic change – to decline from 177 to 138 million persons is a 22% reduction which means birth rates need to increase from 45 to 68 per thousand women aged 15 to 49 years to offset that. This is the most significant determinant of total births in future. More than changes in birth rates.

The Total Births Forecasts

If there had been no change in the one-child policy and recent trends in birth rates by age continued, then the expectation was that total births would continue to decline to 11 million per annum by 2035 and that the peak population of 1.433 would be in 2025 and then decline to 1,334 million by 2045. A decline of 77 million persons from 2020.

That, however, will not be the case given the further relaxation of the birth policy. But by how much can it, or will it, change? Here we have little guidance in the context of China. Historically the number of births has been significantly determined by Government policy. To what extent do individual citizens wish to have more than what was previously allowed? Will this be impacted by potential (but unconfirmed) financial or social incentives to have more children?

In terms of the propensity to have a first child, there is little flexibility. Historic data on births by age of mother show quite clearly that around 97% of women aged 15 to 49 years will have at least one child. The missing 3% is a function of those with fertility issues or choosing to not get married (few children are born outside marriage in China to date).

This means that the propensity to have a first child is a 'given' and if it changed it would most likely decline as attitudes to marriage, family etc change. However, for the period to 2045, it is expected to remain high.

In terms of having a second child, we have some clues, but they need to be taken into context.

First, it must be appreciated that the 'one child policy' was never a one-child policy. With few exceptions, if the couple had a rural Hukou (residency certificate) and their first child was a female then they could have a second child.

Analysis of the cumulative birth rate by age of mother indicates that on average 45% of births in any one year is a second child. In 2019 there had been a total of 390 million births to women aged 15 to 49 years. Of these 269 million were birth of the first child and 121 million (45%) were a second child.

As such that is probably a good conservative estimate of the proportion of couples that would want a second child. The fact that there were 9.7 million additional births in the previous years when the policy was relaxed indicates it could be higher – in the region of 49%. That is considered to be the conservative scenario (see below).

There are, however, no clues as to what proportion of those who have had a second child are likely to want a third. Based on the education profile of the country it is expected to be low but there is nothing to indicate how low.

Forecast Scenarios

Because of the uncertainty of future birth rates this next section examines the number of births in future years under three different assumptions. The scenarios used are:

1: Conservative

Under this scenario, the propensity to have a second child begins at 49% of those who have had a first child. This is justified on the basis that this is consistent with the propensity to have a second child considering the policy changes for 2013 to 2019. It also results in an average birth rate that is consistent with other countries of a similar education and GDP per capita level to that of China. It is then assumed to reduce to 40% by 2045 reflecting the ongoing improvements in education and affluence.

Third child propensity is estimated to be low at 25% of those who have had a second child by 2020 declining to 20% by 2045. Therefore, the propensity of a woman who has had a first child to have a third child in 2022 is on average 25% of 49% (propensity to have had a second). That is 12%.

While discussed in detail later and in the attached tables, it is worth pointing out that this scenario means total annual births will decline from 14.4 million in 2024 to 10.8 million in 2045. The years 2022 and 2023 have a higher number but that is partially a reflection of the 'catchup' after (hopefully) Covid-19 is under control. It indicates a birth rate per thousand of 46 in 2024 which is in line with the historic norm of 44. Because of the aforementioned changing age profile of females between the ages of 15 and 49, it drops to a low of 40 in 2034 and then recovers to 46 by 2045.

2: Positive Scenario

Under this scenario, the probability of having a second child is assumed to start at 60% of those with a first child at least 2 years earlier and declines to 45% by 2045 reflecting a combination of greater willingness to have a second child as a result of relaxed regulations and also possible government incentives.

Obviously, under a scenario of incentives, the propensity to have a third child would also increase and for this scenario, it is assumed to initially be 35% of those with a second child two years previously declining to 25% by 2045 reflecting the ongoing improvements in education and affluence. That means that in 2022 21% of women who have a first child will go on to have a third child.

This indicates total births of 15.8 million in 2024 declining to 11.5 million in 2045. Under this scenario, the average birth rate jumps to 50 per thousand in 2024 and declines to 47 per thousand by 2045. Again, because of the changing age profile, it declines to 43 in 2035 before rising back to 47 by 2045.

3: Optimistic

It is assumed that the propensity to have a second child jumps to 80% of those with a first child in 2022 and declines to 60% by 2045 (again driven by increases in the level of education and affluence). Third child propensity starts at 50% of those with a second child at least 2 years earlier decreasing to 32% by 2045.

This gives an average of 40% of first child mothers having a third child in 2024. This results in an average birth rate of 58 in 2024 which, as shown in Figure 11-5, is just above normative bounds given the education and affluence standard of the population. However, China is a unique society in many ways and global norms do not necessarily apply.

Given the expected change in the age profile of women of childbearing age over the forecast period, the birth rate would reach a low of 50 in 2035 and then lift to 52 by 2045.

Figure 11-5: Comparison of China's Birth Rate with Global Norms in terms of Education

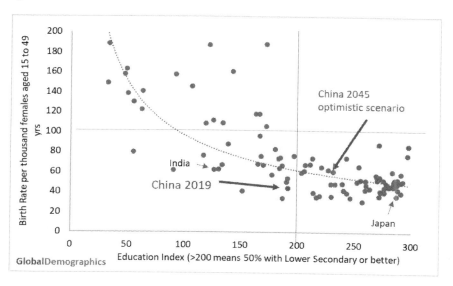

The Results

The next set of charts compares the three scenarios in terms of birth rate statistics. They are also compared with the base case – which is the expected outcome if there had been no change in the Birth Policy to three children in 2021.

Total Births Forecasts

Figure 11-6 shows the impact on total births through to 2045 under each scenario. Under the conservative scenario, it would be 10.8 million per annum by 2045, whereas for the Optimistic Scenario it would be 13.3 million.

Figure 11-6: Total Births by Scenario

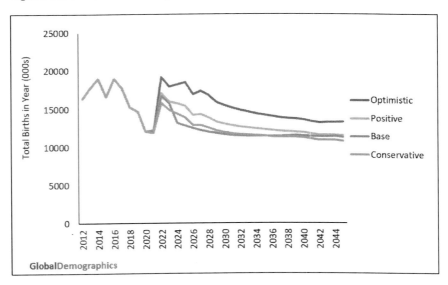

Table 11-1: Births (Millions) per annum

	2012	2015	2020	2025	2030	2035	2040	2045
Optimistic	16.4	16.6	12.0	18.5	15.5	14.2	13.6	13.3
Positive	16.4	16.6	12.0	15.4	13.1	12.3	11.9	11.5
Conservative	16.4	16.6	12.0	13.9	12.0	11.5	11.2	10.8
Base	16.4	16.6	12.0	12.8	11.7	11.4	11.5	11.3

The cumulative number of births between 2022 and 2045 is 291 million for the conservative case versus 365 million for the Optimistic scenario. A difference of 74 million over 25 years. It should be noted that for the same period (2024 to 2045) total deaths would be 378 million. This means that even under the Optimistic Scenario the total population is projected to decline in size.

Changes in Number of Women Aged 15 to 49 Years

That leads nicely to the next chart (Figure 11-7) which shows the projected trend in the number of women aged 15 to 49 under the three scenarios (and base case). What is interesting here is that the impact is very small over 25 years as shown in Figure 11-7.

For obvious reasons, there is no impact before 2037 as the model only changes births in 2022 onward – so the earliest year that any change in birth rate is reflected in the number of women aged 15 to 49 years would be 2038. However, the cumulative additional births between 2022 and 2037 of the Optimistic Scenario over the Conservative Scenario is just 55 million, of which 26 million will be female. This is in the context of a base of 271 million women aged 15 to 49 in 2037.

This is important in the context of this discussion because it is the number of women of childbearing age that is impacting future births most. Only the Optimistic Scenario comes close to slowing the downward trend in the number of women and then only in the last few years. Under the other two scenarios, the number of women aged 15 to 49 continues to decline quite rapidly.

Figure 11-7: Historic and Projected Trend in Number of Women (mns) aged 15 to 49 years

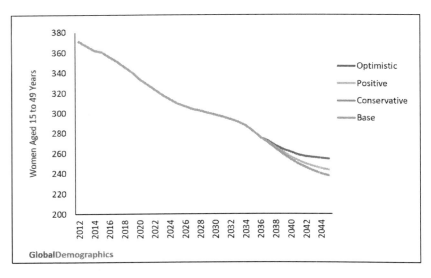

Table 11-2: Women (Mns) Aged 15 to 49 Years

	2012	2015	2020	2025	2030	2035	2040	2045
Optimistic	371.2	360.6	333.9	309.7	298.2	282.0	261.3	254.7
Positive	371.2	360.6	333.9	309.7	298.2	282.0	256.7	243.5
Conservative	371.2	360.6	333.9	309.7	298.2	282.0	254.2	237.8
Base	371.2	360.6	333.9	309.7	298.2	282.0	251.8	232.4

Projected Average Birth Rate

Figure 11-8 shows the impact of these changes on the overall birth rate per thousand women of childbearing age. Here the differences are quite significant. However, it should be pointed out that the start points are assumptions. The conservative starting point is based on the lower bound of the global norm and the optimistic is based on the upper bound of the global norm. See Figure 11-5 earlier.

Figure 11-8: Comparison of Average Birth Rate Per Thousand Women Aged 15 to 49 yrs.

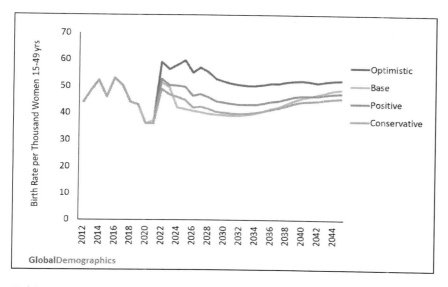

Table 11-3: Average Birth Rate Per Thousand Women Aged 15 to 49 Years

	2012	2015	2020	2025	2030	2035	2040	2045
Optimistic	44.1	46.0	36.0	59.6	51.8	50.5	52.1	52.3
Positive	44.1	46.0	36.0	49.8	43.9	43.7	46.5	47.4
Conservative	44.1	46.0	36.0	44.8	40.1	40.6	44.2	45.6
Base	44.1	46.0	36.0	41.4	39.1	40.6	45.7	48.8

Under the conservative scenario, it is assumed that the average birth rate would rise to 45 per thousand in 2025 and then decline steadily to 45.6 by 2045 – in short, it is relatively static over the 25 years with a decline to 40 per thousand by 2031 as a result of the changing age profile of women in the relevant age range.

In contrast for the Optimistic Scenario, it is assumed to increase to 59.6 per thousand in 2025, and then the combined dynamics of the changing age profile of women aged 15 to 49 and increased education and affluence would result in it dropping to 50 per thousand in 2031 and then lift to 52 by 2045.

Implications for the overall population

It is worth looking at the implications of the different scenarios for the overall population and perhaps, more importantly, the working-age population. Figure 11-9 shows the projected trend for the total population under each of the three scenarios as well under the forecast based on data to 2020 and before the change permitting three children.

Figure 11-9: Projected trend in Total Population

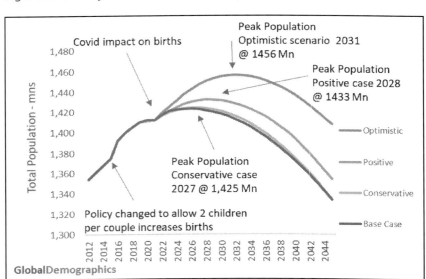

Table 11-4: Historic and Projected Total Population (mns)

	2012	2015	2020	2025	2030	2035	2040	2045
Optimistic	1,354	1,375	1,411	1,438	1,455	1,454	1,437	1,408
Positive	1,354	1,375	1,411	1,428	1,432	1,420	1,394	1,354
Conservative	1,354	1,375	1,411	1,424	1,421	1,404	1,375	1,334
Base	1,354	1,375	1,412	1,423	1,418	1,401	1,373	1,334

The variation is greater under the optimistic scenario. Peak population moves marginally out to 2031 with an extra 55 million persons and then declines to 1,408 million by 2045. That is an additional 74 million persons in 2045 than under the base case.

The range of outcomes in terms of peak population under the three scenarios is from 1,425 million (conservative) to 1,456 million (optimistic). A difference of 31 million on a population of 1,411 in 2020. This is not likely to significantly change any business decisions.

The important point to note here is that under all four scenarios the total population of China will decline between the mid 2020s and 2045.

Implication for the Working-age Population

This carries across to the working-age population – but given that any change in birth policy takes 15 years to impact the working-age population, the effect is less – to the point that it is barely discernible except for the Optimistic Scenario. This is shown in Figure 11-10.

Under the base (historic) case the working-age population was projected to decline from 995 million in 2020 (census) to 814 million in 2045. As reported elsewhere by Global Demographics Ltd, nearly all of this decline is in the rural population. The ongoing rural to urban migration means the urban working-age population is sustained until 2035 and beyond.

Under the optimistic scenario, the working-age population is projected to decline to 847 million compared with the 816 million under the conservative case. In short, under this scenario, the change in the birth policy would mean 31 million more working-age persons by 2045 over the conservative case. This is on a total working-age population of 995 million in 2020. It is not a significant difference.

Figure 11-10: Projected Trend in Working-age Population

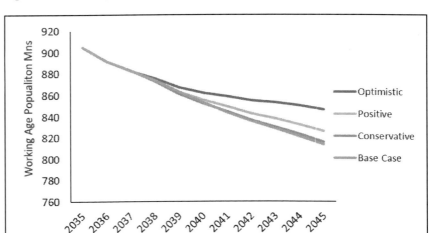

Table 11-5: Historic and Projected Size of the Working-age Population (15 to 64 years) in Mns

	2012	2015	2020	2025	2030	2035	2040	2045
Optimistic	994	1,003	995	988	956	905	862	847
Positive	994	1,003	995	988	956	905	856	826
Conservative	994	1,003	995	988	956	905	853	816
Base	994	1,003	995	988	956	905	853	814

The one potentially significant impact here is that the Optimistic Scenario does slow the reduction in the size of the working-age population.

Implication for the long-term size of the Child Market (0-14 year olds)

The one age segment that a change in the birth rate does directly impact is what is classified as the Child Market – defined as persons aged 0 to 14 years. This age group is important for quite specific products and services including health (vaccines, post-natal care, etc), education, toys, recreation etc.

The key issue here is that the Optimistic Scenario (as one would expect) initially increases and then maintains the absolute size of this age segment until 2038. In contrast, under the base case and the two more conservative scenarios this age group goes into quite a rapid decline in terms of the absolute number of persons. That of course is not positive for the child market.

Figure 11-11 and Table 11-6 show the expected trend for each of the scenarios and how different they are in respect of this particular measure.

Figure 11-11: Projected Size (in Mns) of the 0-14 years Age Segment

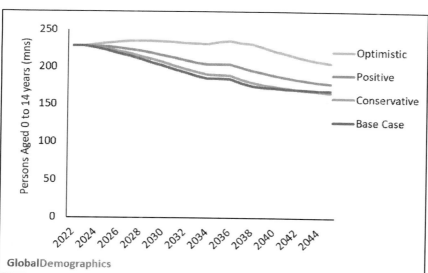

Table 11-6: Historic and Projected Number (in Mns) of Children aged 0-14 Years

	2012	2015	2020	2025	2030	2035	2040	2045
Optimistic	223	229	231	233	234	233	221	206
Positive	223	229	231	227	216	204	189	178
Conservative	223	229	231	224	206	190	174	166
Base	223	229	231	222	202	185	172	169

Note: The kink in the lines for 2036 reflects the projected upsurge in births in 2022 and 2023 post-Covid.

To Conclude

While there are indications that the Government would like to increase the birth rate to sustain the population it is considered unlikely to achieve that. A decline in the total population of China by 2045 is almost inevitable. Analysis of international data indicates that countries with a similar education and GDP per capita profile as China have a birth rate in the region of 40 to 50 per thousand and the efforts of various governments in these countries to increase the rate have not been effective. A simple reality is that the majority of educated people tend to regard 2 children as sufficient if not one.

Secondly, even if the propensity to have children did increase either with or without financial or social incentives, the reality is that there is a significant headwind in terms of the ongoing decline in the number of women of childbearing age. This cannot be reversed before 2035 and as shown in the analysis, even under assumptions of a significant and abrupt increase in the average birth rate from 44 to 59 in 2022 decreasing to 52 by 2045 does not change this scenario – it only slows the decline. It does not stop it. As demonstrated in Figure 11-7, even under the Optimistic scenario with the initial average birth rate set to 59 per thousand, the decline in the number of such women continues through to 2045.

Probably the only effective change is that if the Optimistic Scenario was achieved it would slow the decline in the size of the child segment for a decade – but then it will decline just as steeply as the other scenarios are expected to from 2024.

The reality is that China's population will peak by the mid 2020s and it will decline in size thereafter. It is extremely unlikely that the country can increase its propensity to have children sufficiently to change this outcome.

However, the decline is relatively small and does not reduce the potential size of the urban workforce until after 2045 although the growth rate slows to almost zero after 2035. Hence, with increased productivity per worker, GDP growth is expected to continue to 2045.

The total population of China is expected to peak at 1.433 Bn persons in 2028 and then will decline at quite a rapid rate to reach 1.35 billion by 2045.

At present (2020) China's total population is 1.411 billion, by 2028 it is projected to be 1.433 billion and by 2045 it is projected to be 1.354 billion. This means that by 2045 the total population will have 57 million fewer persons than the 2020 level and 78 million fewer than the peak population which is not significant relative to the total of 1.4 billion. What is important is that the population size is now 'stable' rather than growing which enables it to lift the well-being of the population.

Education

This was the 'magic key' that enabled China to change from being many poor people to a very large middle-class society with ongoing upward potential. It does not require great science to realize that an educated person will be more productive and that in turn lifts the economy, individual earnings, and lifestyles.

Compulsory education was the simple expedient for this. But do appreciate it was facilitated by the aforementioned 'one child policy'. The number of children needing education flattened out as a result of the constraint on births and as such China could focus on lifting the quality of education (reducing class size, better facilities etc.) rather than scrambling to maintain a basic inadequate level just to keep up with the number of school places needed.

In 1992 there were 224 million children aged 5 to 14 years who required an education place. By 2000 this had reduced marginally to 219 million and by 2019 it was 153 million. That is close to a one-third reduction in the number of primary and lower secondary educational places required – which in turn enables an increase in quality.

By way of comparison, consider Nigeria. There are 56 million school-age (5 to 14 years) children today (2020) and in 25 years there will be 95 million. To simply **maintain** its present (inadequate) education level Nigeria will need to increase its education spending by 70% (in real terms).

In China, education enabled the individual to move to urban areas and take on manufacturing and then tertiary level work. This significantly lifted the productivity of the worker. Based on wage differentials between rural and urban workers, it lifted productivity per worker by a factor of 3. Manufacturing and tertiary work is more productive than Primary (agricultural) work – especially in a society where agriculture is still mainly physical labour.

In China, education enabled the individual to move to urban areas and take on manufacturing and then tertiary level work. This lifted the productivity of the worker by a factor of 3.

It is expected that this improvement in the education level of the adult population will continue because as shown in Figure 11-12, the absolute number of persons of 'education age' (realistically ages 5 to 19 with the provision of vocational and tertiary education extending the age range) is reducing steadily allowing a continued focus on lifting the quality of education facilities rather than needing to increase the quantity. This is under the 'Positive' Birth rate scenario discussed earlier in this Chapter.

Figure 11-12: Number of Persons (Nms.) Aged 5 To 19 Years Inclusive.

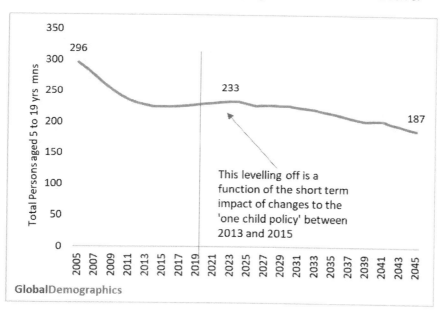

Long term there is no reason why China will not continue to build and leverage its education advantage. The facilities are in place, the demand in terms of the number of persons has levelled off thereby enabling a focus on quality rather than quantity, and Society values it.

Perhaps the only emerging 'issue' here is the dichotomy between the three municipality areas of Beijing, Tianjin and Shanghai and the rest of the country in terms of the number of vocational and tertiary level educated adults. A disproportionate share of such persons is now located in those three Municipalities. This is not a problem except it does tend to create a concentration of an educational elite.

Employment

Working-age Population

This is another area where there is significant change taking place. As a result of the levelling off (over the last decade) and now, projected, decline in the total number of births per annum for the next two decades, the number of persons of working age will decline. What does this mean for the productive power of China and the overall quality of life of its citizens?

Working-age in China for the period to 2045 will be essentially 15 to 64 years although the model used for forecasts allows an increasing proportion of 65 to 74-year-olds to be employed as the life expectancy of the older population increases. Figure 11-13 shows the impact of this increasing age range on the total working-age population.

In addition, Figure 11-13 demonstrates that the total working-age population in China under either definition is in decline. Initially, the decline is small but after 2033 it starts to decline quite rapidly. Using the traditional definition of working age, under the 'Positive Scenario' in terms of births, the number of persons aged 15 to 64 is projected to decline from 995 million to 827 million over the next 25 years. The obvious question is what does this mean for the Chinese economy?

It is necessary to look at the labour supply separately for the urban and rural located populations. It is also necessary to consider the ongoing rural to urban migration. Rural to Urban migration has been running at around 19 million persons per annum.

'Rural to urban' migration is expected to continue through to 2045. Overall, the number of rural to urban migrants per annum is projected to decline from 19 million per annum in 2020 to 15 million by 2045.

Figure 11-13: Projected Trend in the Size of the Working-age Population.

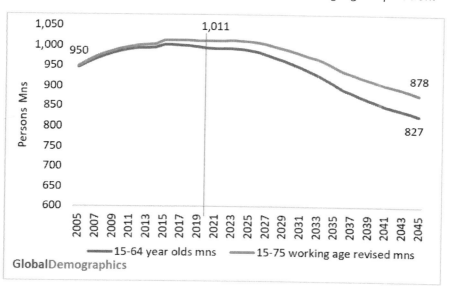

GlobalDemographics

Using the traditional definition of working age, the number of persons in China aged 15 to 64 is projected to decline from 995 million to 827 million over the next 25 years.

As a result, while the *total* number of persons of working age is projected to decline over the next 25 years, all of this decline will be in the rural workforce as shown in Figure 11-14. In contrast, thanks to rural to urban migration, the urban working-age population will continue to grow through to 2033 and only then stay at close to 671 million through to

2045. Given that the urban labour force is the most productive sector of the labour force, this means that the total economy can also be expected to continue to grow for at least to then.

Figure 11-14: Historic and Projected Urban and Rural Working-age Population (15 To 64 Yrs.) in Millions of Persons.

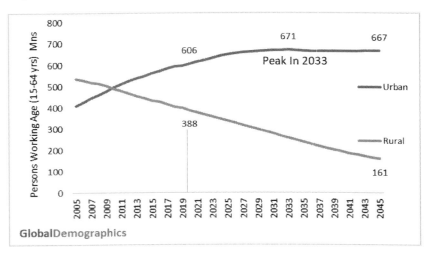

It is in rural areas that the working-age population is declining and as shown in Figure 11-14, it is a very significant decline. The working-age population of rural China is projected to decline from 388 million in 2020 to 161 million in 2045. A reduction of 59%, which is a function of migration and ageing. However, as the agriculture industry is being rapidly mechanized this is not as much an issue as it might at first appear. Productivity per rural worker is increasing rapidly and overall production is maintained.

Employed Persons (The Labour Force)

Because the propensity to be employed in China is both high and stable, the working-age population is the determinant of the trend in the employed labour force. The urban propensity to be employed for males aged 15 to 64 years is 84% and for females, it is 69%. This rate of employment has been stable for the last 15 years, but it is expected to decline slightly over time as affluence and education increase and people consider alternative (less work-intensive) lifestyles. It is high by global norms.

As shown in Figure 11-15 the urban labour force is projected to continue to grow because of the growth of the urban working-age population, more than offsetting a minor decline in propensity to work. Do note that this includes some persons from the age range 65 to 74. They are 1% of the total employed in 2020 increasing to 4% by 2045.

While there is a positive forecast for the size of the urban labour force it is important to note that the projected rate of growth in the urban workforce reduces to almost zero after 2033. For the decade to 2020, it grew at 2.9% per annum. The forecast to 2033 indicates it drops to 1.0% per annum and then there is 0.1% per annum growth through to 2045.

The Urban labour force will continue to grow through to 2033, but there is no further significant increase after that year which will have implications for the growth rate of total GDP thereafter.

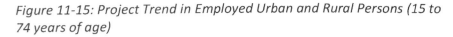

Figure 11-15: Project Trend in Employed Urban and Rural Persons (15 to 74 years of age)

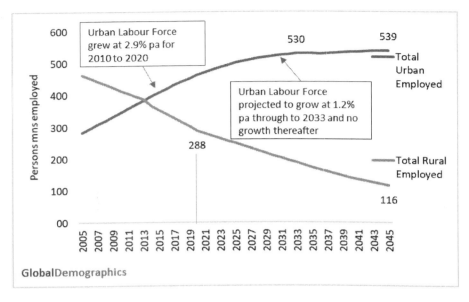

This invariably means that overall GDP growth slows marginally unless the productivity of the worker can be increased at a more rapid pace than in the past to offset this lack of increase in the number of urban workers.

There are considerable differences between provinces in the growth rate of the urban labour force and this is shown in Figure 11-16. This shows the projected growth rate of the **urban** labour force by province considering the age profile of the relevant population, the number of rural to urban migrants, the number of province-to-province migrants and the trend in the propensity of urban persons to be employed.

Figure 11-16: Projected Growth Rate of Urban Employed 2020 To 2030

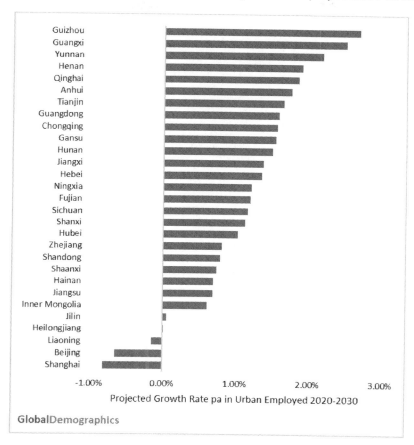

This reveals some interesting sub-trends. Note, for example, that the two large municipalities of Shanghai and Beijing are projected to decline in the number of employed. This is a function of three factors.

1. They are already highly urbanized, so they get a minimal lift from the ongoing rural to urban migration within their province.

2. They are getting expensive and both employers and employees are looking at alternative locations (For example, cities in Jiangsu and Zhejiang Provinces instead of Shanghai).

379

3. These cities already tend to have an older population and as such have a greater proportion of their population leaving working-age.

Finally, a key statistic when looking at employment in a country is the 'dependency ratio'. That is the number of persons supported by each employed person and is the total population less employed population divided by the employed population.

In the case of China, the ratio is very low by global standards at 0.81 in 2020 increasing slowly to reach 1.07 in 2045. The Global average is over 1.1. This is an important measure, as the lower it is the greater the per capita spending power of the household.

Other Population Trends

The Changing Age profile of Urban and Rural Populations

Birth rates, education and employment are of course critical aspects of a society's development, but we also need to look at other aspects. The first of these is the overall age profile of the population of China.

Slowing population growth has been happening for some years now and it means the society has moved away from 'an ever-hungry pyramid' requiring growth of social facilities and infrastructure towards a stable 'square' population profile with stable demand levels for social services (e.g., education and health care).

To demonstrate how the age profile of China has and is projected to change, Figure 11-17 shows the historic and projected age profile for the total population for the years 2005, 2020 and 2045. The overall age profile 'pivots around the central age range of 30 to 54 years. The younger age groups decline in size quite significantly from their 2020 size. Conversely, the Over 60 years age groups grow dramatically compared to their 2005 and even 2020 size.

Probably the single most important point to take from this chart is that the consumer profile of China is changing. For the next 25 years all age groups under 50 years of age, decline substantially in size.

Also, even with this top-loading of the population profile with older people, the employment rate is such that the dependency rate is still low by global standards at 1.07 dependents per worker in 2045. Nonetheless, note should be made of the significant increase in the over 64 years population over the next quarter century. It nearly doubles in absolute size.

Figure 11-17: The Evolving Age Profile of China 2005-2045 (Total Population)

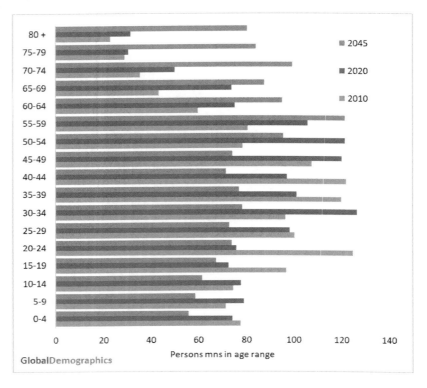

GlobalDemographics

For the next 25 years, all age groups under 50 years of age decline substantially in size. This means that China has a very different consumer profile in 2045 from what it has today.

Urban Consumer Life Stage Segments

Summarizing the population age profile into key consumer life stages gives a good indication of the dominant lifestyles and also likely consumer demand patterns. Due to the differences in age profiles, this needs to be done separately for urban and rural populations.

The specific consumer life stage segments used are 0 to 14 years for the child market, 15 to 24 years for the young adult market: 25 to 44 years for the family stage market: 45 to 64 years for working-age empty nesters and finally 65 + years retired market.

Figure 11-18 shows how the relative size of the key age segments in **urban** areas changed in the last decade and how they are expected to change over the next 25 years.

What should be noted from this chart is the growth in the last decade of the 'Empty Nester' segment, and how that growth stops dramatically after 2030 (specifically 2032). This is important as it is a key consumer segment. Having none, or few, dependents, at least one wage earner, and an established home, this group of people have a high *disposable* income per capita.

Figure 11-18: Historic and Projected Size of Key Life Stage Segments in Urban China. 2010 to 2045.

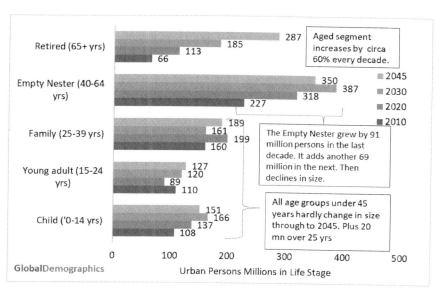

They certainly would have been a key driver behind the growth of retail spending in China for the last decade. From 227 million to 318

383

million in a decade. That was an annual growth rate of 3.4%. From 2020 to 2030 the growth rate drops dramatically to 1.8% per annum (but still adds 69 million persons to the cohort) and then there is a quite abrupt change to a decline after 2032. That is significant – both in nature as well as the implication for consumer spending.

This age group moves into the 65 years and above segment which, as shown in Figure 11-18, grows steadily in the number of persons through to 2045. The concern is that this cohort is more careful spenders because of their age and fixed (pension) income.

The transition of a core number of people (approximately 170 million) from high discretionary spending 'working-age' in 2020 to careful spending 'aged' person by 2045, could have a significant implication for retail spending/consumption in future. Especially as the other (under 45 years) consumer age groups are relatively stable in size for the next 25 years.

This transition of a core number of people (approximately 170 million) from high discretionary spending 'working-age' to careful spending 'aged' person by 2045 could have a significant implication for retail spending in future and global consumption.

Rural Key Life Stage Segments

Not unexpectedly, the rural age profile also changes dramatically over the next 25 years. As shown in Figure 11-19, all the key consumer segments under 65 years of age are projected to decline significantly in the number of persons over the next 25 years. This has an obvious impact on rural retail spending, but also and more importantly, on the size of the rural workforce. However, it is probably not a crisis in that with the mechanization of processes and aggregation of land the demand for physical labour in rural areas has and will continue to decline.

Figure 11-19: Historic and Projected Size of Key Life Stage Segments in Rural China. 2010 to 2045.

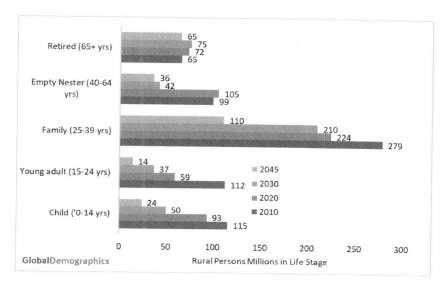

Domestic Migration

There are two aspects of this migration – the well-known Rural to Urban migration and the less well understood Province to Province migration.

Looking first at rural to urban migration, the simple reality is that this will continue to take place as educated young people pursue better work opportunities in urban areas while at the same time agriculture changes dramatically from small, labour intensive, inefficient holdings to large, efficient, and mechanized agricultural farms (the capital for which tends to be urban-based).

While the rural to urban migration trend will continue over the next 25 years it will gradually decline in absolute number for the simple reason that the number of persons in rural areas declines in absolute number – and particularly the younger rural population. Based on that, the forecast for annual rural to urban migration is expected to decline from 19 million in 2020 to around 11 million per annum by

385

2045. Figure 11-20 shows the projected trend in the number of persons aged 20-29 in rural areas which is an effective indicator of the 'stock' of people that will make the move.

Figure 11-20: Historic and Projected Trend in Number of Persons Aged 20 To 29 Years Living in Rural Areas.

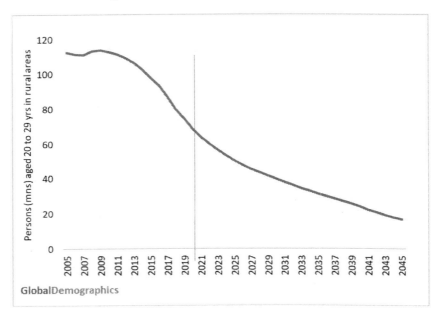

GlobalDemographics

The age profile of rural to urban migrants is changing. Initially, before the year 2000, moving from a rural village to an urban area was probably perceived as a relatively risky/daring move. As such it was constrained to the younger population with the education and skill advantage and higher risk profile. That is less so today, and data indicates that the migrant profile has expanded upwards to include the 40-to 64 year age group.

But do note the point made earlier about labour forces, this continued movement from rural to urban areas is sustaining the growth of the more productive urban workforce and ultimately the growth of the overall economy.

Finally, whereas in the past all rural to urban migration involved a physical relocation of the individuals, in recent years some of the change is a reclassification of counties as urban. Some of the growth involves no population movement at all. This reflects the spread of cities into the outlying towns and townships. As such the demand for additional urban households will not be as great as the migration rate indicates.

The other form of migration to consider is Province to Province migration which is not always appreciated in the context of China. It is significant. For example, Guangdong (and Guangzhou and Shenzhen Cities in that Province) and Shanghai, Zhejiang and Jiangsu provinces have all benefited significantly from Province-to-Province migration. It has happened as those tended to be the provinces where Fixed Capital Investment was greatest and where higher-paying employment opportunities exist.

Just as globally, migrants move to countries where there are better employment/lifestyle opportunities for them so in China people are moving to where there are better employment opportunities and with that, income, and lifestyle.

It is difficult to get a good measure of the province-to-province migration pattern, but the impression given by the data is that it is to the east and south away from central and western provinces.

Wages and Productivity of the Worker

What a country's workers can earn significantly determines the future outcomes of the country. The higher the wages the more able are households to provide adequate nutrition, health care and education which becomes a continuously improving cycle.

The ability to earn a good (by global standards) wage is very much a function of education and health. In that respect, as indicated clearly in the earlier parts of this chapter, China has made significant advances.

However, wages also determine global competitiveness and ultimately the ability of the country to trade. Here China has also been successful – but with a hidden advantage. The average worker in China gets a lower share of their productivity paid out to them than is the norm for other countries.

As shown in Figure 11-21, the share of productivity paid out to the worker in the form of wages has been increasing quite rapidly. From 46% in 2007 to 59% in 2020. However, this compares with a global norm for 2020 of 70%.

This lower wage share enhances the profitability of the enterprises employing persons, which in turn helps lift investment into capital equipment that lifts productivity further. Note that it does not necessarily make the product cheaper – although it helps.

Figure 11-21: Share of GDP Per Worker That is Paid Out in Wages. 2005 to 2020.

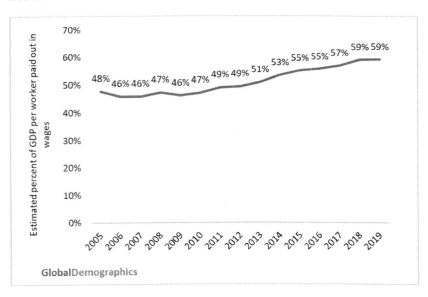

*In 2019 the average worker in China received wages equivalent to
59% of the value of what they produced. The global norm is 70%.*

In part, this lower share of productivity reflects the demand for jobs in
what, historically, was a market of an increasing number of (urban)
working-age persons looking for work and hence with a weak negotiating
position in terms of wages.

However, the reader is referred to Figure 11-15 which shows the trend in
the number of urban working-age persons. In the past, the number of
such persons grew quite strongly (2% per annum). For the next decade, it
slows dramatically and then goes to zero for 2033 to 2045.

This suggests a tighter labour market after 2033 which in turn could push
wages up. But growth in wages may be constrained as Fixed Capital
Investment will probably slow due to two factors – poor return on
investment and accumulated debt. This could mean that the demand for
labour reduces along with the supply. Accordingly, wages are expected to
stay at around 59% of GDP for the forecast period.

Household Incomes

This leads to the issue of household incomes. As mentioned earlier,
there is a significant difference between urban and rural household
incomes.

Figure 11-22 shows the distribution of urban and rural households in
2019 as reported in the Household Income and Expenditure Survey
done annually by the National Bureau of Statistics of China.

The difference between urban and rural households is quite
considerable and in part is an explanation for the rural to urban
migration. It does mean that the two segments (Urban and Rural)
have very different consumer profiles and attractiveness as a market.

Figure 11-22: Distribution of Urban and Rural Households by Income In 2020.

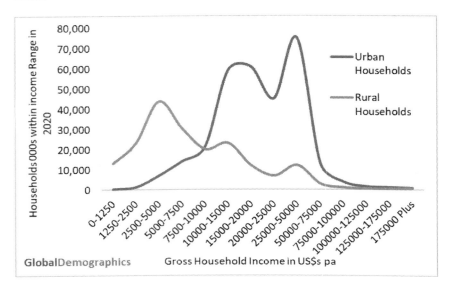

Note: Income segments increase in size above US$25,000 which causes a second peak to appear.

It is estimated by Global Demographics Ltd that in 2020 urban households accounted for 81% of all consumer income (and spending) in China. The model indicates that with increased urbanisation and a continuing income differential between the two groups, by 2045 urban households will account for 86% of consumer expenditure.

Therefore, it is important to look at how the distribution of urban households by income might be expected to change in just the next decade assuming the GDP of China grows at a compound average growth rate (CAGR) of 5.2%[2] from 2020 to 2030. This change in the

---

[2] See Appendix A for more details on GDP growth rates.

distribution of urban households by income is shown in Figure 11-23. There are two key points to note from this chart.

First, in the next 10 years, the middle class (middle third of households by income) will move quite dramatically – from the range of US$15,000 to US$25,000 per annum in 2020 to US$22,000 to US$45,000 in 2030 (in real 2019 values). That is a lot of extra spending power.

Figure 11-23: Projected Distribution of Urban Households by Income 2020 and 2030.

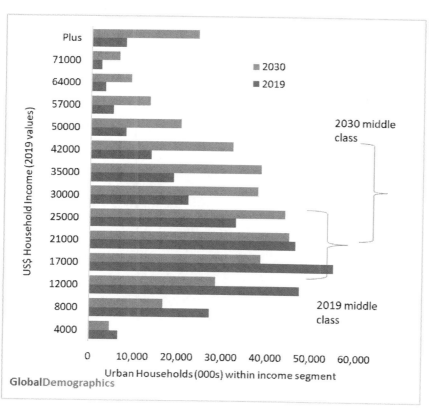

In addition, the higher income segments grow dramatically in absolute size as a result of increased affluence and the number of urban households. In 2020 there are estimated to be 7.9 million households with a gross annual income above US$75,000. The projection is that there will be 24 million such households by 2030 and 52 million by 2045.

In the next 10 years, the household income of the middle class moves quite dramatically from the range of US$15,000 to US$25,000 per annum in 2020 to US$22,000 to US$45,000 in 2030 (in real 2019 values).

The implications of this for the range of products and services sought in future are considerable. Clearly 'Premium' has a future in China. However, it does show how the disparity of incomes in this country is increasing and there need to be questions about the implications of that for social cohesiveness. Will it even be allowed to happen in what is a Socialist State?

The number of high income (US$75,000 and above) urban households in China is projected to increase from 7.9 million in 2020 to 52 million by 2045.

Household Spending

This leads to the issue of propensity to spend. At the time of preparing this book one of the Chinese Government's objectives was to move the driver of the economy from significant annual Fixed Capital Investment at 47% of Gross Domestic Product to increased Consumer spending.

The projected growth in household incomes supports the achievability of this – with average urban household income projected to increase from US$23,895 in 2020 to US$35,088 in 2030 and US$47,352 in 2045 (all in real 2019 values). This forecast is derived from projections in terms of the number of workers, productivity (a function of education and Fixed Capital Resources per worker) and hence wages per worker and number of workers per household.

However, there is one interesting issue that needs to be considered. That is the propensity to spend. Here again, the Chinese consumer tends to be different from the norm as discussed in Chapter 8 (see Figure 8-9). Compared with other countries, the overall propensity of urban households in China to spend is relatively low at 53% of gross household income.

For an urban household with an average income in 2020 of US$24,201, the reported expenditure is US$11,738 and tax at US$2,858 leaving US$9,604 saved which is 40% of gross income.

China is unusual compared with other countries in that the savings rate does not vary by income level. Normally as income increases so does the propensity to save – and that does happen at the very low-income rural levels. But once Gross household income is over US$8,000 it stabilises at around 40%. Analysis by urban and rural households produces almost identical rates of saving at the same income levels.

This savings rate is significantly higher than that of other countries with a similar level of household income. The anecdotal explanation is that the combination of a less than adequate state pension and health service is the key driver. There is historical credence to this, but it should be noted that private expenditure on health in China is declining as a proportion of total health expenditure. This indicates that the Government's free service is improving, increasingly available and increasingly used. This may take some of the pressure of needing to save.

Figure 11-24: Propensity of Urban Households to Save As Percent of Gross Household Income -2019

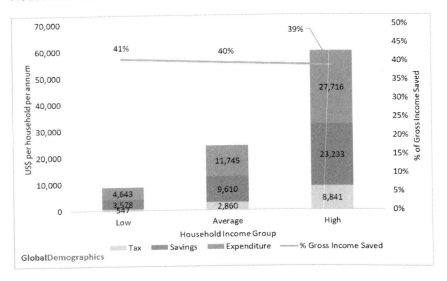

The savings rate may also reduce with generations. The younger better educated population coming through over the next 25 years may well be more confident in their ability to maintain earnings and hence feel less need to put money aside for difficult times. Although counter to that, at the same time, there are increasing options for people to save – it was once only the State Bank – now it includes shares, property, bonds etc.

An alternative anecdotal scenario is that some of this is paying off loans used to purchase property as an investment. While it is effectively a mortgage and should be included in housing expenditure it may not be categorised as such if it is a second home for investment purposes (rent out).

This propensity to save, however, does play an important role. A significant proportion of it went into the State-owned banking system and helped finance the massive Fixed Capital Investment that took place over the last two decades and transformed China's productive capacity. It is not foreign debt and hence is of lower financial risk for the Government.

The Gender Bias

This is often pointed out as being a sociological issue that China is going to have to confront but rarely do the commentators put an order of magnitude on it. It is worth some clarification.

First, it is correct that there is a male bias, and this reflects a bias in births that have existed particularly since the introduction of the One-Child Policy. This bias emerged because those with a rural Hukou (most of the population even in 2020) could have a second child if the first was a female. Consequently – given natural birth order results in 49% of births being female - a high proportion of those rural Hukou couples had a second child and for various reasons that child was significantly more likely to be male than female. As a result, in 2019 for example, 54% of births in total (not just second child births) were male.

To estimate the social impact of this gender birth bias, an assumption must be made about marrying age. Available data indicates that by 2019 the average age difference between a male and a female getting married is decreasing and currently is less than 5 years. Typically, the male is slightly older. For that reason, we have compared within five-year age groups. In addition, the marrying age is defined as 25 to 39 years – it used to be much younger but with education and urbanisation, it has moved out to age 25.

Table 11-7 shows that in 2019 the number of surplus males of marrying age and above is 13 million. This is expected to increase to 18.8 million in 2030 and 31.3 million in 2045. How this discrepancy is handled is uncertain. Do note, however, that this problem is not unique to China.

Table 11-7: Surplus Marrying Age Males. 2019 to 2045.

| Age Group | Males minus Females in age group | | |
	2019	2030	2045
0-4 Yrs	4,834	3,678	2,924
5-9 Yrs	6,133	4,508	3,276
10-14 Yrs	7,223	4,942	3,432
15-19 Yrs	6,552	6,053	3,760
20-24 Yrs	5,981	7,123	4,405
25-29 Yrs	4,094	6,417	4,793
30-34 Yrs	1,550	5,806	5,838
35-39 Yrs	1,137	3,792	6,808
40-44 Yrs	2,175	920	5,946
45-49 Yrs	2,602	444	5,114
50-54 Yrs	1,739	1,441	2,782
55-59 Yrs	521	1,595	-383
60-64 Yrs	514	696	-533
65-69 Yrs	-1,546	-637	203
70-74 Yrs	-1,449	-1,900	-2,216
75-79 Yrs	-2,064	-6,165	-7,252
80 + Yrs	-4,845	-10,456	-19,956
Total Surplus Ages 25 to 59 yrs	13,298	18,819	31,282

Note that the male bias in births is projected to continue to 2045.

This is the age range where surplus males to females is a potential issue.

However, the elderly widow is a growth segment.

To Conclude

So, what does 'China of the future' mean for the world?

First, it has a positive message in that it is a great example of how education can change a country. From a country with population growth out of control and hence overwhelming the education and social system and no improvement in quality of life, to one where population growth is sensible and the resulting improvement in quality and availability of social services leads to a better-quality life. China broke the poverty cycle and other countries could learn from it.

The second significant issue is that the Working-age Empty Nester segment that drove the disposable expenditure category (tourism, wellness, dining out etc.) in the past, is now slowing significantly in growth in the number of persons. This could mean that the growth in demand for discretionary services and products may not be as fast as previously and given the size of this market, that has global implications (Fewer Tourists from China for example).

Finally, it must be noted that claims that it is potentially facing economic growth problems as the working-age population is no longer growing are without foundation. The ongoing movement of labour from rural to manufacturing and tertiary employment will continue and hence the most productive aspect of the labour force continues to grow and with that the overall economy – until 2033. The story changes after that year.

Whereas in the past and as projected to 2033, China had two pistons driving its economic engine – that is growth in productivity per worker and growth in the number of (particularly urban) workers - one of those pistons is now slowing and then stopping – specifically the number of additional urban-based employees.

This means productivity per worker has to grow faster to offset the slower growth in the number of highly productive workers. That is harder to achieve once overall education standards and degree of infrastructure per worker improve significantly – as they have in China. In short, the easy growth path is now over.

The growth of the total economy will slow as a result of

- the inevitable slower growth in the number of productive urban workers (inevitable due to the age profile of the population),
- the slower lift in productivity as a result of now having achieved good standards in terms of education and infrastructure such that the marginal benefit of further investment in either decreases.

- the inevitable slower growth in the number of consumers in the 'higher spend' category of Working-age Empty Nesters after 2030 could impact the consumption side of the economy.

But the emphasis is on growth. The economy is not expected to decline in size just grow slower like other mature economies.

Chapter 12
India – Will the Demographic Dividend be Delivered?

Introduction

With a population in 2020 estimated at 1.38 billion India is the second largest country in the world after China (1.411 billion). India's population has increased rapidly over the last 15 years, adding 211 million people to its 2005 population of 1.15 billion persons. (For reference purposes, the third largest country by population is the United States of America at 320 million – a lot smaller).

In addition, India is also representative of several other countries that are in what might be called a development stage. That is, having a rapidly growing working-age population (which is not particularly well educated). This is often referred to as a 'demographic dividend' which is considered to be a potential boost to the economy and hence society. This Chapter on India will help bring out the issues that these similar countries will face.

As such, what is happening with India's demographics is important.

This chapter will look at the following aspects
- The Changing Age Profile and growth of the population
- The size and nature of the demographic dividend
- Education and labour force competitiveness
- Urbanisation
- The household

The Changing Size and Age Profile of the Population

For reasons discussed later in this chapter, the total population of India is projected to continue to increase. From its current population of 1.38 billion, it is projected to reach 1.487 Bn in 2030 and 1.527 bn in 2041 which is currently projected to be its 'peak' population point. It then declines marginally to 1.522 bn by 2045

This population growth is driven by the number of births and the extent to which they exceed the number of deaths. In the case of India, migration is negative (more leaving than arriving) but not significant in terms of relative size.

Population growth, driven by a combination of births and longer life expectancy, means that the age profile of the overall population is going to change considerably over time and that is as shown in Figure 12-1.

The youngest segment is projected to decline in absolute size over the next 25 years – from 361 million in 2020 to a projected 245 million by 2045. This, of course, is a function of a reduced number of total births due to a combination of a reducing birth rate and, after 2035, a reducing number of women aged 15 to 49 years. Total births have already declined significantly from their historic peak of 384 million in 2008.

Conversely, the aged segment (persons over 64 years of age) starts to grow and is projected to increase from 6% to 13% between 2020 and 2045. This from 91 million to 193 million older persons with attendant social implications.

However, the biggest change in the age profile of the population of India is the 40 to 64 years of age segment. It is now the growth consumer segment. It is projected to grow from 347 million persons in 2020 to 468 million in 2030 and then to 528 million by 2045. India is becoming older and middle-aged.

This is not dissimilar to the scenario that has played out in China over the last decade but what is different in this instance is that it is not until 2022 that the 'Working-age Empty Nester' Segment is the largest consumer life stage segment. In China, it has held that position since 2005.

In contrast, the 'youth' and Family Stage segments (15 to 39 years) are projected to reduce marginally in size through to 2045 - down from 582 million to 554 million.

Figure 12-1: Age Profile of India 2005 to 2045.

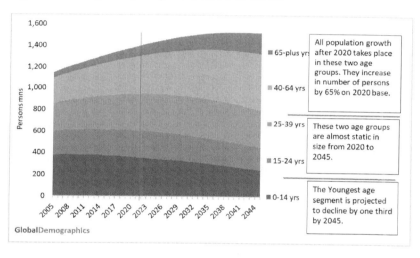

GlobalDemographics

This has a significant implication in terms of the nature of the consumer markets. Youth is no longer a growth segment in terms of the number of persons. The 15-to-39-year age remains important in terms of absolute size but any future growth in its value has to come from growing affluence (and spending per customer) rather than from an increased number of customers.

In contrast, the 40 years and above age group is projected to increase in absolute number by 65% in the next 25 years adding 284 million persons to a base of 437 million. However, it should be noted that these older people do not have a good education or earning history and perhaps are not a 'high value' market opportunity.

It is useful to also look at what is happening in terms of births. This is summarised in Figure 12-2. There are two important trends taking place.

First, the propensity of a woman aged 15 to 49 years to have a child in any one year has declined quite significantly from 95.6 in 2005 to 65.4 in 2020. The model expects this rate of decline to slow (on a global basis that is typical once the rate is below 100) and to stabilise around 40 births per thousand women aged 15 to 49 by 2045.

Figure 12-2: Historic and Projected Trends in Birth Rate, Total Births per annum, and Women of Childbearing Age.

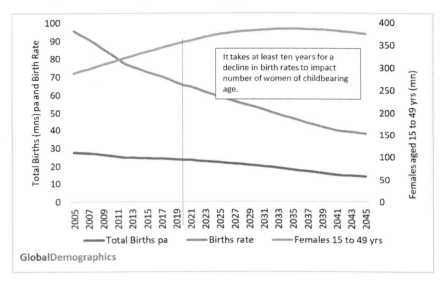

GlobalDemographics

This does result in a reduction in the absolute number of births. The impact is muted initially because, as shown in Figure 12-2, the number of women of childbearing age will continue to increase through to 2035. After that year this stabilises and then starts to decline and with that, annual births decline from 20.4 million in 2030 to 14.4 million by 2045.

The reducing number of births means that the number of school-age children reduces from 244 million in 2020 to 223 million in 2030 and 173 million by 2045. It takes the pressure off the education system and allows it to focus more on quality rather than quantity.

The reducing number of births means that the number of school-age children reduces from 244 million in 2020 to 173 million by 2045. enabling the education system to focus on quality rather than quantity. This benefits society.

Employment

The Working-age Population

The working-age population of India (defined as persons aged 15 to 64 years of age) has been increasing in size at quite a rapid rate. As shown in Figure 12-3, Between 2005 and 2020 it grew at 1.7% per annum, increasing in absolute number by 211 million or 29%.

Figure 12-3: Historic and Projected Trend in The Working-age Population by Age Group.

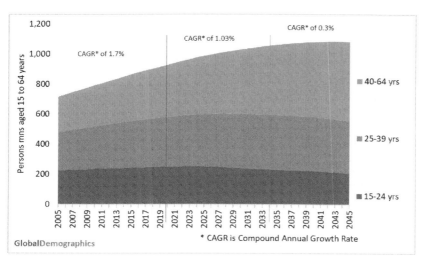

But the growth rate of the working-age population is projected to slow – and significantly. Between 2020 and 2030 there will be an additional 101 million working-age persons in India – an average increase of 1% per annum. From 2030 to 2045 the increase is a more modest 54 million or 0.3% per annum. The growth of the 'demographic dividend is slowing rapidly and to some extent could already be regarded as over. Adding 10 million a year (from 2020 to 2030) to a cohort of 1 billion is not significant.

Whether this Demographic Dividend actually pays out depends on whether a continuing or increasing proportion of these additional working-age persons can find employment and the productivity of those workers are at least maintained if not increased.

The Ability to Find Employment.

It is best to begin this discussion with a look back over the last 14 years for which data is available. That is from 2005 to 2019 inclusive and which excludes 2020 which has uncertain values due to the Covid-19 pandemic. During that period, the working-age population grew from 718 million persons to 916 million. An additional 198 million persons, of which some were seeking employment. (The reader is reminded that not all working-age persons want/enter full-time employment).

Employment statistics indicate that the number of employed persons in that period increased from 424 million in 2005 to reach 468 million in 2019. This means that during that period the *proportion* of working-age persons in employment fell quite significantly – from 59% to 51%. This means that there were potentially 73 million persons who were looking for work in 2019 and not finding it. Figure 12-4 summarises the differences that emerge. This is a significant social issue.

Analysis of the data on the propensity to be employed showed that the shortfall in employment was biased toward females. Male propensity to be employed fell from 83% to 77% between 2005 and 2019. Female propensity to be employed fell from 32% to 21%.

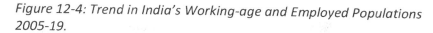

Figure 12-4: Trend in India's Working-age and Employed Populations 2005-19.

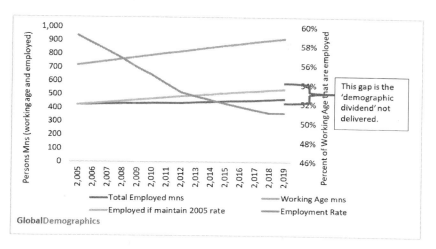

Most importantly it means that *the 'demographic dividend is not being delivered.* This then raises the question – what circumstances must exist for these working-age persons to be able to gain employment? Otherwise, the economic prospects of India are not as good as might be expected. The answer is believed to be education and fixed capital investment.

The Education Dilemma

Education is India's core developmental problem. Unlike China, it has not developed the education system as widely as would be desired. The education profile of the adult population in 2020 does not compare favourably with China or many other countries with similar levels of economic development.

Figure 12-5 demonstrates (based on reported statistics from the relevant Governments) that India is effectively 10 years behind China in terms of the proportion of adults that have an Upper Secondary or better qualification.

Given current trends in improvement (and remember education takes time to be implemented) by 2030, India will start to be competitive with the China of 2020 – but by then China will have improved its education profile further – so the competitive gap remains.

Figure 12-5: India and China Education Profile 2010 to 2045

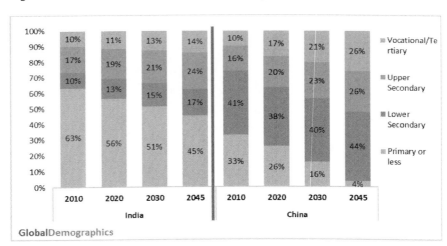

Nonetheless, India must improve its education if it is to lift productivity and become more attractive as an investment opportunity. It is a competitive world. Figure 12-6 shows where India stands in 2019 on the education index relative to some of its key competitors for jobs. The importance and need for this improvement are self-evident.

Figure 12-6: Relative Position of India on Education Index.

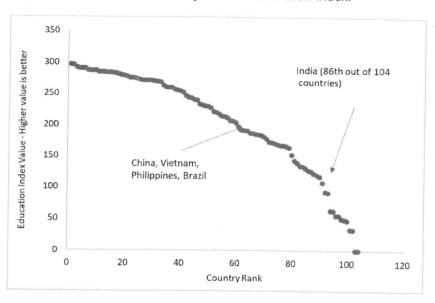

It is good that India now claims that it is in a position where every child aged 5 to 12 is going to school.

The data indicates that the total spend per child of school age in 2019 was US$423 which means that 3.8% of GDP goes on education (public and private spending) - this is low by world standards (even after adjusting for the proportion of the population that is school age) and raises a question as to the quality or availability of education – even after adjusting for cost of labour (teachers).

However, assuming the improvement in education availability is happening then India's adult education profile (labour force skill level) will improve and that is incorporated into the forecasts used for this book. The significant shift is that it starts to fill out the middle skill level which has been effectively missing in India. (Lots of highly educated and poorly educated persons with little in the middle.)

The problem is that it will take 10 years before the current reform (universal education) even starts to impact the labour force. Specifically, a child benefiting from the universality of education introduced last year will not reach the labour force until 10 years later – namely in 2029. Until then it is only possible to expect marginal improvement in the education profile of the working-age population.

Education and Urbanisation

The issue of education has other implications. The lack of provision of universal education has meant that many young people have not been able to move from low paying agricultural work to more productive (and typically higher paying) manufacturing and tertiary work.

In 2005 just 29.2% of the population were urban based – it is now 34.5%. Over the last 15 years after adjusting for births and deaths in each of urban and rural locations only 71 million persons have moved from a rural to an urban environment which is 8% of the rural population in 2005. It reflects the inability of the rural population to be able to do manufacturing and tertiary employment due to a lack of adequate education.

The importance of this is considerable. China lifted the productivity of its workforce by effectively moving 19 million persons a year from low productivity agricultural work to higher productivity manufacturing and then tertiary employment. The difference in productivity is at least a factor of 3.

Implications for Productivity and GDP growth

As shown in Figure 12-7, Productivity per worker has been improving steadily over the last 15 years. Fixed Capital Investment as a percentage of GDP has been high at 39% (2007) but it has trended downward to 29% in 2019 (which is close to the global norm of 27%).

Fixed Capital Investment is important as it creates jobs and then subsequently together with improving the education profile of the labour force lifts the productivity of the worker. The recent decline in Fixed Capital Investment feeds into the forecast productivity per worker which as shown, slows to circa 3% per annum. If Fixed Capital Investment was increased in line with education the gains may be greater in future.

Figure 12-7: Historic and Projected Trends in Fixed Capital Investment, Annual Productivity Growth Rate and GDP Per Worker.

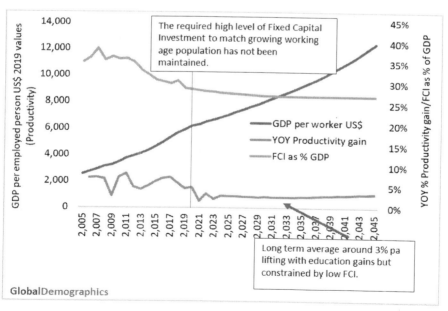

However, household incomes in India are relatively low (See the next section of this Chapter) and consequently the ability to save is low. Because of that, India does not have a substantial pool of domestic savings to draw on. It is reliant on overseas debt. That could inhibit the level of Fixed Capital Investment that takes place.

In the forecasts in this book, it is expected the increased availability of education will mean that urbanisation will increase (assuming it is accompanied by increased Fixed Capital Investment per worker – either private or government) and this, in turn, will help maintain or increase the overall productivity of the labour force.

This obviously will have a beneficial effect on the economy and lifestyle. However, the productivity growth will be around 3% per annum rather than the recently claimed 6% to 7% per annum. This has implications for household incomes as discussed in the next section.

The Household

Number of households

As indicated by the age profile, the average household in India is essentially at the 'family stage'. That is the parents and their children – with a bias toward older children hence the higher-than-normal number of workers per household.

It is expected with the ageing of the society that there will be a reduction in average household size as the older children move out and start their own families over the next 25 years. The forecast in terms of household size is that it reduces from the 2019 level of 3.12 persons per household to 2.59 by 2045. (It was 4.31 in 2010 so it is declining rapidly as the population ages).

That combined with a growing population means that the total number of households will increase significantly over the next 25 years from an estimated 446 million households in 2020 to 588 million in 2045. That indicates a growth rate of 1.1% per annum.

So, the housing market will be under pressure for the next 25 years. But what can they afford?

The distribution of Households by Income

The key issue for India is the need to lift people (and households) out of poverty. Doing this to a meaningful number is predicated on the need to lift employment as discussed above. Education is expected to improve and with that so should employment, productivity per worker and ultimately, household incomes.

Figure 12-8 shows the historic and projected trend in average and median household income. The Median is the income point at which an equal number of households have an income above and below that point. It is usually lower than the average, which is lifted because of a relatively small number of very wealthy households. Median gives a better indication of what the typical household is living on. The further the median is from the average the less equalitarian is the distribution of income in the society. As shown in Figure 12-8 the gap is shown as increasing – but only marginally and so it is not a problem.

The good news is that under the assumptions that.
- The employment rate is maintained or improved and
- The impact of an improving education profile and increased accumulated Fixed Capital Investment per worker on productivity is positive.

Then the average and median household income is projected to increase as shown in Figure 12-8. The expectation is at a sensible but steady 2.36% per annum for the decade to 2030. This does potentially create a meaningful middle class which is generally a good situation for any society.

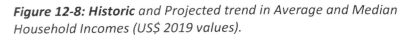

Figure 12-8: Historic and Projected trend in Average and Median Household Incomes (US$ 2019 values).

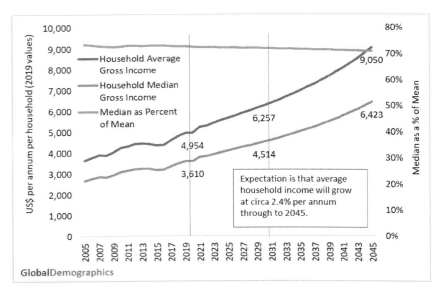

Figure 12-9 shows the changing distribution of households by income from 2009 to 2019 and then as projected for 2030 and 2045. In many ways, the important statistic here is not how much the average or median income has/is projected to increase but rather the extent to which the lowest income segment can be reduced.

While the number of households with an income at or below US$5,000 per annum (and typically with 4 or more persons in them) has and is projected to reduce as a *proportion* of all households – from 81% in 2005 to 68% by 2020 and then to 56% by 2030 - they increase in absolute number through to 2030. This happens because the growth in the number of households is faster than the growth in overall affluence. Fortunately, the number of such households is projected to decrease after 2030 and quite rapidly and significantly. From 290 million to 216 million.

In contrast, the middle-class income segment shows robust growth in terms of the number of households. That is households with a gross income of US$7,500 to US$25,000 per annum. In 2019 there are estimated to be 65 million such households (probably urban based). With the projected trends in productivity per worker, the share of GDP paid in wages and the number of workers per household, it is expected that the number of middle-class households will increase to 116 million by 2030 and then almost double to 215 million by 2045. The income segment of US$25,000 and above (affluent in the context of India) exhibits a similar growth.

Figure 12-9: The Historic and Projected Distribution of Households by Income 2009 to 2045.

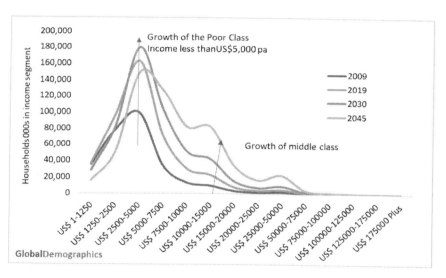

However, Figure 12-9 shows that while the distribution of income, as well as the median, is expected to improve over the next 25 years based on the assumptions outlined in terms of education and employment, nonetheless the socio-economic profile of India remains one of a society with a lot of relatively poor households. These are, most probably, the residual effect of the inadequate education provision of the past and will take time to change. It will change, but it takes more than 25 years to get there. So political patience is required.

Figure 12-10 shows the historic and projected distribution of households by key income segments for selected years. It is of concern that the lowest income group (US$0 to US$5,000) grew in absolute number in the last decade. However, it did reduce as a proportion of all households during that same period. That is, from 77% of households in 2019 to 68% in 2020.

Figure 12-10: The Distribution of Households by Key Income Segments. 2010 to 2045.

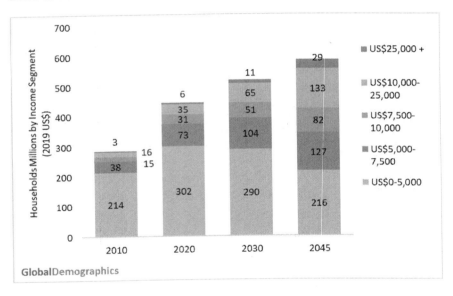

GlobalDemographics

The 'middle class', defined as US$5,000 to US$10,000, is projected to show strong growth and move from 23% of all households to 36% and in the absolute number of households from 104 million to 209 million. This can be expected to create a lift in consumer spending and perhaps some change in retail expectations.

Finally, the high-income segment (in the context of India that is households with an income over US$10,000) is expected to show very significant growth from 41 million to 163 million – and this also will impact retail demand significantly. However, it is just 9% of households in 2020 – but becomes relatively important by 2045 at 28%.

Overall, the expectation is that there will be a significant shift in the distribution of households by income and with that significant change in the size and nature of consumer spending.

The Future Consumer (Life Stages)

The nature of the consumer market in India can also be expected to change quite significantly in the next decade – and not just in terms of growth of the middle class as referred to above but also in terms of the very nature of the consumer. Figure 12-11 shows how the life stage/age profile of India can be expected to change over the next 25 years.

The similarity of the forecast for India to that of China is quite high. As for China, India's 15-to-40-year age groups are projected to be almost static in number through to 2045, and the under 15 years age group is projected to decline significantly in size.

The key consumer growth is the 40-to-64-year age segment. A projected increase of just under 100 million persons in a decade. Furthermore, these will typically be smaller households as the children have left home and as such, they potentially have higher per capita disposable income. Again, the similarity to China is considerable – albeit a decade later. (China's Growth of this age segment is slowing and it is now the 65 plus where the rapid growth is).

Figure 12-11: Projected Change in Size of Consumer Life Stages.

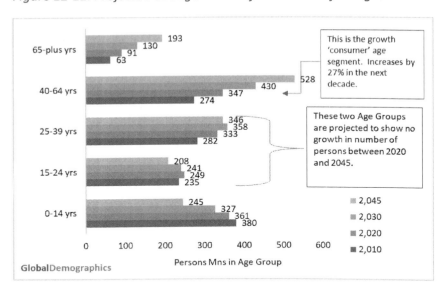

GlobalDemographics

Given this is a high growth segment and one that tends to have slightly more disposable income (although constrained somewhat by overall low relative incomes) it is going to be the market opportunity in India in the next 25 years.

Finally, the aged – that is 65 years and above. It is a small segment in 2020 at 91 million which is just 6% of the total population. It is projected to grow rapidly in the next 25 years to reach 193 million by 2045. It is this segment that is driving the increase in the overall population. Birth rates are declining (as are total births) but because of increased life expectancy, the old are increasing in number.

However, overall, these people have had a low earnings history and hence limited savings and there is limited social support for this age group as well. Therefore, it is unlikely to represent a significant consumer market in the future.

The expectation of a high growth consumer market in India is dependent on one consumer segment – the working-age empty nester. That they will grow in number is inevitable – but will they spend enough to help create

416

an additional eighty-eight million jobs to keep employment levels at the level desired (51% of the working-age population)? An additional 25 million higher spending households will certainly help.

Summary

Perhaps it is a surprising conclusion about India for some, but it is no longer a dynamic young market. True, the 15-to-39-year age group is a very significant number of consumers at 582 million persons in 2020. But that segment hardly changes in size after 2020 and declines from being 42% of the total population to 36%.

It has been replaced by the 40 to 64-year-old who is probably in a smaller household but still earning and with that probably got a higher per capita income. This segment is projected (with some reliability as all the relevant population is already alive in 2020) to grow from 347 million to 430 million in 2030 and reach 528 million by 2045. Very significant growth in a market which is probably (at least in the cities) a relatively aware consumer.

Because there is evidence of improvement in education (albeit rather modest) that may attract Fixed Capital Investment and consequently assist in lifting productivity per worker the economy will likely grow steadily. But probably not spectacularly.

As a society, it will continue to have a significant low-income population for at least 2030 if not longer. That does, of course, raise the potential of social risk.

From the point of view of 'growth,' India is no longer a young market. It is the older middle-aged (40 to 64 years) consumers where the growth is. A product or brand that captures the loyalty of that age group will experience considerable growth.

So much is going right – but the issue of an inadequately educated working-age population remains. It will not disappear by 2045. It is going to take longer. This has risks associated with it. Specifically:

- Inability to find sufficient work opportunities for all who are seeking it. There is evidence that this is already happening.

- The inability to move away from the competitive set of countries that also have large and growing working-age populations which are low skilled/poorly educated.

Chapter 13
Twenty Forty-Five

Introduction

This analysis began with what the world's demographic and socio-economic profile is like now and then the analysis looked at a series of factors that potentially will determine what the world will look like in 25 years' time.

The purpose of this Chapter is to paint what the 2045 picture is expected to be like given the foregoing discussion and assumptions. It is not a conclusion – forecasts by definition are forecasts and the possible outcomes are many and varied. However, with demographics, there is a degree of certainty that can be resorted to in order to gain a picture of what the world might look like in 2045. The focus here will be on the major issues.

To begin, it is interesting to look at the four Country Segments in terms of how they are expected to change on the two key measures used to segment them in Chapter Two. That is the median age and Gross Domestic Product per capita. The result of this is summarised in Figure 13-1. Note that the size of the 'ball' represents the relative size of the total population in each segment.

Not surprisingly on average all four segments get older which means that the centre point for each segment moves to the right in Figure 13-1. However, because of the enduring high birth rate for the Young Poor Country Segment, the median age does not increase nearly as much as it does for the other country segments. Hence the horizontal movement of that country segment is limited. Niger (a country in the Young Poor Country Segment) for example – with a median age of 14 in 2019 increases to 15 years by 2045 and Nigeria (also in that Country Segment) from 17 to 19 years. Many of the 'Young' countries in 2019 remain young through to 2045 due to declining (but high) birth *rates* being more than offset by the inevitable growth in the number of persons in the family forming stage. As a result, total births remain high.

---

*Many of the 'Young' countries in 2019 remain young through to 2045 due to declining (but high) birth rates being more than offset by the **inevitable** growth in the number of persons in family forming stage as a result of high birth rates in the past two decades. Total births, therefore, remain high.*

In terms of Gross Domestic Product per capita, the picture is also one of different rates of overall change. The Older Affluent Country Segment moves from US$49,146 to US$69,765 (1.4% per annum). While the rate of growth is the slowest of all four segments, the absolute amount of increase is a significant sum of money (US$20,000 per capita in real 2019 values).

The Older Low-Income Segment GDP per cap moves from US$10,793 to US$25,261 which is 3.3% per annum. This is particularly driven by China and the combined ongoing increases in the urban workforce (despite a declining working-age population overall) and productivity per worker.

The other two Country Segments show relatively less increase in the absolute amount, but the Compound Average Growth Rate (CAGR) is projected to be 2.03% per annum for the Family Low Income Segment and 2.8% per annum for the 'Young Poor'.

However, do note that while it is good that affluence is increasing in the Young Poor Segment, it remains relatively poor. Gross Domestic Product per capita is projected to lift from US$1,494 to US$3,078, an increase of US$1,500 in 25 years. The Older Affluent Gross Domestic Product per capita *increased* by US$20,000 in the same time period. The gap is widening.

As is apparent from Figure 13-1 the positions are moving apart. The older Affluent gained particularly in affluence (as well as age) the Older Low Income doing strongly on both dimensions, the Family Low income gaining on age, particularly as a result of reducing birth rates whereas the Young Poor got older rather than more affluent.

Figure 13-1: *Plot of the change in the relative position of the Four Country Segments in each of 2020 and 2045 based on the two key criteria for segmentation (Median Age and GDP per cap).*

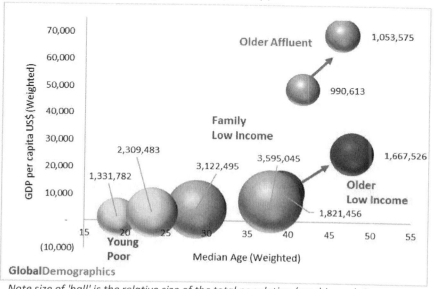

Note size of 'ball' is the relative size of the total population (mns) in each Segment.

The spread between the Country Segments is projected to increase rather than reduce. It is a story of the Young Poor Country Segment being left behind. It is projected to be *relatively* younger and poorer by 2045 than it is in 2020. That is not a good outcome.

The subsequent discussion looks at the current and projected nature of each of the four Country Segments. The objective is to give a picture of what each of these segments is projected to look like in 2045 considering all the changes discussed in the previous Chapters.

421

The Young Poor Country Segment

The profile of this Country Segment
is given in Table 13-1.

Ongoing rapid population growth at
over 2% per annum for the period
2020 to 2045 is probably the single
most important issue for this
Segment. While average birth rates are declining (from 137 to a projected
101 per thousand women aged 15 to 49 years by 2045) the rate of decline
is not sufficient to offset the rapidly increasing number of women aged 15
to 29 years as a result of historic high birth rates.

This increase in women (and couples) of that age range is inevitable as
most are already alive today. This means annual births are projected to
increase from 44 million in 2020 to 59 million per annum in 2045. This in
turn results in the relentless increase of the population with the younger
age groups getting bigger and bigger which in turn results in an increasing
number of births and so the cycle continues.

This, unfortunately, carries over to other aspects of society.

A marginal decline in household size combined with the growth in total
population means the number of households is projected to increase from
284 million to 539 million by 2045 – a 90% increase (2.5% per annum). If
nothing else the home construction market is going to be a growth
segment.

---

*This increase in couples aged 15 to 49 years (those likely to have
children) is inevitable as most are already alive today. This means
that in the Young Poor Countries births are projected to increase
from 44 million in 2019 to 59 million per annum in 2045. A tsunami
of Children.*

The same happens with education. The number of school places offered will need to rise from 338 million in 2020 to 498 million by 2045 if every child aged 5 to 14 years inclusive is to attend school. That is a 47% increase in school facilities which detracts from the ability of these countries to increase spending on education *per child* which is an indicator of quality. It is currently low at US224 per annum per school-age child. It is projected to rise to US$572 by 2045 if the trend in the current allocation of Government spending continues.

Figure 13-2: The Projected Changing Age Profile of the Young Poor Countries 2020 and 2045 – The Poverty Trap Explained.

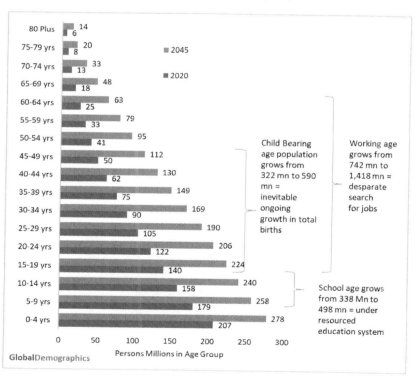

If the number of School-Age Children was not increasing, then the expenditure per child on education could increase so much more and probably to a meaningful level.

Finally, the ageing profile of the population inevitably results in a growth in the number of persons of working age and the number of them seeking work (typically around 64% - or 2 out of 3). There are 742 million working-age persons in 2020 and this is (reliably) projected to be 1,418 million in 2045. That means there has to be a significant increase in employment opportunities in those countries in the next 25 years.

As has been stressed throughout this Book, education is seen as the enabler. A poorly educated working-age population will not attract investment and productivity will not increase (not sufficient capital equipment to leverage labour skills) hence incomes do not increase, and jobs are at risk.

The current and projected spending per school-age child in Young Poor countries is too low to change the competitive position of the labour force of these countries over time.

Maintaining employment is the key issue for this group of countries. If the present level of employment as a percentage of the working-age population is not maintained, then household incomes are at risk (due to unemployment) as is the economy and hence the spending on education and health.

A popular belief is that all these young working-age people are going to be employed (either directly via migration or indirectly via the purchase of goods and services) by the affluent older countries. That is not going to be the case. As shown later in this Chapter these older affluent countries are NOT running out of labour supply, but their number of consumers is first showing slow growth (to around 2030) and then negative growth after that year.

Table 13-1: *Projected Changing Profile of the Young Poor Segment*

		2020	2030	2045
Population				
Total Population	Mns	1,332	1,717	2,309
Population Growth Rate	% pa	2.5%	2.3%	2.0%
Births pa	mns	44	50	59
Birth Rate	per 1000	137	118	101
Growth in Births	% pa	1.5%	1.2%	1.1%
Age Profile				
Median Age	yrs	19	21	23
Percent pop under 40	Perecent	80.8%	78.3%	74.2%
Percent pop 40-64	Perecent	15.8%	17.8%	20.8%
Percent over 64	Perecent	3.4%	3.9%	5.0%
Households				
Households	Mns	284	381	539
Household size	persons	4.7	4.5	4.3
Workers per household	Persons	1.68	1.71	1.72
Education				
School age population	Mns	338	411	498
As % total Population	Percent	25%	24%	22%
Growth rate of school age pop	% pa	2.2%	1.8%	1.3%
% of GDP spent on education	Percent	3.8%	3.8%	4.0%
Spend per school age person	US$ 2019	224	313	572
Education Index	Index	82	111	131
Employment				
Working Age population	Mns	742	1,004	1,418
as % total population	Percent	56%	58%	61%
Growth Rate	% pa	2.9%	2.8%	2.3%
Propensity to be employed	Percent	64.0%	64.3%	64.8%
Total employed	Mns	475	645	918
Growth Rate	% pa	2.5%	2.8%	2.4%
Dependency ratio	Pers per worker	1.80	1.66	1.51
GDP per worker	US$ 2019	4,069	4,954	7,321
Growth in GDP per worker	% pa	1.7%	1.8%	2.6%
Income and Expenditure				
Average Household income	US$ pa 2019	5,599	6,927	10,100
Growth rate	% pa	1.9%	2.0%	2.5%
Avg HH expenditure per cap	US$ 2019	1,128	1,457	2,228
Total expenditure all households	US$ Bn	1,502	2,501	5,146
Growth of total expenditure	% pa	4.7%	4.7%	4.9%
Share of global expenditure		3%	4%	7%
Propensity to spend	Percent	92%	92%	91%
Health				
Index demand	Index	100	147	235
Economy				
GDP per cap	US$ 2019	1,494	1,953	3,078
GDP Growth rate	% pa	1.6%	2.5%	3.1%

Maintaining employment in the Young Poor countries is at risk for two reasons – insufficient education and insufficient global demand for consumer goods and services.

Unless the people in the older Country Segments increase their absolute amount of spending to offset the lack of growth in the number of consumers it does mean the global demand for goods and services will grow at a slower rate – or even stagnate. Projections based on projected income increases and spending trends relative to income indicate that total consumer spending will experience slower growth. Down from 2.3% per annum to 2020, then 2.5% to 2030 and 1.1% per annum from 2030 to 2045.

If employment cannot be maintained, then it is a catastrophe for the countries in the Young Poor Country Segment. To make the point, the number of persons *seeking work* in the next 25 years in this Country Segment increases from 478 million to 918 million. Demand for work nearly doubles. It has implications not only for these countries but also for the more affluent ones nearby – migration will become a necessity, not a life choice, to survive.

Migration will become a necessity, not a life choice, to survive.

However, assuming employment rates are maintained then there are some interesting outcomes. First, household incomes are expected to increase as a reflection of a marginally improving education profile and consequent productivity gains which combined with an increased number of households results in household consumption expenditure projected to grow at 4.7% per annum.

It does not have a big effect on total global consumption expenditure as the spend per household is small – but it does lift it from 3% of global consumption expenditure to a projected 7% between 2019 and 2045. That is a useful increase.

It is interesting as well as it means the high growth area of global consumer spending is in countries where the expenditure per cap per annum is US$1,128 increasing to US$2,228 by 2045. The type of products and services purchased by households with that level of per capita spending is very different from the types of products and services purchased by the Older Affluent households spending over US$10,000 per capita. New products and services and new opportunities.

Finally, two other issues need consideration. The first is the issue of population growth. While belaboured at the start of this section it is worth returning to it. The total population of this Country Segment is projected, with some confidence, to grow from 1.3 billion persons to 2.3 billion.

These are countries where already there are people barely surviving because of poor food production and insufficient access to water. How can this potential disaster of a starving population be averted?

In a similar vein, the demand for health care is potentially going to increase rapidly. Expenditure on health care cannot be forecast as a significant part of it is a function of government policy which is unpredictable. But the likely trend in demand can be projected with some confidence and calculation indicates that the demand index for treatment will go from 100 in 2019 to 235 by 2045.

In short, the health service is going to have to more than double in capacity just to maintain existing care levels. How is that going to be achieved? Especially with many of the health professionals in those countries emigrating to more affluent countries.

If employment can be maintained, then the Young Poor Countries will be a fast-growing consumer market. But at a much lower price point and for a much younger age group than the markets currently dominating consumption.

The Family Low Income Segment

This Country Segment is very different from the preceding one. Specifically, its projected total population growth is quite moderate, and the age profile is changing significantly. This group of countries (and particularly India which is the major proportion of this population) are moving from the Population 'Pyramid' to a Population 'Square' as shown in Figure 13-3.

This is good as it helps these countries break out of the poverty cycle. The pyramid with its ever-increasing number of young people means a country stays poor. It cannot keep up with the ever-growing demand on its social structure such as education, health as well as fixed capital investment. In the case of this Country Segment, the number of births is projected to reduce (by nearly 14 million per annum) which is significant.

With a square population profile, the load is stabilised over time and the increased productivity of the workforce translates directly into increased incomes and improved lifestyles as well as social services.

For this group of countries, the school-age population is projected to decline from 545 million in 2020 to 429 million by 2045. With no change in the budget, the spending per school-aged person would increase by one third as a result. This means the quality of education improves and the society ultimately benefits.

The change in age profile for this Country Segment is very significant. In 2020, 68% of the population was under 40 years of age and the median age was 29 years. By 2045 it is projected that 53% will be under 40 years and the median age will be 38 years. A very different lifestyle profile and consumer.

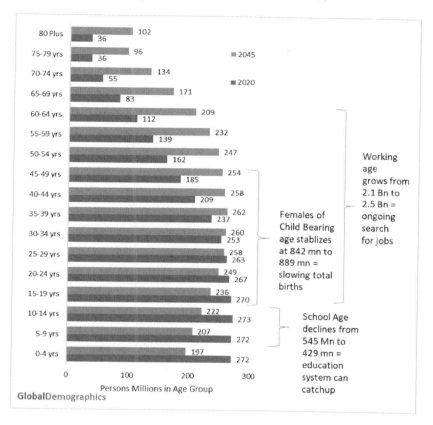

In the Family Low Income Segment, the age profile is changing
significantly. From 68% under 40 years of age to 53% by 2045.

These are societies in transition. Table 13-2 demonstrates the degree of
change taking place in the section labelled 'Population'. The overall
population growth rate drops from 1.2% per annum to 0.3% per annum.
Births drop from 54 million per annum to 39 million.

It is worth noting that while the population is declining, household size is also declining and hence the total number of households is growing – by 41% over the next 25 years. Smaller, older households with a higher income per capita.

With the rebalancing of the age profile of the population, the 'working-age' population is projected to continue to increase in size to 2030 and then such growth slows. This increase in the working-age population is often referred to as the 'demographic dividend' as it will boost the economic growth of these countries. However, that dividend is only 'collected' if the propensity to be employed can be maintained or increased.

With the expected improvement in the education profile of the workforce, the model has assumed that the propensity to be employed will be maintained and improve marginally. But be warned, it is not guaranteed.

India (which is the major player in this Country Segment) has not maintained the rate of employment over the last decade. Its propensity to be employed dropped from 59% in 2005 to 50% in 2019 meaning the 'demographic dividend' did not payout. It is projected that this situation will stabilise given India now has universal education in place, and this will enhance the employability of its labour force. However, it is a warning that this 'dividend' is not a certainty.

It is likely that this Country Segment will be competing with the previous Segment (Young Poor) for job opportunities and with that, for Fixed Capital Investment also. This segment's advantage is its higher education profile (Education Index score of 159 compared to 82 for the Young Poor Countries) and its more stable governments. That is good as the improvement in education means the overall productivity of workers increases. That plus the projected increase in the number of employed persons means total GDP could show good growth – projected to achieve circa 2% per annum through to 2045.

Table 13-2: Projected Changing Profile of the Family Low Income Segment: 2020 to 2045

		2020	2030	2045
Population				
Total Population	Mns	3,122	3,425	3,595
Population Growth Rate	% pa	1.2%	0.8%	0.3%
Births pa	mns	54	48	39
Birth Rate	per 1000	66	54	45
Growth in Births	% pa	-0.6%	-1.1%	-1.3%
Age Profile				
Median Age	yrs	29	33	38
Percent pop under 40	Perecent	67.5%	60.8%	52.6%
Percent pop 40-64	Perecent	25.8%	29.6%	33.4%
Percent over 64	Perecent	6.7%	9.5%	14.0%
Households				
Households	Mns	906	1,095	1,281
Household size	persons	3.4	3.1	2.8
Workers per household	Persons	1.3	1.3	1.2
Education				
School age population	Mns	545	519	429
As % total Population	Percent	17%	15%	12%
Growth rate of school age pop	% pa	0.0%	-0.4%	-1.3%
% of GDP spent on education	Percent	5.1%	5.3%	5.1%
Spend per school age person	US$ 2019	1,276	1,850	3,189
Education Index	Index	159	178	195
Employment				
Working Age population	Mns	2,095	2,338	2,466
as % total population	Percent	67%	68%	69%
Growth Rate	% pa	1.6%	1.0%	0.4%
Propensity to be employed	Percent	57.2%	57.8%	58.7%
Total employed	Mns	1,198	1,352	1,446
Growth Rate	% pa	1.3%	1.1%	0.5%
Dependency ratio	Pers per worker	1.61	1.53	1.49
GDP per worker	US$ 2019	11,183	13,182	17,980
Growth in GDP per worker	% pa	2.4%	1.5%	2.1%
Income and Expenditure				
Average Household income	US$ pa 2019	11,084	12,113	14,927
Growth rate	% pa	0.7%	0.8%	1.4%
Avg HH expenditure per cap	US$ 2019	2,673	3,178	4,272
Total expenditure all households	US$ Bn	8,348	10,884	15,357
Growth of total expenditure	% pa	3.7%	2.4%	2.3%
Share of global expenditure		19%	19%	21%
Propensity to spend	Percent	81%	80%	78%
Health				
Index demand	Index	100	134	178
Economy				
GDP per cap	US$ 2019	4,398	5,338	7,421
GDP Growth rate	% pa	2.7%	1.8%	2.2%

That is expected to carry through to household incomes and then consumption which is projected to grow at 2.4% per annum through to 2030 and 2.3% to 2045. It would lift this Segment's share of global consumption from 19% to 22% by 2045.

But again, note that the average spend per capita per annum is US$2,673 (projected to increase to US$4,272 by 2045) which is much lower than that of the traditional affluent markets. So again, a different consumer and a different product/service range need to be offered. But at a projected 22% of global consumption spending by 2045 this Country Segment is an important market.

One key change in the profile of the consumer is age. As mentioned earlier this Country Segment, as of 2020 is a relatively young society with two thirds under the age of 40 years. By 2045 only 50% will be under 40 years of age. The under 40 population is a large consumer market, but not growing in number, just affluence. The growth market will be the older age groups – growing in the number of consumers and affluence.

Finally, healthcare. The transiting of this population to over 40 years of age carries a cost. The probability of someone getting a chronic condition increases dramatically after age 40 in nearly every society. This group of countries is no exception. It is expected that the demand for health services in this Country Segment will increase by 78% in the next 25 years (compared with the total population growing by 15%). Such an increase in health needs is going to have implications for Government and Private budgets but also of course is a significant market in its own right.

Globally this could be the largest healthcare market in terms of value by 2045. Whereas the older Country Segments are approaching what could be called 'peak aged', this Country Segment is just starting to become 'aged'.

The Older Low Income Country Segment

This is made up of countries where the median age is over 35 years and Gross Domestic Product Per capita is less than US$20,000 per annum. It includes many of the Eastern European Countries as well as Russia and China – with the latter dominating the numbers.

But it is interesting to note that there is a lot of similarity between China and the other countries on birth rates despite China having specific policies on that. If nothing else, it confirms the relationship between education and birth rates.

There is a specific Chapter on what is happening to the demographics of China in this book – that is Chapter 11 – and the reader is referred to that for more detail. China is made up of two populations – urban and rural – and hence the averages for China can be a bit misleading.

That aside, overall, this Country Segment's most unique characteristic is that the total population is declining in absolute number. Down 5.8% by 2045. In part driven by a decline in the number of births, but also by an increasing proportion of the population that is older. From 2025 onward collectively the number of deaths exceeds the number of births. In addition, these countries receive relatively few migrants. They are not wealthy enough.

Overall and as shown in Figure 13-4 the age profile of Country Segment is close to being a 'Square Population Profile' and the number of young people is in decline as a proportion (from 50% to 40%) as is the number of school-age children (from 202 million to 152 million)) and finally their working-age population (from 1,274 million to 1,060 million).

Figure 13-4: The Current and Projected Age Profile of the Older Low-Income Countries 2020 and 2045.

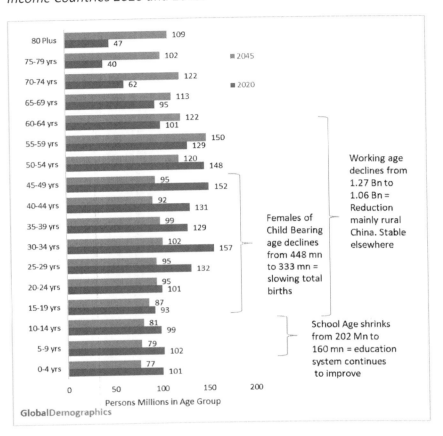

GlobalDemographics

But this is not a doom and gloom scenario. The reduced number of the school-age population reduces demand on the education system allowing a significant lift in quality – and some of the countries in this Segment already have the best-educated working-age populations. As such their upside potential in productivity is considerable if they (like China) can attract fixed capital investment. That of course would translate through to household incomes and consumption power.

There needs to be some explanation in terms of the employed labour force. Particularly in respect of China. With the working-age population

434

in absolute decline, there is the expectation that the economies will suffer as they will have fewer workers. However, be aware that in China, the decline in the working-age population (and Labour force) is entirely rural. Due to ongoing rural to urban migration, the urban labour force continues to grow in size through to 2035 and then stabilise at that number through to 2045.

This benefits China as rural occupations are of much lower productivity than urban ones. Furthermore, it should be noted that this relocation of labour could only happen because China introduced compulsory education to all children, urban and rural, in 1984. An uneducated youth would be of little use in modern industrial society.

China's Urban labour force, which accounts for 83% of total productivity, continues to grow through to 2030 despite an overall decline in China's working-age population. This is because of ongoing rural to urban migration.

The other countries suffer a 10% decline in the size of their labour forces even despite a 4-point increase in propensity to be employed. However, as the overall population is also declining in size, the dependency ratio (the number of dependents per employed person) increases only slowly. Excluding China, it is projected to lift from 1.19 to 1.32 dependents per worker between 2019 and 2045. That is significantly lower than the same measure in the two preceding Country Segments and does not suggest a need for migrant labour. In the case of China, the dependency ratio lifts from 0.9 to 1.19 which is low by global standards and translates into high (but declining) income per capita.

Perhaps the one key problem for this segment of countries is the loss of their skilled labour to countries in the Older Affluent Segment. This applies particularly to those within the European Union. The easy movement of skilled persons from low-income countries to high income countries within the European Union is deskilling some countries (Greece for example) and limiting the ability of those economies to grow.

Table 13-3: Projected Changing Profile of the Older Low-Income Segment:

		2020	2030	2045
Population				
Total Population	Mns	1,821	1,837	1,740
Population Growth Rate	% pa	0.4%	0.1%	-0.4%
Births pa	mns	19	17	16
Birth Rate	per 1000	44	44	50
Growth in Births	% pa	-0.8%	-1.2%	-0.6%
Age Profile				
Median Age	yrs	39	43	47
Percent pop under 40	Perecent	50.2%	43.3%	41.1%
Percent pop 40-64	Perecent	36.3%	38.0%	33.3%
Percent over 64	Perecent	13.4%	18.8%	25.6%
Households				
Households	Mns	652	720	731
Household size	persons	2.8	2.6	2.4
Workers per household	Persons	1.5	1.3	1.1
Education				
School age population	Mns	202	191	160
As % total Population	Percent	11%	10%	9%
Growth rate of school age pop	% pa	0.5%	-0.5%	-1.2%
% of GDP spent on education	Percent	4.0%	3.7%	3.3%
Spend per school age person	US$ 2019	3,860	5,968	9,289
Education Index	Index	205	222	239
Employment				
Working Age population	Mns	1,274	1,214	1,058
as % total population	Percent	70%	66%	61%
Growth Rate	% pa	0.0%	-0.4%	-0.9%
Propensity to be employed	Percent	73.4%	74.1%	75.3%
Total employed	Mns	935	899	796
Growth Rate	% pa	-0.1%	-0.4%	-0.8%
Dependency ratio	Pers per worker	0.95	1.04	1.19
GDP per worker	US$ 2019	20,034	33,119	55,200
Growth in GDP per worker	% pa	6.0%	4.7%	3.5%
Income and Expenditure				
Average Household income	US$ pa 2019	18,535	26,422	37,395
Growth rate	% pa	5.7%	3.3%	2.3%
Avg HH expenditure per cap	US$ 2019	3,899	5,749	8,310
Total expenditure all households	US$ Bn	7,104	10,561	14,457
Growth of total expenditure	% pa	6.1%	3.7%	2.1%
Share of global expenditure		16%	19%	20%
Propensity to spend	Percent	55%	52%	50%
Health				
Index demand	Index	100	131	160
Economy				
GDP per cap	US$ 2019	10,793	16,787	25,674
GDP Growth rate	% pa	5.6%	4.1%	2.9%

The easy movement of skilled persons from low-income countries to high income countries is deskilling some countries (Greece for example) and limiting the ability of those economies to grow.

While there may be fewer workers in future (down 15% in absolute number by 2045 – although most of this is rural China) the increased Fixed Capital per worker and improved education profile are projected to lift the productivity per worker significantly. By 4.7% pa to 2030 and then 3.% to 2045. This results in the average household income lifting by 2.8% per annum to 2045.

That combined with a stable number of households means the total consumption expenditure of this Country Segment will lift by 2.4% per annum and its share of global consumption expenditure from 15% to 18%. The expenditure per cap lifts from US$3,899 to US$8,310 which suggests that this is an increasingly important consumer market.

One advantage of being an older group of countries is that the growth rate of the over 40-year age group is slowing. That in turn means that the demand for health services does not grow as rapidly as it has in the past. To some extent, they are approaching 'peak aged' by 2045. The expected increase in demand for health care for this Country Segment is 1.7% per annum (an absolute increase of 58%) over the next 25 years which is manageable given the projected rate of increase in Gross Domestic Product Per capita.

The key aspect of this Country Segment is that it can move quite quickly to being a much more affluent area. Most of those countries are politically stable and have good education standards. But except for China, they have failed, for various reasons, to attract the investment level to lift educated workers' productivity. That can change and has been factored in the forecasts for them – but they are not expected to get to the level of the Older Affluent Country Segment much before 2045. China is different in that it has the investment but is behind on education – but it is aggressively lifting its education standard and is expected to catch up by 2045. Remember education, unlike fixed capital investment, takes time to change meaningfully.

The Older Affluent Country Segment

This Country Segment is
particularly distinct from the
others on one key dimension– the
productivity of its workforce. It has this advantage for the simple reasons
of (1) good education facilities and history and hence a well-educated
labour force and (2) a stable government and social environment which
has attracted investment for the workforce to leverage.

As a result of having a highly productive workforce and a low dependency
ratio per worker (see Table 13-4), the residents of these countries enjoy a
level of affluence significantly higher than the other Country Segments.

But, and this is the issue for this Segment of Countries, they are not
growth economies – they are stable. Such is their profile that the
potential gains are harder to achieve. The education standard of them is
high, so an additional worker with upper secondary or higher education
has only a very marginal impact.

Similarly, the Accumulated Fixed Capital Investment per worker at
US$119,200 per worker in 2019 is high relative to other Country
Segments. The next closest is the Older Low Income Country Segment at
US$39,156 per worker. This means the average worker in this Country
Segment is well equipped to leverage their skill set and lift their
productivity. But while an extra Fixed Capital Investment of US$1,000 per
worker would help, it is only a 1% lift, compared to it being a 25% lift for
the Young Poor Segment.

It is difficult to create dynamic growth statistics in that scenario. One
possibility is the growth of Artificial Intelligence and Robotics. These may
be game-changers as well as addressing the issue of declining workforce
size.

438

Table 13-4: Projected Changing Profile of the Older Affluent Segment:

Population		2020	2030	2045
Total Population	Mns	991	1,025	1,030
Population Growth Rate	% pa	0.5%	0.3%	0.0%
Births pa	mns	10	10	10
Birth Rate	per 1000	47	47	49
Growth in Births	% pa	-0.5%	-0.1%	-0.2%
Age Profile				
Median Age	yrs	42	44	46
Percent pop under 40	Perecent	53.7%	50.8%	48.1%
Percent pop 40-64	Perecent	32.6%	32.0%	31.2%
Percent over 64	Perecent	13.8%	17.1%	20.7%
Households				
Households	Mns	387	407	413
Household size	persons	2.6	2.5	2.5
Workers per household	Persons	1.2	1.2	1.2
Education				
School age population	Mns	108	103	100
As % total Population	Percent	11%	10%	10%
Growth rate of school age pop	% pa	0.0%	-0.5%	-0.2%
% of GDP spent on education	Percent	4.7%	4.9%	5.0%
Spend per school age person	US$ 2019	21,163	28,335	35,878
Education Index	Index	272	277	280
Employment				
Working Age population	Mns	742	752	727
as % total population	Percent	75%	73%	71%
Growth Rate	% pa	0.4%	0.1%	-0.2%
Propensity to be employed	Percent	64.9%	65.2%	65.6%
Total employed	Mns	481	490	477
Growth Rate	% pa	0.9%	0.2%	-0.2%
Dependency ratio	Pers per worker	1.06	1.09	1.16
GDP per worker	US$ 2019	101,297	120,058	149,205
Growth in GDP per worker	% pa	0.5%	1.6%	1.5%
Income and Expenditure				
Average Household income	US$ pa 2019	82,877	94,593	107,756
Growth rate	% pa	0.9%	1.2%	0.9%
Avg HH expenditure per cap	US$ 2019	28,339	32,228	35,955
Total expenditure all households	US$ Bn	28,073	33,018	37,049
Growth of total expenditure	% pa	1.6%	1.5%	0.8%
Share of global expenditure		64%	58%	52%
Propensity to spend	Percent	86%	84%	82%
Health				
Index demand	Index	100	115	129.74
Economy				
GDP per cap	US$ 2019	49,146	58,414	69,765
GDP Growth rate	% pa	1.3%	1.6%	1.2%

The total population of the Older Affluent Country Segment is now static and to the extent that there is any growth, it is the result of migration. Also as shown in Figure 13-5 these countries effectively have a

'Population Square'. (The tail at the top of this Figure simply reflects longer life expectancy).

Consequently, the working-age population is stable and as these countries already have a high propensity to be employed, the number of employed persons is also stable at 481 million in 2020 and a projected 477 million in 2045.

The total population of the Older Affluent Country Segment is now static and to the extent that there is any growth, it is the result of immigration.

This lack of growth dynamics is not a problem in itself. The dependents per worker are low at 1.06 in 2020 and a projected 1.16 in 2045 – so there is not a shortage of workers to look after the non-working population and incomes are high, meaning lifestyles are good by global norms.

While at 1.6% per annum growth in productivity per worker is lower than that of the other Country Segments, it is positive and in absolute terms is a significant amount of money. This of course translates across to household incomes which are projected to grow at 1% per annum for the period to 2045.

These households are very affluent on a comparative basis   The per capita income is US$ 32,357 in 2019 (projected to be US$43,205 by 2045) and that is significantly more than say the Family Low Income segment's per capita household income of US$3,216 in 2019.

Therefore, it is not surprising that the older Affluent account for a significant, but declining, proportion of global consumption expenditure. In 2020 this Country Segment was an estimated 62% of global household expenditure. It is projected to be 52% by 2045. It is declining in share as a result of the projected increased affluence of the other segments.

Figure 13-5: The Projected Age Profile of the Older Low-Income Countries 2019 and 2045.

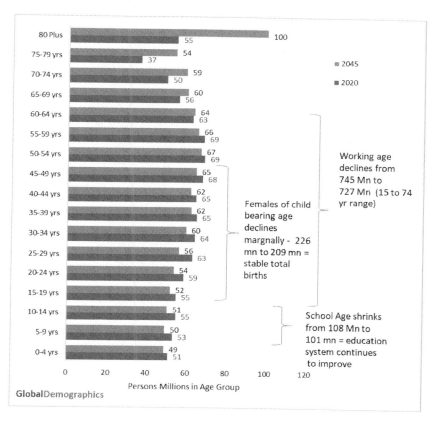

The future growth of consumption expenditure is a function of their increased affluence and the proportion spent whereas in the past it *also* had a growing number of affluent consumers.

As a result, the rate of growth in consumption expenditure by this segment is projected to slow – from 1.6% per annum for the period 2009 to 2019 to 1.1% per annum for the period 2030 to 2045. This is of concern as it is this consumption that drives the demand for jobs and this Country Segment accounts for 62% of it in 2020. As shown earlier, in the Younger Countries the demand for jobs is increasing - significantly. The sociological implications of this are significant.

The rate of growth in consumption expenditure by this segment which accounts for 63% of global consumption is projected to slow which has implications for the demand for workers elsewhere in the world.

Finally, in many respects, this Country Segment is at 'peak aged'. Being a square population age profile, the number of older people will not grow as rapidly in future as it has in the past. This helps the health sector as it means demand stabilises and will lift a more modest 1% per annum (an absolute increase of 29%) over the next 25 years.

The Total Picture

To conclude some useful overall statistics

1. Total global population growth continues, but the growth rate slows – from 1.1% per annum for the period 2009 to 2019 to 0.42% per annum from 2040 to 2045. This is desirable from an environmental point of view as well as a sociological one.
2. Between 2019 and 2045 total births decline very marginally from 128 million per annum to 124 million. Slower population growth is very much a function of increasing deaths as a result of an ageing global population.
3. Some countries are reaching 'peak age'. And their population profile will not change dramatically now. They will tend to consolidate their (relatively affluent) position.
4. The Older Low-Income Countries are potentially the ones with the biggest change in the short term as they leverage their education strength with greater investment and lift their affluence and lifestyle.
5. The Family Stage Country Segment is the one in greatest transition over the entire period – from young populations struggling to improve to more middle-aged and starting to get out

of the poverty trap of a pyramid population. Education is improving and that will help lift all outcomes. The biggest issue here is that developing a better-educated labour force takes time. The change will progress but will not be completed in 25-years' time.

6. In contrast to the three more affluent Country Segments, the Young Poor Country Segment is approaching a crisis. First, their births are out of control, resulting in a population growth these countries simply cannot service. Already there is insufficient nutrition, water, education, and health care in most if not all of them. An extra billion people is going to exacerbate that problem – as these extra billion persons are by definition children (at least for the next 15 years) which will not help lift the economy or productivity.

7. The problem is further exacerbated in that population growth is not easily slowed. Birth rates are declining (albeit too slowly), but the issue is the number of women of childbearing age in these countries is going to increase rapidly in the next 10 years from 321 million to 479 million by 2035 and reach 584 million by 2045. Birth rates have to plummet at unlikely rates to offset this growth in family stage people having children. Unless something draconian, such as the 'One child Policy' of China is introduced, this tsunami of children is going to happen.

8. This is already causing rapid growth in the number of persons looking for work and that will continue through to 2045 – and that is the risk for these societies. There is a real probability that demand for workers will slow as a result of slowing growth in the number of affluent consumers, changing spending habits (in part because of the ageing of the affluent consumer), the growth of robotics and onshoring that is enabled as the work is no longer labour intensive. There simply may not be enough work opportunities.

9. This could create a huge pool of persons (estimated at 400 million) who cannot sustain themselves, let alone any family they might have, and this will result in desperation, conflict, and mass (potentially unfriendly) migration.

Appendix A:
Gross Domestic Product Forecasts

The following pages give the total real Gross Domestic Product numbers and forecasts used for this analysis.

- For the years 2005 to 2019 they are actual

- For the years 2020 and 2021, they are from the IMF
- For the years 2022 to 2045 they are derived from the Global Demographics Population Model

The Global Demographics Model takes into account:

- Size of the working-age population

- Relationship of the Education profile and Accumulated Fixed Capital Investment per worker to productivity (GDP) per worker.
- The trend in Fixed Capital Investment as a proportion of the previous year's GDP
- The trend in Propensity to be employed and hence the number of workers.

Older Affluent Segment

Absolute Amount

Total Real GDP US$ Bn All values are 2019 Real	2005	2010	2015	2019	2020	2021	2025	2030	2035	2040	2045
Australia	931	1,072	1,227	1,354	1,263	1,339	1,449	1,659	1,934	2,238	2,563
Austria	365	389	410	446	415	434	493	534	573	608	642
Belgium	434	467	498	530	493	516	567	590	604	615	625
Canada	1,284	1,445	1,607	1,736	1,627	1,694	1,794	1,884	1,976	2,060	2,144
Denmark	293	296	315	348	325	344	390	411	423	431	436
Finland	235	246	247	269	253	260	288	301	311	319	325
France	2,318	2,415	2,542	2,716	2,519	2,632	2,913	3,009	3,045	3,058	3,062
Germany	3,111	3,299	3,596	3,846	3,577	3,763	4,166	4,388	4,556	4,686	4,803
Hong Kong	242	294	340	366	350	364	370	412	470	526	579
Iceland	17	18	21	24	22	24	29	34	39	43	47
Ireland	215	219	304	389	361	383	700	881	941	969	999
Italy	2,018	1,989	1,922	2,002	1,817	1,904	2,097	2,250	2,382	2,452	2,470
Japan	4,582	4,604	4,837	4,777	4,823	5,121	5,374	5,736	6,080	6,381	6,627
Macao	23	33	61	55	39	52	57	63	69	74	77
Netherlands	745	797	828	909	841	866	1,000	1,076	1,135	1,175	1,200
New Zealand	156	166	192	208	205	230	257	281	300	316	329
Norway	333	349	381	403	378	389	434	440	439	437	433
Puerto Rico	125	117	113	98	95	98	92	87	79	67	55
Republic of Korea	1,029	1,270	1,476	1,642	1,624	1,680	1,954	2,369	2,961	3,752	4,802
Singapore	192	266	331	372	359	370	414	509	645	810	1,003
Slovenia	42	46	47	54	49	52	63	77	92	106	118
Spain	1,203	1,262	1,260	1,394	1,278	1,332	1,654	1,996	2,361	2,684	2,954
Sweden	404	441	491	531	494	520	568	587	602	615	628
Switzerland	541	603	655	703	661	686	755	814	876	934	990
Taiwan	385	476	549	611	623	648	737	853	961	1,059	1,147
United Kingdom	2,338	2,397	2,649	2,827	2,643	2,748	3,024	3,194	3,328	3,415	3,473
United States of America	16,765	17,536	19,546	20,782	20,189	22,152	24,140	26,351	28,131	29,499	30,559

Compound Annual Growth Rate

Total Real GDP Growth rate % pa	2005-10	2010-15	2015-19	2019-20	2020-21	2021-25	2025-30	2030-35	2035-40	2040-45
Australia	2.9%	2.7%	2.5%	-6.7%	6.1%	2.0%	2.7%	3.1%	3.0%	2.8%
Austria	1.3%	1.1%	2.1%	-7.0%	4.5%	3.2%	1.6%	1.4%	1.2%	1.1%
Belgium	1.5%	1.3%	1.6%	-6.9%	4.6%	2.4%	0.8%	0.5%	0.4%	0.3%
Canada	2.4%	2.1%	2.0%	-6.3%	4.1%	1.4%	1.0%	1.0%	0.8%	0.8%
Denmark	0.2%	1.3%	2.5%	-6.7%	5.9%	3.2%	1.1%	0.6%	0.4%	0.3%
Finland	0.9%	0.1%	2.1%	-6.0%	3.1%	2.5%	0.9%	0.7%	0.5%	0.4%
France	0.8%	1.0%	1.7%	-7.2%	4.5%	2.6%	0.7%	0.2%	0.1%	0.0%
Germany	1.2%	1.7%	1.7%	-7.0%	5.2%	2.6%	1.0%	0.8%	0.6%	0.5%
Hong Kong	3.9%	2.9%	1.9%	-4.4%	4.1%	0.4%	2.2%	2.6%	2.3%	1.9%
Iceland	1.1%	2.8%	4.2%	-7.4%	5.9%	5.0%	3.1%	2.8%	2.2%	1.7%
Ireland	0.4%	6.7%	6.4%	-7.1%	6.1%	16.3%	4.7%	1.3%	0.6%	0.6%
Italy	-0.3%	-0.7%	1.0%	-9.2%	4.8%	2.4%	1.4%	1.1%	0.6%	0.1%
Japan	0.1%	1.0%	-0.3%	1.0%	6.2%	1.2%	1.3%	1.2%	1.0%	0.8%
Macao	8.0%	12.8%	-2.5%	-28.9%	33.2%	2.4%	1.9%	1.8%	1.3%	1.0%
Netherlands	1.4%	0.7%	2.4%	-7.5%	3.0%	3.6%	1.5%	1.1%	0.7%	0.4%
New Zealand	1.2%	2.9%	2.1%	-1.6%	12.3%	2.8%	1.9%	1.3%	1.0%	0.8%
Norway	1.0%	1.7%	1.5%	-6.4%	2.9%	2.8%	0.3%	0.0%	-0.1%	-0.2%
Puerto Rico	-1.4%	-0.6%	-3.7%	-3.2%	3.8%	-1.7%	-1.0%	-2.1%	-3.1%	-4.0%
Republic of Korea	4.3%	3.1%	2.7%	-1.1%	3.4%	3.8%	3.9%	4.6%	4.9%	5.1%
Singapore	6.8%	4.5%	2.9%	-3.5%	3.0%	2.9%	4.2%	4.9%	4.7%	4.4%
Slovenia	1.9%	0.4%	3.6%	-8.0%	5.4%	5.0%	3.9%	3.6%	2.8%	2.2%
Spain	1.0%	0.0%	2.6%	-8.3%	4.2%	5.6%	3.8%	3.4%	2.6%	1.9%
Sweden	1.8%	2.2%	1.9%	-6.9%	5.2%	2.2%	0.7%	0.5%	0.4%	0.4%
Switzerland	2.2%	1.7%	1.8%	-6.0%	3.8%	2.4%	1.5%	1.5%	1.3%	1.2%
Taiwan	4.3%	2.9%	2.7%	1.9%	4.0%	3.3%	3.0%	2.4%	2.0%	1.6%
United Kingdom	0.5%	2.0%	1.6%	-6.5%	4.0%	2.4%	1.1%	0.8%	0.5%	0.3%
United States of America	0.9%	2.2%	1.5%	-2.9%	9.7%	2.2%	1.8%	1.3%	1.0%	0.7%

The Older Low-Income Segment

Absolute Amount US$ Bn

Total Real GDP US$ Bn / All values are 2019 Real	2005	2010	2015	2019	2020	2021	2025	2030	2035	2040	2045
Albania	9	12	13	15	15	16	18	24	35	49	67
Belarus	40	57	60	63	59	61	63	68	78	91	109
Bulgaria	46	54	59	68	65	69	74	82	89	95	100
Cuba	64	83	96	100	100	108	111	111	108	103	98
Czechia	178	201	219	246	230	247	290	350	427	515	615
Estonia	23	22	26	31	29	31	40	52	68	87	109
Georgia	9	12	15	18	17	18	21	25	28	32	35
Greece	248	244	200	210	189	198	228	271	312	338	348
Hungary	125	124	137	161	156	162	218	249	264	273	282
Latvia	26	25	30	34	31	33	40	48	58	67	77
Lithuania	37	39	47	54	50	54	62	67	70	71	70
Mauritius	8	10	12	14	13	14	17	21	25	28	31
Poland	341	430	499	592	565	589	681	771	850	911	953
Portugal	217	224	215	238	217	227	283	341	401	454	498
Republic of Moldova	7	8	10	11	11	12	14	16	17	19	20
Romania	154	177	205	250	237	247	297	348	399	449	496
Russian Federation	1,236	1,471	1,603	1,700	1,606	1,662	1,718	1,718	1,702	1,683	1,667
Slovakia	65	83	94	105	99	104	124	150	181	213	244
Thailand	341	410	474	544	507	538	608	713	849	1,004	1,178
Ukraine	147	154	138	154	142	147	170	185	195	200	201
Uruguay	33	45	53	56	54	57	58	58	60	61	62
China	4,652	7,968	11,612	14,993	15,193	16,097	20,302	25,174	29,552	33,169	36,099

Compound Annual Growth Rate

Total Real GDP Growth rate % pa	2005-10	2010-15	2015-19	2019-20	2020-21	2021-25	2025-30	2030-35	2035-40	2040-45
Albania	5.3%	1.8%	3.3%	-5.0%	8.0%	3.6%	6.2%	7.2%	7.0%	6.8%
Belarus	7.3%	1.2%	1.1%	-6.1%	3.5%	0.6%	1.8%	2.7%	3.2%	3.6%
Bulgaria	3.2%	1.8%	3.4%	-4.1%	5.7%	1.7%	2.1%	1.8%	1.3%	0.9%
Cuba	5.4%	2.8%	1.1%	0.4%	7.5%	0.8%	-0.1%	-0.5%	-0.9%	-1.1%
Czechia	2.4%	1.7%	3.1%	-6.7%	7.3%	4.1%	3.9%	4.0%	3.8%	3.6%
Estonia	-0.3%	3.3%	4.4%	-7.7%	7.7%	6.5%	5.4%	5.4%	5.0%	4.7%
Georgia	5.2%	5.0%	4.4%	-4.0%	3.0%	5.1%	3.0%	2.7%	2.4%	2.1%
Greece	-0.3%	-4.0%	1.3%	-10.0%	5.1%	3.6%	3.5%	2.9%	1.6%	0.6%
Hungary	-0.2%	2.1%	4.1%	-3.1%	4.2%	7.7%	2.6%	1.2%	0.7%	0.6%
Latvia	-0.5%	3.6%	3.0%	-9.3%	7.7%	4.8%	3.8%	3.6%	3.1%	2.7%
Lithuania	1.1%	3.8%	3.6%	-8.3%	8.0%	3.7%	1.7%	0.9%	0.2%	-0.2%
Mauritius	4.7%	3.6%	3.7%	-6.8%	5.9%	5.5%	3.9%	3.3%	2.5%	1.9%
Poland	4.8%	3.0%	4.4%	-4.6%	4.2%	3.7%	2.5%	2.0%	1.4%	0.9%
Portugal	0.6%	-0.8%	2.6%	-8.7%	4.8%	5.6%	3.7%	3.3%	2.5%	1.9%
Republic of Moldova	3.3%	5.2%	3.2%	-3.1%	4.1%	4.5%	2.5%	1.9%	1.6%	1.5%
Romania	2.8%	3.0%	5.1%	-5.0%	3.9%	4.8%	3.2%	2.8%	2.4%	2.0%
Russian Federation	3.5%	1.7%	1.5%	-5.5%	3.5%	0.8%	0.0%	-0.2%	-0.2%	-0.2%
Slovakia	4.9%	2.6%	2.9%	-6.3%	4.9%	4.6%	3.9%	3.8%	3.3%	2.8%
Thailand	3.7%	3.0%	3.5%	-6.8%	6.1%	3.1%	3.3%	3.5%	3.4%	3.2%
Ukraine	0.9%	-2.3%	2.8%	-7.7%	3.6%	3.6%	1.7%	1.1%	0.5%	0.1%
Uruguay	6.0%	3.4%	1.5%	-3.0%	5.0%	0.2%	0.2%	0.5%	0.4%	0.3%
China	11.4%	7.8%	6.6%	1.3%	6.0%	6.0%	4.4%	3.3%	2.3%	1.7%

Family Stage Low Income Segment

Absolute Amount US$ Bn

Total Real GDP US$ Bn All values are 2019 Real	2005	2010	2015	2019	2020	2021	2025	2030	2035	2040	2045
Algeria	119	135	159	170	161	171	188	204	221	235	247
Argentina	343	436	469	450	424	443	467	499	555	605	647
Armenia	7	9	11	14	13	14	17	25	36	50	67
Azerbaijan	20	43	48	48	47	47	52	71	105	153	220
Bangladesh	123	165	225	301	307	336	454	580	706	856	1,045
Bolivia	22	27	35	41	40	41	45	47	49	51	53
Brazil	1,391	1,731	1,832	1,840	1,741	1,791	1,867	2,017	2,206	2,368	2,489
Cambodia	11	15	21	27	27	28	36	41	43	45	47
Chile	179	216	261	282	269	283	310	347	386	426	465
Colombia	189	235	295	324	316	328	358	380	398	416	432
Dominican Republic	42	56	71	89	88	92	125	156	186	219	255
Ecuador	71	84	105	107	101	104	116	123	129	134	137
El Salvador	20	22	25	27	26	27	31	33	34	35	36
India	1,166	1,636	2,241	2,895	2,950	3,168	3,680	4,364	5,122	6,029	7,138
Indonesia	531	702	918	1,119	1,125	1,214	1,406	1,545	1,616	1,676	1,743
Iran (Islamic Republic of)	329	400	392	471	469	484	581	798	1,110	1,509	2,011
Kazakhstan	92	125	157	180	176	183	223	269	317	367	418
Malaysia	187	233	302	365	358	390	436	517	614	718	829
Mexico	943	1,015	1,174	1,258	1,175	1,210	1,299	1,370	1,468	1,568	1,665
Morocco	69	88	107	119	114	120	134	155	185	225	281
Myanmar	27	46	66	81	87	94	118	154	200	262	343
Nicaragua	8	10	12	13	12	12	13	14	15	16	18
Panama	27	39	56	65	67	74	82	87	91	94	97
Paraguay	21	28	34	38	38	39	42	45	49	52	55
Peru	114	159	200	227	216	227	258	287	320	355	390
Philippines	171	218	292	377	379	407	519	576	597	609	621
Saudi Arabia	520	595	765	793	775	797	910	990	1,048	1,079	1,083
South Africa	263	307	342	351	331	344	378	398	420	445	470
Sri Lanka	40	54	73	84	84	87	99	111	124	137	150
Tunisia	29	37	40	42	42	43	48	57	68	78	89
Turkey	397	465	656	754	717	753	812	848	887	929	975
Uzbekistan	22	33	47	58	59	63	100	123	131	135	139
Venezuela RB	375	450	419	463	465	467	482	505	521	529	529
Viet Nam	111	151	201	262	272	294	383	549	784	1,093	1,494

Compound Annual Growth Rate

Total Real GDP Growth rate % pa	2005-10	2010-15	2015-19	2019-20	2020-21	2021-25	2025-30	2030-35	2035-40	2040-45
Algeria	2.5%	3.3%	1.7%	-5.3%	6.0%	2.5%	1.6%	1.6%	1.3%	1.0%
Argentina	4.9%	1.5%	-1.0%	-5.7%	4.4%	1.4%	1.3%	2.1%	1.8%	1.4%
Armenia	3.8%	4.4%	5.1%	-1.5%	4.8%	5.1%	7.5%	7.7%	6.8%	6.0%
Azerbaijan	16.4%	2.0%	0.2%	-2.2%	0.7%	2.5%	6.4%	8.0%	7.9%	7.5%
Bangladesh	6.1%	6.3%	7.6%	2.0%	9.5%	7.8%	5.0%	4.0%	3.9%	4.1%
Bolivia	4.6%	5.5%	3.7%	-2.9%	2.9%	2.2%	1.0%	0.8%	0.8%	0.8%
Brazil	4.5%	1.1%	0.1%	-5.4%	2.9%	1.0%	1.6%	1.8%	1.4%	1.0%
Cambodia	6.7%	7.2%	7.1%	-1.6%	6.0%	6.5%	2.4%	1.2%	0.9%	0.9%
Chile	3.8%	3.9%	2.0%	-4.6%	5.2%	2.3%	2.2%	2.2%	2.0%	1.8%
Colombia	4.5%	4.7%	2.3%	-2.4%	3.7%	2.2%	1.2%	0.9%	0.9%	0.8%
Dominican Republic	5.8%	4.9%	5.8%	-1.0%	4.0%	8.2%	4.5%	3.6%	3.3%	3.1%
Ecuador	3.4%	4.4%	0.6%	-6.4%	3.9%	2.7%	1.1%	0.9%	0.7%	0.5%
El Salvador	1.7%	2.6%	2.4%	-5.4%	4.5%	3.5%	1.4%	0.9%	0.6%	0.3%
India	7.0%	6.5%	6.6%	1.9%	7.4%	3.8%	3.5%	3.3%	3.3%	3.4%
Indonesia	5.7%	5.5%	5.1%	0.5%	7.9%	3.7%	1.9%	0.9%	0.7%	0.8%
Iran (Islamic Republic of)	4.0%	-0.4%	4.7%	-0.5%	3.3%	4.7%	6.5%	6.8%	6.3%	5.9%
Kazakhstan	6.2%	4.7%	3.4%	-2.5%	4.0%	5.1%	3.8%	3.4%	3.0%	2.7%
Malaysia	4.5%	5.3%	4.8%	-1.7%	8.9%	2.8%	3.5%	3.5%	3.2%	2.9%
Mexico	1.5%	2.9%	1.7%	-6.6%	3.0%	1.8%	1.1%	1.4%	1.3%	1.2%
Morocco	5.0%	4.0%	2.6%	-3.7%	4.7%	2.8%	3.0%	3.6%	4.1%	4.5%
Myanmar	11.1%	7.3%	5.4%	7.4%	8.1%	5.6%	5.5%	5.4%	5.5%	5.6%
Nicaragua	2.7%	5.5%	0.3%	-6.0%	0.0%	2.5%	1.0%	1.5%	2.2%	2.3%
Panama	7.4%	7.7%	3.5%	3.9%	10.4%	2.4%	1.2%	0.9%	0.7%	0.6%
Paraguay	5.4%	4.0%	3.1%	-1.0%	4.0%	1.6%	1.5%	1.5%	1.3%	1.1%
Peru	6.9%	4.8%	3.1%	-4.6%	5.1%	3.2%	2.1%	2.2%	2.1%	1.9%
Philippines	5.0%	6.0%	6.6%	0.6%	7.4%	6.3%	2.1%	0.7%	0.4%	0.4%
Saudi Arabia	2.7%	5.1%	0.9%	-2.3%	2.9%	3.4%	1.7%	1.1%	0.6%	0.1%
South Africa	3.1%	2.2%	0.7%	-5.9%	3.9%	2.4%	1.0%	1.1%	1.2%	1.1%
Sri Lanka	6.4%	6.2%	3.4%	-0.5%	4.2%	3.3%	2.4%	2.1%	2.0%	1.9%
Tunisia	4.5%	1.8%	0.8%	-0.1%	3.8%	2.6%	3.5%	3.5%	3.0%	2.5%
Turkey	3.2%	7.1%	3.6%	-5.0%	5.0%	1.9%	0.9%	0.9%	0.9%	1.0%
Uzbekistan	8.3%	7.5%	5.4%	1.8%	6.9%	12.3%	4.2%	1.2%	0.6%	0.6%
Venezuela RB	3.7%	-1.4%	2.5%	0.4%	0.5%	0.8%	0.9%	0.6%	0.3%	0.0%
Viet Nam	6.3%	5.9%	6.8%	3.7%	8.1%	6.9%	7.5%	7.4%	6.9%	6.5%

Young Poor Segment

Absolute Amount US$ Bn

Total Real GDP US$ Bn All values are 2019 Real	2005	2010	2015	2019	2020	2021	2025	2030	2035	2040	2045
Angola	77	116	144	142	143	144	174	203	259	323	397
Botswana	10	13	16	18	17	19	21	24	26	28	30
Burkina Faso	7	10	12	16	16	17	21	24	27	29	32
Cameroon	22	26	33	39	38	40	49	58	67	78	89
Chad	7	9	12	11	11	12	14	16	21	28	38
DR Congo	21	28	40	47	48	51	57	66	76	86	99
Egypt	161	217	248	295	307	327	383	462	541	616	689
Ethiopia	25	41	67	93	96	100	152	254	456	859	1,670
Ghana	27	38	53	67	68	72	79	94	111	131	152
Guatemala	47	56	68	77	75	79	94	114	135	155	172
Guinea	7	8	10	14	14	15	17	19	22	24	27
Haiti	6	7	8	8	8	8	9	9	9	9	9
Honduras	15	18	22	25	24	25	30	38	48	61	76
Kenya	46	59	77	96	96	102	116	139	166	193	220
Lao PDR	7	11	16	20	21	23	29	41	57	80	111
Madagascar	9	10	12	14	14	15	18	22	25	29	33
Malawi	4	5	7	8	8	8	10	12	15	17	20
Mali	10	12	14	18	18	18	24	30	35	42	49
Mozambique	6	9	13	15	15	16	19	21	24	27	30
Namibia	8	10	12	12	12	12	14	15	17	19	21
Nepal	16	20	25	31	31	33	44	47	50	52	52
Niger	6	8	10	13	13	14	17	20	24	28	33
Nigeria	256	360	461	466	469	529	700	977	1,319	1,704	2,129
Pakistan	148	175	213	253	249	254	302	353	408	461	509
Rwanda	4	5	8	10	10	11	14	16	17	19	20
Senegal	13	15	18	24	24	26	34	41	46	51	57
South Sudan	0	22	12	13	13	13	13	14	14	15	15
Sudan	15	21	24	25	23	22	28	32	37	42	47
Uganda	15	22	28	35	36	37	46	55	64	74	84
United Republic of Tanzani	28	38	51	65	71	75	91	105	119	134	151
Zambia	10	16	20	23	22	23	28	33	37	42	46
Zimbabwe	0	0	0	0	0	0	0	0	0	0	0

Compound Annual Growth Rate

Total Real GDP Growth rate % pa	2005-10	2010-15	2015-19	2019-20	2020-21	2021-25	2025-30	2030-35	2035-40	2040-45
Angola	8.4%	4.5%	-0.4%	0.3%	0.9%	4.9%	3.1%	5.0%	4.5%	4.2%
Botswana	4.6%	4.8%	3.7%	-5.4%	6.8%	3.6%	2.1%	1.8%	1.6%	1.5%
Burkina Faso	5.5%	5.4%	6.2%	2.0%	5.7%	5.6%	2.5%	2.2%	2.0%	1.9%
Cameroon	3.5%	5.1%	4.1%	-1.2%	4.1%	5.3%	3.4%	3.0%	2.9%	2.8%
Chad	4.9%	4.8%	-1.0%	-0.2%	5.9%	3.7%	3.5%	5.5%	5.8%	5.9%
DR Congo	5.5%	7.8%	4.1%	1.3%	7.2%	2.8%	2.8%	2.8%	2.6%	2.7%
Egypt	6.2%	2.7%	4.4%	4.2%	6.5%	4.0%	3.8%	3.2%	2.6%	2.3%
Ethiopia	10.9%	10.2%	8.5%	3.2%	4.3%	11.0%	10.9%	12.4%	13.5%	14.2%
Ghana	6.5%	7.1%	6.1%	1.5%	5.8%	2.4%	3.4%	3.5%	3.3%	3.0%
Guatemala	3.7%	3.9%	3.2%	-2.0%	5.4%	4.4%	3.9%	3.5%	2.7%	2.1%
Guinea	3.1%	4.6%	8.2%	2.9%	7.5%	3.4%	2.4%	2.3%	2.1%	1.9%
Haiti	1.3%	3.3%	0.8%	-4.1%	1.2%	2.5%	0.8%	0.6%	0.3%	-0.1%
Honduras	3.6%	3.5%	3.8%	-2.4%	4.1%	4.5%	4.6%	4.9%	4.7%	4.5%
Kenya	5.0%	5.5%	5.6%	1.0%	5.9%	3.2%	3.8%	3.5%	3.1%	2.7%
Lao PDR	8.0%	7.8%	6.1%	6.5%	6.4%	6.5%	6.8%	6.9%	6.9%	7.0%
Madagascar	2.8%	2.7%	4.3%	0.4%	5.0%	5.1%	3.6%	3.1%	2.9%	2.7%
Malawi	7.4%	4.1%	3.5%	1.0%	2.5%	5.5%	4.4%	3.9%	3.3%	2.8%
Mali	4.6%	3.6%	5.2%	1.5%	4.0%	6.8%	4.3%	3.6%	3.4%	3.3%
Mozambique	7.5%	7.1%	3.3%	2.2%	4.7%	3.9%	2.6%	2.5%	2.3%	2.2%
Namibia	4.3%	5.2%	-0.2%	-2.5%	3.2%	3.0%	1.8%	1.9%	2.4%	2.3%
Nepal	4.4%	4.3%	5.6%	2.5%	5.0%	7.2%	1.6%	1.1%	0.7%	0.2%
Niger	5.4%	5.9%	5.9%	1.0%	8.0%	4.6%	3.5%	3.5%	3.4%	3.4%
Nigeria	7.1%	5.0%	0.3%	0.7%	12.6%	7.3%	6.9%	6.2%	5.2%	4.6%
Pakistan	3.4%	4.0%	4.5%	-1.5%	2.0%	4.4%	3.1%	3.0%	2.5%	2.0%
Rwanda	8.3%	7.3%	7.0%	3.5%	6.6%	6.2%	2.4%	2.0%	1.7%	1.4%
Senegal	3.4%	4.5%	6.4%	3.0%	5.5%	7.6%	3.6%	2.4%	2.1%	2.1%
South Sudan		-11.7%	1.7%	2.7%	1.6%	0.1%	0.7%	0.7%	0.6%	0.5%
Sudan	6.4%	2.8%	1.0%	-7.7%	-3.1%	6.3%	2.3%	2.9%	2.7%	2.6%
Uganda	8.1%	5.4%	5.3%	3.5%	4.3%	5.4%	3.6%	3.2%	2.8%	2.6%
United Republic of Tanzan	6.1%	6.4%	6.0%	9.8%	5.7%	4.8%	2.9%	2.6%	2.4%	2.4%
Zambia	8.7%	5.2%	3.3%	-3.5%	2.3%	5.5%	2.9%	2.6%	2.3%	2.1%
Zimbabwe	0.5%	7.2%	1.3%	1.4%	5.3%	3.2%	2.6%	2.2%	1.8%	1.7%

Appendix B:
Methodology

Model Overview

The Statistical model developed by Global Demographics is Econometric in nature.

For all data series relevant to the model, we have data series running from 2005 and generally earlier (in some cases from 1994). As such we are in a good position to develop regression type models of the relationship between variables that are sufficiently robust to be used for projections.

Unlike financial/economic models, demographic relationships/variables tend to typically follow steady trends. For example, household size does not significantly vary year on year and generally declines as the age profile of the population and/or affluence increases.

There are two exogenous variables to the model – birth rates and death rates - but in both cases, we check back to ensure their trend is consistent with apparent drivers – affluence and education. All other variables are 'driven' by other preceding variables.

The overall structure of the model can be shown graphically as on the following page. This shows the logical order for 'solving' the model.

Note: While in the following model example specific age groups are shown, the actual model solves for 1 year age steps. The model extends to

the right to cover household Income and Expenditure by user-defined
segments. (Not shown here)

Figure B-1: Diagram of the Demographic Forecasting Model

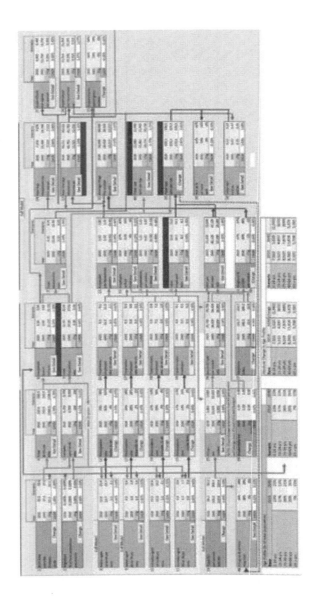

The Modelling Process

Births, Deaths and Migration

The model solves for each country or region on an annual basis – that is, it rolls forward one year for all variables at a time. The equations used are all based on the latest actual data available for the relevant input series.

Births, Deaths and Migration

Birth rates and death rates are exogenous variables. However, both have consistent trends, and we simply project the trend forward. This is done by 1-year gender age groups for deaths and by 5-year age groups from 15 to 49 years for Mothers.

Total deaths are calculated by applying the death rate for each age/gender group to the relevant population of that year to get the total deaths for the year and to give the net number in that age-gender group for the end of the year (subject to migration – see below).

Total births for the year are calculated by applying the Birth Rates to the number of women in each age group the previous year to give total births in the current year. The infant mortality rate is applied to the total birth figure (not by age of the mother).

The model rolls forward one year at a time. All population data is held in a 1-year step age profile.

Immigration is a residual error. Where a country reports a total population figure (which may be annual but more typically 5 yearly) the modal determines the starting population, adds known births, deducts known deaths for the relevant years and compares the resulting total by age and gender with the reported (actual) profile. The difference between the number estimated for each age/gender segment and the reported figure is treated as migration (although it can in part be a measurement error).

That gives a migration (inward or outward) by age gender over time which is trended and applied to the age-gender segments year on year as the model is rolled forward in time.

Households and Household Size

Historic household size is derived from the reported number of households and total population.

The future trend in the distribution of households by size around the mean is derived from the trend in the age profile and GDP per capita of the population. These two variables drive the mean and the variance of the distribution.

Typically, the older and the more affluent the population the smaller the average household size and the longer the tail to the right of the mean.

Employment

Derive the working-age population from the age profile of the population.

For older, more affluent countries, working-age extends to age 74.

Propensity to be employed is a function of historic rate and changes in education by gender and accumulated Fixed Capital Investment. The trend is stable and can be reliably projected.

Applying the propensity to be employed to the working-age population gives the labour force by gender and total employed.

Total employed persons divided by the number of households gives workers per household – this is a significant determinant of household income.

Total population less employed, divided by total employed gives the dependency ratio for the country.

Worker Productivity and Wages

Worker productivity (GDP/number of persons employed) is projected as follows:

- Changes in Accumulated Fixed Capital Investment per worker (10-year depreciation) as this gives a measure of the degree of capital that is available to leverage the skill of the worker.

- Changes in Education Profile of the workforce
- Applied to the long-term historic trend in productivity (which is a function to some extent of government and societal norms).

The share of GDP paid in Wages is a function of

- demand for work (the trend in the proportion of working-age not working),

- education level of workers and
- Accumulated Fixed Capital per worker.

This variable gives the average wage per worker.

Household Incomes and Distribution Thereof

Average household Earned Income is derived from the average wage per worker multiplied by the average number of employed persons per household.

It is subject to the constraints that:

- Average Household income must exceed Private Consumption Expenditure /number of households on the basis that a household cannot (on average) spend more than they earn.

- It is also constrained in that the total income of the average household divided by the number of workers must not exceed 80% of GDP per worker (Long term wages must be below productivity)

The distribution of households around mean income is derived from the historic distribution shape as published by the World Bank – and the correlation of that shape (log-normal distribution) to GDP per capita.

Forward projection of the distribution of households by income uses the coefficients for the log-normal distribution applied to GDP per cap.

Household Expenditure Pattern

Expressed as per cent of gross income spent on each of 12 expenditure standard categories.

Average tax rates are obtained from published tax tables for each country.

Savings is the residual of gross income less tax less expenditure by income level.

Analysis shows that the percentage of gross income spent on each category does not vary much within an income segment. The change in expenditure patterns is more a function of the change in the distribution of households by income.

Modelling Structure

The model is built entirely in Excel using Visual Basic programming in the background.

The advantage is that it is.

- A robust platform.
- Easy to use.
- VBA is widely known (and similar to Python etc) so well understood.

The model is Proprietary to Global Demographics Ltd

Appendix C:

Data Sources

Four Key Sources

1. World Bank
2. United Nations
3. International Labour Organisation
4. World Health Organisation

Global Demographics Ltd uses these because.

- They have established online databases which are updated regularly and have been harmonised in terms of variable definitions and measurement.

- They all have time-series data from the 1990s which we require for building our forecast models.

We supplement these with access to individual country published sources where appropriate – although less so in recent years. The main problem now is Taiwan as its data is not included in many of the Global Organisation Databases for political reasons.

We also cross-check mini census reports against the United Nations population databases in case there is a need for correction. Vietnam recently revised their population upward which was not initially reflected in the UN Database.

United Nations Datafiles Used

Global Demographics Downloads and uses from the United Nations the databases listed below. Please note that these are updated once every five years but are subject to revision on an ongoing basis.

The most recent update is to 2019 which is what we are currently using. As such, there is no need to reference individual country publications.

The web reference for these tables is:
https://esa.un.org/unpd/wpp/Download/Standard/Population/

The specific data tables used are:

Overall population by 5-year age groups by gender.

- WPP2019_POP_F07_2_POPULATION_BY_AGE_MALE.xlsx
"

- WPP2019_POP_F07_3_POPULATION_BY_AGE_FEMALE.xl
sx"

In respect of these tables, we re-express them as continuous 1 year age steps for analysis purposes. While it involves some estimation, the potential error is low as birth rates, death rates and migration age profiles tend to be consistent over time and we can check that the sim of the 5 individual years steps match the 5 age year groups reported by the UN.

Death Rates by age (5 yr.) by gender.

- "WPP2019_MORT_F04_2_DEATHS_BY_AGE_MALE.xlsx"

- WPP2019_MORT_F04_3_DEATHS_BY_AGE_FEMALE.xlsx"

These tables are needed as they, together with the population age profile, allow the determination of the migration by age. The number of persons in the age group at the start of the year, fewer deaths should equal the number of persons in the age group at the end of the year (start of the subsequent year). To the extent that it does not, it is either an error in population measurement (possible but unknown in quantity) or migration (inward or outward depending on country and age group).

Birth data.

These tables provide detailed data on the trend in birth rates by age of mother – which when combined with the trend in the size of relevant age groups of women enables a reliable estimate of the number of births each year by gender. Infant mortality is a necessary measure in some regions.

- WPP2019_FERT_F06_BIRTHS_BY_AGE_OF_MOTHER.xlsx"

- "WPP2019_FERT_F02_SEX_RATIO_AT_BIRTH.xlsx"

- "WPP2019_MORT_F01_1_IMR_BOTH_SEXES.xlsx"

In respect of these tables, we re-express them in 5-year age groups for the age of the mother.

World Bank Database

The World Bank's World Development Indicators online database covers 264 countries and contains 1,440 data series from (in some cases) 1964 to now 2020 (for some variables). It is very complete, has consistently applied definitions enabling comparability and is continuously updated.

We find it more reliable than individual country databases which are often inconsistent in definitions as well as updating policies.

The web reference for this database is.

https://databank.worldbank.org/data/source/world-development-indicators

Variables extracted from this database are:

World Bank Database – Education

Education is a particularly important variable to demographic trends – influencing birth rates, employment and earning capability. The World Bank data series used are:

Collectively these data series enable us to assess.

a) the education profile of the current adult population and

b) the future trend in that given current enrolments and

c) the extent to which the government values education by enabling education in current years.

As there are reasons to believe some governments overstate current enrolments in education, we also used data on expenditure on education (and express it on a per student basis) to validate these claims.

The data series we use for this is below and where a country is under-funding its enrolments we adjust accordingly. This applies mainly to countries on the African Continent.

It is important to make this adjustment as otherwise the work/productive capability of the workforce is overstated.

World Bank Database – Employment

The current levels of employment are important for determining the future levels of household income as well as the GDP of the economy. The measures we use are as listed below. This is based on persons over the age of 14 years.

We do not concern ourselves with the traditional term of working-age – 15 to 64 years – as it is becoming increasingly irrelevant as life expectancy and education improve. Instead, we express employment as a percentage of persons over the age of 14. It assumes child labour does not exist which is not correct but its existence is not measured.

For forecasting purposes, we use the trend in the proportion of persons aged 15+ in employment which tends to be quite stable in overall trend although short term economic shocks can influence it year on year.

World Bank Database – Key Economic Indicators

These are the standard economic indicators used to measure the overall state of the economy of a country. The critical ones from the Global Demographics Model perspective are:

Overall GDP

> This is needed to determine the historic productivity of the workforce taking into account their education profile and the Accumulated Fixed Capital Investment per worker. By knowing these relationships together with the projected trends in education and workforce size we can estimate total GDP, GDP per worker (and hence per household given the number of workers per household) and ultimately a constraint on the estimate of Household income. The series used are:

NY.GDP.MKTP.CD	GDP (current US$)
NY.GDP.MKTP.CN	GDP (current LCU)
NY.GDP.MKTP.CN.AD	GDP at market prices: linked series (current LCU)
NY.GDP.MKTP.KD	GDP (constant 2010 US$)

NY.GDP.MKTP.KD.ZG   GDP growth (annual %)

NY.GDP.MKTP.KN   GDP (constant LCU)

Private Consumption Expenditure

This divided by the number of households gives a reliable measure of the expenditure per annum of the average household (after allowing for expenditure by charities). This in turn provides a measure of the medium-term minimum average household income.

NE.CON.PRVT.CN   Household final consumption expenditure (current LCU)

Fixed Capital Investment per annum

Fixed Capital Investment. This is usefully tracked as a percentage of total GDP the previous year and can be forecast with some reliability based on that trend.

As the resources available to the worker impact productivity per worker, we also express this variable as total FCI over the previous 10 years depreciated at 10% per annum. This is a better indicator of resources than annual FCI which can fluctuate year on year.

NE.GDI.FTOT.CN   Gross fixed capital formation (current LCU)

Total Government Expenditure

A necessary variable against which to compare expenditure on education and health. How seriously does a government take these categories of expenditure?

NE.CON.GOVT.CN   General government final consumption expenditure (current LCU)

Exchange rate to US Dollars

This is necessary to enable comparability between countries on all financial measures.

PA.NUS.FCRF   Official exchange rate (LCU per US$, period average)

Deflator

To enable all financial data to be expressed in real constant value terms (currently 2019). This makes forecasts of financial variables less subjective. Otherwise, assumptions have to be made about future inflation rates.

NY.GDP.DEFL.KD.ZG Inflation, GDP deflator (annual %)

World Bank Database – Household Income and Distribution of Households by Income

This set of variables gives a reliable measure for selected years (vary by country) of the distribution of households/individuals by income. Mathematically the distribution of households by income around the mean can be reliably expressed in a log-normal distribution which requires the median and variance to be estimated. This data helps determine the variance. The last item indicates the mean although please refer to separate pages in this document on how average income (and median) is estimated in our models.

SI.DST.02ND.20   Income share held by second 20%

SI.DST.03RD.20   Income share held by third 20%

SI.DST.04TH.20   Income share held by fourth 20%

SI.DST.05TH.20   Income share held by highest 20%

SI.DST.10TH.10   Income share held by highest 10%

SI.DST.50MD   Proportion of people living below 50 per cent of median
income (%)

SI.DST.FRST.10   Income share held by lowest 10%

SI.DST.FRST.20   Income share held by lowest 20

SI.SPR.PCAP   Survey mean consumption or income per capita, total
population (2011 PPP $ per day)

Household Expenditure Data

There are multiple sources used for this.

Data Published by Individual Countries

67 Countries – all from Europe, North America and Asia as well as some South American Countries do and publish their own 'Household Income and Expenditure Surveys'. For most it is annual but for some, it is every 5 years. They are accessible online.

For many, they also provide a measure of household size by expenditure group

In all cases, they use a standard master group of 12 Expenditure Categories and are generally consistent in terms of what they include in those categories.

In all cases, they provide both the absolute amount spent by the income/expenditure segment as well as the proportion and number of households in each income/expenditure segment. This helps confirm the distribution of households by income data published in the World Bank Database.

The 12 expenditure groups used are:
1. Food and non-alcoholic beverages
2. Tobacco and alcohol
3. Clothing and Footwear
4. Daily use household items and durables
5. Utilities
6. Rent or Mortgage payment
7. Transport
8. Communications
9. Health

10. Recreation
11. Education
12. Other personal use expenditure

Other Countries that do not publish such data.

For the other (typically poor) countries where the Household Income and Expenditure Survey is not done, we use the results of the World Bank's database on Developing Countries Expenditure.

This is available online at the World Bank site and enables the development of the same relationship equations for consumption patterns relative to gross income. As for other countries.

Out of the 117 countries currently in the Global Demographics Database, only 4 do not have expenditure data.

World Bank Database – Healthcare Expenditure and Statistics

The World Bank Database contains some variables which are taken from the World Health Organisation. The ones included in the Global Demographics Database and used for projections are:

SH.MED.BEDS.ZS   Hospital beds (per 1,000 people)

SH.MED.CMHW.P3   Community health workers (per 1,000 people)

SH.MED.NUMW.P3   Nurses and midwives (per 1,000 people)

SH.MED.PHYS.ZS   Physicians (per 1,000 people)

SH.MED.SAOP.P5   Specialist surgical workforce (per 100,000 population)

SH.PRV.SMOK   Smoking prevalence, total (ages 15+)

SH.SGR.PROC.P5   Number of surgical procedures (per 100,000 population)

SH.XPD.CHEX.GD.ZS   Current health expenditure (% of GDP)

SH.XPD.GHED.CH.ZS   Domestic general government health expenditure (% of current
health expenditure)

SH.XPD.GHED.GD.ZS   Domestic general government health expenditure (% of GDP)

SH.XPD.GHED.GE.ZS   Domestic general government health expenditure (% of general
government expenditure)

SH.XPD.OOPC.CH.ZS   Out-of-pocket expenditure (% of current health expenditure)

China

While National Statistics on China are available from the United
Nations and World Bank sites detailed earlier in this document,
the fact is China has a total population of 1.4 billion persons and it
is, therefore, useful to try and get data on a regional basis at least.

As it happens China publishes most of the variables described in
the earlier parts of this document not just at a national level but

also at a Province and Prefecture. There are a few at the County level.

For that reason, we obtain all data for China from the National Bureau of Statistics website at

http://www.stats.gov.cn/enGliSH/

The online database is easily accessed and downloaded and is good for Province level data.

For Prefecture and Country Level data, we purchase each year the following :

- China City Statistical Yearbook
- China Statistical Yearbook (County Level)
- China Population and Employment Statistics Yearbook

Because of the level of detail involved (250 Prefectures and 1,440 Villages and Townships), they are typically not published until after April in the second year following the data year.

Made in the USA
Middletown, DE
05 September 2022

73250721R00263